Developing Country Debt and the World Economy

edited by
Jeffrey D. Sachs

National Bureau of
Economic Research

W9-BLZ-067

Developing Country
Debt and the
World Economy

A National Bureau
of Economic Research
Project Report

Developing Country Debt and the World Economy

Edited by **Jeffrey D. Sachs**

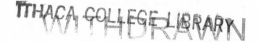

The University of Chicago Press

Chicago and London

JEFFREY D. SACHS is a professor of economics at Harvard
University and a research associate of the National Bureau of
Economic Research.

The University of Chicago Press, Chicago 60637
The University of Chicago Press, Ltd., London

98 97 96 95 94 93 92 91 90   6 5 4 3 2

⊗ The paper used in this publication meets the minimum
requirements of the American National Standards Institute for
Information Sciences—Permanence of Paper for Printed Library
Materials, ANSI Z39. 48-1984.

Library of Congress Cataloging-in-Publication Data

Developing country debt and the world economy / edited by
Jeffrey D. Sachs.
    p.   cm.—(A National Bureau of Economic Research
project report)
  Bibliography: p.
  Includes index.
  ISBN 0-226-73338-6. ISBN 0-226-73339-4 (pbk.)
  1. Debts, External—Developing countries. 2. International
finance. I. Sachs, Jeffrey. II. Series.
HJ8899.D482 1988
336.3′435′091724—dc19   88-20798
                                        CIP

Relation of the Directors to the Work and Publications of the National Bureau of Economic Research

1. The object of the National Bureau of Economic Research is to ascertain and to present to the public important economic facts and their interpretation in a scientific and impartial manner. The Board of Directors is charged with the responsibility of ensuring that the work of the National Bureau is carried on in strict conformity with this object.

2. The President of the National Bureau shall submit to the Board of Directors, or to its Executive Committee, for their formal adoption all specific proposals for research to be instituted.

3. No research report shall be published by the National Bureau until the President has sent each member of the Board a notice that a manuscript is recommended for publication and that in the President's opinion it is suitable for publication in accordance with the principles of the National Bureau. Such notification will include an abstract or summary of the manuscript's content and a response form for use by those Directors who desire a copy of the manuscript for review. Each manuscript shall contain a summary drawing attention to the nature and treatment of the problem studied, the character of the data and their utilization in the report, and the main conclusions reached.

4. For each manuscript so submitted, a special committee of the Directors (including Directors Emeriti) shall be appointed by majority agreement of the President and Vice Presidents (or by the Executive Committee in case of inability to decide on the part of the President and Vice Presidents), consisting of three Directors selected as nearly as may be one from each general division of the Board. The names of the special manuscript committee shall be stated to each Director when notice of the proposed publication is submitted to him. It shall be the duty of each member of the special manuscript committee to read the manuscript. If each member of the manuscript committee signifies his approval within thirty days of the transmittal of the manuscript, the report may be published. If at the end of that period any member of the manuscript committee withholds his approval, the President shall then notify each member of the Board, requesting approval or disapproval of publication, and thirty days additional shall be granted for this purpose. The manuscript shall then not be published unless at least a majority of the entire Board who shall have voted on the proposal within the time fixed for the receipt of votes shall have approved.

5. No manuscript may be published, though approved by each member of the special manuscript committee, until forty-five days have elapsed from the transmittal of the report in manuscript form. The interval is allowed for the receipt of any memorandum of dissent or reservation, together with a brief statement of his reasons, that any member may wish to express; and such memorandum of dissent or reservation shall be published with the manuscript if he so desires. Publication does not, however, imply that each member of the Board has read the manuscript, or that either members of the Board in general or the special committee have passed on its validity in every detail.

6. Publications of the National Bureau issued for informational purposes concerning the work of the Bureau and its staff, or issued to inform the public of activities of Bureau staff, and volumes issued as a result of various conferences involving the National Bureau shall contain a specific disclaimer noting that such publication has not passed through the normal review procedures required in this resolution. The Executive Committee of the Board is charged with review of all such publications from time to time to ensure that they do not take on the character of formal research reports of the National Bureau, requiring formal Board approval.

7. Unless otherwise determined by the Board or exempted by the terms of paragraph 6, a copy of this resolution shall be printed in each National Bureau publication.

(Resolution adopted October 25, 1926, as revised through September 30, 1974)

Contents

Preface

This volume includes 16 papers that were prepared as part of a research project by the National Bureau of Economic Research on Developing Country Debt. These papers examine other debt crises that occurred before World War II, political factors that contribute to poor economic policies in many debtor countries, the role of commercial banks and the International Monetary Fund (IMF) during the current crisis, the effect of developed country economies on the debtors, as well as possible solutions to the debt crisis. In addition, the volume includes summaries of case studies of Argentina, Bolivia, Brazil, Indonesia, Mexico, the Philippines, South Korea, and Turkey.

The findings of NBER's Debt project were presented at a conference for government officials of lending and debtor countries, economists at international organizations, and representatives of banks and other private firms with interests in the debtor countries. The conference was held in Washington, D.C., from 21 through 23 September 1987.

These 16 papers will also be published in longer and somewhat more technical versions. One volume will contain the eight papers on selected topics. Another volume will include studies of the four Latin American countries, while a final volume will have the studies of the other four countries.

We would like to thank the Agency for International Development, The Ford Foundation, Mr. David Rockefeller, the Rockefeller Brothers Fund, and The Tinker Foundation for the financial support of this work. The success of the project also depended on the efforts of Deborah Mankiw, Yasuko MacDougall, Kirsten Foss Davis, Ilana Hardesty, Robert Allison, and Mark Fitz-Patrick.

Jeffrey D. Sachs

1   Introduction

Jeffrey D. Sachs

1.1 Introduction

The Project on Developing Country Debt undertaken by the National Bureau of Economic Research in the past two years seeks to provide a detailed analysis of the ongoing developing country debt crisis. The focus is on the middle-income developing countries, particularly those in Latin America and East Asia, though many lessons of the study should apply as well to the poorer debtor countries in sub-Saharan Africa.

The urgency of the NBER study should be self evident. For dozens of developing countries, the financial upheavals of the 1980s have set back economic development by a decade or more. Poverty has intensified in much of the developing world as countries have struggled under an enormous external debt burden. Moreover, the world financial system has been disrupted by the prospect of widespread defaults on the foreign debts of the developing world. More than six years after the onset of the crisis, almost all of the debtor countries are still unable to borrow in the international capital markets on normal market terms.

Table 1.1 shows several aspects of the economic crisis of the major debtor countries in recent years. Since the dramatic outbreak of the crisis in 1982, economic growth has slowed sharply or has been negative. Per capita incomes in the most indebted countries are still generally well below the levels of 1980. And ominously, dept-export ratios are higher in 1986 than at the beginning of the crisis.

Future growth prospects are clouded by a sharp drop in the share of capital formation in GNP. At the same time, inflation has risen to remarkable levels throughout Latin America. The mechanisms behind the epidemic of high inflations are basically the same that caused the

Table 1.1   The Economic Crisis in the Heavily Indebted Countries

	Average 1969–78	1979	1980	1981	1982	1983	1984	1985	1986
Per capital GDP (annual change)	3.6	3.6	2.6	-1.6	-2.7	-5.5	-0.1	0.9	1.4
Inflation (annual rate)	28.5	40.8	47.4	53.2	57.7	90.8	116.4	126.9	76.2
Gross capital formation (percent of GDP)	n.a.	24.9	24.7	24.5	22.3	18.2	17.4	16.5	16.8
Debt-export ratio	n.a.	182.3	167.1	201.4	269.8	289.7	272.1	284.2	337.9

Source: All data refer to the fifteen heavily indebted countries: Argentina, Bolivia, Brazil, Chile, Columbia, Ivory Coast, Ecuador, Mexico, Morocco, Nigeria, Peru, Philippines, Uruguay, Venezuela, Yugoslavia. Data are from the IMF *World Economic Outlook*, April 1987. Inflation refers to the consumer price index.

n.a. = not available.

hyperinflations in Central Europe after World War I, with foreign debts now playing the role that reparations payments played in the post-World War I crisis.

The NBER Project analyzes the crisis from two perspectives, the individual debtor country, and the international financial system as a whole. A major goal of the country studies is to understand why some countries, such as Argentina or Mexico, succumbed to a serious crisis, while others, such as Indonesia or Korea, did not. Another important goal is to understand why most of the debtor countries have been unable to overcome the crisis despite many years of harsh economic adjustments.

To analyze such questions, the NBER commissioned eight detailed country monographs, covering four countries in Latin America (Argentina, Bolivia, Brazil, and Mexico) and four countries in the Middle East and East Asia (Indonesia, the Philippines, South Korea and Turkey). Each study was prepared by a team of two authors: a U.S.-based researcher and an economist from the country under study.

The choice of countries was dictated by several considerations. First, the project aimed to include the countries with the largest external debt, since their behavior is most important from a global economic point of view. Second, the project was designed to investigate both successes and failures in external debt management. Thus, we have countries that succumbed to serious crisis, and have so far not recovered (Argentina, Bolivia, Brazil, Mexico, and the Philippines); a country which succumbed to crisis but has recovered in substantial part (Turkey); and two countries that did not succumb to an external debt crisis (Indonesia and South Korea). Third, the project aimed to compare countries that varied widely in economic structure, particularly in the structure of international trade. Thus, as shown in table 1.2, our case studies include countries heavily dependent on primary commodity exports (Argentina, Bolivia, Indonesia); countries with a mix of commodity and manufactured exports (Brazil, Mexico, the Philippines, and Turkey); and a country almost wholly dependent on manufactured exports (South Korea).

The economic performance of the eight NBER countries is summarized in table 1.2. The table shows the very broad range of experiences. Economic growth is strong, and inflation relatively low, in South Korea, Indonesia, and Turkey. The Latin American economies all have low growth (negative in per capita terms), and very high inflations. The Philippines has low growth but also low inflation. The external debt burden, measured by the debt-export ratio, is heaviest in Latin America and the Philippines, and relatively light in Indonesia and South Korea. Turkey is ranked in the middle. As shown in the final column of the table, two countries (Indonesia and South Korea),

Table 1.2   Economic Performance in the Eight NBER Countries

	GDP 1980–85	Inflation 1980–85	Primary Share of Commodities in Exports, 1985	Debt-Export Ratio, 1985	Debt Rescheduling 1975–86
Argentina	−1.4	342.8	82	576	Yes
Bolivia	−4.5	569.1	94	601	Yes
Brazil	1.3	147.7	59	417	Yes
Indonesia	3.5	10.7	89	191	No
Mexico	0.8	62.2	73	445	Yes
Philippines	−0.5	19.3	49	563	Yes
South Korea	7.9	6.0	9	156	No
Turkey	4.5	37.1	46	315	Yes

Source: World Bank, World Development Report, 1987. GDP and inflation measures are annual rates of change.

escaped a debt crisis altogether, though Indonesia's debt position remains somewhat precarious. Turkey's crisis came in the late 1970s, before the onset of the global crisis. The Latin American economies and the Philippines have all been engaged in repeated reschedulings since 1982–83.

The individual country studies can answer only some of the questions about the crisis, since global factors have undoubtedly been key to many of the developments in the past few years. Indeed, as Lindert and Morton stress, international debt crises have been a recurrent part of the international financial landscape for at least 175 years, in the 1820s, the 1870s, 1890s, and 1930s. It is important to understand the fundamental properties of the international macroeconomy and global financial markets which have contributed to this repeated instability.

The NBER studies in this project that take a global or "systemic" perspective cover several important topics, including: the history of international sovereign lending (Eichengreen, and Lindert and Morton); the nature of negotiations between the commercial banks and the debtor countries (Krugman); the role of the International Monetary Fund and World Bank (Sachs); the global linkages between debt and macroeconomic policies in the industrial countries (Dornbusch); the appropriate role for long-term structural adjustment policies in the debtor countries (Edwards); the political factors within the developing countries that contribute to economic crisis versus stabilization and growth (Haggard and Kaufman); and possible new approaches to the global management of the crisis (Fischer).

1.1.1   The Creditor and Debtor Views of the Crisis

The international debt crisis has already given rise to many oversimplified interpretations, most of which can be dismissed on the basis of the studies in the NBER project. Simple ideas abound on this topic, often because they serve particular vested interests. Creditors want to blame the crisis on the policy mistakes of the debtor governments. Debtors want to blame the crisis on the macroeconomic and trade policies of the creditor governments. Both sides are keen to neglect the more nuanced historical record.

The mainstream creditor interpretation (as expressed variously by the United States government, the international institutions, and the commercial banks) can be summarized as follows. The debt crisis emerged largely because of the policy mistakes of the debtor governments. Loans were wasted by inefficient state enterprises, or were squandered in capital flight. "Successful" governments were those like South Korea, which pursued free-market economic policies, while unsuccessful governments smothered economic growth with government regulations. With sufficient economic reforms, including trade liberalization and an encouragement of foreign direct investment, the debtor countries will be able to grow out of the current crisis.

Most creditors have also maintained that the only proper way to manage the current crisis is to insist that the debtor governments honor their debts in full, since to do otherwise would threaten the international financial system. To grant debt relief to the debtors, they also suggest, would hurt the debtors more than it would help them, because it would cut the debtors off from future borrowing from the world financial markets, and thereby hinder their economic growth.

The debtor perspective, of course, differs at key points. Debtor governments hold that the crisis erupted because of the rise in world interest rates, the fall in commodity prices, and the collapse of world trade at the beginning of the 1980s. They blame the macroeconomic policies of the creditor governments, particularly the U.S. fiscal policies, for many of the global shocks. Debtor governments typically downplay the role of debtor country policies in the crisis, and often state that advocates of "free-market policies" in response to the crisis are simply serving foreign interests (e.g., multinational firms) at the expense of the domestic interests. Many debtor governments argue that successful adjustment will require some debt relief. One reason for this pessimism is the view that attempts to honor the debt burden through increased exports would simply promote offsetting protectionist pressures in the creditor economies.

The evidence from the NBER study belies many of the points commonly made by both the creditors and the debtors. The historical record and the recent experience certainly call into question the creditors' optimism with respect to rapid adjustment with growth in the debtor countries, but also the debtor's pessimism about the *long-term* results of adjustment policy. The historical record is rather clear on

the long-run benefits of macroeconomic stabilization and a shift towards outward-oriented trade policies (though the studies by Edwards,
Sachs, Collins and Park, and Celâsun and Rodrik, make clear that
outward orientation is not the same as trade liberalization, a point
sometimes missed in the current debate). The country experiences
also suggest, however, that outward-orientation requires a sustained
period of heavy investment in the export sector, as well as a sustained
period of macroeconomic stability, both of which are difficult to achieve
under conditions of financial crisis.

Both the historical record and the recent difficulties of short-run
adjustment in the countries under study highlight the debtor countries'
need for a financial "time out" from the crisis, in the form of a sustained
reduction in the debt-servicing burden as a prerequisite to economic
recovery. The historical cases studied by Eichengreen, and by Lindert
and Morton, show that such a financial time out has often come in the
form of a unilateral reduction of debt payments imposed by the debtor
country, followed by a renegotiation of the terms of the debt contract
that results in a measure of debt relief (we will use the term debt relief
to signify a reduction in the contractual present value of debt
repayments).

The NBER study offers fresh evidence on several important issues,
in addition to the ones just mentioned: the sources of the debt crisis
(and of debt crises in the past); the patterns of economic adjustment
in a debtor country after a debt crisis gets underway; the nature of
bargaining between debtors and creditors; and the role for public policy
in easing or eliminating the global crisis. These subjects are now taken
up in detail in the following sections.

1.2 Origins of the Debt Crisis

The debt crisis arose from a combination of policy actions in the
debtor countries, macroeconomic shocks in the world economy, and
a remarkable spurt of unrestrained bank lending during 1979–81. The
"unsuccessful" adjusters (all but Indonesia and South Korea among
the countries in the NBER study) fell prey to a common pattern of
policy actions: chronically large budget deficits; overvalued exchange
rates; and a trade regime biased against exports in general, and agriculture in particular. These policies would have hindered economic
performance in most circumstances, but they provoked a deep crisis
when combined with severe shocks to world interest rates, exchange
rates, and commodity prices, in the early 1980s. The crisis was greatly
exacerbated because the commercial banks provided copious financing
for the bad policies of the developing countries for many years, particularly during 1979–81, and then abruptly withdrew new credits starting in 1982.

1.2.1 The Role of Global Shocks

The importance of global macroeconomic changes in provoking the debt crisis have been widely noted (see Sachs 1987 for a review of this issue). As is well known, the growth of the eurodollar market and the OPEC price shocks of 1973–74 put in motion a period of rapid bank lending to the developing countries. During the period 1973–79, the export proceeds of the developing countries boomed, while nominal interest rates on the loans were low, contributing to the happy state of affairs that debt-to-export ratios remained modest despite heavy borrowing by the developing countries. Indeed, for the non-oil LDCs as a whole, the debt-export ratio was lower in 1980 than in 1973, while for the Western Hemisphere LDCs, it was only marginally higher in 1980 compared to 1973 as can be seen in table 1.3.

At the end of the 1970s, therefore, the pace of international lending did not seem to pose a serious danger to the commercial banks or to the world economy. But few observers fully appreciated how much this happy state of affairs depended on nominal interest rates remaining below the growth rate of dollar exports of the borrowing countries (put another way, *real* interest rates remaining below the growth rate of *real* exports). Even worse, almost nobody properly understood that the era of high export growth and low interest rates would come abruptly to an end at the end of the 1970s.

In the happy case that interest rates are below export growth rates, borrowers can borrow all the money needed to service their loans without suffering a rise in the debt-to-export ratio (since exports will grow faster than the debt). In other words, the borrower does not have to contribute any of its own resources to servicing its debts. Once the interest rate rises above the export growth rate, however, then the country cannot simply borrow the money to service its debts without incurring a sharply rising debt-to-export ratio. Sooner or later, the country will be cut off from new borrowing, and it will have to pay for its debt servicing out of its own national resources, i.e., by running trade surpluses vis-à-vis the rest of the world.

The remarkable fact is how abruptly the interest rate–growth rate relationship was reversed as of 1980, as shown in figure 1.1. Extremely

Table 1.3   **Debt-Export Ratios, 1973 to 1986 (selected years)**

(percent)	1973	1980	1981	1982	1983	1984	1985	1986P
Non-oil LDCs	115.4	112.9	124.9	143.3	152.8	148.3	162.0	162.2
Western Hemisphere	176.2	178.4	207.9	273.1	290.4	275.2	296.2	331.3

Source: International Monetary Fund, *World Economic Outlook,* April 1986 and October 1986 editions.
PPreliminary.

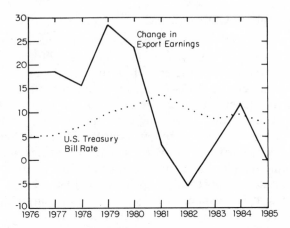

Fig. 1.1   Interest rates and annual change in non-oil export earnings

tight monetary policies in the industrial countries, designed to fight inflation, provoked a sharp rise in interest rates, an industrial country recession, and a steep fall in the export prices and terms of trade of the developing countries. The debt crisis followed relentlessly upon the resulting rise in interest rates and the collapse in developing country export earnings. All of a sudden, all of the debt warning signs started to fly off the charts, as seen by the rapid increase in the debt-export and debt-service ratios after 1980. Commercial bank lending dried up once the debt-export ratios started to soar. Total gross bank lending to the non-oil developing countries rose by 24 percent in 1980 over 1979, 18 percent in 1981, and only 7 percent in 1982.

1.2.2   The Role of Bank Lending Behavior

Few observers perceived the risks of international lending as of the end of the 1970s, least of all the lenders themselves. Lindert and Morton, as well as Eichengreen, suggest that in earlier historical experiences as well, lenders lost sight of the inherent risks of cross-border lending. In the late 1970s, bankers adopted the credo of the worlds' leading international banker, Citicorp Chairman Walter Wriston, who justified the heavy international lending with the declaration that "countries never go bankrupt." In the mid- and late 1970s, the commercial banks were making enormous profits on their cross-border lending to the developing countries. In Citicorp's case, overall international operations accounted for an astounding 72 percent of overall earnings in 1976, with Brazilian operations alone accounting for 13 percent of the bank's earnings (Makin 1984, 133–34).

The banks had the recent loan experience to back them up. As already pointed out, the combination of high export growth rates and low interest rates meant that debt-to-export ratios remained under control despite the heavy lending. There was no real evidence, of course, that the countries would be willing or able to pay back their loans, or even service them, *with their own resources,* but that did not seem to matter: New lending to repay old loans made sense in the circumstances.

One can fault the banks severely for not looking more deeply at the quality of economic management in the developing countries during this period. Few banks, apparently, were concerned with the question of whether the debtor countries would be willing and able to service their debts if debt servicing had to come out of national resources rather than out of new loans. This issue seemed to be an abstract concern, at least through the end of the 1970s.

What is truly remarkable about the bank behavior is not the lending during 1973–79, but rather the outpouring of new lending during 1980–81, even after the world macroeconomic situation had soured markedly. In table 1.4 we see the astounding fact that in a mere two years, 1980 and 1981, total bank exposure nearly doubled over the level of 1979 in the major debtor countries. In the two years *after the rise in real interest rates,* the commercial banks made about as many net loans to the major debtors as during the entire period 1973–79.

This late burst of lending is all the more remarkable, and difficult to justify, in light of the enormous capital flight that was occurring at the same time, as shown in table 1.5. In the case of Argentina, of the tremendous rise during 1980 and 1981 in the overall gross debt of the country, 84 percent was offset by the outflow of private capital, according to the estimates of Cumby and Levich (1987). For Venezuela, the offset is well over 100 percent. I will discuss the origins of the capital flight in more detail in section 1.2.4 below.

Table 1.4   **Net Liabilities of Countries to International Banks in the BIS Reporting Area ($ billion)**

Country	December 1979	December 1981
Argentina	5.3	16.3
Brazil	28.8	44.8
Mexico	22.5	43.4
Subtotal	56.6	104.5
Indonesia	−0.1	−1.5
Malaysia	−1.3	0.2
South Korea	7.2	13.7
Thailand	1.6	1.8
Subtotal	7.4	15.2

Source: Bank for International Settlements, ''The Maturity Distribution of International Bank Lending,'' various issues.

Table 1.5   Capital Flight and Change in External Debt During 1980 and 1981
                   for the Major Debtors

	Capital Flight (Sum, 1980 and 1981)	Change in Gross Debt	Ratio: (1)/(2)
Argentina	12.8	10.8	0.84
Brazil	19.8	1.9	0.10
Mexico	35.1	15.6	0.44
Venezuela	7.8	13.0	1.67

Source: Cumby and Levich (1987), tables in data appendix. The capital flight variable is according to the World Bank definition reported by the authors.

New market-based lending by the commercial banks to the developing countries virtually disappeared after 1982. Even where lending continued, the transfer of net resources to the country (i.e., new lending minus total debt servicing on existing debt) was almost everywhere negative: The debtor countries paid more to the commercial banks than they received in new funds. Some countries received so-called "involuntary loans" as part of financial workout packages, usually linked to an IMF program. In such involuntary lending, the banks agreed to contribute new funds on a pro rata basis, relative to their exposure at an initial date. Even in this case, however, the new lending was invariably less than the amount of debt service payments due from the country to the bank creditors, so that the net resource transfer to the country remained negative.

The heavy commercial bank lending, particularly during 1979–81, certainly created the potential for a serious international banking crisis. As shown in table 1.6, the cross-border exposure of the U.S. money-

Table 1.6   U.S. Bank Assets in the Debtor Countries Nine Major Banks

	End-1982	Mid-1984	March 1986
Total Exposure ($ billion)			
All LDCs	83.4	84.0	75.6
Latin America	51.2	53.8	52.2
Africa	5.6	4.9	3.6
Exposure as Percentage of Bank Capital			
All LDCs	287.7	246.3	173.2
Latin America	176.5	157.8	119.7
Sub-Saharan Africa	19.3	14.3	8.1

Source: Federal Financial Institutions Examination Council, "Country Exposure Lending Survey," various statistical releases. End-1982 from statistical release of October 15, 1984; March 1986 from release of August 1, 1986. Exposures are calculated using data for "Total Amounts owed to U.S. banks after adjustments for guarantees and external borrowing." Total exposures are calculated for All LDCs (OPEC, Non-Oil, Latin America (Non-Oil Asia, Non-Oil Africa); Latin America (Non-Oil Latin America plus Ecuador and Venezuela); and Africa (Non-Oil Africa plus Algeria, Gabon, Libya and Nigeria).

center banks at the end of 1982 to all of the developing countries equalled nearly three times total capital, and to Latin America alone amounted to almost two times bank capital. This exposure was very highly concentrated: about three-fourths of all U.S. commercial bank lending to more than 40 LDCS was centered in just four countries: Argentina, Brazil, Mexico, and Venezuela. Such normal prudential rules as limiting exposure to any single borrower to 10 percent of bank capital were also honored in the breach. The 10 percent rule was skirted by major U.S. banks by counting all different types of public-sector borrowers in one country (e.g., state enterprises, central government, etc.) as distinct borrowers, even though they were all backed by the same "full faith and credit" of the central government, and therefore reflected nearly identical credit risks.

1.2.3 The Role of Debtor Country Policies

In the easy money period of the 1970s, the policies of the debtor countries did not loom large. After all, loans were not serviced out of the country's own resources, but rather out of fresh borrowing. In this sense, the countries were never tested as to whether the loans were being put to good use, and whether the economic policies were sound. Nor were there many complaints about the policies of most of the debtor countries, with the exceptions of Jamaica, Peru, and Turkey, which rescheduled ahead of the rest of the other countries.

It is only with the emergence of the debt crisis itself that the soundness of the early borrowing was determined. Which countries could service their debts without a crushing blow to the domestic economy? Which countries would lack the economic or political stamina to maintain debt servicing? To some extent, of course, the answer turned on the amount of the borrowing itself relative to national income. But many other factors were of crucial significance: the extent to which the debt was held by the public versus the private sector; the distribution of production between tradables and nontradables; the uses to which the earlier borrowing had been put (consumption, fixed investment, financing of private capital fight); and so forth. In all cases, these various issues depended integrally on the types of policies that the various borrowing governments had been following, and on the motivations for the foreign borrowing in the first place.

The NBER studies suggest that two fundamental dimensions of policy require emphasis: fiscal policy and trade policy.

1.2.4 The Role of Fiscal Policy

Many of the policy actions in the debtor countries were not "mistakes" or technical misjudgments, but were the result of deeper political instabilities. The economies in Latin America, in particular, are deeply driven by great inequalities of income, which in turn prompt fierce political conflicts. The chronically large budget deficits in these countries are a reflection of these political conflicts. In some of the cases under study, the governments were too weak to resist the demands for spending from various highly mobilized social groups. In the most pathological cases, the political battle degenerated into a battle of "ins" versus "outs," with the ins using the apparatus of the government for narrow personal gain. The worse excesses of this sort are seen in the Philippines under Marcos, and in several Bolivian regimes in the late 1970s and early 1980s.

At the same time, the governments either could not, or chose not to, raise taxes on the economic elites. On both the spending and revenue sides, therefore, political institutions repeatedly failed to keep the demands for government spending in line with the government's limited tax collections. Foreign borrowing in the 1970s and early 1980s provided a short-term way out of these political dilemmas, by allowing governments to finance large budget deficits without incurring high inflationary costs in the short term. Simply put, the governments could borrow from abroad, rather than face the monetary consequences of borrowing directly from the central bank. Once the net capital inflows ceased in the early 1980s, and governments had to start making net payments abroad, the inflationary consequences emerged, as governments were not able to reduce expenditures and raise revenues sufficiently in response to the shift from net inflows of foreign capital to net outflows. They instead turned to printing money to make up the shortfall in foreign lending.

One of the most talked about, and misunderstood, phenomena in the debt crisis is that of "capital flight." Capital flight refers to the accumulation of foreign assets by the private sector of an economy, often at the same time that the public sector is incurring sharply rising external debts. As an example, while the Mexican government accumulated debts of approximately $75 billion to foreign creditors, the Mexican private sector accumulated claims abroad in the amount of perhaps $40 billion. This conjunction of heavy public debt and large private assets is mainly a reflection of the loose fiscal policies that we have been emphasizing.

The predominant mechanism of capital flight in the late 1970s and early 1980s worked as follows. Suppose that the government increases transfer payments to the private economy. In order to finance those transfer payments, it borrows from the central bank. The central bank financing causes in incipient rise in the money supply as the government spends the borrowed funds. The higher money balances lead to a weakening of the exchange rate as the private sector, flush with cash, attempts to convert some of the increased transfers into foreign currency. This creates the tendency toward higher inflation (the weakening of the currency would tend to raise the domestic prices of imports, exports, and import-competiting goods). In order to stabilize the price level, the central bank keeps the exchange rate from depreciating, by selling foreign exchange in return for the domestic currency (the excess money balances are thereby drained from the economy). The central bank runs down its reserves, and the private sector increases its foreign asset holdings.

To maintain an adequate level of reserves, the central bank itself might then turn to the world capital markets for a foreign loan to replenish its reserves. Over time, the result would be the growing foreign debt of the central bank, and growing private sector claims held in the form of foreign currency (and perhaps actually held abroad). The phenomenon is labelled "capital flight," but is simply the consequence of (1) large fiscal deficits; and (2) an anti-inflationary policy of pegging the nominal exchange rate.

As noted later, the fiscal consequences of the foreign borrowing in the 1970s were exacerbated by a common practice of policy actions in the 1980s. When the financial crisis erupted in 1981 and 1982, many *private* firms that had borrowed heavily from abroad were put into financial distress. In country after country, governments took over the private debt on favorable terms for the private sector firms, or subsidized the private debt service payments, in order to bail out the private firms. This "socialization" of the private debt resulted in a significant increase in the *fiscal* burden of the nation's foreign debt.

1.2.5   The Trade Regime

To the extent that foreign borrowing finances efficient investment in an economy above the level that would otherwise be financed with domestic savings, the foreign borrowing could well be prudent and welfare enhancing. The key condition is that the investment project yield a return that is above the world cost of capital, when the project's costs and returns are measured at appropriate shadow prices (i.e., at prices that take into account the distortions in incentives in the borrowing economy). Of course, much of the heavy foreign borrowing did not finance investment at all. It was used, instead, to finance current consumption spending as well as capital flight by the private sector.

It is well known from trade theory that strongly protectionist policies drive an important wedge between market prices and shadow prices, and thereby tend to lead to important distortions in the allocation of investment spending. In particular, investment is allocated too heavily towards nontradables and import-competing goods, and too little towards exportables. The result is that investments that may be profitable at market prices may be unprofitable at appropriate shadow values. Brecher and Díaz-Alejandro (1977), among others, demonstrated that foreign borrowing to support such misallocated investment is almost surely welfare worsening.

There is considerable evidence from the earlier NBER studies of Bhagwati (1978) and Krueger (1978), Balassa (1984), Sachs (1985), and others, that economies with heavily protectionist trade regimes fare less well in overall economic performance than economies with more balanced trade regimes. The superior performance of so-called "outward-oriented" regimes appears to involve not only a better allocation of investment spending along the lines just suggested, but also other factors that are more difficult to quantify (such as improved technology transfer from abroad, higher savings rates, more market competition, and a tendency towards better exchange rate management).

The country studies in the NBER project support earlier findings on the superiority of outward-oriented regimes. By far the most successful performer in the NBER study is South Korea, the quintessential outward-oriented economy. Outward-orientation is generally measured by the overall incentives of the trade regime on the production of exportables relative to import-competing goods. The evidence described by Collins and Park suggests that the overall effect of trade incentives in Korea is to favor exportables, as opposed to the trade regimes in Latin America which have typically been anti-export biased (and favorable to import-competing sectors). As shown by Woo and Nasution, the Indonesian trade regime under Soeharto seems to lie between the outward orientation of the South Korean case, and the inward orientation of the Latin American cases.

In addition to tariffs and quotas, the management of the nominal exchange rate can have an important bearing on the relative profitability of exports versus import-competing goods. When the nominal exchange rate is overvalued, to the extent that the central bank *rations* the sale of foreign exchange for current transactions, the result is typically an implicit tax on exports, even if no tariffs or trade quotas are imposed. A black market for foreign exchange results from the rationing, allowing a rise in the domestic price of import-competing goods (which at the margin are imported at the black market rate). Exporters, on the other hand, typically must surrender foreign exchange at the overvalued official rate. The typical result of the foreign exchange rationing, therefore, is to lower the relative price of exports, and to bias production away from the export sector.

As shown in Sachs (1985), and confirmed again by the country studies, the East Asian economies (South Korea and Indonesia in the NBER sample) never allowed a substantial black market premium to develop during the 1970s and 1980s, while the Latin American economies all had phases of substantial black market premia on their currencies.

Another dimension of policy is the balance of incentives between tradables as a whole relative to nontradables (e.g., construction and services). Even when foreign exchange is not rationed, so that a black market premium does not arise, the failure to devalue the nominal exchange rate in line with domestic inflation can result in the fall in tradables prices relative to nontradables prices, with the result that production of both exportables and import-competing goods (at least those import-competing goods not protected by quotas), are hurt relative to the production of nontradables. The Korean authorities clearly managed the nominal exchange rate throughout the 1970s and 1980s with a eye to maintaining a rough constancy in the price of tradables relative to nontradables. Indonesia, as well, stands out as a rare case in which devaluations of the exchange rate (in 1978, 1983, and 1986) were undertaken explicitly in order to keep tradable goods prices in line with rising nontradable goods prices, even before a balance of payments crisis occurred.

Turkey provides a particularly interesting example regarding the trade regime, as documented by Celâsun and Rodrik. During the 1970s, Turkey was afflicted by a chronically overvalued exchange rate (with a large black market premium), import rationing, and an overall anti-export bias. After the onset of the debt crisis at the end of the 1970s, the government moved to a strategy of export-led growth. This policy was based initially on a significant depreciation of the nominal exchange rate, which succeeded in raising the relative price of tradables, and of nearly unifying the black market and official exchange rate. Later, during the 1980s there was a progressive liberalization of the trading system. The results were impressive: nontraditional export growth was rapid, and provided the basis for overall growth of the economy in the 1980s. In their paper, Celâsun and Rodrik discuss at some length the contribution of the Turkish policy changes versus other special factors (e.g, the Iran-Iraq war) in promoting the export boom.

As already noted, the Latin American regimes have all been characterized by a considerable degree of import protection and general anti-export bias. In many cases, the exchange rate was allowed to become severely overvalued in the real terms (with a considerable black market premium on foreign exchange), with the exchange rate moved only in the midst of an extreme balance of payments crisis. As with the budget, the exchange rate policy appears to reflect political conditions in Latin America as much as technical mistakes. The chronically overvalued exchange rate favors urban workers and the protected manufacturing sector at the expense of the agricultural sector, which has been politically weak in most countries since the Great Depression.

There are some additional lessons regarding the trade regime that are raised by the country studies. Contrary to a common view, outward orientation in the NBER sample of countries is not at all the same thing as a free-market trade policy (see also Sachs 1987 for a further elaboration of this distinction in the experience of the East Asian economies). The outward-oriented countries in the study, South Korea, Indonesia (to some degree), and Turkey in the 1980s, all had successful export growth with continued import restrictions and heavy government involvement in managing trade. The key instruments in stimulating exports was not import liberalization *per se,* but rather: (1) a realistic and unified exchange rate; (2) heavy investment in the exporting sectors, often spurred by government subsidies and direct credit allocations; and (3) an array of additional financial incentives for exporters.

More generally, the South Korean case belies the simple position often taken by the United States government and the IMF and World Bank, that "small" government, as opposed to effective government, is the key to good economic performance. As the study by Collins and Park makes clear, the government of South Korea played a leading role in organizing economic development. The government was sufficiently powerful, however, to be able to generate significant budget surpluses to finance domestic investment, and to pursue a long-term policy of export-led growth. Also, given Korea's relatively equal distribution of income (the result in large part of extensive land reform in the late 1940s and early 1950s), the government was able to devote its attention to matters of efficiency rather than redistribution.

Another interesting aspect of the experience of South Korea and Turkey is the blurring of the distinction over time between import-competing firms and exporting firms. It is notable that in both countries much of the export boom of the 1980s was based on investments during the 1970s in heavily protected industries, which became profitable for export in the 1980s. Moreover, at the time that the investments were made, they were decried by economists as an inefficient allocation of investment spending, with the incorrect argument (in hindsight) that such industries could not be expected to export in the forseeable future. As it turned out, productivity improvements together with a modest depreciation of the real exchange rate and an export-promoting regulatory environment were enough to make these sectors profitable for export in the 1980s.

This finding is both good news and bad news for those who are hoping for a major export boom in the Latin American debtor countries. On the one hand, formerly protected industries can probably become exporting industries with only moderate changes in the real exchange rate. On the other hand, export promotion did not come out of thin air in South Korea and Turkey, but rather out of heavy investment expenditure during the 1970s. Since the burden of debt servicing is now causing a major drain on investment spending in the heavily indebted countries, the base for future export promotion is jeopardized. The authors of the studies for Argentina, Bolivia, Brazil, and Mexico all highlight this dangerous situation with regard to current investment spending.

1.3 Adjustment to the Debt Crisis

The NBER case studies examine in great detail the process of adjustment once a debt crisis begins. The patterns of adjustment in the eight countries under study certainly belie the easy optimism of the creditor community in the years after 1982. An external debt crisis sets in motion a process of economic deterioration that is extremely difficult to limit in the short term. Early optimistic forecasts of a rapid recovery in the debtor countries, such as William Cline (1984) or Rimmer DeVries, relied on models that projected debtor country performance purely on the basis of external variables (e.g., world growth, interest rates, etc.). These studies neglected the internal economic disarray in the debtor countries that is caused by a sudden cutoff in foreign lending, combined with a sharp fall in commodities prices and a sharp rise in world interest rates.

The creditor community forecast a relatively smooth transition for economies that fell into debt crisis. Since the inflow of new capital declined sharply after 1982, the debtor economies had to shift from a position of current account deficits (i.e., net foreign borrowing) to a position closer to current account balance. Initially, it was felt, this would be brought about through a reduction of imports; subsequently, exports would grow over time in line with the growth in the markets in the industrial economies. The debtor economies would shift smoothly to a trajectory of export-led growth. Along this path, exports would exceed imports to the extent necessary to finance interest servicing on the foreign debt.

According to forecasting models such as Cline's (1984), the success of this strategy depended centrally on the external variables facing the debtor country: industrial country growth, world commodity prices, and world interest rates. Assuming an adequate trajectory for these variables (3 percent OECD growth; gently rising commodities prices; and gently declining world real interest rates), the recovery would take care of itself. The OECD growth rates and world interest rates turned out to be close to Cline's estimates, while the economic recovery in the debtor nations did not, by and large, materialize. Part of the discrepancy in Cline's forecast and the actual historical outcomes may have resulted from the decline in commodities prices after 1984, but a much larger part of the failure of Cline's model resulted from his neglect of the internal economic effects of an external debt crisis.

Remember that the debtor economies were hit by three simultaneous shocks: a cutoff in lending, a rise in world interest rates, and a fall in most commodities prices. The cutoff is new lending required that the current account balance move from deficit to near balance, and that the trade balance move from deficit to surplus (with the surplus required to finance the sharply higher interest payments on the foreign debt). Cline stressed the required adjustment in trade flows, but not the equivalent required shifts in savings and investment. Since the net foreign capital inflows before 1982 were financing domestic investment in excess of domestic savings, the cutoff in lending required a fall in investment relative to savings. As was shown in table 1.1, the common pattern was a sharp fall in the national investment rate after 1982. This fall in investment expenditure was bound to have deleterious effects on future growth prospects.

The cutoff in lending had particularly destabilizing effects since most of the foreign funds had been financing government deficits. All of a sudden, governments had to start making significant net resource transfers abroad. The sudden shift *in the public sector* from positive to negative net resource transfers is shown in table 1.7, and is most dramatic for Argentina, Bolivia, and Mexico (the shift for Brazil is delayed until 1985–86, as is the case in Indonesia and the Philippines). Governments were therefore required to cut their noninterest deficits sharply, or to shift the method of their finance. Most of the governments undertook harsh cuts in public sector investment, but dramatic as those cuts were, they were insufficient to eliminate the financing gap left over by the shift from net capital inflows to net capital outflows.

Governments therefore shifted to new forms of financing. Increased domestic bond finance tended to raise real interest rates substantially,

Table 1.7   **Net Resource Transfers to the Public Sector (medium- and long-term debt, public and publicly guaranteed)**

Country	Averages for period, percentage of GNP:		
	1981–82	1983–84	1985–86
Argentina	2.2	−1.5	0.1
Bolivia	0.0	−5.1	0.6
Brazil	0.2	0.8	−2.2
Mexico	1.8	−3.5	−0.8
Indonesia	1.4	1.9	−0.4
Philippines	2.0	2.0	−0.6
South Korea	1.3	0.7	−1.6
Turkey	0.0	−0.4	−0.6

Sources: Net resource transfers are defined as net loans minus interest payments, on medium- and long-term debt on public and publicly guaranteed debt. Data are from the World Bank, *World Debt Tables, 1987–88,* and earlier for 1979–81. GNP data are from the IMF, *International Financial Statistics Yearbook.*

while domestic money finance tended to raise inflation. Usually, governments struggled with some combination of lower public sector investment, higher internal real interest rates, and higher inflation. By 1987, very high inflation rates were deeply entrenched in the major debtor countries of Latin America, as shown by the data in table 1.8. These adverse developments often undermined the fiscal situation even further. Higher inflation reduced the real value of tax collections, while higher real interest rates increased the burden of servicing the stock of internal public debt. As recessions developed in the debtor countries, under the weight of higher real interest rates, reduced commodity prices, and falling public spending, the tax base fell in line with shrinking national income.

The adverse effects of the cutoff in lending were greatly exacerbated by the simultaneous deterioration in the terms of trade for most of the debtor countries. It *cannot* be claimed, as some have tried, that the commodity price decline was the major cause of the debt crisis, since some countries such as Bolivia and Mexico fell into crisis even though commodity prices were strong by historical standards. Nonetheless, for almost all countries, prices for commodity exports fell in real terms after 1981, and thus exacerbated the capital market shocks. The decline in export prices lowered national income, and further squeezed government revenues, since the revenue base in most of the debtor countries was either directly or indirectly tied to commodity exports (directly through exports by state enterprises, as in Bolivia and Mexico; indirectly through commodities taxes, as in Argentina).

A successful strategy of debt servicing with growth requires the development of new exports. In general, however, major new export

Table 1.8   **Inflation Rates, 1985–87, Selected Latin American Debtor Countries**

| | Inflation Rate[a] | | |
Country	1985	1986	1987[b]
Argentina	385.4	81.9	175.0
Bolivia	8,170.5	66.0	10.5[c]
Brazil	228.0	58.4	366.0
Ecuador	24.4	27.3	30.6
Mexico	63.7	105.7	159.2
Peru	158.3	62.9	114.5
Venezuela	5.7	12.3	36.1

Source: Economic Commission for Latin America and the Caribbean (ECLAC), "La evolucion economica en America Latina en 1987," January 1988.

[a]Consumer Price Index, variations of December over December of previous year.
[b]Preliminary.
[c]November to November.

sectors require heavy investment. A devaluation can sometimes produce a rapid increase in exports (as happened in South Korea and Turkey after 1980, and Brazil after 1983), but only if there is substantial excess capacity resulting from earlier investments (or if there is a sharp domestic recession, which may free up domestic capacity for export if the country produces tradables that are consumed domestically). Also, increasing the capacity of export industries often requires both public and private investment. New export sectors generally require new infrastructure in transport, communications, and perhaps port facilities, that usually are in the domain of public investment. Unfortunately, public sector investment has been among the hardest hit areas of government expenditure in the crisis countries of Argentina, Bolivia, Brazil, Mexico, and the Philippines.

1.3.1 Further Adverse Feedbacks in Adjusting to the Crisis

Adjustment to the external shocks has required enormous relative price changes within the debtor economies, but contrary to simple theory, those relative price changes have often intensified the crisis itself—at least in the short term. The inevitable effect of the cutoff in foreign lending, higher world interest rates, and adverse commodity price shocks, was a significant decline in domestic demand in the debtor economies, and therefore a sharp fall in the price of nontradables relative to tradables (i.e., a sharp depreciation of the real exchange rate, defined as the price of tradables relative to nontradables). This rapid shift against nontradables is, in principle, the motive force behind the desired shift in resources to tradables production. In practice, however, the rapid collapse of nontradables production had several highly deleterious effects in the economies under study, that in fact may have impeded the longer term reallocation of resources.

Most important, the collapse of nontradables prices led to financial distress for much of the nontradables sector. Not only did the profitability of nontradables production suffer when the real exchange rate depreciated, but nontradables firms that had incurred dollar-denominated debts found themselves unable to service their debts (the decline in the relative price of nontradables meant that nontradables output prices failed to keep pace with the rising cost of foreign exchange, which had to be purchased to service the debts). In many cases, the domestic commercial banks had borrowed internationally and then relent the borrowed funds in dollar-denominated loans in the domestic capital markets to firms in the nontradables sector. When firms in the nontradables sector could not pay back their debts, much of the banking system was put in jeopardy in Argentina, Bolivia, and Mexico. Note that firms in the tradables sector were typically better prepared to service their dollar-denominated debts, since tradables output prices moved in tandem with the price of foreign exchange.

In turn, the collapse of the banking industry disrupted financial intermediation more generally. With banks at risk, domestic residents demanded a significant risk premium over foreign interest rates in order to maintain funds in the national banking system. Several governments in Latin America were forced to take over many banks directly, or at least to take over the bad loans of much of the banking system. With many large conglomerates (known as *grupos* in Latin America) in financial distress, even the export-sector parts of the conglomerates were unable to attract new credits. (For a more general discussion of the role of the *grupos* in the Latin American financial structure, see Galbis 1987.)

Note that the central government faced the same problems as an overindebted firm in the nontradables sector. Since the public sector debts were heavily dollar-denominated, while much of the tax base was effectively linked to nontradables production, the shift in the terms of trade against nontradables tended to exacerbate the fiscal deficits. Put another way, the domestic currency value of the government's external debt rose sharply relative to the domestic currency value of the government's tax revenues. Thus, in Brazil, for example, what looked like a moderate fiscal burden of the foreign debt suddenly became enormous after the real exchange rate depreciations during 1980–82.

Once a government's fiscal situation has seriously deteriorated, a fiscal crisis can become self-fulfilling, as argued recently by Guillermo Calvo (1987). The fear of high future inflation, for example, can raise nominal interest rates, and thereby raise the interest costs for the government. Higher interest costs in turn widen the fiscal deficit and make inevitable the high future inflation. This kind of adverse feedback has apparently contributed to the sustained high interest rates in many of the debtor countries in recent years.

Despite the centrality of the public-sector budget in the origin and development of the crisis, there are profound difficulties in measuring and forecasting the fiscal position. Even the IMF auditing of the fiscal accounts, as recorded in the IMF's Government Finance Statistics, are inadequate to the task.

There are several kinds of measurement problems, many with economic significance. First, actions with fiscal consequences (e.g., actions that increase the public debt or the money supply) are made not only by the central government, but also be regional governments, parastatal enterprises, development banks, and the central bank. Often, the finance minister has little ability to measure, much less control, the consolidated public sector accounts. In most of the countries under study, the various governmental entities outside of central government can gain direct access to the central bank, or can get government guarantees for foreign borrowing, without the authorization of the finance minister.

Another problem is that private-sector obligations often quickly become public-sector obligations when a financial crisis hits, a point that we have already noted several times. Domestic firms cry for bailouts, and foreign creditors often insist as well that the central government make good on the private-sector debts. The government takeover of the debt can be partially disguised (or at least hard to measure) if the takeover comes in the form of special exchange rates for debt repayments, subsidized credits, or other off-budget means of bailing out private debtors.

The net result of this fiscal complexity is that many countries are forced to rely heavily on inflationary finance even when the measured central government budget seems close to balance. Cardoso and Fishlow discuss, for example, the data problems in Brazil, where several years of triple digit inflation were accompanied by measured deficits near zero. The small measured deficits led some to conclude that the inflation was purely an "inertial" phenomenon. This view was tested in the ill-fated Cruzado Plan, which attempted to use a wage–price–exchange rate freeze to break the inertia. After the collapse of the Cruzado Plan, most observers now concede that large fiscal deficits are the driving force of the high Brazilian inflation.

1.4 Renegotiating the Foreign Debt

The historical record, and the country experiences, speak strongly on another point. To get out of a debt crisis, countries have almost always required a sustained period of time in which the debt-servicing-burden is sharply reduced or eliminated. This financial "time out" has come about through a combination of a negotiated reduction of payments (as in the case of Indonesia during 1966–71), a substantial increase in official lending (as in the case of Turkey during 1979–81), or an unilateral suspension of debt-servicing payments (as in the case of Bolivian commercial bank debt, 1986–87). In recent years, most countries have not been able to achieve a significant "time out" through conventional negotiations. The Turkish bailout in 1979–81, for example, is an important exception that proves the rule. The generous official lending to Turkey during 1979–81 came mainly because of Turkey's geopolitical significance as a NATO ally on Iran's border, rather than as the result of conventional debtor country negotiations.

The NBER historical studies also make clear that debt relief has played an important role in the resolution of the earlier crises. Relief has come in many forms (e.g., debt repurchases at a discount, and conversions of debt into new debts with a lower servicing burden) that might prove to be relevant in the present circumstances. The studies by Lindert and Morton, and Eichengreen, both demonstrate that previous debt crises have usually ended in some forgiveness. A compromise is typically reached in which the debtors service some, but not all, of the debt that is due. *A partial writedown of the debt is the norm, not the exception.* In the past, the compromise was typically reached as the result of bilateral negotiations between debtors and creditors. Lindert and Morton suggest that the involvement in the 1980s of third parties (mainly the creditor governments and the international institutions) has hindered the effective (though often messy) process for arriving at a solution to excessive debt.

The creditor view that debt relief would be harmful even for the recipient debtor countries, because these countries would be closed' out of capital markets for many years in the future, is not supported by the historical experience. Both Lindert and Morton, and Eichengreen, find that countries that have achieved partial debt relief have not lost access to the markets to any greater extent than countries that continue to pay their debts. In the aftermath of global debt crises, neither "good" debtors nor "bad" debtors have been able to borrow.

History offers an ironic example why. Argentina was the only country in South America to service the federal debt in the 1930s, under terms laid down by onerous treaties with Great Britain. The nationalist backlash against foreign influence helped to sweep Juan Perón into power. Perón's populist policies more than undid any beneficial reputational effects that Argentina might have garnered from its debt repayments in the 1930s.

1.4.1 Debt Management during 1982–87

The management of the crisis since 1982 has so far differed from the historical experience, at least in the sense that negotiated debt relief has so far played little role in the resolution of the crisis. Indeed, because of creditor government fears over the possibility of an international banking crisis, the whole thrust of creditor government policies since the crisis began has been to *avoid* debt relief, by pressuring the debtor countries to remain current on their interest servicing. (See Sachs 1986 for an elaboration of this interpretation of creditor government policies.)

The standard form of debt management was set in the aftermath of the Mexican crisis in mid-1982. The events in Mexico prompted strong and almost immediate actions in support of Mexico from the official financial community, under the leadership of the United States. Within days of Mexico's announcement that it would be unable to meet its debt-servicing obligations, the U.S. government arranged for several forms of emergency official finance. On the other side, the U.S. government pressed hard on Mexico to maintain interest servicing to the commercial banks. In November 1982, an agreement was reached between Mexico and the IMF.

One novelty of the Mexican agreement was to link the IMF financing with new "concerted" lending from Mexico's bank creditors. The IMF declared that it would put new money into Mexico only if the existing bank creditors also increased their loan exposure. The requisite agreement with the commercial banks (involving a loan of $5 billion, which covered a portion of Mexico's interest costs in 1983) took effect in early 1983. Additionally, the Mexican debt was rescheduled. Crucially, while the rescheduling called for a postponement of repayments of principal, the rescheduling also provided for *the continued and timely payments of all interest due*. In fact, the spread over LIBOR (London interbank offer for dollar deposits) on Mexican debt was increased in the agreement, so that in present value terms, there was no sacrifice by the banks in the debt-rescheduling process.

The Mexican agreement was quickly improvised, but it nevertheless became the norm for the dozens of reschedulings that followed. Like the Mexican program, virtually all of the debt restructurings have had the following characteristics:

1. The IMF has made high-conditionality loans to the debtor government, but such loans have been made contingent on a rescheduling agreement between the country and the commercial bank creditors.
2. The commercial banks have rescheduled existing claims, by stretching out interest payments, but without reducing the contractual present value of repayments.
3. The debtor countries have agreed to maintain timely servicing of interest payments on all commercial bank loans.
4. The banks have made their reschedulings contingent on an IMF agreement being in place.
5. The official creditors have rescheduled their claims in the Paris Club setting, and have also made such reschedulings contingent on an IMF agreement.

In the original conception of the debt management strategy, the concerted lending was to play a key role in guaranteeing that countries received an adequate amount of international financing in order to stabilize and recover. In fact, after 1984, the amounts of concerted lending dropped off sharply. Moreover, as shown in table 1.9 (from Sachs and Huizinga 1987), only the *largest* debtors, with the greatest bargaining power vis-à-vis the commercial banks, have been able to obtain concerted loans with any regularity. In the table, we measured

Table 1.9   **Medium-Term Concerted Lending as a Percentage of Debt
Outstanding and Disbursed from Financial Markets[a]**

	1983	1984	1985	1986	Average 1983–1986
Argentina[b]	12	18	0	0	8
Bolivia	0	0	0	0	0
Brazil	11	14	0	0	6
Chile	35	16	9	0	15
Colombia	0	0	29	0	7
Congo	0	0	0	9	2
Costa Rica	0	0	0	0	0
Dominican Rep.	0	0	0	0	0
Ecuador	20	0	0	0	5
Gabon	0	0	0	0	0
Guatemala	0	0	0	0	0
Honduras	0	0	0	0	0
Ivory Coast	0	0	4	0	1
Jamaica	0	0	0	0	0
Liberia	0	0	0	0	0
Madagascar	0	0	0	0	0
Malawi	0	0	0	0	0
Mexico	11	6	0	8	4
Morocco	0	0	0	0	0
Nicaragua	0	0	0	0	0
Nigeria	0	0	0	4	1
Panama	0	0	3	0	1
Peru	16	0	0	0	4
Philippines	0	18	0	0	5
Senegal	0	0	0	0	0
Sudan	0	0	0	0	0
Togo	0	0	0	0	0
Uruguay	18	0	0	0	5
Venezuela	0	0	0	0	0
Yugoslavia	41	0	0	0	10
Zaire	0	0	0	0	0
Zambia	0	0	0	0	0

Sources: World Bank, *World Debt Tables, 1986–87;* IMF, *International Capital Markets, 1986.*
Taken from Sachs and Huizinga (1987).

[a]For each year t, we calculate the ratio of the concerted loan CL_t, to the disbursed debt in year $t - 1$, $D_t - 1$.

[b]In 1987 Argentina received a concerted loan amounting to 6 percent of its 1986 outstanding loans.

the size of converted loans in a given year as a proportion of disbursed debt at the end of the preceeding year. On average, this ratio is far higher for the large debtors (Argentina, Brazil, Chile, and Mexico) than for the rest of the countries. Indeed, the fifteen smallest debtors in the table had 3.4 percent of the debt at the end of 1983, but received only 0.3 percent of the concerted loans during 1984–86.

We should stress as well that the whole notion of "new" money in the concerted lending agreements is misleading, in the sense that most "new money" packages after 1982 have involved considerably less in new loans than was due to the same creditors in interest payments. Thus, even when Mexico or Argentina gets a new concerted loan, the check is still written by the country to the creditors, since the new loan only covers a fraction of the interest that is due to the creditors. The fact of negative net resource transfers points up one of the fallacies in a popular argument as to why debtor countries should not default. It is sometimes said that if a country defaults, it will not be able to attract new bank money. This is obviously not a major concern to a debtor country if the reduction in interest payments achieved by default systematically exceeds the amounts of new money that the country is able to borrow by not defaulting.

1.4.2   The Default Decision

It remains to ask why the debtor countries have by and large continued to service their debts fully in the 1980s, despite the fact that this has resulted in large net resource transfers to the creditors, at considerable economic cost to the debtor countries. In part, the answer may be simply one of time. In the first years of the crisis, most countries accepted the creditors' arguments that the crisis could be quickly resolved. As that has not come to pass, more and more countries are taking unilateral actions with respect to debt servicing. By the end of 1987, several Latin American countries had unilaterally suspended at least part of the interest servicing of the debt, including: Bolivia, Brazil, Costa Rica, Dominican Republic, Ecuador, Honduras, Nicaragua, Panama, and Peru.

Another aspect of the debt-servicing policies involves the balance of power between debtors and creditors. Debtor governments fear the retaliation of the commercial banks, especially in the form of a cutoff in trade credits. Ironically, those countries that have suspended interest payments in recent years (e.g., Brazil, Ecuador, and Peru), have generally been able to maintain their trade credit lines, though at the cost of a higher risk premium on the short-term borrowing.

Another kind of retaliation that is feared is a reaction by the creditor governments (especially the United States), either within the financial sphere or more generally in other areas of foreign relations. Countries fear that if they suspend interest servicing, they may lose access to support from the IMF, the World Bank, the Paris Club (for a rescheduling of debts with official bilateral lenders), foreign aid agencies, and export credit agencies. Moreover, debtor governments fear that the leading creditor governments might withdraw other forms of foreign policy support (e.g., involving trade policy, security assistance, etc.), and might even back political opponents of the regime.

The United States government has repeatedly warned would-be recalcitrant debtors that nonpayments of interest on the foreign debt constitutes a major breach of international financial relations, and a major breach of normal relations with the United States. Countries that choose default with their bank creditors are forced into the position of simultaneously choosing a hostile action vis-à-vis the United States government. Most finance ministers, and their presidents, do not have the stomach for such a confrontation, which takes steady nerves and a considerable capacity to explain the crisis to the domestic populace.

A final and often overlooked reason that countries do not default involves the domestic political economy of the debtor country. In the case of a unilateral suspension of debt payments, some sectors and classes of the economy will tend to gain and others will tend to lose. Gainers from tough bargaining will usually include the nontradables sectors, urban workers, and landless peasants producing from the domestic market. Losers will include the tradables sectors (both because of repercussions on the exchange rate, and because of possible retaliation), and the domestic financial community, which has a stake in harmonious financial relations with the foreign banks. Left-wing governments, such as Alan Garcia's in Peru, are therefore more likely to please their working class constituency by taking a hard line on the debt than are governments oriented to exporters and the banking community. Most developing country governments, however, have sufficiently close ties with leading bankers (domestic and foreign) and leading exporters, that they are unwilling to run the risk of an overt international confrontation.

1.5 New Approaches to Managing the Debt Crisis

The unsatisfactory economic performance of most of the debtor countries in the past five years has led to continued suggestions for new approaches to international debt management. The NBER studies by Fischer, Krugman, and Sachs consider several alternatives that have been widely discussed, as well as some new proposals. Edwards and Sachs discuss the appropriate role of the international institutions, and the appropriate kinds of policy reforms, for overcoming the crisis.

All of the authors stress that a workable solution to the debt crisis will differ across countries. Some countries, such as Bolivia, Sudan, or Zaire, clearly can service only a small faction of their debts on market terms. When Bolivia tried to meet its debt-servicing obligations during 1982–84, the result was a hyperinflation (the links of debt servicing and hyperinflation are explained by Morales and Sachs). Other countries can service some, but perhaps not all of their debts at normal market terms. Thus, a real case-by case approach would recognize the need for substantial debt relief for some of the poorest and weakest economies, and perhaps some lesser degree of relief for the other debtor countries.

1.5.1 The Case for Debt Relief

Krugman and Sachs both illustrate the efficiency case for debt relief (see also Sachs 1988 for a further analysis). A heavy debt burden acts like a high marginal tax rate on economic adjustment. If the economy successfully imposes austerity, much of the benefit accrues to the foreign creditors. Partial debt relief can therefore be Pareto improving (i.e., to the benefit of *both* creditors and debtors), by improving the incentives for the debtor country to take needed adjustment actions. In political terms, partial debt relief can strengthen the hand of moderates, who would pay some but not all of the debt, against the hand of extremists, who would like to service little or none of the debt.

Debt relief is extremely difficult to negotiate, for several reasons. First, because each debtor country has many types of creditors, and the various creditors have the incentive to let the *others* grant the debt relief while they individually try to hold on to the full value of their claims. Second, the linkage between debt relief and improved economic policies is not sufficiently tight to make debt relief an obvious proposition for the creditors. Even if creditors understand that the existing overhang of debt acts as a major disincentive to policy reform in the debtor countries, they might be skeptical that debt relief alone would be sufficient to lead to policy reforms. The creditors tend to view debt relief as throwing away money, i.e., giving up the potential of getting fully repaid, with little tangible benefit. As Sachs points out, the strongest case for debt relief can be made if the relief can be explicitly conditioned on particular policy reforms in the debtor countries.

Fischer offers an analysis of a broad range of proposals for modifying the current management of the crisis, dividing his analysis between those alternatives that would merely restructure the debt, and those that would effectively cancel part of the debt. In the first group, he considers debt-equity swaps, and echoes the conclusions of Krugman that debt-equity swaps are unlikely to be a major vehicle for resolving the crisis. Indeed Krugman shows how such swaps can very easily be detrimental to the debtor country.

Among proposals that would offer partial forgiveness to the debtor countries (i.e., an explicit writedown of part of the present value of the debt), Fischer focuses heavily on the idea of creating an International Debt Discount Corporation (IDDC). The IDDC would buy developing country debt from the banks in exchange for claims on the institution, and in turn collect from the debtor countries. The basic idea is that the IDDC buy the debt at a discount, and then cancel some of the debt due from the debtor country. Calculations in Sachs and

Huizinga (1987) show that the IDDC, far from hurting the commercial banks, could actually raise their market value, because the bank stock prices have *already* been deeply discounted in view of their LDC debt exposure.

Fischer stresses, however, that the most likely scenario is that partial relief will result from bilateral negotiations between creditors and debtors (as in the historical examples described by Eichengreen, and by Lindert and Morton) rather than through a single international relief operation.

1.5.2 Breaking the Cycle of Failed Reforms

I have stressed that policy "mistakes" in the debtor countries are often not mistakes (in the sense that the government misunderstands the implications of its actions). Rather they are often symptoms of deeper political or economic problems in the debtor countries. The diagnosis that a budget deficit is too large, and therefore should be reduced, is not a complete diagnosis. In the abstract, most finance ministers understand that excessive inflation, or excessive foreign borrowing, result from excessively large budget deficits. At the same time, they are often unable or unwilling to do much to reduce the deficits. In order to improve the design of stabilization programs, and to improve the effectiveness of conditionality, we must therefore give greater emphasis as to why the political process produces the excessive deficits. The papers by Haggard and Kaufman, Sachs, and Edwards, as well as the country monographs, all emphasize the political context in which various economic policies are pursued.

The basic ideas in most stabilization programs supported by the IMF and World Bank are quite straightforward, and aim to reduce budget deficits, achieve a real exchange rate depreciation, and open the economy to international trade. The sobering point is that programs of this sort have been adopted repeatedly, and have failed repeatedly, in the countries under investigation during the past 30 years. A major goal must be to understand why such programs typically fail.

Consider the case of Mexico and Argentina, for example. As the Mexican case study by Buffie and Krause makes clear, the "standard" package has been attempted in 1971, 1977, and 1983. In the first two cases, at least, major parts of the package were abandoned early on. Similarly, in Argentina, the "orthodox" package has been tried under Perón, in 1951; Onganía, in 1967 (the so-called Krieger-Vasena program); Viola, in 1977–81 (with Martinez de Hoz as finance minister); and to some extent, Alfonsin, since 1985. Again, the staying power of the orthodox program has been very weak in Argentina. (Very recently, this weakness was again underscored by the electoral losses of Alfonsin's Radical party and the electoral resurgence of the Perónists.)

I have already noted that part of the problem with program implementation lies in the deep political and class cleavages that afflict most of the countries under study, combined with weak political institutions and fragmented political parties that fail to keep pace with rapid increases in political and social mobilization. The result, as pointed out by Samuel Huntington in an influential treatise, is that "cliques, blocs, and mass movements struggle directly with each other, each with its own weapons. Violence is democratized, politics demoralized, society at odds with itself" (Huntington 1968, 262). This is certainly an apposite sketch of Argentina, Bolivia, Brazil, the Philippines, and Turkey at various times in recent history. In the end, governments alternate rapidly between civilian and military regimes, and budgets are exploited for short-term political advantage rather than long-term economic strategy.

Interestingly, Huntington suggested that political stability in modernizing societies can best be achieved through an alliance of an urban ruling elite with the rural masses. Ideally, according to Huntington, that alliance is cemented through agrarian reform and the organization of party support in the countryside. Among the countries under study in the NBER project, Indonesia and South Korea most closely fit Huntington's characterization, as the governments have sought stability through an important base of rural support. (In the case of Indonesia, however, Soeharto's stress on his rural constituency was combined, early in his rule, with violent repression of his rural opposition.) In none of the Latin American countries in the NBER study have governments recently looked to the rural sector as the principal locus of political support. An apparent exception to this rule in Latin America is Colombia (which unfortunately was not studied in the NBER project), which is also the only major South American economy to have avoided a debt crisis.

Haggard and Kaufman identify several other features of the political landscape which affect a government's capacity to carry out necessary economic adjustments, including: the administrative capacity of the governments, the pattern of trade union organization, and the susceptibility of the political institutions to electoral business cycles.

Sachs stresses that the normal problems of carrying out a reform program are greatly exacerbated by the overhang of foreign debt. Not only is the economic adjustment process made more difficult, but the political difficulties of reform are deepened as well. To the extent that the reforms serve mainly to raise the amount of foreign debt servicing, and so act as a tax on the domestic economy, they will find little political support domestically. Indeed, the government will be heatedly attacked for caving in to the interests of the foreign creditors. Adding debt relief as a part of the package of reform and adjustment could greatly enhance the likelihood that the economic program will in fact be carried out and sustained.

Sachs also explores whether changes in the nature of IMF/World Bank conditionality could increase the chances of compliance with programs monitored by these institutions. He argues that the nature of negotiations between the IMF and the debtor countries seems almost programmed to undermine the political legitimacy of Fund programs, thereby reducing their chance of success. In recent years, IMF programs have been unrealistically harsh, as they reflect the priorities of the private creditors rather than the realities of economic adjustment. Though the IMF has not yet acknowledged the possibility, there are times when debts to private sector creditors cannot and will not be paid in full. Designing programs based on the opposite assumption is bound to lead to frustration and failure.

Moreover, the style of negotiations seems problematic. Most IMF programs are negotiated between a technocratic team in the debtor government and the IMF staff, under conditions of secrecy. The letter of intent with the IMF is generally not made public by the debtor government. The result is that the agreement with the Fund often has little internal political support, and calls for actions by parts of the government (e.g., the legislative branch) or the private sector (e.g., the union organizations) that were not parties to the agreement. Since the actions are typically things that the government must do "down the road", the programs are signed, and then not adequately implemented.

With regard to the substantive design of adjustment programs, Edwards disputes the notion that dramatic liberalization is helpful in the context of a debt or stabilization crisis, suggesting that dramatic liberalization has little basis in either theory or history. Edwards argues that rapid trade liberalization is likely to generate adverse employment effects in the short term, as occurred in the liberalization programs in Argentina, Chile, and Uruguay in the 1970s. Similarly, abrupt devaluations are likely to result in output losses and unemployment in the short run.

1.5.3 The Global Macroeconomic Setting

Even with debt relief, political resolve in the debtor countries, and well-designed economic reform programs, the chances for economic recovery in the debtor countries wil depend on an adequate international economic environment. Dornbusch suggests that the probability of a "soft-landing" as the U.S. reduces its external deficits is rather low. In the Dornbusch view, a successful adjustment path for the U.S. will require a period of progressively tighter fiscal policy combined with expansionary monetary policy, with a strong likelihood of rising inflation in the United States as the dollar continues to weaken. Dornbusch suggests that "the monetary authorities would have to be sufficiently accommodating and impervious to inflation, and asset holders would have to be patient, sitting out the dollar depreciation without a stampede." He concludes that "this does not seem to be a high-probability scenario."

On the other hand, by stressing the crucial importance of interest rates, Dornbusch does signal one possible macroeconomic bright spot for the crisis. There are several signs at the end of 1987 of a persistent downward trend in the level of U.S. real interest rates, related to reductions in the U.S. budget deficit, easier monetary policy, and perhaps an incipient rise in U.S. private savings. A sustained reduction in real interest rates below the export growth rates of the debtor countries could significantly meliorate the crisis, in the same way that the sustained rise in real interest rates at the beginning of the 1980s was a decisive international shock that ushered in the crisis.

References

Balassa, Bela. 1984. Adjustment Policies in Developing Countries: A Reassessment. *World Development* 12 (September): 955–72.

Bhagwati, Jagdish. 1978. *Anatomy and consequences of exchange control regimes.* Cambridge, Mass.: Ballinger Publishing Company.

Brecher, Richard, and Carlos Díaz-Alejandro. 1977. Tariffs, foreign capital, and immiserizing growth. *Journal of International Economics* 7 (4): 317–22.

Calvo, Guillermo. 1987. Servicing the public debt: The role of expectations. Philadelphia: Penn.: University of Pennsylvania. Mimeo.

Cline, William. 1984. *International debt: Systemic risk and policy response.* Washington, D.C.: Institute for International Economics, July.

Cumby, Robert, and Richard M. Levich. 1987. On the definition and magnitude of recent capital flight. NBER Working Paper no. 2275 (June). Cambridge, Mass: National Bureau of Economic Research.

Galbis, Vincente. 1987. La liberalization del sector financiero bajo condiciones oligopolicas y las estructura de los holdings bancarios. In *Estabilizacion y ajuste estructural en America Latina,* ed. Santiago Roca. Lima, Peru: IDE/ESAN. [English language version is published in *Savings and development* no. 21 (1986), Milan, Italy.]

Huntington, Samuel. 1968. *Political order in changing societies.* New Haven, Conn.: Yale University Press.

Krueger, A. 1978. *Foreign trade regimes and economic development: Liberalization attempts and consequences.* Cambridge, Mass.: Ballinger Publishing Company.

Makin, John. 1984. *The global debt crisis.* New York: Basic Books.

———. 1987. Trade and exchange-rate policies in growth-oriented adjustment programs. In *Growth-oriented adjustment programs,* ed. Vittorio Corbo, M. Goldstein, and M. Khan. Washington, D.C.: International Monetary Fund and The World Bank.

————. 1988. The debt overhang of developing countries (paper presented at memorial conference, WIDER, Helsinki, Finland, 1986). In a conference volume in memory of Carlos Díaz-Alejandro, ed. Ronald Findlay and Jorge de Macedo. Forthcoming.

Sachs, Jeffrey, and Harry Huizinga. 1987. The U.S. commercial banks and the developing-country debt crisis. *Brookings Papers on Economic Activity* 2: 555–601.

I Country Studies

2   Debt and Macroeconomic Instability in Argentina

Rudiger Dornbusch and Juan Carlos de Pablo

2.1 Introduction

In l985, after 40 years of financial instability, Argentina reached once again near-hyperinflation conditions. Budget deficits were the immediate cause, but the deeper roots must be seen in ill-fated policy experiments of the l970s. The destructive pendulum between populists and market-oriented reformists has meant that much of national wealth is held abroad, taxes are paid by only a few, and the general atmosphere is one of skepticism about everything Argentine. Mallon and Sourrouille (1975) have drawn attention to this steady conflict when they write,

> Decision makers in Argentina have quite consistently attempted to adopt policy positions that seemed designed to tear society apart rather than to forge new coalitions. . . . Major policy disagreements in modern Argentina history have their main roots in the conflict between two divergent streams of thought: liberalism of the British Manchester School variety and what can be called national populism. . . . In general, the liberals have stood for the virtues of a society open to international opportunities and influences, whereas, the national populists have emphasized indigenous, autonomous development (p. 11).

Our study investigates the interaction between domestic macroeconomic instability and external constraints. We study these relationships by focusing on the past decade in which four very different periods can be distinguished:

Rudiger Dornbusch is Ford International Professor of Economics at the Massachusetts Institute of Technology and a research associate of the National Bureau of Economic Research. Juan Carlos de Pablo is a professor of economics at the Catholic University of Argentina and an editorial writer for *El Cronista Comercial*.

1. The Martinez de Hoz period of the second half of the 1970s when external debts were accumulated in the context of an incompatible mix of policies: persistent deficits, a strongly overvalued currency, and liberalization of capital flows.
2. The period running from the end of the 1970s to the hyperinflation. In this period debt and foreign exchange problems, war and domestic politics are the reasons for an inflation explosion.
3. The Austral stabilization plan.
4. The post-Austral quest for a resumption of growth.

2.2   A Long-Run Perspective

Although we only focus on the past ten years we place our analysis in a long-run context. This is appropriate since debt problems and financial crises are at least 100 years old in Argentina. One hundred years ago Argentina's inability to service foreign debt nearly brought down the City of London in the famous Baring panic of 1890; the Tornquist monetary reform dates back to 1899.

It is important to view developments in this long-term perspective because it highlights how Argentina has lost its position in the world economy steadily during this century.[1] Carlos Díaz Alejandro (1970, 1) reminds us of this decline:

> It is common nowadays to lump the Argentine economy in the same category with the economies of other Latin American nations. Some opinion even puts it among such less developed nations as India and Nigeria. Yet most economists writing during the first three decades of this century would have placed Argentina among the most advanced countries—with Western Europe, the United States, Canada, and Australia. To have called Argentina "underdeveloped" in the sense that word has today would have been considered laughable.

If in 1900 Argentina had a U.S. standard of living, then the decline has been long and deep. Summers and Heston (1984) estimate that in 1950 Argentina had only 41 percent of the U.S. standard of living (against 80 percent in Australia and Canada). By 1985 the standard of living had slipped to only 30 percent of the U.S. level. Figure 2.1 shows the level of per capita real income in Argentina over the past 45 years.

There is a striking difference between the steady expansion of the thirty years to 1975 and the stagnation and decline that have occurred since then. The contrast could not be stronger: From 1945 to 1975 per capita income grew at an annual rate of 1.7 percent. From 1975 to 1985 it fell at an annual rate of 1.7 percent.

The other dimension in which Argentine performance has shown a dramatic deterioration is inflation and fiscal stability. Of course, there have been frequent precedents of massive inflation and depreciation.

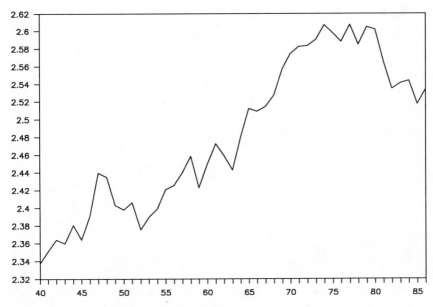

Fig. 2.1   Real per capita GDP (logarithm)

But the experience of the past decade, with two near hyperinflations, stands out. In 1899 *Banker's Magazine* already reported of South Americans and their currency: [2]

> [They] are always in trouble about their currency. Either it is too good for home use, or, as frequently happens, it is too bad for foreign exchange. Generally, they have too much of it, but their own idea is that they never have enough . . . the Argentines alter their currency almost as frequently as they change presidents. . . . No people in the world take a keener interest in currency experiments than the Argentines.

The experience with the destruction of the financial system in the past 15 years has certainly reinforced that keen interest and expertise. Figure 2.2 shows the *monthly* rate of inflation since 1970. In interpreting the graph one should bear in mind that a monthly rate of inflation of 6 percent corresponds to 100 percent per year, and 22 percent per month yields an annual rate of 1,000 percent. Inflation passed 2,000 percent both in the Perónist period of 1975–76 and again in the pre-Austral period of early 1985. At no time in the past ten years did it fall below 100 percent for any length of time.

The third broad feature that we want to draw attention to concerns the real exchange rate. This is a key price in any economy and even more so in Argentina. Figure 2.3 shows the real exchange rate measured

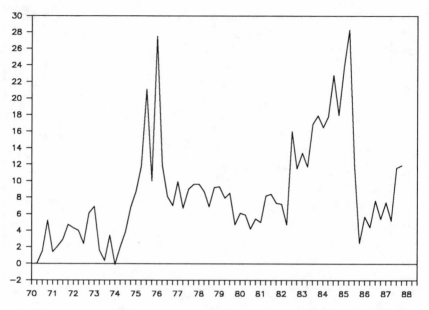

Fig. 2.2   Inflation rate of the CPI (quarterly average of monthly rates)

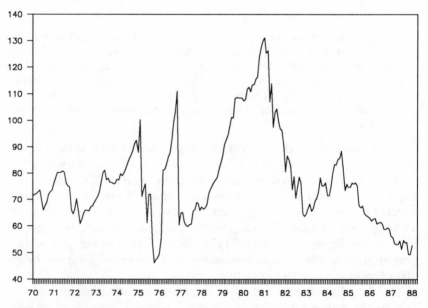

Fig. 2.3   Real exchange rate (index 1980–82 = 100)

as the ratio of Argentine manufactured prices relative to those of her trading partners.[3]

The extraordinary variations in Argentina's external competitiveness are tied closely to the macroeconomic policy mistakes, capital flight induced by these mistakes, and the present debt crisis. The outstanding episode, clearly apparent in figure 2.3, is the real appreciation of 1979–81. For the period 1970–78 the real exchange rate averaged 73; it increased to 108 over the next three years before declining back to an average of 75 in the 1982–86 period. By March 1987 it had fallen to almost a third of the peak value during the period of most extreme overvaluation. The swings in the real exchange rate capture best the seesaw nature of Argentine policies. In some periods unimaginable damage is done to the productive and financial structure and then a period of repair follows where austerity and real depreciation restore the base for yet another political, fiscal, or foreign exchange adventure.

Table 2.1 shows the debt accumulation over the past 15 years. There is considerable uncertainty about the size of the external debt prior to the late 1970s and available estimates from various official sources vary widely. Estimates of the BCRA (Banco Central de la Republica Argentina) show that the debt varied between $2.5 and $3 billion in the 1960s, starting at about the same level as it ended. But from 1970 on, external debt steadily increases both for the private and for the public sector. Between 1970 and 1977 the external debt rises by $6 billion and in the next four years by more than $30 billion.

With this broad overview of the past decade we now turn to a review of the principal episodes. We use these episodes to describe and explain their relevance to the debt problem, or the role of the external debt in creating domestic macroeconomic difficulties. A brief chronology of dates and important facts helps place the events in context.

2.2.1 The Martinez de Hoz Period (3/1976–3/1981)

When de Hoz assumed power as finance minister of the military government, consumer prices in the previous month had increased at

Table 2.1   **Argentina's External Debt ($ billion and percentage)**

	1975	1978	1979	1982	1985
Total external debt ($)	7.9	12.5	19.0	43.6	48.3
Public ($)	4.0	8.4	10.0	28.6	40.0
Reserves ($)	0.6	5.8	10.1	3.0	6.0
Net debt/exports (%)	260	110	120	540	520
Debt/GDP (%)	18.6	23.9	30.2	60.3	64.5
Interest payments/GDP (%)	0.7	1.4	1.4	2.4	5.7

Sources: World Bank, BCRA, and Morgan Guaranty Trust.

an annual rate of 5,000 percent and output had declined sharply. The black market premium for foreign exchange exceeded 200 percent.[4] The new program was to stabilize the macroeconomy, as a first priority, and then to renovate industry and financial markets. Macroeconomic stabilization was under way quite rapidly so that inflation soon fell to less than 150 percent.

A financial reform was implemented in June 1977 that aimed to liberalize capital markets and link Argentina more effectively with the world capital market. Already in late 1976 foreign exchange transactions were completely liberalized *on capital* account and this was done so effectively that for the next four years the black market premium was zero. Figure 2.4 shows the black market premium and brings out the striking interlude of free capital mobility between the Perónist period and the aftermath of the collapse of Martinez de Hoz's policies.

Inflation failed to decline further once it had come to the 150 percent range. To make further inroads, policymakers opted for what Fernandez (1985) has called an "expectations management approach." Beginning in 1979 they pre-fixed the rate of exchange depreciation with a *tablita*, announcing ahead of time gradually declining rates of depreciation. These announcements were repeated on a rolling (though shortening) basis so as to create an environment where economic agents could discern a government commitment to disinflation embodied in the timetable for declining rates of exchange depreciation.

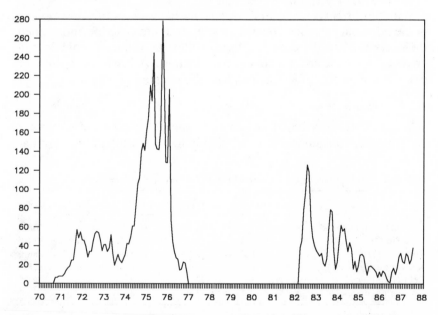

Fig. 2.4   Exchange rate gap, parallel/official (Australs per $US)

This policy was expected to reduce inflation through three separate channels. First, reduced rates of depreciation would directly reduce the rate of import price inflation. Second, reduced depreciation would enforce a discipline on domestic price setters. Third, in an environment where inflation to a large extent depended on expectations, the rule or precommitment introduced a fixed point around which expectations could rally. Needless to say, the intellectual underpinnings of such a program relied on the belief that the "law of one price" would be strongly operative.

Inflation responded to this policy and gradually fell throughout 1980 to reach a bottom well below 100 percent. But gradually, during 1978–80, the *real* exchange rate appreciated because inflation consistently outpaced the rate of depreciation. We saw in figure 2.3 that the cumulative overvaluation reached 50 or even 60 percent. But while the overvaluation ultimately led to capital flight and collapse of the financial system, the early stages were quite the opposite. The high interest rates— relative to world rates and the preannounced rate of depreciation— gave rise to an (almost) risk-free speculation in favor of Argentine assets. As a result, private-sector borrowing abroad increased to take advantage of the relatively low foreign interest rates and a massive capital inflow developed. This is shown in table 2.1 in the large increase in Central Bank reserves between 1978 and 1979 and the matching increase in private external borrowing.

The trade and employment effects of the overvaluation were slow to come. Díaz Alejandro (1964) has shown that the real income effects of a real depreciation tend to be dominant in the early stages, before substitution effects take over. For the real appreciation of 1977–80 the reverse applied: The increase in real income created an expansion in demand and thus seemed to validate the Martinez de Hoz approach by creating inflation reduction with rising real income. This factor was reinforced by the fact that trade protection, even with liberalization measures, kept the economy relatively closed, which dampened the disinflation effects of the *tablita* but also the effects in the real sector.

By 1979–80 the overvaluation had become so extreme that financial markets increasingly took the view that depreciation would have to come sometime. Even though the government asserted that the policy would be continued, and could be financed, speculation increasingly went in the direction of dollar purchases. The regime of unrestricted capital mobility introduced in late 1976 facilitated this capital flight to the maximum. Hence, in 1980–81, the Central Bank and public sector enterprises were forced to borrow massively abroad to obtain the foreign exchange which was then sold in support of the exchange rate policy. Private speculators in turn bought the dollars and applied them abroad. With the round trip complete, commercial banks in New York,

Zurich, and Tokyo had lent to the government the resources to finance capital flight which returned to the same banks as deposits. Of course, capital flight was not limited to dollar deposits. Investments in financial markets were important as was real estate abroad.

A variety of estimates is available on the accumulation of external assets by Argentines during this period. These estimates are typically formed as residuals from debt and balance-of-payments data. They are obtained by deducting from the recorded increase in gross external debt the current account and recorded capital flows in the form of direct investment and changes in reserves. Dornbusch (1985), for example, calculates that capital flight in 1978–82 amounted to $23.4 billion. In a review of various estimates, the IMF (Watson et al. 1986, 142) reports capital flight amounting cumulatively to about $15 billion in 1979–81. Rodriguez (1983) estimates that between 1979 and 1982 the external assets of Argentineans increased from $10 billion to $34 billion. The estimates would have to be revised upward to the extent that underinvoicing of exports and overinvoicing of imports was a significant channel of capital flight in this period.

Both the fact of and the motivation for the wave of capital flight in the late 1970s are very clear. Unlike in other debtor countries, as for example Brazil or Chile, mismanagement of the exchange rate combined with an opening of the capital account are the almost exclusive explanations for the massive debt accumulation. One must understand the particular background to appreciate that in Argentina's case the government has an external debt, but the private sector has external assets of at least half the size. Moreover, that process was carried further over the next few years as the government increasingly took over all external debt in the course of sustaining failing financial institutions. In 1980 about half of the debt was owed by the public sector, and in 1985 that share had increased to 82 percent.

2.2.2 From Martinez de Hoz to Alfonsin (3/1981–12/1983)

The end of the military government did not come easily. The Martinez de Hoz overvaluation had sown the seeds of financial destruction, but the actual unraveling came only over the next four years. The world economy contributed to the difficulties of the debt crisis: Sharply declining commodity prices and much higher interest rates brought with them difficulties in servicing the external debt.

But domestic events certainly were the dominant factor. First came the undoing of the overvaluation. This started with the change of presidents: The incoming president, months before taking office, declined to comment on his exchange rate policy. This served as an obvious indication to anyone that devaluation was ahead and hence capital flight became massive. Central Bank reserves declined by more than $5 billion and public external debt increased sharply. Finally Martinez de Hoz was forced by his successor, not yet in office, to bring his own expectations management and credibility approach to an end by devaluing the currency.

Over the next three years exchange depreciation and inflation became endemic, rising from less than 100 percent to 600 percent at the time Alfonsin took office. Changes in public finance and financial markets were particularly important in this period. Exchange control was instituted once again, and the black market premium reemerged (see figure 2.4). The Central Bank, in an effort to assure continuing trade flows, started exchange rate guarantee programs only to find that it could never sustain the guaranteed exchange rates. As a result of losing a string of bets in the foreign exchange market, the budget deteriorated dramatically. The deterioration was reinforced by financial failures that turned up in the public-sector, by the burden of external interest payments, and by deteriorating terms of trade. The conflict in the South Pacific added to the loss in confidence and devastation of public finance.

The economics of this period of deterioration can be expressed in terms of a simple model of deficit finance and of financial markets. Suppose the budget deficit represents a fraction, g, of national income, and let velocity of high-powered money be an increasing function of the rate of inflation. Then it can be shown that the rate of inflation, p, will be an increasing (and steeply rising) function of the deficit, but it will also depend on financial institutions.

(1) $$p = (ag - y)/(1 - bg).$$

The higher the level of noninflationary velocity, a, and the more responsive velocity is to inflation as measured by the parameter b, the more dramatic the inflation impact of budget deficits.

This framework helps to identify the interaction of deficits, external debt service, real depreciation, and financial markets in generating the inflation explosion of 1981–84. Increasing burdens of debt service, because of higher interest rates and real depreciation, increased the budget deficit ratio, g, and hence raised money creation and inflation. The institutional response of financial markets to higher inflation aggravated this impact by a flight from money. The reduction in money holdings was facilitated by an increasing range of interest-bearing substitutes. As these came increasingly into play, velocity sharply increased (a and b in [1] above increased) and that meant the inflation rate associated with a given deficit ratio also escalated.

The 1981–84 period thus represents an unraveling of the artificial stability of the late 1970s. Several events, each in itself extraordinary, combined to make the crisis large: The initial overvaluation had been extreme, the financial sector had been allowed to become overexposed in speculation, private capital flight had been massive, and finally the world economy turned unfavorable just at the wrong time. Each of these factors deteriorated the budget and hence reinforced inflation.

2.2.3 Alfonsin (1/1984–)

These difficulties carried over to the beginning of the Alfonsin administration. Large real wage increases in 1983–84 created problems for the budget and for the external balance. Inflation rapidly escalated and negotiations with creditors and the IMF did not bring a solution.

The inflation issue soon became the single most pressing problem. In early 1985 annualized monthly rates of inflation rose toward 1,500 percent and beyond. The possibility of a hyperinflation was entirely realistic since the inflation process itself eroded the real value of tax collection as well as the financial system, so that ever more money needed to be created to finance an ever-widening deficit. Because IMF programs seemed unable to cope with the inflation problem on a timetable and in a fashion that was politically acceptable, and because the sheer pace of disintegration was so rapid, the government considered extreme measures. The monetary reform known as the Austral Plan was just that, an all-out attempt to stop hyperinflation.

The details of the June 1985 Plan of Economic Reform, which is now called the Austral Plan, were as follows:

- A real depreciation and a sharp increase in real public sector prices. An export and import tax, a forced saving scheme, and accelerated tax collection.
- A wage–price–exchange rate freeze.
- A new money, the Austral, and a promise not to create money to finance the budget.
- A conversion scale for existing contracts that would adjust them so as to keep real burdens unchanged in the face of the unanticipated reduction in inflation.
- An IMF agreement and a rescheduling agreement with the creditors.

The stabilization immediately reduced inflation to levels of only 1–2 percent per month. The decline in inflation and the fiscal measures brought about a rapid and major shift in the budget. High real interest rates and the budget improvement created an atmosphere of at least temporary stabilization. The black market premium vanished. For a country that had been on the verge of hyperinflation the stabilization created an immense relief, but it also left considerable skepticism as to the possibility of stopping inflation by edict. The skepticism extended in particular to the government's ability to achieve sufficient budget control to permanently reduce the need for inflationary money creation.

But even if skepticism persisted, the stabilization proved to be an important political move and as such a stepping stone for a more fundamental stabilization. A public opinion survey presents an assessment over time of the public response to policy and management. The data are reported in table 2.2.

This was not the first time Argentina had used wage-price controls to stop inflation. Indeed, in 1975–76 this was tried, and the experience ended in an outburst of repressed inflation. The Austral Plan has in fact not brought price stability. Inflation today is back to the 100–200 percent rate. But the important achievement is that inflation was brought down from more than 2,000 percent and that this was accomplished without a decline in economic activity, rise in unemployment, or reduction in the purchasing power of wages.

Today there is little risk that in the near term the stabilization will collapse. That confidence makes it possible and fruitful for the government to concentrate on the two key issues: How to achieve further budget improvement so as to bring inflation down to less than 20 percent and how to restore investment and growth. External debt and debt service have a bearing on each of these questions.

2.3 Investment, Debt, and the Budget

The budget influences inflation as well as investment and growth because it influences the distribution of resources in the economy. If the government commands a large share of the resources less is left for the private sector. The government may use these resources to service the external debt by means of noninterest external surpluses; it can use the resources to support consumption; or it can make them available for investment. The possible choices of budget strategy then are to service the debt, sustain consumption, or use resources for growth. Table 2.3 shows the budget of the consolidated government.

Two points must be distinguished when looking at the budget impact on the economy. One is the *way* in which the government finances its outlays, i.e., by regular taxes, by borrowing, or by the inflation tax. The second, possibly related, is how the tax system determines the allocation of resources among sectors. To illustrate, the government

Table 2.2   **Response to the Austral Plan (percentage of the sample responding positively)**

	1984 Dec.	May	1985 Aug.	Dec.	1986 Apr.
Austral Plan			74	68	52
Economic management	19	10	40	35	19
Government in general	46	35	57	52	36
President Alfonsin	72	64	74	71	64

Source: La Nación.

Table 2.3   Budget (percentage of GDP, budget basis)

	Expenditure	Revenues	Budget Deficit
1980	43.9	36.4	7.5
1981	49.1	35.8	13.3
1982	48.2	33.1	15.1
1983	51.6	34.8	16.8
1984	46.2	33.4	12.8
1985	47.4	41.5	5.9
1986	43.4	39.8	3.6

Source: BCRA

can replace the inflation tax with outright taxes and there will be little effect in the aggregate except that inflation will decline. But if the inflation tax declines without an offsetting increase in outright taxes then an offsetting reduction in absorption needs to occur: Either the government cuts its spending or it reduces its debt service.

For the country at large there is a trade-off between consumption, investment, and net resource transfers abroad. These points can be brought out by looking at the GDP identity:

(2)   Output = Net Resource Transfer Abroad
              + Investment + Consumption,

where consumption denotes private- and public-sector consumption, and investment, likewise, includes the private and public sectors. With a given amount of resources or output available (because the economy is fully employed already) the budget and the external debt strategy now determine inflation and growth.

To show the range of options we can look at two particular scenarios. One possibility is to keep budget adjustments to a minimum, not to interfere with consumption and yet foster growth via increased investment. That strategy requires, as (2) shows, that resource transfers abroad can no longer occur or must even be reversed. In a second scenario the government seeks both investment and continued, partial debt service. In that case the resource shortage calls for crowding out of consumption by outright taxation or by the inflation tax.

Over the past few years crowding out of investment, not consumption, has been the rule. By maintaining relatively tight money and a strongly competitive exchange rate the government has crowded out private investment, with consumption and transfers abroad absorbing the available resources. The adverse effect of positive and often high real interest rates on investment is all the more punishing in that uncertainty about future budget trends, debt service, and hence interest rates, makes it unwise to repatriate capital or risk borrowing.

Figure 2.5 shows the extraordinarily low rate of investment (as a percentage of GNP) in Argentina. Net investment in fact is zero or negative. With productive capacity not expanding, or even shrinking, there is no source of growth in the standard of living. Hence the question is whether the current policy mix can be sustained much longer without doing irreparable damage to the productive system and thus to the long-run viability of the economy. The flourishing of the underground economy is certainly a warning signal of a very undesirable trend.

IMF programs for Argentina, in the absence of an official change in the debt strategy, anticipate that the current account deficit gradually declines as a ratio of GDP and ultimately turns toward surplus. The 1986 program, for example, anticipated that by 1990 Argentina's current account would reach a modest surplus of 0.2 percent of GDP. That means, of course, net resources transfers in the full amount of interest liabilities and no "new money" except for principal. This strategy, if it is to be consistent with even moderate growth of the economy's supply side, requires a major shift in the budget to contain consumption. That can take the form of a much higher inflation tax or a much higher outright form of taxation.

Latin American leaders advocate a different scenario. They claim that net resource flows need to be reversed and that the noninterest

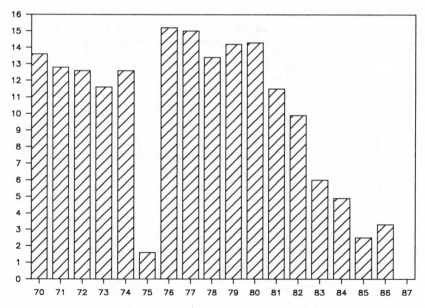

Fig. 2.5   Private investment (percentage of GDP)

surpluses can come down. Resources need to be transferred inward again, they argue, so that they can supplement scarce domestic saving in financing domestic investment. Such a reversal of resource flows encounters the problem of creditworthiness. If now debtor countries like Argentina experience difficulties in servicing the debt, is it plausible that yet more debt should be added. Feldstein (1987) has made the case that some countries, in particular Brazil, can both borrow and grow without risking the buildup of an unsustainable debt. It is difficult to see that possibility in Argentina, except in the context of a major restructuring of the public sector.

But if increased reliance is placed on external resources by reducing net transfers abroad, the question must be asked how the extra space thus gained should be used. Once again a fiscal reform could translate these resources into growth of productive capacity. Using them for consumption would simply reduce creditworthiness and thus presage yet another financial crisis sometime in the future.

Argentina thus faces a critical juncture in respect to fiscal policy. Fiscal choices today are critical because they affect inflation and growth and because there is little room left for mistakes. The external debt service is a key variable because it presently absorbs resources that could be available for growth. But resource savings due to reduced external debt service (assuming there is no debt forgiveness) can only be used productively if fiscal reform translates them into sharply higher investment and growth. The critical decisions to make that possible have as yet not been reached. Moreover, if capital markets are unwilling to lend on a major scale then most of the growth must be financed by reduced consumption. Thus the policy mistakes of the 1970s directly translate into a growth crisis for the 1980s.

The present effort to stabilize the budget and hence bring about growth and financial stability goes in its implications much beyond the economic sphere. Political and institutional instability in Argentina resembles that of the Weimer Republic and Central Europe in the 1920s or the Fifth Republic in France. The political instability in turn influences economics because it stands in the way of continuity and farsightedness in economic policies. If, as has been the case in Argentina, the average tenure of a central bank president is less than a year, this is certainly not conducive to a long view. The attempt at reconstruction underway today is thus of extraordinary significance. This also implies that increased flexibility of external constraints associated with debt service assumes particular importance.

Appendix

Table 2.4   **Key Macroeconomic Variables**

	GDP[a] Growth	Inflation[a] (CPI)	Budget[b] Deficit/GDP	Noninterest[b] Current Account/GDP	Real[c] Exchange Rate	Terms[c] of Trade
70	5.4	21.7	2.0	0.3	56.7	106.6
71	3.7	39.1	4.6	−0.6	49.7	116.4
72	1.9	64.1	6.1	0.2	52.9	125.7
73	3.5	43.8	8.6	1.5	58.6	134.6
74	5.7	40.2	8.5	1.3	71.2	117.8
75	−0.4	335.1	15.6	−2.2	36.9	111.5
76	−0.5	347.5	10.6	2.9	46.4	95.8
77	6.4	160.4	5.0	3.9	50.7	92.7
78	−3.4	169.8	6.7	4.9	64.7	83.5
79	6.7	139.7	6.7	−0.1	83.4	88.4
80	0.7	87.6	8.6	−6.1	100.0	100.0
81	−6.2	131.3	18.0	−2.7	69.5	113.8
82	−4.6	209.7	18.9	3.3	48.9	98.5
83	2.8	433.7	17.8	3.9	58.8	94.1
84	2.6	688.0	13.8	4.2	58.4	101.7
85	−4.5	385.0	5.1	6.2	48.9	88.4
86	5.7	81.9	4.7	1.9	45.2	78.4

[a]Percent per year.
[b]Percent of GDP.
[c]Index 1980 = 100.

Table 2.5   **The External Sector**

	Current Account		Interest[a] Payments	Noninterest[a] Current Account	Terms of[c] Trade	Debt[b] GDP	Real Exchange[c] Rate
	$[a]	% of GDP[b]					
70	-159.0	-0.8	-222.5	63.6	106.6	16.7	56.7
71	-389.0	-1.8	-255.9	-132.8	116.4	18.2	49.7
72	-223.0	-1.0	-273.0	50.0	125.7	21.8	52.9
73	721.0	2.7	-317.0	1,038.0	134.6	20.0	58.6
74	127.0	0.4	-298.0	425.0	117.8	20.4	71.2
75	-1,284.0	-3.5	-460.0	-824.0	111.5	18.6	36.9
76	665.0	1.7	-465.0	1,130.0	95.8	18.6	46.4
77	1,290.0	3.0	-370.0	1,660.0	92.7	19.2	50.7
78	1,833.0	4.0	-405.0	2,238.0	83.5	23.9	64.7
79	-537.0	-1.0	-493.0	-44.0	88.4	30.2	83.4
80	-4,767.0	-7.6	-947.0	-3,824.0	100.0	37.3	100.0
81	-4,714.0	-7.4	-2,965.0	-1,749.0	113.8	48.1	69.5
82	-2,357.0	-3.8	-4,403.0	2,046.0	98.5	60.3	48.9
83	-2,461.0	-3.8	-4,983.0	2,522.0	94.1	59.5	58.8
84	-2,391.0	-3.5	-5,273.0	2,888.0	101.7	60.5	58.4
85	-953.0	-1.5	-4,879.0	3,926.0	88.4	60.5	48.9
86	-2,645.0	-4.0	-3,934.0	1,289.0	78.4	—	45.2

[a]Million $US.
[b]Percent of GDP.
[c]Index 1980 = 100.

Table 2.6   Key Relative Prices^a (Indices 1980 = 100)

	Agriculture/ Nonagriculture (wpi)	Real Public- Sector Prices	Real Wages	Terms of Trade	Real Exchange Rate	Relative Price of Land
70	119.05	106.30	—	106.6	56.69	190.16
71	132.14	100.13	263.25	116.4	49.69	216.39
72	152.38	97.64	216.16	125.7	52.92	308.20
73	141.67	107.61	267.77	134.6	58.62	249.18
74	123.81	151.71	264.36	117.8	71.15	337.70
75	97.62	158.53	217.64	111.5	36.92	319.67
76	104.76	131.63	124.01	95.8	46.46	478.69
77	111.90	130.05	83.01	92.7	50.69	393.44
78	109.52	133.60	79.59	83.5	64.69	124.59
79	110.71	104.59	70.73	88.4	83.38	93.44
80	100.00	100.00	100.00	100.0	100.00	100.00
81	90.48	115.88	106.46	113.8	69.54	63.93
82	103.57	111.29	139.89	98.5	48.92	103.28
83	107.14	131.50	152.54	94.1	58.77	159.02
84	101.19	147.24	142.94	101.7	58.38	145.90
85	85.71	159.97	110.34	88.4	48.92	—
86	109.52	147.77	110.06	78.4	45.15	—

^aDeflated by GDP deflator.

Table 2.7   Inflation and the Financial Sector

	Inflation	Budget Deficit/GDP	Base/GDP	M1/GDP	M2/GDP	M3/GDP	M4/GDP
70	21.7	2.03	0.12	0.15	0.25	0.25	0.25
71	39.1	4.58	0.10	0.13	0.22	0.23	0.23
72	64.1	6.10	0.09	0.11	0.19	0.21	0.21
73	43.8	8.60	0.13	0.11	0.20	0.22	0.22
74	40.2	8.52	0.14	0.14	0.25	0.27	0.28
75	335.1	15.59	0.16	0.09	0.14	0.16	0.17
76	347.5	10.56	0.14	0.07	0.11	0.12	0.16
77	160.4	5.04	0.16	0.06	0.14	0.15	0.16
78	169.8	6.67	0.14	0.06	0.18	0.18	0.20
79	139.7	6.65	0.09	0.06	0.19	0.19	0.21
80	87.6	8.56	0.08	0.07	0.21	0.21	0.23
81	131.3	17.97	0.09	0.05	0.20	0.20	0.22
82	209.7	18.78	0.29	0.05	0.17	0.16	0.19
83	433.7	17.76	0.29	0.04	0.13	0.14	0.14
84	688.0	13.79	0.20	0.04	0.11	0.12	0.12
85	385.0	5.10	0.12	0.05	0.11	0.11	0.13
86	81.9	4.70	0.09	0.05	0.14	0.16	0.18

Table 2.8   The Budget and Interest Payments (percentage of GDP)

	Budget Deficit	Interest on Foreign Debt	Interest on Domestic Debt	Operational Deficit
61	3.79	0.02	0.06	3.71
62	6.80	0.04	0.05	6.71
63	6.59	0.02	0.07	6.50
64	5.60	0.03	0.09	5.48
65	2.87	0.03	0.05	2.79
66	3.65	0.03	0.05	3.57
67	1.83	0.03	0.03	1.77
68	1.72	0.03	0.04	1.65
69	1.28	0.03	0.03	1.22
70	2.03	0.15	0.26	1.62
71	4.58	0.21	0.27	4.10
72	6.10	0.31	0.25	5.54
73	8.60	0.18	0.36	8.06
74	8.52	0.18	0.61	7.73
75	15.59	0.16	0.53	14.90
76	10.56	0.15	1.33	9.08
77	5.04	0.14	1.00	3.90
78	6.67	0.17	1.76	4.74
79	6.65	0.10	1.93	4.62
80	8.56	0.30	1.55	6.71
81	17.97	3.47	2.75	11.75
82	18.78	4.36	3.87	10.55
83	17.76	2.44	0.54	14.78
84	13.79	2.81	0.34	10.64
85	5.10	2.60	0.13	2.37
86	4.70			

Notes

1. See Ford (1983), Williams (1971) and Díaz Alejandro (1970) for Argentine economic history prior to World War II.
2. Quoted by Cardoso (1987) and Ford (1983, 92).
3. This is the series reported regularly by Morgan Guaranty Trust, *World Financial Markets*. We are indebted to Rimmer de Vries for making available the historical series.
4. On the Peronist experience see, in particular, Di Tella (1983) and de Pablo (1982; 1984).

References

Calvo, G. 1986. Incredible reforms. University of Pennsylvania. Mimeo.
Cardoso, E. 1987. Latin American debt: Which way now? *Challenge* (May).
Cavallo, D. 1984. *Volver a crecer*. Buenos Aires: Sudamericana-Planeta.
Cavallo, D., and A. Pena. 1983. Deficit fiscal, endeudamiento del gobierno y tasa de inflacion: Argentina 1940–82. *Estudios*, no. 26, April–June.
Dagnino Pastore, J. M. 1983. Progress and prospects for the adjustment in Argentina. In *Prospects for adjustment*, ed. J. Williamson. Institute for International Economics, MIT Press.
de Pablo, J. C., ed. 1980. *La economia que yo hice*. Buenos Aires: El Cronista Comercial.
————. 1981. *El processo economico*. Buenos Aires: El Cronista Comercial.
————. 1982. *Economia politica del Peronismo*. Buenos Aires: El Cid.
————. 1984. *Politica economica Argentina*. Buenos Aires: Ediciones Macchi.
di Tella, G. 1983. *Argentina under Peron 1973–76*. New York: St. Martin's.
Díaz Alejandro, C. 1964. *Exchange devaluation in a semi-industrialized country*. Cambridge: MIT Press.
————. 1970. *Essays on the economic history of the Argentine Republic*. New Haven: Yale University Press.
Dornbush, R. 1985. External debt, budget deficits and disequilibrium exchange rates. In *International debt and the developing countries*, ed. G. Smith and J. Cuddington. Washington, D.C.: The World Bank.
Dornbusch, R., and M. Simonsen. 1987. *Inflation stabilization with incomes policy support*. New York: Group of Thirty.
Feldstein, M. 1987. Muddling through is just fine. *The Economist* (London), 27 June.
Fernandez, R. B. 1985. The expectations management approach to stabilization in Argentina 1976–82. *World Development* 13, no. 8 (August): 871–92.
Fernandez, R. B., and C. A. Rodriguez. 1982. *Inflacion y estabilidad*. Buenos Aires: Ediciones Macchi.
Ford, A. G. 1983. *The gold standard 1880–1914: Britain and Argentina*. (Reprint) New York: Garland.
Harberger, A. 1985. Lessons for debtor country managers and policy makers. In *International Debt and The Developing Countries*, ed. G. Smith and J. Cuddington. Washington, D.C.: The World Bank.
Heyman, D. 1986. *Tres ensayos sobre inflacion y politicas de estabilizacion*. Doc. no. 18. Buenos Aires: CEPAL.
Instituto de Estudios Economicos sobre la Realidad Argentina y Latinoamericana. *Estatisticas de la evolucion economica de Argentina. 1913–1984.* (Published in *Estudios* 9, no. 39, July–September, Cordoba).
McCarthy, D. 1987. Argentina towards the year 2000. The World Bank, mimeo.
Mallon, R., and J. Sourrouille. 1975. *Economic policy making in a conflict society*. Cambridge: Harvard University Press.
Morgan Guaranty Trust. *World Financial Markets*, various issues.
Nogues, J. 1986. The nature of Argentina's policy reforms during 1976–81. World Bank Staff Working Paper no. 765. Washington, D.C.: World Bank.
Pazos, F. 1972. *Chronic inflation in Latin America*. Westport, Conn.: Praeger Publishers.
Ramos, J. 1986. *Neoconservative economics in the Southern Cone of Latin America, 1973–83*. Baltimore, Md.: Johns Hopkins University Press.

Rodriguez, C. A. 1983. *Politicas de estabilizacion en la economia Argentina, 1978–82. Cuadernos de Economia* (April).

Watson, M. et al. 1986. *International capital markets: Developments and prospects.* IMF Occasional Paper no. 43 (February). Washington, D.C.: International Monetary Fund.

Williams, J. H. 1971. *Argentine international trade under inconvertible paper money. 1880–1900.* (Reprint) New York: AMS Press.

World Bank. 1987. *Argentina. Economic recovery and growth.* Report no. 6467-AR. Washington, D.C.

3   Bolivia's Economic Crisis

Juan Antonio Morales and Jeffrey D. Sachs

3.1   Introduction

By any standard, Bolivia's economic crisis in the 1980s has been extraordinary. As seen in table 3.1, Bolivia's economic debacle of recent years is striking even in comparison with the poor performance of Bolivia's neighbors. Like its neighbors, Bolivia suffered from major external shocks, including the rise in world interest rates in the early 1980s, the cutoff in lending from the international capital markets, and the decline in world prices of Bolivia's commodity exports. But the extent of economic collapse in the face of these shocks suggests that internal factors as well as the external shocks have been critical to Bolivia's economic performance. The Bolivian hyperinflation of 1984–85, for example, which was one of the most dramatic inflations in world history, is the only 20th century hyperinflation that did not result from the dislocations of war or revolution. One major theme of our work is that the recent economic crisis in Bolivia is a reflection of political and economic conflicts in Bolivian society that have undermined the development process throughout this century.

Table 3.2 gives a brief political chronology of Bolivia since the Revolution of 1952. The most striking aspect of the chronology is the instability of constitutional rule in the country. The Revolution of 1952 was led by the National Revolutionary Movement, the MNR, which governed Bolivia for 12 years, winning elections in 1956 and 1960. The military toppled the civilian regime in 1964, and ruled without interruption until 1978. A period of political chaos followed during 1978–

Juan Antonio Morales is a professor of economics at the Universidad Católica Boliviana, La Paz. Jeffrey D. Sachs is a professor of economics at Harvard University and a research associate of the National Bureau of Economic Research.

Table 3.1   Economic Performance in the 1980s, Selected Countries

	GDP Growth (annual rate) 1980–85	Inflation (annual rate) 1980–85	Debt-GNP[a] Ratio 1985	Terms of Trade, 1985 (1980 = 100)
Bolivia	−4.5	569.1	136.8	86
Latin America				
Argentina	−1.4	342.8	56.4	88
Brazil	1.3	147.7	43.8	87
Mexico	0.8	62.2	52.8	98
East Asia				
Malaysia	5.5	3.1	62.0	85
Indonesia	3.5	10.7	36.6	97
Korea	7.9	6.0	43.0	105

Source: World Bank, *World Development Report 1987.*
[a]Medium-and long-term debt, public and private.

82, with a rapid alternation of military and civilian rule. Civilian rule was restored in 1982, with the accession to power of Siles Zuazo.

As in other Latin American nations, the alternation of power also reflected an alternation between populist and antipopulist politics. In Bolivia, however, this alternation has been particularly sharp. Generally, the military rule was antipopulist, and especially antilabor. There was, however, a brief populist phase of military rule under General Torres in 1970–71, which coincided with the leftist military government in Peru under Velasco. The civilian governments have all drawn their leaders from the MNR, though the civilian governments have varied widely in their policies, with populist phases during 1952–56 and 1982–85, and conservative phases during 1956–64 and 1985 to the present.

The chronic political instability, and more specifically the swings between populist and antipopulist politics, reflect the deeper divisions in the Bolivian economy and society. Not only is Bolivia's distribution of income and wealth highly unequal, but the various sectors in Bolivian society are highly mobilized to do battle over their shares of income and wealth. Since the Revolution, all of the social factions have looked to the central government to satisfy their particular distributional agenda, and the battle for political power has also been a battle for a share of the national pie. The battle over shares has been particularly damaging since it has occurred in the context of a secular decline in the earnings of Bolivia's key mining sector. That decline not only made the need for a coherent development strategy particularly urgent, but also heightened the sense of desperation in the distributional battle.

The result, not surprisingly, has been a government stretched far beyond its fiscal capacity; an economic environment inimical to long-term investment; and an inability of the key political actors to settle

Table 3.2   Brief Political Chronology, 1952–1985

1952	Bolivian Revolution, carried out by National Revolutionary Movement (MNR), under leadership of Dr. Víctor Paz Estenssoro.
1952–56	Presidency of Paz Estenssoro; sharp rise in inflation, to 178.8% in 1956.
1956–60	Presidency of Hernán Siles Zuazo (MNR); economic stabilization under U.S. and IMF supervision and finance.
1960–64	Second presidency of Paz Estenssoro.
1964	Third presidency of Paz Estenssoro; Paz Estenssoro deposed in military coup led by General René Barrientos Ortuno.
1964–66	Co-presidency of Alfredo Ovando Candía and Barrientos Ortuno.
1966–69	Civilian presidency of Barrientos (dies in plane crash, April1969).
1969	Vice-president Luis Siles Salinas becomes president; deposed in coup by Ovando Candía.
1970	Ovando Candía deposed by General Miranda. Miranda deposed by General Juan José Torres.
1971	Torres rules left-wing radical government. Deposed in coup, jointly sponsored by the military, FBS, and MNR.
1971–73	General Hugo Banzer Suarez rules with MNR support.
1974–78	Banzer presidency under military rule; MNR withdrawal from government in 1974.
1979	Pereda becomes president in election marked by accusation of fraud. Pereda deposed by General David Padilla, who calls for 1979 election.
1979	Election results in stalemate (no majority); Senate President Walter Guevara Arze serves as interim president. Guevara deposed by Colonel Natusch Busch; Busch resigns in 15 days. President of Chamber of Deputies, Lidia Gueiler, becomes interim president.
1980	Electoral stalemate. Gueiler deposed in coup by Major General Luis Garcia Meza.
1981	Garcia Meza forced to resign in favor of General Bernal. General Bernal resigns in favor of General Torrelio.
1982	General Torrelio deposed in coup by General Vildoso Calderon. Congress reconvenes; names Siles Zuazo as president.
1985	Siles Zuazo announces early elections. Paz Estenssoro becomes president. New economic policy declared on 29 August 1985.

on a sustained strategy for national economic development. The failure of economic development has taken its toll. Bolivia is the poorest country in South America, with a per capita income of about $500, and the second poorest in the Western Hemisphere, behind Haiti. Between 1952 and 1985, GNP grew at the meagre annual rate of 2.4 percent.

In the next section of this chapter, we extend this analysis as to why Bolivia has failed to develop a workable strategy of long-term development. We then turn to an analytical chronology of the recent economic crisis, and highlight how the crisis has emerged from the longer-term failures that we have stressed. To understand the proximate economic determinants of the crisis, we highlight the critical linkages between foreign borrowing, the exchange rate, and inflation, that are key to understanding both the onset of the hyperinflation and debt crisis, and the progress that has been made since 1985 in overcoming the crisis. While major reforms have been begun by the present government, many of the deepest problems in Bolivian society that contributed to the crisis remain unresolved. We underline these areas of remaining difficulty, and discuss various policy options for addressing them.

3.2   The Long-Term Problems of Bolivian Economic Growth

Bolivia's problems begin with the inherent difficulties of growth in a landlocked mining economy centered in breathtaking, yet forbidding, terrain more than 14,000 feet above sea level. Bolivia is a very large and sparsely populated country. Its area is greater than the combined areas of the United Kingdom, West Germany, and France, with a population of only 6 million. The country is divided geographically between the Andean highlands, where the mining industry is located, and the lowlands to the east, where petroleum products and commercial agriculture are situated. From the beginning of colonial development, Bolivia's political and economic center of gravity has been in the highlands. The secular decline of the mining sector has led in recent decades to a shift in economic and political activity to the east.This shift, which is the cause of significant political conflict, has been accelerated by the recent sharp crash of tin prices in October 1985.

Bolivia's economy since the colonial period has been based on mining, first silver, from the colonial period until the late 19th century, and then tin in the 20th century. With population centered in the highlands and neighboring valleys, transport costs are extremely high. Therefore, while it has been profitable for Bolivia to export minerals such as silver and tin that have a high value added per unit weight, and therefore a low share of transport costs per unit value, Bolivia has been unable to overcome the transport costs for almost any kind of manufactured product. The problem of transport costs was greatly exacerbated by Bolivia's loss of its littoral on the Pacific Coast, in the traumatic War of the Sea against Chile and Peru in 1879.

The requirement of high value added per unit weight in Bolivian exports helps to explain Bolivia's only real diversification of exports in recent years: coca leaf derivatives (the precursors of cocaine) and petroleum products. Petroleum products, particularly natural gas exported to Argentina, can be carried out of the country by pipeline, while coca leaf can be profitably transported even if carried on a peasant's back. Table 3.3 shows Bolivia's concentration of noncoca exports in recent years. Among Bolivia's measured exports (i.e., excluding coca), tin and petroleum products usually accounted for much more than half of total exports during the 1960s, 1970s, and 1980s. Coca exports in the 1980s are generally estimated to equal the sum of tin and natural gas exports.

Many of Bolivia's problems can be seen as the tragic playing out of the secular decline in the mining sector, a process that has been underway

Table 3.3   Relative Shares of Tin and Natural Gas in Total Exports of Bolivia

Year	As % of Merchandise Exports
1952	59.9
1953	64.2
1954	55.2
1955	56.0
1956	55.1
1957	58.9
1958	56.1
1959	68.2
1960	71.0
1961	87.3
1962	89.7
1963	80.6
1964	80.8
1965	80.5
1966	70.2
1967	58.5
1968	58.9
1969	57.3
1970	52.0
1971	58.4
1972	61.3
1973	57.2
1974	46.6
1975	48.1
1976	47.9
1977	62.4
1978	72.0
1979	65.9
1980	63.6
1981	68.3
1982	73.5
1983	77.6
1984	86.1
1985[a]	89.7

Source: Central Bank of Bolivia, *Boletin Estadistico,* various issues.
[a]Estimate.

derway for at least half a century. (See Malloy 1970 for an authoritative account of 20th century Bolivian history before the Revolution, with an emphasis on the secular decline of the tin sector starting in the late 1920s.) Actually, Bolivia's first deep crisis came with the depletion of silver deposits and the fall of world silver prices at the end of the last century. Good fortune, however, pulled Bolivia out of crisis when a boom in world demand for tin followed the development of the modern canning process. The apogee of modern Bolivian economic development relative to the neighboring countries was reached in the first two decades of the 20th century, when tin was intensively developed, and when export earnings provided the basis for a major extension of the country's infrastructure, including roads and the railway system.

Tin lodes were increasingly exhausted in the 1920s, and Bolivia began to lose export competitiveness with other producers. When tin prices collapsed at the start of the Great Depression, Bolivia became the first country in that crisis to default on its sovereign foreign debt, in January 1931. Bolivia was also the last country in Latin America to settle these defaulted debts after World War II.

The collapse of tin undermined both the economy and the political system, known as the Rosca, which was managed heavily in favor of the three tin magnates, Patino, Hochschild, and Aramayo. The public finances, which relied heavily on tin exports and international trade generally, were gravely weakened, and the financial problems generally undermined the central government. Thus, the period between 1931 and the Revolution of 1952 was an era of political uncertainty and unrest. Bolivia lost the bloody and costly Chaco War to Paraguay in the mid-1930s, an experience that heightened the political mobilization of workers and the middle classes unhappy with the leadership of the oligarchy. A military government with a mixed fascist and revolutionary orientation came to power in 1943, but was deposed in 1946. The oligarchy regained control in 1946, but was swept aside by the Revolution of 1952.

The leaders of the Bolivian Revolution of 1952 drew inspiration from the Mexican Revolution, and from Mexico's Institutional Revolutionary Party (the PRI), in the formation and policies of the Bolivian MNR. The experience under the Rosca had thoroughly discredited private wealthholders as a class capable of leading national development. The revolutionary leaders looked to the public sector as means of growth that would be broadly based and equitable. They put in place an economic system, which can broadly be called state capitalism, that assigned the bulk of capital formation to the public sector, both for infrastructure and for industrial production in state enterprises. The leading state enterprises were COMIBOL, the national tin company, and YPFB, the state petroleum company.

It should be stressed that the reliance on the state sector was guided by political considerations as well as by an ideology of economic development. The revolutionary movement, after toppling the oligarchy, was hardly interested in returning power to a small class of wealthholders. Indeed, given Bolivia's highly unequal income distribution, the problems of establishing a political equilibrium together with mass participation (indeed mass political mobilization) were evident. A large state sector was viewed as providing a political answer to the distributional bind. As seen in table 3.4, Bolivia's income distribution remains, despite the Revolution, highly unequal. The Revolution did succeed, particularly through land reform, in raising the income share of the poorest 20 percent of households above the shares found in several other Latin American countries.

Despite the great variation of governments after 1952, one aspect of the model of state capitalism remained fairly constant. Whether the government was of the populist left, as under the military leader General Torres in 1970–71, or of the right, as under the military regime of General Hugo Banzer during 1971–78, the state was looked to as the guiding force of development. As shown in table 3.5, a large fraction of total national investment, generally more than half in the 1960s and 1970s, was invested directly by the public sector. This predominant role of the state is, of course, not unusual for late developers, as was elegantly demonstrated by Gerschenkron many years ago in the case of the European latecomers. And as stressed in Sachs (1987) the state has played a very large, and apparently successful, role in spurring economic development in Japan, Korea, and Taiwan. What has been distinctive in the Bolivian case, however, has been the fundamental

Table 3.4 **Income Distribution in Selected Countries**

	Year	Bottom 20%	Top 20%	Ratio, Top to Bottom
Bolivia	1970	4.0	59.0	14.8
Latin America				
Argentina	1970	4.4	50.3	11.4
Brazil	1972	2.0	66.6	33.3
Mexico	1977	2.9	57.7	19.9
East Asia				
Malaysia	1973	3.5	56.1	16.0
Indonesia	1976	6.6	49.4	7.5
Korea	1976	5.7	45.3	7.9
Taiwan	1976	9.5	35.0	3.7

Source: World Bank; national sources for Taiwan.

Table 3.5   Public and Private Participation in the Gross Capital Fixed
                   Formation

	Public		Private		Total	
Year	Amount	%	Amount	%	Amount	%
1958	203.0	42	206.0	58	489.0	100
1959	213.0	40	313.0	60	526.0	100
1960	281.2	44	355.8	56	637.0	100
1961	239.1	45	292.2	55	581.3	100
1962	452.0	54	382.7	46	834.7	100
1963	576.0	62	348.3	38	924.3	100
1964	570.1	60	387.6	40	957.7	100
1965	451.1	43	599.7	57	1,050.8	100
1966	478.3	50	470.8	50	949.4	100
1967	581.6	50	574.1	50	1,155.7	100
1968	929.0	52	841.0	40	1,770.0	100
1969	910.5	59	633.4	41	1,543.9	100
1970	1,002.0	56	790.0	44	1,792.0	100
1971	1,170.0	40	781.0	40	1,951.0	100
1972	1,548.0	59	1,075.0	41	2,823.0	100
1973	1,690.0	37	2,829.0	83	4,519.0	100
1974	2,199.0	34	4,351.0	66	6,550.0	100
1975	3,711.0	41	5,344.0	59	9,055.0	100
1976	5,949.0	56	4,736.0	44	10,655.0	100
1977	7,930.0	64	4,484.0	36	12,414.0	100
1978	10,216.0	66	5,180.0	34	15,396.0	100
1979	8,928.0	58	6,378.0	42	15,306.0	100
1980	9,767.0	50	7,361.0	42	17,328.0	100
1981						100
1982						100

Source: Ministry of Planning and Central Bank of Bolivia.

disjunction between the *weak capacity* of the state on the one hand, and the *responsibilities* invested in the state on the other.

The whole concept of more equitable growth through a large state sector collapsed in a mass of inconsistencies over the 30 years between the Revolution and the onset of the Bolivian hyperinflation. During the post-Revolution period, leftist leaders were always too weak politically to satisfy their redistributional aims. To the extent, for instance, that they aimed to raise public-sector salaries or to increase public-sector investment and employment, they lacked the capacity to tax income and wealth necessary to finance the larger state sector. If necessary, the Bolivian army was prepared to intervene to forestall populist or redistributionist actions, as it did in 1971. For these reasons, leftist or populist leaders have been constantly forced to rely on inflationary finance or foreign aid and foreign borrowing to carry out their distributional and developmental goals. The first high inflation in Bolivia came in the wake of the Revolution, and the second came with the left-wing government of Siles Zuazo in 1982.

Leaders on the right, such as Barrientos and Banzer, were not interested to limit the power of the state, but rather to use the state to satisfy a different agenda. While governments on the left sought redistribution through higher wages and a larger role for public-sector workers, governments on the right sought instead to bolster favored segments of the private sector through generous government subsidies. Governments of the left have generally paid for higher public salaries through printing money (i.e., the inflation tax) or through foreign borrowing, since they have been forestalled from raising taxes. Governments on the right, on the other hand, have rejected higher taxes outright, and have instead sought to finance the government through a reduction of public-sector wages (often with overt repression of labor), and also through foreign borrowing. Note one common theme of both types of governments: let the foreigners pay!

The conflict over income distribution continues to have a number of profound effects on economic policy and economic performance. The first effect that we have noted is fiscal indiscipline, since powerful high-income groups veto the income and wealth taxes that would be needed to finance a large public sector. A second effect is the deep politicization of almost all instruments of economic policy. There are few economic policy tools in Bolivia that are judged mainly on the basis of efficiency rather than distribution. Exchange rate changes, for example, typically have been avoided in Bolivia until currency overvaluations reach absurd proportions, for fear of a resulting distributional battle. Similarly, public-sector prices have often been stuck at levels far below market clearing rates, for the same reason, despite the often devastating fiscal consequences. A third effect of the continuing battle over income distribution is the uncertainty for private investment spending that is created by the alternation between leftists and rightist regimes with widely varying agendas. A fourth effect has been the degeneration of politics into a fierce battles of the "ins" versus the "outs." With the state viewed as an instrument of redistribution, succeeding governments came to view the public purse and public enterprises as private slush funds, to be used for personal gain or political patronage. Malloy and Gamarra (1987) have termed this condition "neopatrimonialism."

3.3   Origins of the Debt Crisis: The Banzer Era

As shown in table 3.6, Bolivia's external debt rose dramatically in the 1970s, mostly during the Banzer era. Bolivia's rapid accumulation of external debt in the 1970s reflected three forces at work. Part of the foreign borrowing financed a plausible attempt to generate a more

Table 3.6   **Bolivian External Debt, 1970–85**

$ millions	1970	1975	1980	1981	1982	1983	1984	1985
Total debt[a] (MLT public and publicly guaranteed)	481.7	824.4	2,228.6	2,679.2	2,769.1	3,105.1	3,203.5	3,259.3
Debt/GNP (%)	46.3	46.2	78.1	89.3	102.6	111.5	115.9	124.8
Debt/Exports (%)	232.6	166.7	213.1	262.3	301.5	345.4	377.8	441.9

Source: World Bank, *World Debt Tables*, 1986–87 edition.

[a]Debt outstanding and disbursed, medium- and long-term maturities, on public and publicly guaranteed debt.

diversified export base through various investment projects. Some of these projects, such as natural gas exports to Argentina, proved successful. Others, such as investment in crude petroleum production, proved to be failures. Less benignly, the foreign borrowing also reflected an attempt to finesse the internal distributional conflict on borrowed money and borrowed time. The government did not attempt to raise taxes (and indeed rejected a detailed tax reform proposal of the Musgrave Commission). Third, and most perniciously, some of the foreign borrowing had the purpose and effect of enriching a narrow set of private interests via the public sector's access to foreign loans. Similarly, an overvalued exchange rate, maintained through foreign borrowing, became a channel for capital flight for the wealthier individuals.

The economic record of the Banzer years look quite good when taken in isolation. Bolivian GDP growth averaged 5.4 percent per year, which was far above the average of 2.4 percent during the whole period 1952–85. Prices were rather stable except in 1974, following a major devaluation of the Bolivian peso. Investment as a share of GNP reached historical highs, as did government revenues relative to GNP, though the gap between government expenditures and government revenues widened. In an era of easy foreign finance, however, the gap was readily filled by eager foreign bankers. Few observers at the time realized the precariousness of the Banzer boom, built as it was on a temporary commodity boom, easy access to foreign finance, and a narrow political base.

Banzer's rule lasted for seven years, an extraordinary stretch by Bolivian standards. For three years, Banzer ruled with the support of both leftist and rightist political parties. As Malloy and Gamarra (1987, 103) indicate, Banzer jettisoned these parties in 1974 when he recognized that "they were rump factions who represented little more than cliques whose primary purpose was to lay claim to public-sector jobs." From 1974 to 1978, Banzer ruled with the support of private-sector business, the military, and some technocrats. Because of the booming economy, Banzer enjoyed the support of the urban middle classes, and even some favored labor groups such as the railway workers, but faced continued strong opposition from most of organized labor, and the leftist parties.

Another important dimension of support and opposition to Banzer was regional. The eastern part of the country, and especially Banzer's home province of Santa Cruz, provided strong support and were major beneficiaries of Banzer's policies. Groups in this region were favored with grants of property rights over public lands, and with generous subsidized credits. An important illustration of how the government distributed public revenues to private supporters is the case of loans for large-scale cotton production in the Santa Cruz region, made by the government Agricultural Bank (Banco Agricola Boliviano) between 1972 and 1975. Tens of millions of dollars were loaned to a small number of large landowners during an incipient cotton boom. The Bolivian producers sold their crops forward on world markets, but then tried to renegotiate when the spot market prices rose above the forward contract price. They failed in the renegotiations, and in the end, much of the cotton remained undelivered. The growers quietly defaulted on the Agricultural Bank loans and the government absorbed the losses with no attempt to collect or to foreclose on any property. To this day, the bad cotton loans have undermined the solvency of the Agricultural Bank.

In 1975, the Banzer regime announced a five-year development plan which encapsulated the governing philosophy. The plan aimed at export promotion led by state investment. The public sector was targeted with 71 percent of total investment over the period, focussed heavily on hydrocarbons, mainly in the Santa Cruz region. Financing of the plan was to rely on the profits from petroleum exports, which in the event never materialized, and on foreign borrowing, which did. Most of the plan however was never implemented.

In 1977 and 1978, General Banzer faced growing pressure from the Carter administration for a return to democracy. An election was called, but was annulled after charges of massive fraud. When Banzer then tried to remain in office, he was ousted in a coup. There ensued a four-year period of intense political instability, with several interim presidents, coups, and deadlocked elections, producing in all nine different heads of state between Banzer and Siles.

Bolivia reached its political nadir in 1980 and 1981, when General Garcia Meza deposed the interim president Lidia Gueiler. The Garcia Meza regime was deeply implicated in the burgeoning cocaine industry, and therefore never received international support, except for the backing from the similarly corrupt and violent military regime in Argentina. Capital flight reached new highs in the period, with errors and omissions in the balance of payments in 1980 and 1981 totalling $590 million, or about 10 percent of 1980 GNP. The commercial banks stopped all lending, and negotiated an emergency rescheduling agreement which was soon defaulted upon. The rest of the international community also ceased new lending, except for two important loans from the Argentine regime.

Not one of the heads of state during this chaotic period had the political backing to address the acute economic problems facing the country. Banzer's strategy of foreign borrowing had run its course, with insufficient export earnings and government revenues to show for it. The various goverments following Banzer during 1978–82 were in no position to raise taxes or enforce economic austerity, and so they resorted to printing money when the flow of foreign money changed from net inflow to net outflow. On top of the problem of obtaining fresh credits, commodity prices started to slide in 1981, and interest rates on the existing international loans soared. By October 1982, when the Siles Zuazo government came to power, the economy was in a sharp downward slide. Real GNP had declined by an estimated 0.9 percent in 1981 and by 8.7 percent in 1982. The price level had risen by 308 percent in the 12 months preceding Siles's accession to power.

3.4   The March to Hyperinflation

It is important to appreciate the political implications of Siles's accession to power in 1982. The new administration represented the first elected government in 18 years, so that pent-up social and economic aspirations were sure to boil over early in the term. Siles represented the left wing of the MNR, and governed in a coalition with various leftist parties, including the Communist Party of Bolivia. In the early phase of the administration, organized labor gave support to the new government, but only in return for significant wage increases. Ultimately, when the financially strapped government was unable and unwilling to grant wage increases to keep ahead of the accelerating inflation, organized labor turned bitterly against the government. General strikes by organized labor in 1984 and 1985 killed the final two stabilization attempts of the Siles administration.

The hyperinflation under Siles was not so much a result of an explosion of new spending as the inability to restrain spending in the face of falling foreign loans, falling tax revenues, and higher debt service payments abroad. The coalition members were never able to agree on policies to restrain spending, while the government's right-wing opponents in the Bolivian Congress rejected all proposals to broaden or even stabilize the tax base. At a fundamental level, moreover, the coalition government failed to realize that the deepening crisis was an indictment of the system of state capitalism itself, and especially of the financial limitations of that system. To the end, the Siles administration defended the logic of a large state enterprise sector, even as it tried to squeeze key state enterprises in order to support the finances of the rest of the government.

The hyperinflation and debt crisis developed as Bolivia's net resource transfers from the rest of the world turned negative in 1982. Seignorage financing (i.e., printing money) substituted for the decline in foreign resource flows. Table 3.7 demonstrates this shift in foreign resources for a subset of loans, the medium- and long-term public or publicly guaranteed loans. We see that for 1979 through 1981, new net borrowing

Table 3.7   Bolivia's Debt Servicing of Medium- and Long-Term
                   Public-Sector Debt

	1980	1981	1982	1983	1984
Net interest payments	163.9	171.0	180.9	172.8	201.3
Official creditors	42.8	50.3	66.2	64.7	166.2
Private creditors	121.1	120.7	114.7	108.1	35.1
Net new lending	341.9	263.2	88.6	−18.0	60.5
Official creditors	191.0	163.9	103.0	13.5	63.3
Private creditors	150.9	99.3	−14.4	−31.5	−2.9
Net resource transfer	178.0	92.1	−92.2	−190.8	−140.8
Official creditors	148.2	113.6	36.8	−51.3	−120.9
Private creditors	29.8	−21.4	−129.1	−139.5	−37.9
Net resource transfers Total, % of GNP	6.2	3.1	−3.4	−6.9	−5.1

Source: World Bank, *World Debt Tables,* 1985–1986 edition.

by the public sector exceeded the interest payments on the public debt. In 1982, however, net new lending plummeted, so that the transfer of resources to Bolivia (net new loans minus interest payments) turned sharply negative. As a percentage of GNP, net resource transfers on the loans in table 3.7 shifted from 6.2 percent of GNP in 1980, to 3.1 percent of GNP in 1981, to −3.4 percent of GNP in 1982, and to −6.9 percent of GNP in 1983.

The jump in seignorage, which fueled the hyperinflation, is the mirror image of the declining net resource transfer from abroad. As the government devoted an increasing share of resource to foreign debt servicing, it resorted to printing money to finance the balance of its domestic spending. Figure 3.1 shows this pattern clearly. Seignorage jumped in mid-1982, several months before Siles's term began. Aside from seasonal spikes in seignorage in the fourth quarter of most years (associated with a Christmas wage bonus for public-sector workers), seignorage remained at a high plateau of about 12 percent of GNP annually until stabilization was achieved in late 1985. Note that the decline in net resource transfers (a shift of about 10 percent of GNP), and the rise in seignorage, are of about the same magnitude.

The relative constancy of government seignorage does not reflect a stable level of government spending, taxes, and monetary emission. Rather, the constancy of the seignorage collection hides a process of fiscal collapse in which tax revenue collections all but disappeared, while government spending (particularly on public investment projects) was cut back sharply in a vain attempt to catch up with the moving target of falling tax collections. Meanwhile, the monetary emission

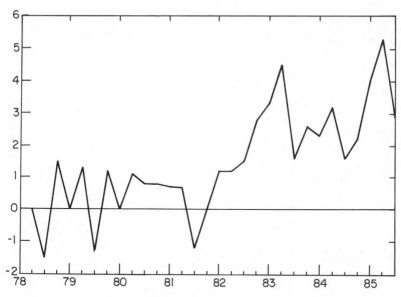

Fig. 3.1   Seignorage per quarter (percentage of annual GNP)

prompted repeated and accelerating depreciations of the exchange rate, which then fed into inflation. As inflation accelerated, the demand for real money balances fell, so that a constant rate of seignorage collection as a percentage of GNP was associated with an accelerating inflation and a falling level of real money balances.

Government revenues in Bolivia in the early 1980s relied heavily on three main forms of taxes: internal taxes (mainly sales, property, and income taxes); taxes on trade (mainly tariff collections); and taxes on hydrocarbons and minerals (mainly paid by COMIBOL and YPFB). As shown in figure 3.2, each of these taxes plummeted as a percentage of GNP. Overall, revenues of the central administration (the TGN) fell from more than 9 percent of GNP in 1980 to just 1.3 percent of GNP in the first nine months of 1985. The proportion of TGN expenditures backed by TGN revenues fell from 65.5 percent in 1979 to just 6.9 percent in the first nine months of 1985.

As is well known from the studies of Olivera (1967) and Tanzi (1977), inflation itself can be a major factor in undermining the government revenue collections. In Bolivia, several particular institutional factors were at work. With income taxes, simple lags in collection reduced the real value of collections almost to nothing by 1985. Similarly, property taxes and several excise taxes were stated in specific, rather than ad valorem, terms. Thus, as the price level rose, the real value of the tax

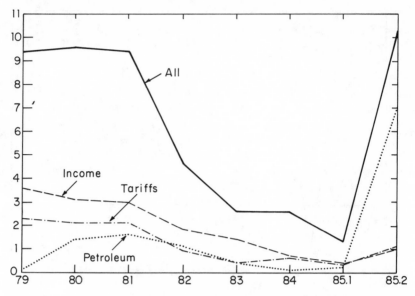

Fig. 3.2   Tax revenues as a percentage of GNP (by category of tax)

collections fell. Tariff revenues declined for several reasons. The down-
turn in economic activity reduced imports, and therefore tax collections. Equally important, the official exchange rate was persistently
overvalued relative to the black market rate. This had the effect of
encouraging smuggling, on which tariffs are typically not collected.
Even when goods were imported legally, however, the tariff in pesos
was collected on the basis of the official exchange rate, and therefore
the real value of the tariff collections was substantially reduced. The
taxes on mining and hydrocarbons were similarly squeezed. The overvalued exchange rate reduced the profitability of the state enterprises
in these sectors, and they therefore paid their taxes to the central
government on a sporadic basis only. Indeed, the central bank made
large transfers to the state enterprises to keep them functioning despite
the squeeze on their operating revenues.

It is more difficult to offer an account of spending patterns by the
central government during the hyperinflation period, because of serious
data limitations. The following major points seem clear, however. There
was a sharp squeeze on public investment spending rather than wages
and salaries as the Siles government attempted to cope with the growing
fiscal crisis. Union opposition successfully forestalled any serious attempts to reduce public sector real wages or public employment, until

the end of the hyperinflation. Until the spring of 1984, the government squeezed internal spending and relied on monetary emission to make room for interest servicing on the foreign debt. In the spring of 1984, the government finally quit debt service payments on the government debt to the commercial banks. By this time, ironically, the rising inflation had so ravaged the tax system that even with the suspension of interest payments, the deficit on a cash-basis remained enormous, so that the resort to seignorage finance was hardly slowed.

There are many particular features of public finance in this period that help to give a deeper insight into the dynamics of the hyperinflation. In a foolhardy attempt to restrain inflation, the government resorted continually to ineffectual price controls, overvalued and multiple exchange rates, and other forms of intervention. These policies had no effect on the general price level, but they frequently threatened the solvency of private and public firms. In response, the government would typically find some indirect way to compensate the firms for the intervention measures, and thus the direct price control measure would show up as an indirect fiscal subsidy, adding to the government's need for inflation finance.

While the hyperinflation was a disaster for the economy and Bolivian society as a whole, many well-connected rent-seeking individuals made considerable fortunes in the course of the hyperinflation. Anybody with access to official foreign exchange from the central bank could become wealthy almost instantly during the period, by purchasing cheap dollars at the central bank and selling them at a several hundred percent profit in the black market. Similarly, commercial bankers, who took deposits at zero interest and lent money at high nominal interest rates, shared in the government's seignorage gains. Moreover, the government extended large amounts of low-interest loans during the period, often to politically powerful landowners, which effectively became grants as a result of the inflation. Price controls on public-sector goods, including flour and petroleum products, generated opportunities for lucrative smuggling operations. All of these opportunities for gain provided a powerful constituency of those who wanted to see the hyperinflation continue.

3.5 The Stabilization Process

The inflation under Siles went from annual rates of several hundred percent in 1982 and 1983 to several thousand percent in 1984 and 1985. According to Cagan's classic definition of hyperinflation (price increases exceeding 50 percent per month), the true hyperinflation began in May 1984 and ended in September 1985, upon the accession to power of the Paz Estenssoro government. It should be noted that Siles tried several times to implement a comprehensive stabilization program (during November 1982, November 1983, April 1984, August 1984, November 1984, and February 1985), but in each of these cases, some combination of Siles's political opponents in Congress, and his ostensible "allies" in organized labor, torpedoed the adjustment efforts.

The successful stabilization program was carried out by the newly elected center-right government of Paz Estenssoro. The government came to power in rather inauspicious circumstances, after another election which failed to produce a clear majority for one of the candidates. The program of the Paz administration was unveiled only three weeks after the government came to power. The program was remarkably wide ranging, and indeed radical, encompassing not only plans for macroeconomic stabilization, but also for trade liberalization, administrative and tax reform, and deregulation and privatization in the domestic market. The so-called "New Economic Policy" was nothing less than a call to dismantle the system of state capitalism that had prevailed over the previous thirty years.

The fiscal part of the program was to operate on five fundamental bases:

1. A stable unified exchange rate backed by tight fiscal and monetary policies
2. Increased public-sector revenues, via tax reform and improved public sector prices
3. A reduced public-sector wage bill, through reductions of employment in state enterprises (particularly COMIBOL) and reduced rates of real compensation
4. An effective elimination of debt servicing, through a combination of rescheduling with official creditors, and a unilateral suspension of payments to private creditors until a more fundamental debt settlement could be arranged
5. A resumption of concessional foreign financial assistance, from foreign governments and the multilateral institutions

The leading trade union organization, which had opposed and mobilized against similar, indeed far less dramatic, policy packages under Siles, called for a general strike in opposition to the program. But after three years of accelerating inflation, and the sense of chaos in early 1985, the new government clearly had the upper hand. A temporary state of siege under the constitution was declared, and the strike was quickly broken.

The fiscal measures, combined with a buildup of internal arrears by the central government, were sufficient to obviate the need for fiscal credit from the central bank to support government spending. The

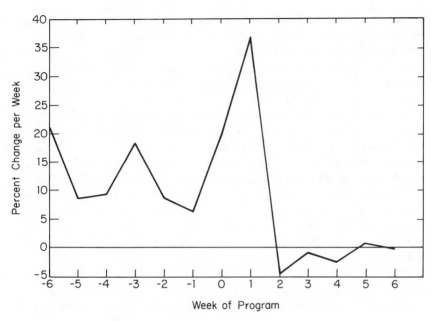

Fig. 3.3   Weekly inflation rates (week 0 = 8/26 – 9/1)

exchange rate stabilized almost immediately, and with a stable exchange rate, the price level stopped rising. As shown in figure 3.3, the
remarkable break in the hyperinflation began no more than one week
after the inception of the program! Inflation fell from a rate of more
than 50 percent per month to price stability almost immediately. The
key to price stability proved to be a stable unified exchange rate, protected by tight fiscal and monetary policies. When the government
deviated from that policy temporarily at the end of 1985, the high
inflation quickly surged again, but this time it was stopped by a reas-
sertion of fiscal discipline. From February 1986 to July 1987, the inflation rate has averaged only 10–15 percent at an annual rate, one of the
lowest inflation rates in Latin America.

One key aspect of the stabilization should be highlighted, to contrast
the case of Bolivia with those of Argentina, Brazil, and Peru. The
Bolivian stabilization was highly orthodox with respect to monetary,
fiscal, and pricing policies (though it was "heterodox" in its continued
suspension of foreign debt payments). The stabilization program es-
chewed all wage and price controls as part of the anti-inflation effort,
and indeed freed many controls at the inception of the program. It is
likely that the hyperinflation had obviated any need for price controls
as part of the anti-inflation effort, since the high inflation rates had

eliminated all vestiges of long-term contracts, and therefore all vestiges of inertial inflation. Peso prices were basically being set at the end of the hyperinflation by converting dollar prices of goods into pesos at the spot market exchange rate. Thus, by stabilizing the exchange rate, the inflation rate was immediately stabilized to the prevailing rate of dollar inflation in world markets.

In reality, stabilization is a cumulative process, not an event. While prices quickly stopped rising, fiscal reform has been underway for two years, and the results are still unsatisfactory in major areas. The government has had to proceed gradually along three major dimensions: (1) a rebuilding of the national tax system, which had virtually collapsed by the end of the hyperinflation; (2) a reestablishment of normal relations with the government's various creditors, both internal and external; and (3) a restructuring of the public sector, to provide for a more durable solution to the fiscal crisis. Let us consider each of these in turn.

The restoration of a stable revenue base has proceeded in stages. The immediate and crucial actions of the Paz government were the raising of public-sector prices and the unification of the exchange rate. In addition, some back taxes on hydrocarbons and tin were also collected at the outset of the stabilization program, to give the government some fiscal breathing space. Eight months later, the Bolivian Congress approved the government's tax reform measures, which most importantly instituted a national value added tax of 10 percent. (Characteristically, the Congress postponed a tax on land wealth until 1988.) Implementation of the tax measures has been slow and uneven however, despite the formation of a new Ministry of Taxation. Administrative difficulties and political pressures from powerful groups have slowed the introduction of the new taxes.

Even more difficult, perhaps, has been the process of extricating the government from an enormous overhang of national debt. The Banzer government bequeathed a highly indebted public sector to Siles, and the Siles administration bequeathed a truly bankrupt public sector to Paz. Not only were payments to all international creditors, both public and private, deeply in arrears by 1985, but payments internally to various creditors were also in default.

With respect to the international creditors, the government has sought substantial debt relief. For foreign governments that are creditors of Bolivia, the government has rescheduled payments via the Paris Club. For multilateral creditors, including the World Bank and the IMF, the government has become current on payments, partly on the view that it stands to receive net resource inflows from the multilateral agencies. For private foreign creditors, mainly the commercial banks, the government has maintained a suspension of interest payments, and has been negotiating with the creditors for a "fundamental" solution to that part of the debt, by means of some mechanism of debt repurchase and cancellation.

The indebtedness problems are also severe internally, though measured internal debt is rather low. The Siles administration failed to honor many internal obligations, to private suppliers as well as to regional corporations and other quasi-official entities. In many cases, promises for transfer payments were made by the Siles government as a way to buy time or support, in full knowledge that the obligations could not be met. Thus, as revenues under the current government have increased, the pressures for renewed payments on various outstanding commitments have also risen. The government has been forced into negotiations on many of these ostensible claims, and each negotiation has generated a domestic political battle that threatens the fragile fiscal equilibrium.

Since the Bolivian government does not have the benefit of a bankruptcy proceeding that would partially cancel its outstanding debts once and for all, it will continue for many years to be buffeted by various claimants. Each creditor has the incentive to fight bitterly for full payment on its claims, and thereby to beat the other claimants, even though all creditors well recognize the impossibility that the total sum of claims can be met. This "grab race" among the various creditors, which is precisely what is blocked by formal bankruptcy proceedings, leads to a constant and bruising political battle between the government and its various creditors, a battle which continues to put the government at political jeopardy.

The third part of the stabilization process cited earlier is the reform of state administration. Under Banzer and Siles, the central government had grown to extravagant proportions, since much of the government had degenerated into a patronage machine. This bloated and unwieldy state mechanism was already on the verge of collapse before the end of 1985, when suddenly tin and petroleum prices plummeted on world markets. To preserve fiscal balance, the government had to launch a bruising, indeed brutal, battle to reduce the employment in COMIBOL and YPFB. Although fiscally necessary, the results are stunning, and indeed reflect a social tragedy. COMIBOL has reduced its employment from about 30,000 workers in 1985 to just 7,000 as of 1987. Many of these workers are unemployed, or marginally employed, or have gone to the coca growing region to find work. The mining towns themselves have been decimated. Employment in YPFB has also been reduced, though not as dramatically, from 9,000 workers in 1985 to about 5,000 in 1987.

3.6   Beyond Stabilization to Economic Growth and Development

The stabilization has eliminated much of the panic conditions that surrounded the hyperinflation in 1984 and 1985. Virtually complete price stability has been reestablished in Bolivia during 1986 and 1987. It is evident, however, that many of the deeper problems in the Bolivian economy and society that helped to cause the hyperinflation remain in place, and in some cases have deepened. We now mention some of the challenges that remain in converting the current stabilization period into the first phase of sustained economic development.

There are three sociopolitical cleavages that are serious obstacles to economic stability and long-term growth: the cleavages of income distribution, ideology, and region.

The income distributional cleavage remains profound, and is the source of considerable political conflict. The key political problem is to moderate the nearly continuous confrontation between powerful social groups, such as organized labor and private capital, and the various regional forces. The state capitalist model attempted to finesse the income distribution problem through a combination of the inflation tax, heavy foreign borrowing, and internal repression of the lower classes. None of these alternatives is effective for a long-term development strategy.

A key to a more equal distribution of income in Bolivia is an increased tax burden on the higher-income individuals. Balancing the budget by eliminating basic services, such as health and education, is likely to be considerably more regressive distributionally than equity and stability increased taxes on higher incomes. Progressive taxation might include a tax on land holdings, and higher taxes on luxury consumption goods. A second kind of policy to promote a more equal distribution of income would be greater public spending on education in the rural sector, where most of Bolivia's poorest citizens live. Investment in the human capital of the rural peasantry is a key factor in long-term economic development.

The second division to overcome is ideological, involving competing conceptions of the role of government. With the evident failures of state capitalism in the past two decades, there is a temptation on one side for a strict laissez-faire economic approach, and on the other side, for a fortified socialism. A more modulated approach is more likely to succeed. Such an approach would recognize the government's responsibilities for infrastructure, and social investments in health and education, but also recognize the limitations to the role of the state in the productive sector. Part of the push toward laissez-faire in Bolivia is a frank acknowledgment of the limited capacity for honest, capable public adminstration in the country. But this limitation could be lessened by a concerted effort to raise the standards and capacity of the state bureaucracy. A determined effort at improved training of civil servants is vital in this regard.

The third division is sectoral and regional. Mining and petroleum products can no longer be the basis of a vibrant Bolivian economy. Nor can coca production. Export diversification will require a turn to agriculture and light manufacturing, which in turn will surely entail some geographical shift in the locus of economic activity from the highlands to the lowlands. This kind of shift can be politically destructive if not handled with foresight and planning. To accomplish this restructuring, future governments will have to tread carefully between goals of allocating investment expenditures heavily towards the new sectors and regions, and the need to distribute the burdens and benefits of public spending in a politically stabilizing manner.

References

Dunkerley, James. 1984. *Rebellion in the veins.* Thetford: The Thetford Press.

Malloy, James. 1970. *Bolivia: The uncompleted revolution.* Pittsburgh: University of Pittsburgh Press.

Malloy, James, and Eduardo Gamarra. 1987. The transition to democracy in Bolivia. In *Authoritarians and democrats: Regime transition in Latin America,* ed. James Malloy and Mitchell Seligson. Pittsburgh: University of Pittsburgh Press.

Morales, Juan Antonio. 1987. Inflation stabilization in Bolivia. Working Paper no. 01/87. La Paz: Universidad Católica Boliviana (IISEC).

Olivera, Julio. 1967. Money, prices and fiscal lags: A note on the dynamics of inflation. *Banca Nazionale del Lavoro Quarterly Review* 20: 258–67.

Sachs, Jeffrey. 1986. The Bolivian hyperinflation and stabilization. NBER Working Paper no. 2073 (November). Cambridge, Mass.: National Bureau of Economic Rearch.

———. 1987. Trade and exchange rate policies in growth-oriented adjustment programs. In *Growth-oriented adjustment programs,* ed. Vittorio Corbo, Morris Goldstein, Mohsin Khan. Washington, D.C.: International Monetary Fund and The World Bank.

Tanzi, Vito. 1977. Inflation, lags in collection and the real value of tax revenue. *IMF Staff Papers,* 24: 154–77.

4 The Macroeconomics of the Brazilian External Debt

Eliana A. Cardoso and Albert Fishlow

4.1 Introduction

Brazil has been a central participant in the developing country debt experience. In quantitative terms, Brazil's $110 billion debt accounts for some 10 percent of the total debt of developing countries.[1] In qualitative terms, Brazil's strategic use of debt in the 1970s and subsequent adjustment difficulties in the 1980s epitomize the possibilities and risks inherent in reliance on foreign capital inflows. Brazil's large resource transfer to its creditors and low investment rate since 1982 point up the medium-term problem of sustaining adequate rates of economic development faced by other debtors. Finally, Brazil's evolution from diligent conformity to the rules of the game to its current moratorium symbolizes both the continuing precariousness of the present debt regime and the apparent inability to devise durable solutions.

Brazil's experience is distinctive, however, in three dimensions. First, a long tradition of inflation, and hence explicit indexing of wages, rents, financial assets, and the exchange rate, introduce special problems of adjustment to the sequence of balance of payments shocks since 1973. Second, Brazil is a continental economy, with limited reliance on trade. Export performance, although much improved relative to earlier periods, has remained somewhat erratic; the internal market has exercised much greater appeal. Shortage of foreign exchange for essential imports has always lurked as a potential constraint to economic expansion. Third, there is an imperative for rapid economic growth, which on the whole has been satisfied. In the postwar period, Brazil's trend rate of

Eliana A. Cardoso is an associate professor of international economics at the Fletcher School of Law and Diplomacy, Tufts University. Albert Fishlow is a professor of economics at the University of California at Berkeley.

expansion of over 6 percent is one of the highest for developing countries. That standard is a constant source of pressure upon policymakers, whether under military or civilian government. Recession is not a permissible option. In combination, these three characteristics define very narrow limits for economic policy. They help to explain both why debt has proved so seductive but also difficult to manage, and why return to sustained economic growth and reasonable inflation rates is closely tied to more adequate treatment of the debt problem.

4.2 The Debt Strategy of the 1970s

The first oil shock caught Brazil at the height of its economic "miracle": a product growth of 10 percent a year that had prevailed since 1968. The economy was showing clear signs of overheating, and excess demand for imports. As the leading developing country importer of petroleum, and one whose industry and transport were centered on the car and truck industry, the blow was especially severe. To make matters even more delicate, a political transition was in its initial stages, for which continuing prosperity was regarded as a necessary condition. These circumstances predisposed Brazil to an adjustment strategy based upon high, although slower, rates of growth, and one in which there was more reliance upon government-stimulated import substitution investment than upon market driven responses to changes in exchange rates or relative prices of petroleum. External debt played a central role in that strategy through its financing of increased investment rates and of large trade and current account deficits. By permitting gradual rather than immediate accommodation, the negative real income effects of the shock could be postponed and go unnoticed in the midst of continuing growth.

If there was demand for debt, there was also supply. Brazil was a favored and privileged participant in the Eurocurrency market. It had started to borrow early, even before the oil shock, and its rapid growth and level of industrialization qualified the country as highly creditworthy. The Brazilian economic technocracy was held in high regard, and its political stability was not in doubt.

The strategy succeeded in sustaining high rates of growth: Between 1973 and 1979 Brazilian product expanded at a rate of 7 percent, well above the average for developing country oil importers as a whole. It did so, however, at the expense of a very rapid increase in medium- and long-term net debt: $5.3 billion at the end of 1972 to $31.6 billion at the end of 1978. The 35 percent annual rate of debt growth was also well above the 25 percent for oil importers. More significantly, the Brazilian net debt-export ratio had almost doubled and was about three times as great as the developing country average.

Brazil had thus become much more vulnerable to changes in the international economy as a result of its adjustment style. Import-substituting industrialization was itself highly import intensive in its early stages, and despite increasing export subsidies, the domestic market was clearly the priority. Oil imports continued to expand, while export performance lagged: Even though sales of industrial products increased, total export volume stagnated between 1973 and 1978. Improved terms of trade were an important factor in helping the trade balance through 1977.

At the same time, there were signs of an accumulating domestic disequilibrium as the ambitious investment plan was followed. Government expenditure outran its finance, and monetary accommodation was increasingly necessary to sustain direct outlays and mounting indirect incentives. The level of inflation had doubled from its pre-oil shock of 20 percent, and only a stop-and-go macropolicy and increasing direct controls prevented the situation from getting even more out of hand.

4.3   The Second Oil Shock and Subsequent Adjustment

Even on the eve of the second oil shock, Brazil faced the need for a midterm modification of strategy. Such was the proposal of Mario Simonsen, to whom economic policy had been entrusted in the Figueiredo government installed in March 1979. He sought to reduce the government deficit and to finance less of it through credit. In addition, he sought to expand the use of price signals, including more aggressive exchange rate devaluation, as well as to accept the more modest rates of growth implicit in a stabilization policy.

This approach, labeled "recessionist" by Brazilian critics, yielded to a more ambitious supply-side plan undertaken by Simonsen's successor, Antonio Delfim Neto, the author of the earlier "miracle." Priority was given to expenditure and credit expansion to finance investment in the agricultural and energy sectors. A maxi-devaluation of 30 percent, the first departure from the crawling peg implanted in 1968, would ease the foreign exchange constraint. Macroeconomic policy would contain inflation by reducing interest rates (a significant cost component), and by changing expectations through preannounced internal monetary correction and exchange rate devaluation at 45 percent and 40 percent, respectively.

Heterodoxy did not work this time. The balance of payments, under pressure from the oil price increase and a 7 percent product increase, registered a record current account deficit of $12.4 billion in 1980. Inflation reached a three digit level, reflecting excess demand, the increases of public-sector prices, the effects of devaluation, and the consequences of a new wage law mandating a shorter adjustment lag. New finance was necessary, adding not only to the registered medium-and long-term debt, but increasingly to short-term liabilities.

The deterioration in creditworthiness enforced a foreign exchange constraint and, in October 1980, a more orthodox package of fiscal and monetary restraint was fashioned. Banks then agreed to new loans in 1981 to meet immediate needs. But the financing, since it was increasingly allocated to debt service, did not leave a margin for real growth. Brazil reluctantly entered into a lengthy period of adjustment through recession that was to last until 1983, provoking a decrease in absolute income of 4 percent that was greater than the fall in the 1930s.

The sudden decline in the availability of bank financing for debtors in 1982, after the Mexican de facto moratorium in August, was a major reason for this poor performance. Coming just when interest rates were rising sharply, and OECD countries were opting for reduced demand to control inflation, the capital supply shock left no alternative but contraction. Try as Brazil might in September and October to emphasize its continuing creditworthiness, replete with its own austerity program, the application for an IMF extended facility loan immediately after the November elections was a foregone conclusion.

Brazil's experience under the aegis of the Fund was tumultuous, as the submission of seven letters of intent over a two-year period suggests. There was reason for the two waivers, three modifications of targets, and two suspensions that characterized the relationship.

First, the initial program retained the limited and unrealistic financing requirements that the Brazilian authorities themselves had calculated in their effort to bypass the Fund. Such an underestimate required larger domestic financing of the rising interest debt service, and thereby made internal targets equally erroneous. Even the reduced disbursements agreed upon were not made in a timely fashion, complicating the situation more. Noncompliance was self-fulfilling.

Second, the standard nominal target for public-sector borrowing requirements, which is the centerpiece of an IMF stabilization program, did not easily conform to a highly indexed economy. The recorded increase in nominal government borrowing necessarily accommodated to the realized rate of inflation (and the exchange rate for a large part of the debt) since the outstanding principal was automatically revalued. Higher than projected inflation rates quickly absorbed all available finance for monetary and exchange correction, suggesting that policies were unrealistically stringent. This soon became apparent after another maxi-devaluation in February 1983 and led to an amended letter even before the first had been considered by the board. By the fourth letter in November, the Fund finally accepted the concept of an operational deficit purged of monetary and exchange correction that more adequately measured the management of fiscal policy. This innovation has become characteristic of arrangements with other Latin American countries as well.

The third reason for agreement changes was that there was a marked divergence between internal and external performance. Contrary to the IMF model tying the improvement in the balance of payments to reduction in domestic credit and inflation, the Brazilian external accounts improved partially at the expense of higher inflation and larger public-sector deficits. Pervasive indexation projected exchange devaluations into higher rates of inflation. Export surpluses absorbed domestic saving and exerted upward pressure on interest rates that were applied to growing internal debt. Despite these interactions, and the Brazilian subordination of internal targets to external priorities, the Fund's preoccupation with inflation and deficits was persistant and became a source of continuing friction.

Brazil's trade balance improved more rapidly than had been expected, due to the jump in exports in 1984. Surpluses of $1 billion a month, adequate to meet interest payments, obviated the need for new private capital inflows in 1985. This led to suspension of the IMF agreement as well as postponement of the planned multiyear rescheduling with the banks. The new civilian government, free from the requirements of external creditors, soon opted for a more expansionist policy based upon increased internal demand. Gross domestic product grew more than 8 percent in 1985.

Accelerating inflation, however, remained a concern and provoked popular discontent and political dissatisfaction. The response was the *Plano Cruzado*, in the mold of programs launched within the year in Argentina and Israel. It was a bold, and temporarily successful, attempt to match the success that had been achieved on the trade account with a recession-free solution to inflation that had escalated, by February 1986, to an annual rate approaching 400 percent.

4.4 Stopping Inflation

The basis of the *Plano Cruzado* was the recognition that indexing played a central role in projecting past increases in price into the future:

$$p_t = a \cdot p_{t-1} + b \cdot gap_t + c \cdot e_t,$$

where p is the rate of inflation, gap is a measure of excess demand, and e is an indicator of supply shocks. Past inflation is built into current cost through its effect on wages, the exchange rate, and public sector prices. Excess demand measures the degree to which cost increases will be absorbed, but also the extent to which cost increases can be averted, as for example by increased labor turnover to avoid mandated wage increases. Shocks record the effect of independent internal and external effects upon prices: harvests, oil prices, devaluation, etc. Where such a process has long been operative, as in Brazil, the role of nominal demand in stopping inflation is weak relative to the replicative effects of formal indexation. Moreover, any escalation of prices from supply shocks get permanently embedded in the inflation rate. Endogenous increases in velocity and money supply accommodate increases in prices.

To stop inflation effectively under such conditions requires a coordinated standstill of wages and prices. Indexing is nothing more than an automatic incomes policy to guard against erosion of real returns. The essence of the Cruzado Plan was to substitute a sophisticated price and wage freeze, where the latter took into explicit account the staggered contract period and thus the average level of real earnings over the preceding six months. Financial contracts also had to be rewritten to account for anticipated inflation in future payments. The new currency, which progressively appreciated against the old, facilitated the adjustment.

A neoclassical alternative approach would have consisted of an announcement of a new and credible noninflationary monetary regime, and a simultaneous wage recontracting. In conditions of hyperinflation, prices and wages tend to be measured in terms of foreign currency. It is not difficult, therefore, simply to rescale and stop inflation flat, as long as monetary and fiscal policies assure that the conversion holds. In Brazil, short of that degree of inflation, the freeze of the Cruzado Plan was a more feasible way of breaking the vicious circle. Nonetheless, it required that other sources of inflation be eliminated.

As it turned out, however, they were not. After an initial euphoric reception, the price freeze instead became the principal and preferred instrument of anti-inflationary policy. Politics had much to do with the decision. An impending election in November became the critical horizon around which all planning was centered. Critical decisions were postponed, and those intermediate measures taken to restrain the overheating economy were consciously diluted. Remonetization of the economy to satisfy increased demand for money balances and to prevent excessive real interest rates had gone too far. Fiscal policy, instead of being neutral, as the authors of the Cruzado Plan had hoped after the December tax increases, was expansionary. And wage policy encouraged, rather than restrained, the increases in real wages that had been on the rise since the expansion in 1985.

As shortages developed, expectations of resurgent inflation encouraged speculative accumulation of inventory and real assets, but not longer-term investment. Since the exchange rate had been held constant, it was becoming overvalued relative to repressed inflation, leading to disincentives to export. Consequently, the trade balance underwent rapid deterioration in the last quarter of the year, and reserves were drawn down. When new increases in the excise tax (100 percent on beer and cigarettes and 80 percent on cars) were finally announced immediately after the election, they were too little and too late. Efforts to purge the price index, and hence prevent it from influencing wage demands, encountered popular resistance. Thereafter, decontrol proceeded irregularly until the freeze was formally lifted in February 1987. Unchecked by the force of past, low-inflation inertia, prices exploded and were joined by wages triggered by the 20 percent annual threshold of the *escala movel* (sliding scale) that had been added to the Cruzado Plan. Interest rates registered ever increasing inflationary expectations that became reflected in actual price increases. The finance minister, Dilson Funaro, had gone from hero to villain in the space of six months. Even the proclamation of a moratorium on interest payments on the medium- and long-term commercial debt could not save his job.

The Cruzado Plan, which had been so promising, had failed and accelerating inflation remained. Its treatment was to require still new emergency measures and another freeze put in place by the successor finance minister, Luiz Carlos Bresser Pereira. The prospect of more conventional stabilization, predicated upon some reduction of real wages and slower demand growth, has unleashed a profound debate within the majority party, the Partido do Movimento Democratico Brasileiro (PMDB). Central to success will be the ability to gain control over government expenditures, not only of the Federal government but of heavily indebted states and municipalities.

Comparison of the earlier 1964–67 success in reversing accelerating inflation with the failure of the Cruzado Plan suggests three lessons. The first is that it was easier to gain control over the fiscal deficit in 1965, when the inherited public debt from the past was small and external assistance was forthcoming. By contrast, the debt-income ratio in 1986 stood at 50 percent, and a large transfer of resources amounting to 4 percent of product was necessary to service external interest.

The second lesson is to avoid excess boldness in policy implementation. The Cruzado Plan aimed for zero inflation and abolished indexation, while the program of 1964–68 introduced indexing as a way of reducing the real misallocations inherent in living with some inflation. Indexation is a source of inflation propagation, but it is also protection against rapid inflationary acceleration of the kind that occurred in early 1987. Adjustment triggers without caps and financial assets tied to the short-term interest rate created a volatile climate whose end result was inflation that reached almost 30 percent a month, or twice what had provoked the Cruzado Plan.

Third, distributionally neutral disinflation is theoretically attractive but difficult to manage. Incomes policy is a necessary means of achieving coordination and a reduction in inflation, but not sufficient by itself to sustain it. In 1964, residual wage repression was the element that underwrote continued progress in reducing the rate of inflation. Real wages were supposed to be maintained at their previous average, but the nominal wage adjustments were based upon prospective inflation rates much lower than realized. In 1986, real wages were increasing at the expense of profit margins, and provoked shortages, black markets, and disordered growth. In this case, it eventually meant that disinflation not only was checked, but that further costs were incurred through a deterioration in the balance of payments. Neither the 1964 nor the 1986 program were implemented as planned.

4.5 External Debt, Budget Deficits, and Inflation

The budget deficit is central not only to the failure of the Cruzado Plan, but to the acceleration of inflation and high real interest rates of the 1981–84 stabilization period. Adding considerably to the complication of fiscal policy is the multiplicity of budgetary concepts, ranging from inclusion of monetary and exchange correction that is self-financed, to a cash-flow measure that excludes the implicit subsidies of the monetary authorities. We add another in table 4.1: a deficit measure corrected for inflation, based upon the real increases in the money stock and debt required to finance public sector expenditures. This, like the others, is large and above target, and has the added advantage of relating directly to the issue of financing.

In Brazil, because of its more sophisticated financial market and the attempt to comply with monetary targets, increases in debt rather than changes in the real monetary base and the inflation tax were used to

Table 4.1   **Different Measures of the Budget Deficit as a Share of GNP**

Year	Increase in Total Debt/GDP	Deficit Corrected for Inflation/GDP	FGV[a] measure/GDP	BRPS[b] /GDP	Operational[c] Deficit/GDP
1982	29.9	8.4	3.7	15.8	6.6
1983	60.5	15.2	4.1	19.9	3.0
1984	60.7	4.6	4.7	23.3	2.7
1985	65.6	6.1	n.a.	27.8	4.3

Source: Cardoso and Reis (1986), and Banco Central of Brazil, *Brasil Programa Econômico*, February 1987.

[a]Calculated on cash-flow basis, excludes the monetary authorities' deficit.
[b]Borrowing requirement of the public sector, calculated on accrual basis, excludes the monetary authorities' deficit.
[c]Subtracts monetary correction from BRPS.

finance the deficit. As external resources became more limited, increases in the internal debt were the necessary vehicle. This process required ever higher real interest rates, that crowded out private investment, provoked in turn higher public interest expenditure and deficits, and pushed up private financial costs. Real devaluation in 1983 had the effect of significantly increasing internal debt through an exchange rate–based revaluation of principal greater than the inflation rate.

A simple two equation model incorporating debt finance in an open economy and specifying inflation dynamics brings out the essential elements of this interaction. The first equation combines the government budget constraint and the balance of payments definition:

(1) $$\mu = a/h - \pi$$

where μ is the growth rate of the real monetary base; a is the sum of the domestic deficit financed by increases in the monetary base and of the net trade and nonfactor service surplus; h is the real monetary base; and π is the rate of inflation.

The second equation describes changes in inflation as a function of excess demand. Inertial inflation is built in. Inflation accelerates when the actual real interest rate $(i - \pi)$ corresponding to goods and money market equilibrium, is below the full employment real interest rate, r, determined by permanent government expenditure, G, and the net trade and nonfactor service surplus, NX:

(2) $$\pi = \sigma[\, r(G, NX) - (i - \pi)]$$

Figure 4.1 shows how Brazilian inflation between 1979 and 1985 increased despite reductions in the real monetary base. The two equations are graphed. Since a reduced monetization of domestic deficits offsets the export surplus, the schedule $\mu = 0$ is held constant. The other, $\pi = 0$, shifts to the left as government expenditure increased and larger trade surpluses were necessary to pay interest on the external debt. The economy adjusts in a cyclical fashion; inflation no sooner subsides before another increase in excess demand sends both inflation and the required real interest rate up again.

In late 1986 and 1987, the acceleration in inflation after the failure of the Cruzado Plan can also be explained within the context of the same model. But now, with monetization of the larger deficit, the $\mu = 0$ schedule also shifts, but to the right. The increase in the money supply lowers nominal interest rates and stimulates demand, pushing up the inflation rate. Gradually, inflation catches up with money growth and then exceeds it, reducing real cash balances and increasing the real interest rate. There is, therefore, a direct linkage between the growing inability to finance the public sector deficit externally after 1979, and

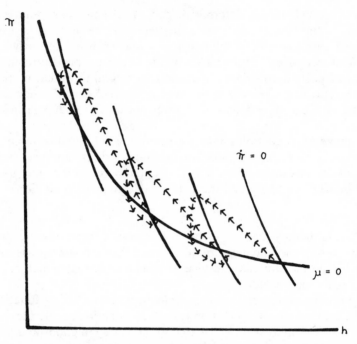

Fig. 4.1   Successive increases in the full employment real interest rate

domestic inflationary impulses. The debt problem went much deeper than the immediate effects of the balance of payments.

4.6   Import Substitution and Export Diversification

From the standpoint of the balance of payments, Brazil was especially vulnerable to the oil, interest rate, and debt shocks because of its longstanding emphasis on import substitution industrialization. There was no margin of substantial competitive imports to be reduced easily. Trade was reduced to little more than 5 percent of total gross product. In addition, Brazil remained very dependent on imported oil. Import substitution had worked in Brazil, unlike many other countries, because of the size of the market; indicators like effective protection typically underestimate the competitiveness of the industrial sector because they generalize exaggerated tariffs to all domestic prices.

By 1964, after more than a decade of grappling with foreign exchange constraint, it was clear that trade liberalization and greater attention to exports were necessary. New and sizable incentives were conceded to exports of manufactured products principally through tax rebates of various kinds and subsidized credit. In 1968 the exchange rate policy was converted to a crawling peg, limiting the variations of real exchange rates that earlier prejudiced export profitability. Performance improved markedly after 1968, with export receipts more than doubling by 1972. In addition to the diversification into industrial goods, increases in the volume and prices of nontraditional primary exports played an important role. These favorable results gained Brazil access to the Eurocurrency market and underwrote the even more rapid growth of imports that accompanied the economic "miracle."

The surge in the trade deficit in 1974 and continuing imbalance thereafter brought a resurgence of import controls and the ambitious import substitution with debt adjustment strategy described earlier. The appreciation of the real exchange rate was offset by larger export incentives that provoked increased resistance from the industrialized countries, particularly the United States. Export performance was irregular and disappointing over this interval; real growth stagnated between 1973 and 1978, and was an important reason for reliance on continuing debt. Improved terms of trade averted worse. Imports meanwhile were increasingly made up of oil and its derivatives, which went from 10 percent to almost a third of total imports.

Brazil, in common with other indebted countries, was forced into a massive reduction of imports after 1981. It did, however, achieve a large rise in exports in 1984, producing trade surpluses of more than $12 billion in that year and in the following year. The same pace was followed in the first 9 months of 1986 until the Cruzado Plan unravelled. These results permitted interest obligations to be paid without resort to much new bank borrowing. They also led some Brazilians to the conclusion that high rates of growth could be resumed in the future without fear of again encountering an exchange rate constraint.

Closer analysis of Brazilian import demand and export supply cast doubt upon the validity of such an inference. There is no decisive evidence in favor of structural reduction of import elasticities in the 1980s. Higher rates of sustained growth are therefore likely to encounter much more than proportional import growth, particularly with increases in the investment rate. Relative price elasticities are low, on the other hand, limiting the impact of real devaluation. For exports, while manufactured products show a more than unitary real price elasticity, primary products, still more than a third of the total, are less sensitive. The influence of industrialized country income is also smaller and less reliable for primary products than for manufactured goods. The key point, however, is the large and consistently statistically significant influence of capacity utilization upon both import demand and export supply. Prosperity rapidly diminishes the trade surplus by augmenting imports and reducing exports.

The very favorable performance of the 1980s is thus not yet fully persuasive of Brazil's ability to keep imports down at abnormally low levels or its capacity to sustain competitiveness with other exporting developing countries. Nor is international trade likely to be the engine of growth that it was before the oil shocks. Over the next few years projections show a rather slowly growing market with weak commodity prices. In order to revive the Brazilian economy, continued efforts to stimulate exports are necessary as well as a better international economic climate.

4.7   Debt and Growth

The debt problem is not simply one of macroeconomic adjustment, straining the balance of payments, and contributing to fiscal deficits and inflation. The debt problem is also a development problem.

Export surpluses to satisfy external interest obligations that have averaged more than 5 percent of gross product since 1984 imply correspondingly lower rates of investment. The real interest rates needed to restore macroeconomic equilibrium crowd out private-sector capital formation; they do not reduce consumption. This large decline of investment rates and relative constancy of the consumption ratio is widespread, and Brazil is prototypical. Investment averaged 21.6 percent of gross product in 1980–82, and only 17.7 percent in 1984–86.

Such investment rates are incompatible with the sustained recovery needed to absorb new entrants to the labor force, let alone to assure the continuing advances in productivity required to compete successfully in world markets. Only in an expanding economy, moreover, will it be possible to bring the public sector into better balance, and to achieve the increases in domestic saving implied by inevitably smaller future foreign savings. Durable structural reforms do not emanate from either stop-and-go macroeconomic policies or shock treatments intended rapidly to restore equilibrium. Only in an expanding economy will it be possible to service the debt reliably and continuously. A low-growth economic equilibrium in Brazil, especially under welcome transition to democracy, translates into a political and social disequilibrium. The first obligations to go, as the February moratorium already shows, are debt service.

Analyses that limit their scope to projecting the balance of payments are not only frequently overoptimistic about future imports and exports, but also miss the critical importance of the reverse resource transfer burdening an adequate recovery. Enormous trade surpluses are not in Brazil's immediate future. Nor should they be. An efficient international capital market should be expected to channel larger foreign savings to a country like Brazil that has a demonstrated record of sustained growth.

The implication is either larger capital flows or a reduction in external interest payments. Neither seems entirely likely to emerge from simple muddling through. The capital inflows required are large, and there is little indication that they will be forthcoming under present arrangements. Martin Feldstein's calculations for Brazilian net borrowing in *The Economist* (27 June 1987) are made to seem eminently reasonable. Yet the net annual borrowing of $4 billion needed in the next few years is much greater than achieved in any year since 1982. If capital inflows had been larger, as the Baker Plan was supposed to have accomplished, then there would have been no moratorium, and very probably, a much more successful outcome to the Cruzado Plan.

Feldstein is correct regarding Brazil's capacity to absorb more debt productively and eventually to outgrow it in a world that was certain. Debt-export and debt-product ratios readily improve if modest trade surpluses are sustained and growth rates approximate the interest rate. This is the argument in support of more lending. Even if it were available, however, which remains a large question mark, such a course is not without peril. The problem is the projected 1987 debt-export ratio of 4.7 from which Brazil starts. That leaves Brazil extremely vulnerable to changes in interest rates, higher oil prices, slower industrialized country growth, and domestic policy mistakes. The trouble with muddling through is that the growth rates of developing countries have been the residual adjustment variable rather than a target to which capital flows reliably accommodate.

The case for some debt relief is made by market prices that value Brazilian debt at a discount of up to 40 percent. Such valuations imply an expectation of less than full debt service on outstanding loans. If large voluntary lending were available, Brazil would have an incentive to do better than predicted in order to qualify for needed additional capital. Since it is not, an alternative solution is to substitute a more certain asset, from the World Bank perhaps, yielding less, with the difference passed along in lower debt service to Brazil (and other countries) in return for policy conditionality. Now that banks have begun to adjust more realistically through loan loss reserves and larger capitalization, there is less risk to the financial system. Now that countries have made significant adjustment to the shocks of the last decade, Brazil included, there is the possibility of stimulating a return to needed higher rates of economic development.

Appendix
Brazilian Economic Performance: 1971–86

Table 4.2   Real Rates of Growth of Production Year

Year	Gross Domestic Product	Industry	Agriculture
1971	12.0	12.0	11.3
1972	11.1	13.0	4.1
1973	13.6	16.3	3.6
1974	9.7	9.2	8.2
1975	5.4	5.9	4.8
1976	9.7	12.4	2.9
1977	5.7	3.9	11.8
1978	5.0	7.2	−2.6
1979	6.4	6.4	5.0
1980	7.2	7.9	6.3
1981	−1.6	−5.5	6.4
1982	0.9	0.6	−2.5
1983	−3.2	−6.8	2.2
1984	4.5	6.0	3.2
1985	8.3	9.0	8.8
1986	8.2		

Table 4.3   Rates[a] of Growth of Money and Prices

Year	Monetary Base	Money Supply M1	Augmented[b] Money Supply M4	Wholesale Prices, Internal Supply Total	Foodstuffs
1971	36.3	32.3	n.a.	21.4	30.2
1972	18.5	38.3	n.a.	15.9	16.1
1973	47.1	47.0	n.a.	15.5	12.4
1974	32.9	33.5	40.6	35.4	37.4
1975	36.4	42.8	57.5	29.3	33.0
1976	49.8	37.2	55.3	44.9	50.1
1977	50.7	37.5	49.1	35.5	37.5
1978	44.9	42.2	53.2	43.0	51.9
1979	84.4	73.6	65.1	80.1	84.8
1980	56.9	70.2	69.1	121.3	130.8
1981	78.0	87.2	141.7	94.3	85.9
1982	87.3	65.0	105.7	97.7	98.9
1983	96.3	95.0	150.2	234.0	299.5
1984	243.8	203.5	291.9	230.3	223.7
1985	202.8	328.2	302.4	225.7	
1986	293.5	303.8	102.5	62.6	

[a]December to December of indicated year.
[b]Includes time deposits and federal government debt.

Table 4.4   **Balance of Payments and Debt ($ billion)**

Year	Exports[a]	Imports[a] Total	Imports[a] Fuel	Net Interest	Current Account	Net Capital Inflows	Surplus	Level of Reserves	Level of Debt[b]
1971	2.9	3.2	0.4	0.3	-1.3	1.8	0.5	1.7	6.6
1972	4.0	4.2	0.5	0.4	-1.5	3.5	2.4	4.2	9.5
1973	6.2	6.2	0.8	0.5	-1.7	3.5	2.2	6.4	12.6
1974	8.0	12.6	3.0	0.7	-7.1	6.3	-0.9	5.3	17.2
1975	8.7	12.2	3.1	1.5	-6.7	5.9	-1.0	4.0	21.2
1976	10.1	12.4	3.8	1.8	-6.0	6.9	1.2	6.5	26.0
1977	12.1	12.0	4.1	2.1	-4.0	5.3	6.0	7.3	32.0
1978	12.7	13.7	4.5	2.7	-6.0	9.4	3.9	11.9	43.5
1979	15.2	18.1	6.8	4.2	-10.0	7.7	-3.2	9.7	49.9
1980	20.1	23.0	10.2	6.3	-12.4	9.7	-3.4	6.9	53.8
1981	23.3	22.1	11.3	9.2	-11.0	12.8	0.6	7.5	61.4
1982	20.2	19.4	10.5	11.4	-16.3	7.9	-8.8	4.0	69.7
1983	21.9	15.4	8.6	9.6	-6.8	2.1	-5.4	4.6	81.3
1984	27.0	13.9	7.3	10.2	0.0	0.2	0.7	12.0	91.1
1985	25.6	13.2	5.7	9.7	-0.3	-2.7	-3.5	11.6	95.9
1986	22.4	12.9		9.1				6.8	101.5

Source: Conjunctura Economica, various issues, and Banco Central of Brazil, Monthly Bulletins, various issues.

[a]FOB.

[b]Registered; excludes interbank liabilities and short-term debt.

Table 4.5   **Investment and Saving Shares in GDP 1970 – 1985**

Year	Gross Domestic Investment[a]/ GDP	Non Factor Current Account[b]/GDP	Net Factor Payments Abroad[c]/GDP	Net Foreign Savings/ GDP	Gross National Savings/GDP
1970	21.5	−0.5	−0.8	1.3	20.2
1971	21.9	−1.7	−0.9	2.6	19.3
1972	22.1	−1.7	−0.9	2.6	19.5
1973	22.4	−1.2	−0.9	2.1	20.3
1974	23.9	−5.9	−0.9	6.8	17.1
1975	25.0	−4.0	−1.4	5.4	19.6
1976	23.3	−2.4	−1.6	4.0	19.3
1977	21.3	−0.7	−1.6	2.3	19.0
1978	21.1	−1.2	−2.2	3.4	17.1
1979	20.3	−1.9	−2.6	4.5	15.8
1980	21.1	−2.1	−3.1	5.2	15.9
1981	21.2	−0.3	−4.0	4.3	16.9
1982	21.2	−0.6	−5.1	5.7	15.5
1983	16.9	2.4	−5.7	3.3	13.6
1984	16.4	5.6	−5.7	0.1	16.3
1985	16.3	5.2	−5.4	0.2	16.1

Sources: Conjuntura Econômica, various issues, and Banco Central of Brazil, *Monthly Bulletins,* various issues.
[a]Changes in stocks are excluded.
[b]Excludes factor payments.
[c]Includes reinvested profits.

Table 4.6   Brazilian Foreign Debt and Reserves ($ billions)

Year	Medium- and Long-Term (1)	Short-Term (2)	Total Debt (1) + (2)	Gross Reserves	Reserves Net of Liabilities of Monetary Authorities	Ratio of Gross Interest to Exports	Ratio of Debt to GDP
1965	3.644		3.644	0.483	-0.777		
1966	3.666		3.666	0.421	0.412		
1967	3.281		3.281	0.198	-0.617		
1968	3.780		3.780	0.257	-0.488		
1969	4.403		4.403	0.657	0.143		
1970	5.295		5.295	1.187	0.786		
1971	6.622		6.622	1.723	1.413		
1972	9.521		9.521	4.183	3.706		
1973	12.572		12.572	6.416	5.994		
1974	17.166		17.166	5.269	4.870		
1975	21.171		21.171	4.041	3.688	.215	.20
1976	25.985		25.985	6.544	5.657	.206	.21
1977	32.037	3.700 NB	35.737	7.256	6.216	.203	.22
1978	43.511	4.600 NB	48.111	11.895	11.535	.264	.25
1979	49.904	6.200 NB	56.104	9.689	9.443	.351	.24
1980	53.848	10.800 NB	64.648	6.913	5.163	.370	.26
1981	61.411	14.100 NB	75.511	7.507	5.695	.435	.27
1982	70.198	13.067 CB	83.265	3.994	-2.332	.621	.30
1983	81.319	10.313 CB	91.632	4.563	0.086	.469	.45
1984	91.091	10.948 CB	102.039	11.995	5.096	.424	.48
1985	95.857	9.269 CB	105.126	11.608	4.400	.438	.47
1986	101.540	9.032 CB	110.572	6.760	0.771	.449	.42

Sources: Banco Central of Brazil and Nogueira Batista (1985).

(1) Medium- and long-term debt outstanding at the end of the year.

(2) Non-registered debt.

NB = Nogueira Batista's estimates.

CB = Central Bank figures.

Table 4.7   Real Exchange Rates and Terms of Trade (1977 = 1)

Year	(1)	(2)	(3)	(4)	(5)
1970	1.059	1.218	1.620	0.936	0.89
1971	1.059	1.168	1.479	0.932	0.82
1972	1.027	1.126	1.380	0.942	0.87
1973	0.952	1.092	1.085	0.977	0.95
1974	0.929	1.067	0.901	0.978	0.78
1975	0.925	1.034	0.986	0.955	0.76
1976	0.969	1.025	1.056	1.101	0.85
1977	1.000	1.000	1.000	1.000	1.00
1978	0.896	0.916	1.056	1.105	0.86
1979	0.819	0.815	0.986	1.153	0.79
1980	0.766	0.714	0.944	0.951	0.65
1981	0.929	0.866	1.127	0.909	0.55
1982	0.981	0.941	1.296	0.896	0.54
1983	0.812	0.723	1.056	0.811	0.53
1984	0.849	0.723	1.056	0.738	0.58
1985		0.714		0.803	0.55
1986					

(1) Ratio of domestic wholesale prices to foreign wholesale prices times exchange rate.
(2) Ratio of Brazilian export prices of manufactures to export prices of competitors times exchange rate.
(3) Ratio of domestic prices of manufactures to export prices of manufactures.
(4) Ratio of domestic construction prices to prices of domestic manufactures.
(5)Terms of trade: export prices divided by import prices.

Note

1. Selected data relating to Brazilian macroeconomic performance and debt are found in the Appendix.

References

Arida, Pérsio, and André Lara-Resende. 1985. Inertial inflation and monetary reform. In *Inflation and indexation: Argentina, Brazil, and Israel*, ed. John Williamson. Washington, D.C.: Institute for International Economics.
Batista, Paulo Nogueira. 1983. *Mito e realidade da dívida externa brasileira.* Rio de Janeiro: Paz e Terra.
———. 1985. International flows to Brazil. Mimeo. Rio de Janeiro: Fundação Getúlio Vargas.
Cardoso, Eliana. 1987. *Inflation, growth, and the real exchange rate: Brazil and Latin America, 1850–1983.* New York: Garland Publishing.

————. 1987. Latin American debt: Which way now? *Challenge* (May–June): 11–17.

Cardoso, Eliana, and Rudiger Dornbusch. 1987. Brazil's tropical plan. *American Economic Review* 77, no. 2 (May): 288–92.

Cardoso, Eliana, and E. Reis. 1986. Deficits, dividas e inflacao no Brasil. *Pesquisa e Planajamento Econômico* (December): 575–98.

Díaz Alejandro, Carlos. 1983. Some aspects of the 1982–1983 Brazilian payments crisis. *Brookings Papers in Economic Activity* 1: 515–52.

Dornbusch, Rudiger. 1985. The Larida proposal: Comments. In *Inflation and indexation: Argentina, Brazil, and Israel*, ed. John Williamson. Cambridge: MIT Press.

————. 1987. The world debt problem. New York: The Twentieth Century Fund.

Dornbusch, Rudiger, and Mário Simonsen. 1987. *Inflation stabilization with incomes policy support*. New York: Group of Thirty.

Fishlow, Albert. 1988. Tale of two presidents. In *Democratizing Brazil: Problems of transition and consolidation*, ed. Alfred Stepan. Oxford: Oxford University Press.

————. 1984. The debt crisis: Round two ahead? In *Adjustment Crisis in the Third World*, ed. R. E. Feinberg and V. Kallab. Washington, D.C.: Overseas Development Council.

————. 1985. The debt crisis: A longer perspective. *Journal of Development Planning* no. 16: 83–104.

————. 1985. Lessons from the past: Capital markets during the 19th century and the interwar period. *International Organization* 39, no. 3: 383–439.

Goldsmith, Raymond. 1986. *Desenvolvimento financeiro sob um século de inflação: Brasil, 1850–1984*. São Paulo: Harper & Row do Brasil.

Simonsen, Mário Henrique. 1983. Indexation: Current theory and the Brazilian experience. In *Inflation, debt, and indexation*, ed. Rudiger Dornbusch and Mário Henrique Simonsen. Cambridge: MIT Press.

5 The Conduct of Economic Policies in Indonesia and Its Impact on External Debt

Wing Thye Woo and Anwar Nasution

5.1 Introduction

Our aim is first to explain why Indonesia did not experience an external debt crisis in the 1982–84 period as did most of the Latin American countries, and then, on the basis of our analysis, make recommendations to deal with Indonesia's present debt situation. We hope that the lessons drawn will be useful as well in the design of adjustment policies for other countries experiencing debt-servicing difficulties. Our study goes beyond the normal economic analysis by giving detailed attention to the Indonesian historical and political setting within which decisions about policies are made.

We conclude that the major reason for the absence of a 1982–84 debt crisis was the satisfactory management of the exchange rate, a task that was made easier because there were neither burgeoning budget deficits nor extended periods of loss of control over monetary growth. The absence of protracted exchange rate overvaluation from 1979 onward was fundamental in maintaining a strong nonoil tradable sector. The nonoil tradable sector was able to earn enough foreign exchange to service Indonesian debts when the external shock of high interest rates increased debt-service payments and the recession in industrialized countries lowered the price of oil. We also want to emphasize that the absence of extended exchange rate overvaluation kept the external debt down by not encouraging capital flight. We ascribe this use of the exchange rate to protect the tradable sector as much to the existence of an influential political constituency consisting of (comparatively)

Wing Thye Woo is an assistant professor of economics at the University of California, Davis. Anwar Nasution is lecturer in monetary economics, Faculty of Economics, at the University of Indonesia.

neoclassical economists, Javanese peasantry and Outer Island residents, as to balance-of-payments considerations.[1]

This chapter is organized as follows: sections 5.2 and 5.3 explore the historical and political dimensions of economic policymaking, and section 5.4 verifies the veracity of our political economy approach by looking at the distributional consequences of the fiscal system. Section 5.5 reviews the conduct of monetary policy and finds that the choice of the monetary control mechanism in the 1970s was influenced by political economy considerations. Section 5.6 shows how exchange rate management since November 1978 has been sensitive to both the economic viability of the agricultural export sector and the balance-of-payments position. Section 5.7 identifies three factors—concessional loans, prudent debt management, and export orientation—responsible for the non-crisis outcome in 1982–84, and then estimates their relative contribution. Section 5.8 discusses the prospects of Indonesia avoiding a future external debt crisis, and the role for policy in ensuring such an outcome.

5.2   Political and Economic Instability, 1950–65

An understanding of the economic conditions prior to the establishment of the New Order government in 1966 is important because the economic policies of the 1950–65 period left a very strong imprint on the institutional memory of the new government, especially insofar as it resides in the person of President Soeharto. During this period, the Indonesian government was preoccupied with domestic political and military problems, with the restoration of sovereignty on West Irian, and with political recognition in world forums. Little attention and resources were devoted to economic development.

An increasingly difficult budget situation made inflation a major problem. Taxes on trade were the major source of government revenue, but the overvalued multiple exchange rate system was reducing the profitability of the tradable sector, causing it to shrink. The twin rebellions on the islands of Sumatra and Sulawesi in 1958 constituted a simultaneous supply and demand shock to the budget. The rebellions forced large increases in military expenditure at the same time that the government revenue base was reduced because both of these islands were important sources of export tax revenue. The monetization of the budget deficits raised the average 1958–61 inflation rate to 25 percent from the 1950–57 average of 17 percent.

The budgetary pressures grew steadily worse, resulting in a period of high inflation in 1962–65. Between 1962 and 1964 both money supply and the cost-of-living index roughly doubled every year, and by the end of 1965 they were doubling every few weeks. Economic growth slowed to 0.8 percent per year in this turbulent period. The evolution of the export-to-GDP ratio tells the story of economic decline very well; it fell from 8.7 percent (1951–57) to 6.8 percent (1958–61), and then to 1.1 percent (1962–65).

The internal political struggle culminated with the abortive coup by military personnel sympathetic to the Indonesian Communist Party (PKI) on the night of 30 September 1965. The political instability aggravated the economic instability. The increasing economic difficulties speeded up the transfer of authority from President Soekarno to the anti-Communist General Soeharto in the following year.

5.3   The Political Economy Factors in Policymaking

The economic chaos of the 1958–65 period left such a deep impression that the new Soeharto government has had a "balanced" budget rule since 1968. In reality, this rule amounts to refusing to finance the deficit through money creation and to limiting the deficit to the availability of foreign loans, which is officially described as foreign "revenue".[2] Another consequence of the chaos was the recognition that the exchange rate is an extremely potent policy instrument that can effect large-scale economy-wide resource reallocation and income redistribution.

President Soeharto has been in power since October 1965 and has not faced any serious challenges to his rule since the 1974 riots. The Indonesian political system can be described as a bureaucratic-authoritarian state with implicit corporatist features. We can identify three political concerns that have significantly influenced his choice of economic policies. The first is avoiding conditions favorable to the revival of the PKI. Since the PKI was primarily a Javanese peasant-based movement, the policy implication is that conditions in the rural area must be improved. The second concern is to display equitable treatment of the Outer Islands, given their long history of secessionist movements. Since the economy of the Outer Islands depends heavily on tree crop exports, this further strengthens the case for promoting agricultural development. It must be added that Soeharto, because of his peasant origin, has consistently shown a strong personal commitment to eliminating rural poverty. Soeharto's third concern is one common to all politicians: the maintenance of his power base.

Political patronage has often taken the form of trade restrictions to benefit specific groups. It would not be correct, however, to attribute all trade restrictions to rent-seeking motivation. Ideology also plays an important role. Soeharto, like most members of the 1945 generation who fought in the bitter war for independence, is influenced by an economic nationalism which is congruous with Indonesian political nationalism. Dutch economic policies were seen as designed to impose a plantation economy on Indonesia to serve the need of Dutch manufacturing industries for raw materials. In reaction, the generation of 1945 regards industrialization as synonymous with economic development. The policy translations of economic nationalism are establishing high trade barriers to induce the development of a manufacturing sector, and enacting foreign investment laws more strict than those of neighboring countries.

The primary reason why Indonesia sometimes pursues a contradictory mix of liberalizing and protectionist policies is because of the above political, ideological, pecuniary, and personal elements working themselves through two groups of contending presidential economic advisors, popularly referred to as the technocrats and the technicians. The technocrats are mostly economists of neoclassical persuasion who work at the Ministry of Finance and the National Planning Body (BAPPENAS). Their acceptance of the comparative advantage principle leads them to emphasize the development of the nonoil export industries, particularly agricultural commodities and labor-intensive manufactured goods. This has meant a favorable treatment of the agricultural sector because it supplies about 80 percent of nonoil exports. Exchange rate devaluations rather than the removal of trade barriers on imported inputs are used to promote exports. This is because the technocrats control the ministries that oversee macroeconomic policies, but not the Ministry of Trade and the Ministry of Industry which have authority over quantitative restrictions. Their policies find favor with the president because they address his political concerns for raising rural income and for maintaining equitable treatment toward the main islands.

The second group of economic advisors, the technicians, is an amorphous collection of technicians-turned-managers, military advisors, and economists with structuralist inclinations. The technicians are united by their common belief in the general validity of the infant industry argument, and by their common rejection of foreign capital ownership. They see state enterprises—like the oil company, Pertamina, until its downfall—as the vehicle to achieve these two objectives. This position allies the technicians with members of the intelligentsia who see the state enterprises as the way to counterbalance Chinese domination of the corporate sector.

The technicians' push for import-substitution industrialization has also won them the support of the army, the most powerful constituency in the country. Thanks to the dual function (*dwifungsi*) doctrine that legitimizes military participation in economic development, the expansion of state enterprises translates directly into more managerial positions for senior military personnel. It must be noted that since most of the import-competing industries are set up in urban Java, the higher prices of manufactured goods represents an implicit tax on the residents in the rural sector and in the Outer Islands.

In looking at the political setting within which policies are chosen, we have identified an important political coalition of technocrats, Outer Islanders, and rural residents which favors a policy package emphasizing the maintenance of a competitive exchange rate. Since a debt crisis occurs when a government runs out of a foreign reserves—either to service its guaranteed external debts or to permit private residents to convert their domestic currency to service private external debts—such a policy package reduces the probability of a debt crisis by keeping the (foreign exchange earning) nonoil export sector healthy.

5.4 The Fiscal System

The most notable feature of the 1970s is the central government's increasing reliance on oil as its chief source of revenue. Oil revenue as a share of total federal revenue rose from 26 percent in 1969–70 to peak at 71 percent in 1981–82. Nonoil revenue normalized by GDP fell from the 1969–71 average of 8 percent to the 1980–82 average of 6 percent. The fiscal danger of such a narrow tax base was brought home dramatically in 1982 when the global recession caused oil prices to collapse. Oil revenue, expressed in 1980 rupiahs, fell from Rp 7.8 billion in 1981–82 to Rp 6.9 billion in 1982–83, causing real total revenue to fall for the first time since the Soekarno years.

It was clear that greater internal resource mobilization was necessary. A completely revised personal and corporate income tax code came into force in January 1984, a value-added tax in April 1985, and a consolidated property tax in 1986. The result was that real nonoil revenue (1980 prices) rose from Rp 3.6 billion in fiscal 1983 to Rp 4.7 billion in fiscal 1986. It is important to note that the oil revenue contributed to "undertaxation" in a subtle way which led to greater external debt accumulation. The two OPEC price increases encouraged undertaxation by giving Indonesia access to external credit on very favorable terms.

Woo's (1987a) examination of the fiscal system supports our claim that the technocrats favor an economic strategy that leads to resource transfers to the Javanese rural areas and the tree crop industries in the Outer Islands. The secular decline in trade taxes and the low taxation of land relative to income reflect Soeharto's political concerns about communism and secession, as well as the technocrats' neoclassical inclination toward the comparative advantage doctrine. This favorable tax treatment of the agricultural sector improves the rural-urban terms of trade and hence encourages the production of tradables, the presence of which determines a country's ability to service its debts.

In examining government expenditure, Woo (1987a) surmised from fragmentary evidence that government spending was more likely to display a rural rather than an urban bias. In the absence of more detailed data, disproportionate weight was given to the budget allocations for fertilizer subsidies, irrigation projects, rural school programs, the village public works programs, and food subsidies. With better data, we were able to garner stronger evidence to support the hypothesis that budget allocations were very sensitive to interisland equity. There is in fact evidence that interisland equity takes precedence over rural-urban equity. This is consistent with our conjecture that the concern for rural development is based more on the eradication of poverty than on narrowing the rural-urban gap.

The analysis in this section sets the stage for the following discussion in which we find that political economy factors have been important in determining the debt outcome. To the extent that people are consistent in their actions, the fact that the technocrats implemented, with Soeharto's approval, a fiscal policy that favored the tradable sector means that they would also advocate a similarly-oriented exchange rate policy. Such an exchange rate policy, as we will see, yields side effects which are salutary to external debt servicing.

5.5   Monetary Policy and Financial Structure

While the balanced budget policy of the Soeharto government effectively ended the creation of money to finance budget deficits, it could not prevent monetary policy from moving in tandem with fiscal policy during the 1970s. This is because the main instrument for monetary control prior to April 1974 was the extension of central bank credits to the banking system, state enterprises, and private companies. Since these credits were extended for a contracted time period, the government was not in a position to engineer quick increases or reductions of the money stock. This meant that with the maintenance of a fixed dollar-rupiah exchange rate, the conversion of the oil revenue from dollars to rupiahs in order to finance the expanded government expenditure automatically increased the money supply. Thus, when the price of oil quadrupled at the end of 1973, encouraging the government to increase its spending, the monetary authorities lost control of the money supply. Reserve money grew 57 percent in 1974 and the inflation rate for that year was 41 percent. The Central Bank responded to this monetary anarchy by setting lending ceilings on the banking system in April 1974.

It is understandable to use lending ceilings as a shortrun, stopgap measure to control monetary growth, but Indonesia continued to rely upon them for monetary control until June 1983, despite their well-known deleterious effects. The reason is that the credit ceilings gave the government an additional instrument to consolidate its political base. Over time, Bank Indonesia was instructed to introduce detailed ceilings by type of credit for each bank through an extensive selective credit system featuring subsidized interest rates to achieve other goals. For example, banks were assigned a civic function by their restricting certain credit only to *pribumis* (indigenous people) and establishing credit for them as a priority in order to enhance *pribumis* participation in economic activities. The highest priority items were the financing of rural participation in the government's rice intensification program, and the financing of a scheme to stabilize the price of rice. Since most priority credits were handled by the state banks, the policy of ceilings with selective credit became one of the major tools protecting the state banks from competition with private banks. Since the state banks also have a wider network of branch offices than the private banks, this mechanism of monetary control preserved the dominant position of the state banks. In the absence of pressure to innovate in order to be more efficient, the Indonesian financial system remained underdeveloped.

One of the policy responses to the external shocks of the 1980s was an overhaul of the financial structure which was announced in June 1983. The financial reform package included partial deregulation of interest rates, elimination of credit ceilings, and reduction in the scope of Bank Indonesia's subsidized credits to state-owned banks. To increase the amount of central bank instruments for open market operations, Bank Indonesia began reissuing Debt Certificates (SBI) in February 1984 and introduced Money Market Instruments (SBPU) in January 1985.

It is clear that the financial instruments SBI and SBPU still do not provide sufficient control over monetary aggregates. This is evident in the way the money supply had to be contracted in response to a speculative run on the rupiah in June 1987. The minister of planning, in addition to asking Bank Indonesia to sell Rp 800 billion of open market instruments, ordered the state enterprises to withdraw Rp 1.3 trillion from state banks to be placed in central bank securities.

This action reveals that the market for both SBI and SBPU is still too shallow. It may be difficult to increase their role if the financial markets remain underdeveloped. Financial deepening is an important priority, but not only because of the need to enhance the effectiveness of the monetary instruments. Financial deepening would also better mobilize (and maybe increase) domestic savings, reduce the dependence on external credit, and improve the overall allocation of capital within the economy. A boost to financial deepening would be the privatization of some of the state-owned enterprises, and an easing of external debt service would be achieved if foreigners were allowed to buy into these enterprises.

5.6 Exchange Rate Policy

Indonesian exchange rate policy is characterized by three distinct phases in the 1966–87 period. The first phase is from October 1966 to July 1971, in which there was a steady dismantling of the multitiered exchange rate system into a unified exchange rate. This phase revealed a readiness to have medium-sized devaluations at short intervals in order to restore competitiveness eroded by the high inflation in Indonesia.

In the second phase, from August 1971 to October 1978, there was a fixed exchange rate. The reason for this remarkable stability is straightforward: the balance of payments was very strong throughout the period. The rapid development of the oil sector together with the 1973 OPEC price increase caused Indonesian oil exports to grow as follows (in U.S. $ billion): 0.4 in 1969, 0.9 in 1972, 5.2 in 1974, and then 7.4 in 1978. The result was the swelling of the nongold reserves (measured in the number of weeks of imports they could support): 8.1 in 1969, 19.1 in 1972, 20.2 in 1974, and 20.4 in 1978. The macroeconomic conditions also did not warrant any additional stimulus which a devaluation would bring. The sustained high income growth rates of this period—7.9 percent per year—were achieved with substantial overheating of the economy. The average 1973–78 inflation rate was 22 percent compared with 8 percent in 1970–72.

The third phase involved three large devaluations in November 1978, March 1983, and September 1986, separated by moderately long periods of gradual exchange rate depreciation. There are two, mutually compatible, explanations for the 50 percent devaluation in 1978. The first explanation views the November 1978 devaluation primarily as an anticipatory action to the inevitable dropoff in oil export earnings due to resource depletion.

The second explanation emphasizes the economic difficulties and political tensions associated with the reallocation of resources being forced upon the economy by the overvalued exchange rate. The overvaluation of the rupiah was the result of maintaining the exchange rate at 415 rupiahs to the dollar despite the large domestic inflations from 1974 to 1977. This meant that Indonesian producers of tradables were experiencing a profit squeeze. The prices of their output were fixed by international competition, but the prices of their domestic inputs were being driven up by the double-digit inflation. The result was reports of increasing unemployment in the tradables industries, particularly in the labor-intensive agricultural export sector. Indonesia was suffering from the "Dutch disease." In this view, the 1978 devaluation was as much due to political concern about worsening conditions in the countryside, as to economic concern about the desirability of the resulting composition of economic activities. After all, the level of reserves in 1978 could sustain the existing amount of imports much longer than was possible at any time during the 1969–76 period (see table 5.1, column e).

It must be stated that the deleterious effects of the Dutch disease on the nonoil export sector are not obvious. Nonoil nonLNG exports, whether measured in physical units *or* in dollars *or* in the units of imports for which they can be exchanged, show steady growth throughout 1972–78 (see table 5.1, columns a, b, and c). The production disincentive faced by the nonoil export industries is clearly seen only when one measures the amount of local purchasing power of their exports (see column d). Even though the nonoil exports were bringing in increasing amounts of foreign goods, the steady real appreciation of the exchange rate meant that the nonoil export industries were not being paid a greater number of baskets containing the mix of goods typically consumed by Indonesians. In terms of foreign purchasing power, the nonoil export industries increased their revenues by 32 percentage points between 1973 and 1978, but their revenues were unchanged if measured in terms of local purchasing power.

More direct evidence of the production disincentive is the movement of prices of tradables relative to prices of nontradables, PT/PN. The three proxies of PT/PN in table 5.1 show an average decline of 29 percent between 1973 and 1978.[3] The 50 percent nominal exchange rate devaluation caused PT/PN to increase by 29 percent, almost restoring the profitability of the tradable sector.

The speed and size of the response of nonoil nonLNG exports were impressive. Export volume went up by 36 percent in one year, raising dollar earnings by 52 percent. The 32 percent growth in foreign purchasing power in 1979 translated into a domestic purchasing power increase of 78 percent.

We interpret the quick and large response to the devaluation as proof of the Dutch disease, the mounting severity of which since 1974 caused excess capacity in the traditional export industries to increase. Small producers of tree crops were spending more and more of their time in nontradable activities. Meanwhile, the real prices of their agricultural products sank as a constant nominal exchange rate was maintained in the face of large domestic price increases.

Table 5.1   **Background to the November 1978 Devaluation**

Performance of Nonoil NonLNG Exports (1974 = 100) and Foreign Reserves Position

	(a)	(b)	(c)	(d)	(e)
	Nonoil nonLNG exports measured in terms of:				Nongold Reserves Measured in
	Physical Volume	US$	Foreign Purchasing Power	Domestic Purchasing Power	Number of Weeks of Current Level of Import
1969	n.a.	28.6	52.2	51.6	7.8
1970	n.a.	33.6	58.5	60.1	8.1
1971	73.9	36.0	59.4	66.9	8.7
1972	83.4	40.0	60.2	73.7	19.1
1973	96.3	73.2	91.1	103.2	15.3
1974	100.0	100.0	100.0	100.0	20.2
1975	99.6	82.6	74.2	69.5	6.4
1976	111.9	115.2	103.8	80.8	13.7
1977	121.0	159.7	133.0	100.9	20.9
1978	118.0	166.4	123.0	103.6	20.4
1979	160.0	253.7	162.4	184.6	29.3
1980	144.5	276.4	155.9	170.8	25.9

Indicators of Tradable-Nontradable Price Ratio (PT/PN), 1974 = 100

	1971	1972	1973	1974	1975	1976	1977	Jan-Oct 1978	1979	1980
Import price index[a]	75.0	82.2	91.6	100.0	87.2	74.5	66.3	65.3	73.7	70.5
Nonoil export price index[a]	63.9	65.8	91.6	100.0	66.4	65.6	71.7	70.4	93.3	93.8
Competitiveness measure[b]	114.1	127.1	120.3	100.0	87.3	74.8	74.2	79.6	111.3	101.1

Notes: Physical volume (col. a) from deflating rupiah value series by nonoil export price index. Foreign purchasing power (col. c) from deflating US$ value series by export unit value of industrial countries. Domestic purchasing power (col. d) from deflating rupiah value series by Indonesian CPI.
[a]Deflated by Jakarta CPI housing component.
[b]The competitiveness measure is from inverting the Morgan Guaranty real exchange rate.

The March 1983 and September 1986 devaluations were undertaken to boost nonoil exports in the face of large declines in oil export earnings. Manufacturing exports grew very rapidly after the March 1983 devaluation. They jumped (in US $ million) from 850 in fiscal 1982, to 1480 in fiscal 1983, and to 2166 in fiscal 1984. The strong export responses to the 1978 and 1983 devaluations indicate that export-oriented industrialization is a real possibility as long as favorable relative prices are maintained through appropriate exchange rate and trade policies.

While it is clear that negative external demand shock had a role in worsening the balance of payments from 1983 to 1986, we want to point out that there were also internal developments during this period that caused substantial movements in relative prices which were unfavorable for the tradable sector. Specifically, we are referring to the widespread use of quantitative restrictions (QRs) in the 1980s. Of the 5,229 items imported in 1985, 1,484 required import licenses and 296 were under quotas. The import licenses were usually given to only two or three traders, or to the few firms producing the competing goods domestically, and thus conferred a monopoly position to their holders. The range of activities protected by import licenses accounted for 32 percent of total domestic value added, excluding construction and services. If the petroleum sector, which requires no protection, is also excluded, then the coverage is 53 percent of total domestic value added.

The implication of this microeconomic distortion for exchange rate management is profound. The intrusion of this distortion since late 1982 and its quick metastasis across the tradable sector renders invalid trying to draw conclusions about production incentive by examining the movements of the macroeconomic proxies for PT/PN. Output prices of tradables are set by international competition, while those of nontradables (which are generally very labor-intensive) are set by the domestic cost structure, the level of which is primarily determined by domestic wages on the supply side and domestic macro conditions on the demand side. Hence, the introduction of a quota on an imported input to the tradable sector will reduce the profitability of the tradable sector without any change in PT/PN.

The point we want to emphasize is that although the Morgan Guaranty competitiveness index in predevaluation 1986 shows almost the same value as in postdevaluation 1979 (110 versus 111), it does not mean that the August 1986 exchange rate was not overvalued. In order to have the 1986 nonoil export supply schedule in the same position within the familiar Marshallian price-quantity space as in 1979, a devaluation was warranted, especially in light of the shrunken gap between output and input prices.[4] It is of course an empirical question how much the additional nonoil export earnings would have been in the absence of QRs, especially in comparison to the fall in oil export earnings. The current account deficit would still have widened in 1986, but it may not have doubled as it did.[5]

5.7 External Debt Management

The Soeharto government is no stranger to external debt management: it inherited an external public debt of $2 billion. It cut its teeth on the economic stabilization and rehabilitation program of 1966, within which the rescheduling of the Soekarno debts and arranging for new capital inflows to support the balance of payments were key components. Given the desperate situation of Indonesia, the western countries set up the Inter-Governmental Group on Indonesia (IGGI) to ensure a long-term coordinated plan of official assistance. IGGI was generous both in the amount and the terms of assistance. In the 1967–70 period, it gave an average of $477 million a year, with a repayment period of 25 years which included 7 years of grace and an interest rate of 3 percent.

The mix of generous external assistance and corrective economic policies undertaken by the Soeharto government imparted a new dynamism to the Indonesian economy. The annual average growth rate from 1968 to 1972 was 8.2 percent compared to the average rate of 1.2 percent in the preceding five years. By 1974, the international credit markets had rescinded whatever credit restrictions they had imposed on borrowing by the Indonesian government in the aftermath of Soekarno's economic Armageddon. The reasons for this change were threefold: one, the avalanche of oil revenue increased the creditworthiness of the Indonesian government; two, the boom in commodity prices in the early 1970s; and, three, the decreased lending opportunities in the OECD countries whose medium-term economic prospects were rather bleak after the 1973 OPEC price increase.

On consumption-smoothing grounds, the readmission into the external credit market resulted in a net gain to Indonesian national welfare. This welfare gain was not without its price: Indonesia was now exposed to two kinds of new risks. The first risk is systemic in nature and is a threat to every country with external debts. The second is the possibility of imprudent borrowing by Indonesia. This danger was realized in February 1975 when the state oil company, Pertamina, could not roll over a $400 million short-term loan and defaulted.

It could be cogently argued that the Pertamina crisis was a blessing in disguise. The government, by denying all state-owned enterprises direct access to the external credit market after the Pertamina embarrassment, did not have as large a publicly-guaranteed external debt when 1982 began as it otherwise would have had.

A common explanation for an external debt crisis puts the blame on excessive budget deficits that force the government to borrow from abroad. The statistic usually cited in support of this fiscal imbalance view is the ratio of official long-term debt to GNP, DGNP.[6] The official long-term debt is taken to represent the cumulated amount of fiscal deficits financed by external borrowing, and the normalization by GNP is to indicate the extent to which the country has been made to live beyond its income by the budget deficits.

The fiscal imbalance explanation of an external debt crisis points out that DGNP for Mexico rose from 9.1 percent in 1970 to 18.7 percent in 1981, the eve of the debt crisis; and for Brazil it rose from 7.1 percent to 17 percent. It is true that the Mexican and Brazilian governments increased their budget deficits significantly during this period, but it is not true that they had been more profligate than the Indonesian government. The 1981 DGNP for Mexico, Brazil and Indonesia is 18.7 percent, 17.0 percent, and 17.7 percent, respectively. There are just not enough differences in the 1981 DGNPs to explain why Indonesia avoided a debt crisis in the two years that followed.

It must be mentioned that DGNP is a flawed indicator of public profligacy. First, the stock of long-term official debt can understate as well as overstate borrowing for budgetary reasons. This is because the government can borrow short term to finance budget deficits and long term to finance foreign market interventions. Second, DGNP is a measure of profligacy only in the sense of living beyond income, and not in the sense of being unable to service the acquired external debt. To indicate the latter one would have to normalize the external debt by the level of exports—the foreign exchange earning capacity of the country.

As pointed out earlier, a debt crisis occurs not only when the government does not have the reserves to service the loans it has guaranteed, but also when it does not have the reserves to enable private domestic residents to convert their service payments on the nonguaranteed debts from domestic currency to foreign currency.[7] To take the second cause of a debt crisis into consideration, we define the total external debt service to be the sum of external short-term debt plus the debt service on all external long-term debt, publicly-guaranteed and private nonguaranteed. We include short-term debt in our definition because we are interested in the financial resilience of a country to sudden protracted credit squeezes in international credit markets that make short-term borrowing extremely expensive, if not occasionally impossible. After all, the 1973–74 credit crunch did precipitate the 1975 Pertamina debt crisis in Indonesia, and the 1980–81 financial squeeze precipitated the PEMEX crisis in Mexico.

Since the reserve position of the country is crucial for avoiding debt crises, it is not appropriate to assess the country's ability to pay by looking at the total external debt service with respect to its income. A more appropriate indicator is the debt-service ratio, DSO—the total external debt service normalized by the level of exports—because the official reserve position is determined primarily by the ability of the export sector to earn foreign exchange.

Table 5.2 summarizes the basis for our choice of three factors to explain why Indonesia did not experience a debt crisis in 1982–84 as did Mexico and Brazil. Again, the three factors are concessional loans, high export orientation, and prudent management of the maturity structure.

Concessional loans. A high proportion of Indonesia's external debt was borrowed at fixed concessionary rates from IGGI (see items b and

Table 5.2   Debt and Export Characteristics of Mexico, Brazil, and Indonesia

	1980	1981	1982	1983	1984	1985	1986
a. All Short- and Long-Term Debt Service as Ratio of Exports (%)							
Mexico	103.6	117.1	138.9	80.8	69.0	66.5	n.a.
Brazil	114.5	113.6	146.0	104.5	72.1	72.6	n.a.
Indonesia	25.1	26.1	39.0	41.7	43.3	51.6	67.6
b. Proportion of Publicly-Guaranteed Long-Term Debt that has Variable Rate (%)							
Mexico	71.5	75.4	76.7	82.7	83.6	80.1	n.a.
Brazil	61.0	67.1	69.3	70.1	73.1	71.5	n.a.
Indonesia	16.2	17.8	20.0	22.8	23.7	21.7	n.a.
c. Effective Interest Rate for All Long-Term Debt (%)							
Mexico	22.8	20.1	20.8	15.9	18.0	16.1	n.a.
Brazil	23.3	23.7	23.0	13.9	11.7	11.2	n.a.
Indonesia	15.5	16.6	16.1	14.6	15.8	16.6	14.5
d. Export to GNP Ratio (%)							
Mexico	13.7	13.2	17.9	21.5	20.1	17.8	n.a.
Brazil	9.6	10.2	8.7	12.4	15.3	14.0	n.a.
Indonesia	29.7	27.9	23.6	25.8	25.7	25.1	22.6
e. Proportion of Debt that is Short Term (%)							
Mexico	28.3	32.1	30.5	11.1	6.8	5.8	n.a.
Brazil	19.3	19.2	19.3	14.9	11.6	10.8	n.a.
Indonesia	13.3	14.4	18.1	15.6	16.8	14.8	12.2

Sources: All calculations are based on data in World Bank, *World debt tables (1986/87).*
1986 figures for Indonesia are from World Bank, Indonesia, *Strategy for economic recovery* (May 1985).
Note: Effective interest rate is calculated by (debt service/debt).

c). This "IGGI effect" explains why the effective interest rate on Indonesian long-run debt averaged 16 percent against the 20 percent paid by Mexico and Brazil. Another result was that only about one-third of Indonesian debt was denominated in dollars compared to 90 percent of Mexican and Brazilian debt. This meant that the large appreciation of the dollar from 1979 to 1982 did not raise the effective interest rate for Indonesia as much as it did for Mexico and Brazil.

High export orientation. The availability of significant amounts of other tradables prevented Indonesia's debt-servicing capacity from collapsing as did Mexico's when the price of oil dropped in early 1982. Appropriate exchange rate policies by Indonesia, exemplified by the 1978 devaluation, ensured a diversified export bundle as well as a high export orientation. The average 1980–82 export/GNP ratio was 27 percent for Indonesia, but only 14 percent for Mexico and 9.5 percent for Brazil (see item d). Indonesia's political concern to keep the agricultural sector vibrant no doubt helped to maintain the observed export orientation.

Prudent management of the maturity structure. This was evident in that only 14 percent of Indonesia's debt in 1981 was short term, compared to the 19 percent for Brazil and 32 percent for Mexico (see item e). The shock of the 1975 Pertamina crisis caused official borrowing in Indonesia to take place very cautiously with regard to exposure in the short-term credit market. We can also refer to this third factor as the Pertamina legacy.

Capital flight has often been mentioned as a cause of the debt crisis in some Latin American countries.[8] We suspect, however, that imprudent maturity structure management may have contributed more to the Mexican debt-servicing difficulties than capital flight per se. To see this, we allowed capital flight to have the maximum impact on the actual DSO by assuming that Mexico financed the capital flight entirely with short-term debt.[9] We find that DSO in 1982 would have dropped from 138 percent to 64 percent if financing were done with long-term loans instead. Without capital flight, DSO would have been 45 percent. In short, the major reason Mexico's DSO was so high was that the way in which the government financed the capital flight added 74 percentage points. Capital flight per se added only 19 percentage points.

Our conclusion of imprudence in management of maturity structure can be shown in another way. To see that much of the Mexican short-term debt consisted of borrowing by the government rather than by commercial credits to finance imports, we recall that the Indonesian government, since the 1975 Pertamina crisis, had avoided short-term external borrowing as much as possible. Assuming that the Indonesian ratio of short-term debt to imports reflects normal trade financing, we can attribute 77 percent of Mexican short-term debt in 1981 and 1982 to government borrowing. The 1981 and 1982 figures for Brazil are 68 percent and 57 percent, respectively.

There is a trade-off in external debt management between generally lower interest payments and predictability of debt-service payments. Short-term liabilities pay lower interest rates most of the time, but it is risky to rely on a strategy which rolls over a large amount of short-term debt every period. An unforeseen credit crunch would force the country to increase borrowing in order to cover its interest payments. If this credit squeeze were to persist for more than three years, and was accompanied by a prolonged fall in the country's exports, the extra borrowing would be difficult to sustain as the situation increasingly smacked of a Ponzi game.

5.8 Conclusions and Prospects

To quantify the relative importance of the three factors in explaining the absence of an Indonesia debt crisis, we calculated what the total debt-service ratios in the 1980–82 period would have been if Indonesian debt was paying the same effective interest rates as Mexico, as well as bearing the same maturity structure, and if the Indonesian export-GNP ratio was identical to Mexico's.[10]

The average values of the six possible decompositions of the effect of each factor and the range of values achieved are reported in table 5.3.

The decomposition identifies the export orientation of Indonesia as the most decisive factor in why Indonesia's total debt-service/export ratio was so low compared with Mexico's. Export orientation explained 31 of the 54 percentage point difference, accounting for 57 percent of the gap. The Pertamina legacy was of moderate importance. It contributed 18 percentage points, accounting for almost a third of the gap. Concessional interest rates and currency composition of debt played only a minor role in reducing the debt-service ratio, less than 6 percentage points.

Our finding that the IGGI effect contributed so little toward the reduction of the 1980–82 debt service/export ratio is surprising because many of the informed observers we talked to cited foreign concessionary loans as the primary reason for the absence of an Indonesian debt crisis. Our point is that while the $1 billion saved annually in reduced debt service during 1980–82[11] is a large sum of money, this amount would have been easily swamped by a Mexico-style loss of reserves if the Indonesian government had tried to prop up an overvalued exchange rate and was then forced to finance capital flight. Similarly, if exports were 12 percent below actual value because of an overvalued exchange rate, as suggested by the 1965–68 experience, the loss in foreign reserves would also have greatly exceeded this $1 billion saving.

Our conclusion is that Indonesian exchange rate policy was the most important reason why Indonesia was able to meet its debt commitments

Table 5.3   Average Values and Range of Values Achieved

	Average Value	Range of Values for Each Factor
Hypothetical 1980–82 average total debt-service ratio when Indonesia had all 3 Mexican features	84.4	
Contribution of (in percentage points):		
IGGI	5.8	3.7 – 8.4
Maturity management	17.7	12.0 – 23.8
Export orientation	30.8	23.6 – 37.8
Actual 1980–82 average total debt-service ratio	30.1	

in the 1982–84 period. The conduct of this exchange rate policy was greatly facilitated by the existence of a political lobby that promoted exchange rate protection, and by the memory of the economy-wide negative effects of exchange rate overvaluation. The fact that neither the budget deficits nor the money growth rates departed from their historical range for extended periods also helped to make exchange rate management easier.

While the decline of oil prices in early 1982 did make debt management more difficult—the total debt-service ratio rose from 26 percent in 1981 to 39 percent in 1982—it was still far from a crisis situation. The subsequent collapse of agricultural commodity prices and the rapid descent of the price of oil in 1986 from $28/barrel in January to $10/barrel in August have produced a more ominous situation. The fall in export earnings from $21 billion in 1982 to $15 billion in 1986 has caused the total debt-service ratio to soar to 68 percent.

While our analysis would place great emphasis upon an aggressive competitive real exchange policy to reduce the probability of a debt crisis through its effects on exports and capital flight, there are a number of other policies which can also be implemented given the recent drastic jump in the debt service–export ratio. The supplementary policies can be divided into two groups: (1) those that affect the debt service directly, and (2) those that affect export earnings.

Policy measures that could ameliorate the debt service burden directly, through reduction of foreign borrowing, are:

a. Cuts in the budget deficits by controlling spending and increasing taxes. This would keep fiscal policy consistent with exchange rate policy. The tax reforms since January 1984 have raised domestic revenue considerably, but their implementation has not been wholly satisfactory. While the number of registered taxpayers has increased to 995,000 at the end of 1985 from 550,000 before the tax reform, only 50 percent of the companies and 70 percent of registered individual taxpayers actually filed tax returns in 1985.

b. Maintenance of an anti-inflationary posture in monetary policy. This would make real exchange rate management easier by keeping trade deficits down and capital flight low.

c. Amending the balanced budget rule to allow internal financing of government deficits. As long as there is no automatic monetization of budget deficits, it may make little sense not to amend the balanced budget practice in order to reduce reliance on external funds. The deepening of the domestic market in government securities would make open-market operations by the central bank easier. The addition of this monetary tool to SBI and SBPU would tend to enhance monetary control, and thus macroeconomic stabilization efforts.

d. Acceleration of the development of the domestic financial system. Besides further deregulation of the financial sector, financial deepening could be boosted by the privatization of many of the state-owned enterprises. The balance-of-payments position would be improved if the government were to allow foreigners to purchase shares in the former state enterprises. A developed financial market could lower intermediation costs, allow better monetary control, and, possibly, encourage savings.

e. Liberalization of the controls on foreign investments in the manufacturing and agricultural sector, especially in industries which produce primarily for the export markets.

A second group of supplementary external debt management policies would be those which focus on the denominator of the debt-service ratio. Our analyses indicate that the viability and expansion of the Indonesian export sector depends crucially on:

a. The elimination of the wide array of monopoly import licenses. The present efforts to replace import licenses with tariffs is a second-best solution. The growth of manufactured exports, spurred by access to cheaper inputs, would not only increase foreign exchange earnings but would also diversify the export bundle, hence reducing the sensitivity of the debt-service ratio to the prices of a few key commodity exports.

b. The expansion of the tree crop sector. Indonesia has cheaper labor than Malaysia, and with additional investments in transportation, Indonesia could potentially outproduce Malaysia in rubber and palm oil. In addition to earning more foreign exchange, the strategy of accelerating the growth of agricultural export industries would promote a more equitable, rural-urban—as well as inter-island—growth pattern, and ease population pressure on the urban areas.

A final cautionary word on external debt management from the political perspective is pertinent. The Pertamina crisis has led to close supervision by the Ministry of Finance of external borrowing by all state enterprises, making it unlikely that a debt crisis would ever again emerge from the external adventurism of an economic fiefdom. The new danger now may be the absorption of private external debts in order to save large domestic firms when they get into financial problems, as in the Indocement case. In July 1985, Indocement, the biggest cement company in Indonesia, began to experience cash flow problems because the recession-induced collapse of the construction industry led to a cement glut. The response of the Indonesian government was to inject US$325 million in cash to acquire a 35 percent share of the company, and to form a consortium of four state banks to "convert into a rupiah liability a US$120 million syndicated loan that Indocement took out in 1981."[12]

In a few more such rescues are allowed, then the habit may well be impossible to break without the government having to put to the test the source of its political legitimacy—the cohesiveness of the bureaucratic and military elite. Given the widespread participation in large private business ventures by government officials and their family members, the selective use of financial rescue will threaten the political unity of the group. If this kind of political pressure were to be able to completely eradicate the already blurred line between public and large private enterprises, then the vulnerability of Indonesia to a debt crisis would be greatly increased. External debt management would become impossible because no one would know what the size of the sovereign debt really is, and the size of this debt could increase very quickly given the openness of the private capital account.

Notes

1. The concept of exchange rate protection is developed in detail by Corden (1982).

2. The "balanced" budget rule ceased to be a binding constraint on expenditure after the 1973 OPEC-1 price increase. The Indonesian government (perhaps until very recently) was pretty much able to get whatever amount of credit it wanted. This budget rule does not prevent the financing of nonbudgetary expenditure by money creation, e.g., central bank credits to state agencies.

3. The first two PT/PN proxies are calculated from table 3 in Warr (1986), but some of our figures differ from those in his table 4.

4. We are abstracting from natural growth considerations here to make this point within a static context.

5. Current account expressed as a percentage of GDP.

6. A textbook exposition of this fiscal cause of external debt crisis is Rivera-Batiz and Rivera-Batiz (1985, 557–61).

7. If a private borrower could not come up with the service payments in domestic currency for his private nonguaranteed external debt, we do not consider it a *national* debt crisis because the government did not cause the default (except in the broadest sense of not creating more favorable macroeconomic conditions, if it were able to do so).

8. For example, Dornbusch (1987); Lever and Huhne (1986); and Cline (1984).

9. Kahn and Haque (1987) estimate cumulated Mexican capital flight up to 1982 to be $29 billion. Actual short-term debt in 1982 is $26 billion.

10. This decomposition of DSO is from Woo (1987b).

11. This is calculated assuming that Indonesia would pay the same effective interest rate as Mexico.

12. Quote is from *Far Eastern Economic Review*, 25 July 1985. The *Asian Wall Street Journal Weekly* (12 May 1986) put the cash injection at US$360 million.

References

Cline, William. 1984. *International debt: Systemic risk and policy response.* Washington, D.C.: Institute for International Economics.
Corden, Max. 1982. Exchange rate protection. In *The international monetary system under flexible exchange rates,* ed. Richard Cooper et al. Cambridge, Mass.:Ballinger.
Dornbusch, Rudiger. 1987. The world debt problem: Anatomy and solutions. Study paper for the Twentieth Century Fund, New York.
Kahn, Mohsin, and Nadeem Haque. 1987. Capital flight from developing countries. *Finance and Development* 24(1):2–5.
Lever, Harold, and Christopher Huhne. 1986. *Debt and danger: The world financial crisis.* Boston, Mass.: Atlantic Monthly Press.
Rivera-Batiz, Francisco, and Luis Rivera-Batiz. 1985. *International finance and open economy macroeconomics.* New York: Macmillan.
Warr, Peter. 1986. Indonesia's other Dutch disease: Economic effects of the petroleum boom. Working papers in trade and development no. 86/2. Research School of Pacific Studies, Australian National University.
Woo, Wing Thye. 1987a. The dead hand of history in Indonesian economic policymaking. Macroeconomic working paper series no. 43 (April). Economics Department, University of California at Davis.
———. 1987b. Indonesian external debt situation: Performance and prospects. Macroeconomic working paper series no. 48 (November). Economics Department, University of California at Davis.

6 External Debt and Macroeconomic Performance in South Korea

Susan M. Collins and Won-Am Park

6.1 Introduction

In 1981, South Korea was the world's fourth largest debtor country and in the midst of an economic crisis. It had accumulated $17.6 billion of debt within three years, raising its debt stock to $32.4 billion and its debt/GDP ratio to 49 percent. Output had declined by 4.8 percent in 1980, compared to average growth rates in excess of 9 percent during 1970–79. Inflation had doubled from 14.4 percent in 1978 to 28.7 percent in 1980.

Korea's adjustment to the 1979–82 debt crisis has been remarkable. By 1986, it had substantially reduced the debt burden. Inflation had fallen to just 3 percent, while the government budget deficit had been cut in half. Exports grew by 15 percent, fueling a 12.5 percent increase in output, and a current account surplus nearly 5 percent of GNP. At the same time, real wages, per capita income, and consumption all increased, and the country maintained historically high levels of fixed capital formation.

In stark contrast, the 1986 *World Development Report* (p. 54) describes the plight of 17 of the middle income debtor countries as follows:

> The bulk of the adjustment has been undertaken through lower demand, which has meant, in practice, reducing imports and investment. . . . GDP has stagnated since 1980, and per capita incomes

Susan M. Collins is an associate professor of economics at Harvard University and a faculty research fellow of the National Bureau of Economic Research. Won-Am Park is a fellow of the Korea Development Institute.

The research for this project was done while Professor Collins was an Olin Fellow at the NBER. Generous financial support from the Olin Foundation is gratefully acknowledged.

have declined substantially. . . . Yet the main indicators of debt at the end of 1985 were close to their previous peaks. Despite their adjustment efforts, these countries seem to be as far as they ever were from reconciling growth and credit worthiness.

The purpose of this chapter is to summarize the findings of an in-depth analysis of Korea's macroeconomic performance, policy and prospects, with primary focus on its experience with external debt.[1] The chapter begins with an overview of Korea's experience. Four questions emerge from our summary:

1. What caused Korea's debt crises?
2. How was Korea able to achieve rapid, successful recovery?
3. What role has external borrowing played in the experience? and
4. Are there lessons for other debtor countries?

Answering these questions involves synthesizing a number of inter-related factors. In section 6.3 we summarize our conclusions about each of these factors individually. Section 6.4 puts the pieces of the puzzle together and examines the general implications, answering questions 1 through 3. The final two sections of the chapter discuss the lessons to be learned by other debtors and the prospects for Korea.

6.2   Overview of Korea's Macroeconomic Experience

Korea's macroeconomic history can be divided roughly into five periods. The early period, from 1945 to 1953, was one of continued disruption. First came the division into North and South Korea at the 38th parallel after World War II. The South was left with rich agricultural lands and light manufacturing industries, but almost no heavy industry or power facilities. Attempts to begin economic recovery were interrupted by the devastation of the Korean War which is estimated to have killed over one million people and destroyed over one-third of South Korea's physical capital.

Another significant event during this period, with lasting implications for Korean development, was a major land reform. During 1947–49, farmland previously owned by Japanese landlords, was either redistributed or sold, dramatically decreasing the concentration of land ownership. This is perhaps the most important factor in explaining the relatively egalitarian distribution of income in Korea.

The second period, (1953–60) was one of slow recovery, financed by massive foreign aid, primarily from the United States. Foreign aid inflows averaged nearly US $300 million per annum during 1955–59, reaching 16 percent of GNP in 1957. Inflation rates jumped to 60 percent immediately following the War, while output growth remained moderate. Under the complex system of trade restrictions erected by the Syngman Rhee dictatorship, exports grew by only 1.3 percent per year. In contrast, the third period, from 1960–73, saw a dramatic economic turnaround fueled by rapid rates of export growth. Exports grew by 40–50 percent per year during 1960–73, while output grew by more than 10 percent during 1965–73.

The economic transition coincided with a change in political regime and economic policy. Syngman Rhee was forced to resign in 1960 after a student uprising. The new government, led by Chang Myon, collapsed in May 1961 following a military coup led by General Park Chung Hee, who remained president of Korea until a second coup in 1979.

Under General Park, Korea switched from an import-substitution strategy to an active export-promotion strategy. The first of a series of Five-Year Plans, initiated in 1962, identified investment and export-led economic growth as the number one priorities. Other hallmarks of the strategy were extensive government intervention in domestic and international capital markets, the development of close links between government and industry, import liberalization, and the more active use of exchange rates to maintain competitiveness.

Foreign aid inflows fell dramatically during the period. During 1960–64, they averaged $210 million per year, over ten times the average annual accumulation of external debt. This inflow dropped to $110 million per year during 1965–69, just one-third of the average annual debt accumulation, and only $28 million per year during 1970–74, or 0.03 percent of the debt accumulation. Foreign aid to Korea had essentially ended by 1975.

Gross fixed investment was raised from 15 percent of GNP in 1965 to 26 percent in 1969 (table 6.2). To finance the investment, declining foreign aid flows were replaced by increased reliance on external borrowing and by increased domestic savings. Firms (especially exporters) were given strong incentives to borrow abroad. A system of loan guarantees substantially reduced the risks and the real cost of borrowing abroad was negative. External debt jumped to 27 percent of GNP by 1969.

Difficulties emerged during 1970–72. As growth slowed, domestic savings dropped, increasing the current account deficit and reducing Korea's debt service ability. A devaluation to stimulate exports exacerbated repayment difficulties for externally indebted firms. The government bailed them out, and continued to pursue its investment strategy, combined with further depreciation and some monetary and fiscal restraint. Taking advantage of strong world demand, exports grew by 90 percent in 1973, stimulating a record 16 percent output growth, a spurt in domestic savings, and pulling Korea out of the first period of debt difficulties.

Table 6.1   Korea's External Debt, 1960–86 (millions of U.S. dollars)

Debt	1961	1962	1963	1964	1965	1966	1967	1968	1969
Total foreign debt	83	89	157	177	206	392	645	1,199	1,800
Foreign direct investment	—	1	3	6	16	21	34	49	56
Foreign debt/GNP	3.9	3.8	5.8	6.2	6.9	10.7	15.1	22.9	27.2
Foreign debt plus direct investment/GNP	3.9	3.9	5.9	6.4	7.4	11.3	15.9	23.9	28.0
Debt service ratio[1]	8.6	0.8	1.0	2.6	5.0	3.2	5.4	5.4	8.6

Debt	1970	1971	1972	1973	1974	1975	1976	1977	1978
Total foreign debt	2,245	2,922	3,589	4,257	5,933	8,443	10,520	12,649	14,823
Foreign direct investment	81	117	175	329	486	549	650	741	830

	1978	1979	1980	1981	1982	1983	1984	1985	1986
Foreign debt/GNP	28.7	31.2	34.0	31.5	32.0	40.5	36.7	33.8	28.5
Foreign debt plus direct investment/GNP	29.7	32.4	35.6	34.0	34.6	43.1	38.9	35.8	30.1
Debt service ratio[1]	18.5	21.0	18.7	14.8	14.4	14.4	12.1	11.1	13.9

Debt	1979	1980	1981	1982	1983	1984	1985	1986
Total foreign debt	20,287	27,170	32,433	37,083	40,378	43,053	46,762	44,510
Foreign direct investment	866	873	975	1,044	1,112	1,222	1,456	1,891
Foreign debt/GNP	32.5	45.0	49.0	53.5	53.1	52.3	56.3	46.8
Foreign debt plus direct investment/GNP	33.9	46.5	50.4	55.0	54.6	53.7	58.0	48.8
Debt service ratio[1]	16.3	18.5	20.1	20.6	18.8	20.1	21.4	—

[1]Includes interest on short-term debt.

Table 6.2   Major Economic Indicators (1964–73)

	1964–65	1966–67	1968–69	1970	1971	1972	1973
GNP growth rate	7.7	9.7	12.3	9.7	9.1	5.3	14.0
Export growth rate	42.1	35.4	39.5	34.2	27.8	52.1	98.6
Inflation (CPI)	18.1	11.0	15.5	15.9	13.5	11.7	2.3
Current account (%GNP)	0.3	−3.7	−8.4	−7.7	−8.9	−3.5	−2.3
Fixed investment (%GNP)	15.0	21.0	26.5	24.7	22.5	20.4	23.2
Domestic savings (%GNP)	14.0	17.0	20.0	18.0	16.0	18.0	24.0
M2 growth rate	33.8	61.7	66.7	27.4	20.8	33.8	36.4
Budget deficit (%GNP)	—	—	—	1.6	2.3	4.6	1.6
Growth rates:							
Nominal wages	20.3	19.9	30.6	26.9	16.2	13.9	18.0
Real wages	1.6	8.1	16.9	9.3	2.4	2.0	14.3
Labor productivity							
Valued added	2.9	3.9	13.3	22.3	13.9	5.0	5.0
KPC index[1]	13.2	10.9	23.2	12.7	9.6	8.8	8.8
Terms of trade	84.6	97.1	101.0	100.0	99.2	98.7	93.7
Real effective exchange rate	116.7	104.3	98.0	100.0	105.6	114.1	132.5
Won/$	263.0	269.0	282.0	310.6	347.2	392.9	398.3

Sources: Economic Planning Board, Major statistics of Korean economy, review issues, and Bank of Korea, Economic statistics yearbook.
Note: National income data prior to 1970 are based on 1975 constant prices, old SNA (U.N. Standard of National Accounts). 1970–73 data are based on new SNA.
[1]From Korea productivity center, output per production worker.

The fourth period (1973–78) includes a second period of rapid debt accumulation, economic difficulty, and recovery (table 6.3). It also coincided with a major shift in economic strategy—a renewed industrialization, coupled with increased government intervention.

The "Big-Push" was a massive investment program in heavy and chemical industries, initiated in 1973 because policymakers feared that Korea's comparative advantage was shifting away from light industry. The program coincided with a resurgence in inflation, a slowdown in export growth, a rise in the incremental capital-output ratio, and a deterioration in the distribution of income. Import restrictions and credit rationing increased. In addition the exchange rate was fixed (1975–79) and allowed to appreciate in real terms. Although widely viewed as a policy mistake, some of the investments (steel and autos) have begun to pay off.

Economic growth again slowed during 1974–5 in the aftermath of the oil price rise. Domestic savings again dropped, increasing the borrowing necessary to finance the investment program. Korea elected to "borrow her way" through the crisis so as to fulfill planned investment and to relax monetary and fiscal policies. As world demand recovered

Table 6.3   Major Economic Indicators (1973–78)

	1973	1974	1975	1976	1977	1978
GNP growth rate	14.1	8.5	6.8	13.4	10.7	11.0
Export growth rate	98.6	38.3	13.9	51.8	30.2	26.5
Inflation (CPI)	3.1	24.3	25.3	15.3	10.1	14.4
Current account (%GNP)	−2.3	−10.8	−9.1	−1.1	0.0	−2.1
Fixed investment (%GNP)	23.2	25.6	25.3	24.4	27.3	31.3
Domestic savings/GNP	22.8	19.9	19.1	23.9	27.5	28.5
M2 growth rate	36.6	24.0	28.2	33.5	39.7	35.0
Budget deficit/GNP	1.6	4.0	4.6	2.9	2.6	2.5
Growth rates:						
Nominal wages	18.0	35.3	27.0	34.7	33.8	34.3
Real wages	14.3	8.8	1.4	16.8	21.5	17.4
Labor productivity						
Value added	5.0	2.4	2.2	2.4	10.3	12.6
KPC index[1]	8.8	11.4	11.6	7.5	10.5	11.9
Terms of trade	136.2	110.9	100.0	114.1	122.0	127.9
Real effective exchange rate	117.1	101.1	100.0	93.6	94.6	97.8
Won/$	398.3	404.5	484.0	484.0	484.0	484.0

Source: Economic Planning Board and Bank of Korea.
Note: Based on new SNA method.
[1]From Korea Productivity Center, output per production worker.

during 1976–78, high growth rates resumed raising domestic savings and improving the debt position.

In 1979, Korea again underwent a shift in economic strategy. Motivated by concern over rising inflation rates and economic distortions from the Big Push, a new stabilization plan included monetary and fiscal restraint plus the gradual reduction of price controls, import restrictions, and financial market interventions.

However, 1979–82 were years of crisis for Korea. The assassination of President Park in 1979, together with a disastrous agricultural harvest and the second oil shock, all contributed to a severe economic and political crisis in 1980. The military assumed effective control of the country in May 1980 under General Chun Doo Hwan. He was elected president in 1981 and his term ended in 1988.

The poor performance in 1979–82 is documented in table 6.4. Output stagnated, actually declining during 1980. As domestic savings plunged, the current account deficit mushroomed, financed by massive external borrowing. Korea accumulated over $22 billion of debt during 1979–82, raising its debt stock to 53.5 percent of GNP.

During 1980–81, the exchange rate was devalued, however the direction of monetary and fiscal policies alternated. Korea continued to

Table 6.4   Major Economic Indicators (1978–86)

	1978	1979	1980	1981	1982	1983	1984	1985	1986ᵖ
GNP growth rate	11.0	7.0	-4.8	6.6	5.4	11.9	8.5	5.4	12.5
Export growth rate	26.5	18.4	16.3	21.4	2.8	11.9	19.6	3.6	14.6
Inflation (CPI)	14.4	18.3	28.7	21.3	7.2	3.4	2.3	2.5	2.3
Current account (%GNP)	-2.1	-6.8	-8.8	-7.0	-3.8	-2.1	-1.7	-1.1	4.9
Fixed investment (%GNP)	31.3	33.2	32.3	28.7	30.5	31.3	31.3	30.8	31.3
Domestic savings (%GNP)	28.5	28.1	23.5	23.5	24.0	27.9	30.3	30.7	34.8
M2 growth rate	35.0	24.6	26.9	25.0	27.0	15.2	7.7	15.6	18.6
Budget deficit (%GNP)	2.5	1.4	3.2	4.7	4.4	1.6	1.4	1.0	1.8
Growth rates									
Nominal wages	34.3	28.6	22.7	20.1	14.7	12.2	8.1	9.9	9.1
Real wages	17.4	8.7	-4.7	-2.6	6.9	10.4	5.7	7.3	6.7
Labor productivity									
Value added	12.6	16.0	-3.9	11.1	-1.8	4.2	12.0	-0.8	7.6
KPC index[1]	11.9	15.9	10.6	18.1	7.8	13.6	10.5	7.1	13.6
Terms of trade	117.8	115.3	100.0	97.9	102.2	103.1	105.3	105.9	114.7
Real effective exchange rate	109.0	97.2	100.0	103.6	103.2	110.6	114.4	121.2	139.2
Won/$	484.0	484.0	607.4	681.0	831.1	775.8	806.0	870.0	881.5

Source: Economic Planning Board and Bank of Korea.

Note: Based on new SNA method.

[1]From Korea Productivity Center, output per production worker.

ᵖPreliminary.

borrow heavily to maintain investment. By 1982, growth was still low by Korean standards (5.4 percent) and exports stagnated, but inflation and the current account deficits had fallen significantly. The government initiated a more expansionary policy to stimulate growth.

As world demand recovered and the terms of trade improved during 1983–84, Korea again underwent a remarkable economic recovery. Growth rates spurted. Savings rose reducing the current account deficit. Authorities responded to the 1985 slowdown in export growth as world demand stagnated with a 6 percent real depreciation in 1985, and a further 15 percent real depreciation in 1986.

By 1986, the economy was booming, inflationary difficulties had been resolved and there was a substantial trade surplus. In contrast to many of the other large Third World debtor countries currently negotiating rescheduling arrangements with their creditors, Korea not only met all debt service obligations, but was in a position to actually reduce her debt stock by $2.25 billion.

6.3 The Individual Factors

6.3.1 External Debt

Foreign capital inflows have played a critical role throughout Korea's recent development. The preceding discussion has already emphasized the importance of foreign aid in the decade following the Korean War and documented the rapid accumulation of external debt, concentrated during 1966–69, 1974–75, and 1979–82.

Rapid growth of output and especially exports has meant that Korea's actual debt burden grew much more slowly than the nominal debt stock. Although the debt (denominated in U.S. dollars) grew at an average rate of 34.6 percent in the 18 years from 1964 to 1982, the debt-to-GNP ratio reached 53.5 percent, while the ratio of debt service to exports reached only 20.6 percent. Korea ranked only 11th in terms of her debt/GDP ratio and 15th in terms of her debt-service ratio.[2] Korea's growth performance is a key piece in the puzzle of its quick adjustment to the 1979–82 debt crisis.

External borrowing in Korea was used primarily to finance current account deficits. In particular, there has been little capital flight. This suggests an analysis of domestic savings and investment as the key to explaining debt accumulation, because the current account deficit, or foreign savings, finances the portion of investment not financed domestically.

It is also notable that Korean debt has been carefully monitored by the Ministry of Finance since the borrowing began in the early 1960s. Applications for loans must be approved, and the government has actively used the allocation of foreign (and domestic) credit as part of an industrial policy, providing growth incentives for particular industries and firms.

Borrowing is a central component of economic planning in Korea. In many periods, the amount of borrowing required to finance desired investment was forecast quite accurately, however unexpected external and internal developments during 1974–5 and 1979–81 meant that in these years the forecast turned out to be a sizable underestimate. At any rate, the Korean government has maintained excellent debt statistics throughout the period. It was thus not faced with the additional difficulty of faulty or incomplete information when responding to the 1979–80 crisis.

6.3.2 Economic Growth

Korea's phenomenal growth rates since 1965 have been well documented. Of particular significance is that Korea was able to avoid the dramatic slow-down which most of the other fast growers experienced after the first oil price shock. A detailed analysis of the economic sources of Korea's growth identifies fixed capital accumulation as the central factor.

During the 1960s, Korean growth was attributable to a combination of increased factor accumulation, improved resource allocation, economies of scale, and technological improvement. Fixed capital accumulation accounts for 1.1 percent average annual growth during 1963–72. In contrast, capital accumulation accounts for a growth rate of 2.6 percent during 1973–82. Korea offset reductions in factor productivity after the first oil shock with a substantial increase in investment.

Increased labor has also played a key role. The average work week increased throughout the period to 54.8 hours, placing Korea at the top of the International Labor Organization's list. Furthermore, the work force is well educated and disciplined.

It is interesting to point out that the sources of Korean growth are quite different from the sources of Japanese growth during its 1953–71 rapid acceleration period. Factor accumulation explains only 45 percent of the Japanese growth rates as compared to 60 percent of the Korean growth rates.

A decomposition from the demand side identifies exports as the ''engine of growth'' during 1975–85, as well as during the earlier period. It is important to stress the role of exports because, as mentioned above, exports generate the foreign exchange essential to repaying external debt.

Investment demand has also been consistently strong. However, since import requirements for investment ranged from .38 to .48, investment has been only a moderate source of demand for domestic output. Finally, we point out that government consumption has played at best a minor role.

The data also document that labor productivity has consistently grown faster in the manufacturing than in the nonmanufacturing sector. The domestic price of manufactured goods—a proxy for the "tradable goods sector"—rose relative to the price of other—nontraded—goods throughout the 1960–85 period. However this real appreciation has represented technical progress and not a deterioration in external competitiveness or a reallocation of resources away from the production of tradables.

One of the most enviable aspects of Korea's recent recovery has been trade balance improvement combined with growth. In contrast, most debtor countries have achieved trade surpluses through recession induced reductions in imports. In fact, the very low income elasticities of Korean imports during 1981–83 are unusual by Korean standards. They are explained in large part by disastrous harvests during 1978–80, necessitating a surge in food imports, followed by a very favorable harvest during 1981–2 which both raised domestic output and reduced imports. Exports did not begin to recover (in value terms) until 1983, and this turnaround is explained by a combination of increased world demand, a terms of trade improvement, the lagged impact of a real depreciation, and numerous investments targeted to export industries gradually coming on stream.

6.3.3 Investment and the Five-Year Plans

Korea instituted a series of five-year economic plans, beginning in 1962. The first step in the formulation of these plans has been to determine the investment required to achieve a desired rate of growth. Thus, investment for growth has been the number one priority, while external borrowing emerges at the other end as the residual—the gap between investment and available domestic financing. In the mid-1960s, it was an important supplement to declining foreign aid. More recently it has been used to substitute for shortfalls in domestic (especially household) savings.

The plans identify particular sectors of the economy for growth with overwhelming focus on exports. Furthermore, the government has actively controlled the allocation of credit, thereby playing a key role in determining the industrial concentration of capital accumulation.

Even the best plan will have little impact if it cannot be implemented. A large part of the success of the five-year plans is attributable to Korea's centralized decision making combined with a very close link between government and business. Authorities maintain current data, including information about individual firms' performance. Decisions are made quickly, and policies are pragmatic, often involving direct intervention at the firm level. One implication of this approach has been that, by selecting previously successful firms to undertake new projects, the government has helped to create a number of large conglomerates (*chaebol*) and a highly concentrated industrial structure.

6.3.4 Savings Behavior

Korea's savings rate has risen from 14 percent in 1965 to over 34 percent in 1986, however, the remarkable secular increase has been interrupted periodically. These plunges have accelerated foreign borrowing so as to finance desired rates of investment, leading to a "crisis."

Two aspects of savings behavior are especially notable. First, savings declines are primarily attributable to drops in household savings, and not to deteriorating government budgets. Second, current account improvement during the adjustment has not been brought about by cuts in investment to close the gap. Instead, the key has been the recovery of household savings, supplemented by increased government savings.

Disaggregation shows that both the secular rise and the plunges occurred in the household sector. The performance is explained quite well by a model in which the marginal propensity to consume out of permanent income is higher than that out of transitory income. Thus, Korea's strong growth, leading to upward revisions in permanent income, accounts for the secular rise in savings, while growth slowdowns account for the 1970–71, 1975, and 1980–81 plunges, as households reduced savings to smooth consumption. Although interest rates are estimated to affect savings positively, we do not find the estimates to be significantly different from zero.

6.3.5 Exchange Rate Policy

Overall, Korea has followed a consistent, credible exchange rate policy, maintaining a competitive, sometimes undervalued, real exchange rate with low variance. In the adjustment to external imbalance during both 1974 and 1980, the policy packages included a substantial (20 percent) one-time devaluation in addition to a change in the exchange rate regime.

The nominal exchange rate was fixed to the U.S. dollar during 1975–79, during which time authorities did permit a 14 percent real appreciation. Since 1980, the exchange rate has been continually adjusted vis-à-vis a basket of currencies. The real exchange rate depreciated by 6 percent during 1980–82, and by a further 14 percent during 1982–86. There has been gradual appreciation during 1987.

6.3.6 Wages and Competitiveness

Even more striking than Korea's success in maintaining external competitiveness throughout most of the 1965–86 period is the fact that real depreciations were often (e.g., 1973, 1983–86) accompanied by real wage increases. Again, rapidly increasing labor productivity is the key to the puzzle, providing a buffer which can be split between increased competitiveness and increased real income.

During 1965–72, real wages grew at an average annual rate of 9.0 percent while productivity (using the value added measure) grew by 14.4 percent. However, during 1973–79, real wages grew by 12.5 percent, outpacing the 11.1 percent productivity growth. Shortages in skilled labor associated with the Big Push toward heavy industrialization, led to rapid nominal wages gains. Unit labor costs, measured in dollars, grew 2.3 times as quickly for Korea as for Taiwan, a major competitor in third markets.

It is important to point out that real wages declined both at the outset of Korea's export led growth and as Korea reestablished her competitive position after the 1975–79 real appreciation. During 1960–64, the average annual real wage decline was 1.96 percent, despite 7.46 percent productivity growth. Real wages fell at the beginning of the adjustment (1981–82) with all of the productivity gains going to reduce unit labor costs. This, plus exchange rate depreciations dramatically improved Korea's competitive position since 1982.

We note a few other characteristics of Korea's labor market. Worker organizations are extremely weak. There is evidence that they have increased job security, but not that they have influenced wages. Bonuses average 15 percent of employee compensation, which enhances flexibility. Finally, the fact that wages are not indexed to past inflation rates has meant that inflation shows little inertia.

6.3.7   Trade Policy

Korea's switch from a policy of import substitution to one of export promotion during 1960–64 is well known. However, despite the liberalization of many import restrictions, trade policies continued to play a central role. In particular, tax preferences and interest rate subsidies became important mechanisms to subsidize domestic industries after 1965. Through the mid-1970s, export incentives were maintained with little variability. Subsidies were used to compensate exporters during periods of real appreciation.

Import restrictions increased during the Big Push and have been gradually relaxed since 1980. Quantitative restrictions, domestic content, and other regulations have remained critical, so that tariff rates substantially underestimate the degree of protection. For example, the share of manufactured items subject to import restriction jumped from 34 percent in 1968 to 61 percent in 1978. These restrictions have been important in developing "infant industries" such as automobiles and steel, allowing Korea to become competitive enough to begin exporting these products. The restrictions help to explain why almost all Korean imports are raw materials, intermediate products, or capital goods, with consumer products amounting to less than 5 percent of Korean imports.

Korea also stands out in not maintaining a structure of protection which penalizes agriculture. The political economy of that outcome is clearly linked to the relatively equitable income distribution due primarily to the land reform.

6.3.8   Industrial Policy

Korea has been extremely successful in selecting "growth industries," and in managing the industrial transition for these infant industries. A large part of its success lies in the development of credible, comprehensive strategies in which investment projects to promote exports formed the cornerstones of its five-year macroeconomic plans.

Korean businesses targeted for expansion have not been concerned about policy inconsistencies or government policy reversals. They have been given preferential access to domestic credit, to external funds, and to imported materials. The government has maintained its commitment, bailing out firms threatened with bankruptcy during downturns or financial panics. It has also created a few conglomerates which are enormous, even by world standards.

In retrospect, some of the policies were mistakes, particularly during the 1974–79 Big Push. For example, government intervention led to substantial overcapacity in petrochemicals. However, the entire policy should by no means be written off as a mistake. Many of the investments in heavy industries are beginning to pay off and exports of these products are growing rapidly.

6.3.9   Fiscal Policy

Fiscal policy in Korea is perhaps most notable for the role it did not play in accumulation of external debt. Government savings has been positive in every year since 1962.

The budget deficit (which includes public investment as an outlay) has been kept under control, ranging from 1 percent to 4 percent of output. A tax reform and switch to value added taxation in the 1970s did succeed in raising revenues from 15 percent to 18 percent of GNP. Large deficits in 1975 and 1980–81 are attributable primarily to increased expenditures in the Grain Management Fund. Social expenditures, such as education and housing, have been low historically, but rising over time. Since 1980, they have amounted to 30 percent of total government expenditures. Indicators of fiscal stance show that fiscal policy has been countercyclical, used by the government in attempts to "fine-tune" economic performance.

Overall, fiscal deficits have not been financed through rapid money creation. The deficits themselves have been relatively small. Also authorities have alternated between domestic and foreign credit. For example, after jumps in the banking sector credit to the public sector during 1980–81, net credit was reduced during 1982–84.

6.3.10   Monetary Policy

The banking system, including the Bank of Korea, has been monitored by the Ministry of Finance since 1962 so that macroeconomic policy making is extremely centralized. We highlight four aspects. The first is the key role for credit allocation in the industrial strategy, as discussed above. A second objective of monetary policies (especially interest rate adjustments) has been to increase household savings. As discussed above, it is very difficult to quantify how large a part this tactic has played in raising savings rates.

Third, Korean financial markets have three levels. The official banking sector is highly controlled, although there has been some liberalization since 1982, including the privatization of five commercial banks. There is also a partially controlled nonbank financial sector, and an unorganized curb market. The latter two have added flexibility to Korea's financial system, providing credit (often at high interest rates) to those firms which were not given access to scarce bank credit. Since a 1982 financial scandal, however, the curb market has shrunk considerably. Nonbank financial institutions have been growing rapidly, accounting for one-half of all deposits of banks plus nonbanks in 1985, as compared to one-fifth in 1978.

Korea's financial system has been anything but a unified system in which credit is allocated by market forces. While it is certain that the outcomes under such a system would have been different, it is very difficult to assess whether they would have been "better" or "worse." To us, the most sensible conclusion is that the Korean government successfully used an active and pervasive policy of intervening in financial markets to promote its growth objectives.

Finally, there has been some movement toward financial liberalization of the banking sector. But unlike the trade liberalization, the changes so far seem to have been greater on paper than in practice. Credit allocation remains a cornerstone of Korean industrial policy.

6.3.11   Two Themes

Two unifying themes emerge from our investigation of these ten pieces in the puzzle of Korea's successful performance. The first is the importance of rapid growth rates (particularly of exports), rising labor productivity, and expanding human and physical capital resources. These factors gave Korea the leeway to borrow heavily while keeping the burden of debt repayments manageable and to avoid squeezing real incomes while increasing international competitiveness. The rapid productivity growth in export and import competing goods has eased the problem of mobilizing and transferring domestic resources so as to pay external debts.

The second theme is the usage of active, interventionist government policy which is credible, consistent, and coherent. These policies placed investment to promote exports as the number one priority and led the economy through a fundamental industrial restructuring.

6.4 Implications: A Synthesis

In this section, we synthesize the pieces discussed above in order to answer the questions posed at the outset. The first question, important in distinguishing Korea's experience from that of many other debtor countries, is why the debt crises occurred.

Since 1965, Korea has been vulnerable to external and internal shocks because of a determined investment policy that left no buffers between desired investment and domestic savings. External borrowing was treated as the buffer, or residual.

The country has been hit by a number of external shocks, in particular oil price and interest rate changes, but the role of internal "shocks" must not be underestimated. During 1974–75, deterioration in the terms of trade accounts for only a part of the current account deficit. Like 1970–72, this period seems better described as a slowdown than as an economic crisis. External factors were more important during 1979–80. However, the crisis would have been much less severe if these had not been exacerbated by the agricultural disaster, political turmoil, and previous policy mistakes.

How was Korea able to recover so quickly from slowdowns and crises? We believe the central factor has been successfully distinguishing between permanent and temporary shocks, and responding appropriately. The devastation of the Korean War was clearly a permanent shock. In designing and carrying through the impressive structural readjustment of the 1960s, policymakers learned how to put together an adjustment package that worked.

They chose to embark on another structural readjustment during 1973–79 because of pessimistic forecasts for medium-term growth if Korea were to remain on the same industrialization path pursued during the 1960s. In contrast, Korea borrowed to smooth adjustment to the 1973 jump in oil prices because the shock was judged unlikely to alter the medium- to long-run prospects for heavy industry. However, policymakers have not been rigid. A third shift in focus came as doubts emerged about the efficacy of further heavy industrialization, and the economy found itself saddled with the massive debts accumulated during 1979–80.

The point is closely linked to the role of external debt in Korea's adjustment. The debt has been used to supplement domestic savings in financing investment, enabling faster rates of growth. The debt has also been used to smooth over temporary shocks, without jeopardizing the on-going structural adjustment plan. However, Korea has been admirable in not using external borrowing to avoid undertaking a structural readjustment.

What is the adjustment package that has worked for Korea? The centerpiece has been a comprehensive export focused investment plan, operationalized through competitive exchange rates, credit rationing, tax and other incentives for targeted industries, trade policies, and allocation of external credit. Initial declines in real wages have helped to boost competitiveness, but once the investment-growth cycle has been put on track, productivity gains have been split between raising wages and enhancing competitiveness.

Traditional macroeconomic "stabilization" tools—monetary expansion and fiscal deficits—have been important in the passive sense that they have been kept in line. Fiscal deficits have remained small and authorities have been careful to limit domestic credit expansion to the public sector. However, these policies played at best a supporting role in pulling Korea out of slowdowns and crises. Both were quite variable with many reversals during 1980–81. By the time a definite monetary/fiscal expansion emerged in 1982, Korea was already well on the way to recovery.

Good fortune has also helped Korea to recover. In particular, the first oil shock gave Korea an unexpected boost during 1976–78 through revenues from construction in the Middle East. The recent recovery was fueled by terms of trade improvements beginning in 1981.

6.5 Lessons for Other Debtors

We begin by pointing out two lessons that, most certainly, cannot be learned from the Korean experience. The first is how to design "short-run, macroeconomic stabilization" packages. There are no "quick fixes" in Korea's recent history.

The second is the benefits of liberalized trade regimes and (domestic and international) capital markets. Active intervention has been a mainstay of Korean policy. However, there are numerous examples of extensive intervention in other countries which have coincided with poor economic performance. Korea does contain lessons about which types of intervention are likely to be effective.

We draw four lessons from Korea's experience. A first lesson is the value of credibility, consistency, and coherence in economic policy. As in Korea, this may well necessitate coordinated trade, industrial and credit policies in order to promote infant industries. It certainly includes maintaining a competitive real exchange rate together with a sustainable fiscal policy, and moderate monetary growth.

A second lesson is the value of a long-term structural adjustment policy with investment in exports as the top priority. When things have gone well in Korea, high rates of investment have stimulated growth, raising both domestic savings and export earnings and enabling Korea to finance the external debts. When difficulties emerged, Korea consistently avoided cutting investment so that the economy was poised to resume growth when external and/or internal conditions improved.

Of course, the difficulty with such an investment program is that it must be financed, and extensive borrowing can lead to repayment difficulties. The Korean experience highlights the value of external borrowing in enabling an investment policy to be carried through, as distinguished from external borrowing used to avoid structural adjustment.

Finally, Korea's ability to recover from downturns emphasizes the value of monitoring economic performance and maintaining accurate statistics for key variables.

6.6 Prospects

The prospects for rapid growth to continue over the short to medium term are excellent. Our view is based both on Korea's recent good fortune (especially the decline in oil prices and interest rates and the appreciation of the Japanese yen) and on Korea's very competitive position as a result of 1985–86 real depreciations and the heavy investments over the past decade which are beginning to pay off.

We look at two of the many policy issues facing the government. First, some gradual real appreciation is unlikely to disrupt growth prospects, and may well be important to mitigate protectionism in the United States.

Second, many have expressed surprise that Korea has decided to reduce the external debt. There remain many high-return investments. There are also arguments for borrowing so as to take advantage of current favorable external conditions through investment and stockpiles. On the other hand, Korea does have a substantial external debt and reducing it will reduce the potential for future debt crises. Furthermore, careful forward-looking decision making has been an asset in the past. Caution today may well pay off handsomely as external conditions become less favorable down the road.

In addition to important social and political issues, there are two difficulties facing the country. Continued access especially to U.S. markets is critical for continuation of Korea's export led growth. Current efforts to identify new markets for Korean products and to reduce dependence on the United States are timely given the uncertainties about U.S. trade policy.

Finally, shifts in Korea's industrial mix have created a new domestic policy problem—how to respond to the difficulties of declining industries. The options, involving distribution and efficient resource allocation, are important and controversial. Thus, incorporating declining industries into an industrial policy which has successfully targeted growing industries poses a fundamental challenge to Korean economic planning. Hopefully, Korea's response will result in new lessons.

Notes

1. Readers are referred to the detailed study for further discussion of points made in this chapter (see the country studies for this project). The study also contains a comprehensive list of references. A brief list is provided at the end of this chapter.
2. These data, for 1983, are quoted from Aghevli and Marquez-Ruarte (1985, table 6, p. 21).

References

Aghevli, B., and J. Marquez-Ruarte. 1985. *A case of successful adjustment: Korea's experience during 1980–84.* IMF Occasional Paper no. 39. Washington, D.C.: IMF.

Amsden, A. 1986. Growth and stabilization in Korea: 1962–84. Paper prepared for the World Institute for Development Economics research conference project on Stabilization Programs in Developing Countries, Helsinki, Finland.

Cho, Y. J. and D. Cole. 1986. The role of the financial sector in Korea's structural adjustment. Paper prepared for the KDI and World Bank conference on Structural Adjustment in a Newly Industrialized Country: Lessons from Korea, (June). Washington D.C.

Dornbusch, R., and Y. C. Park. 1987. Korea's growth policy. *Brookings Papers on Economic Activity* 2.

Frank, C., K. S. Kim, and L. Westphal. 1975. *Foreign trade regimes and economic development: South Korea.* New York: Columbia University Press.

Haggart, S., and C. Moon. 1986. Industrial change and state power: The politics of stabilization in Korea. Mimeo, Harvard University.

Hong, W. T. 1979. *Trade, distortions and employment growth in Korea.* Seoul, Korea: Korea Development Institute.

Kim, K. S., and J. K. Park. 1985. *Sources of economic growth in Korea: 1963–1982*. Seoul, Korea: Korea Development Institute.

Kincaid, R. 1983. Korea's major adjustment effort. *Finance and Development* (December).

Krueger, A. 1982. *The developmental role of the foreign sector and aid*. Cambridge: Harvard University Press.

Lindauer, D. L. 1984. Labor market behavior in the Republic of Korea: An analysis of wages and their impact on the economy. World Bank Staff Working Paper no. 641. Washington, D.C.: World Bank.

Mason, S. E., et al. 1985. *The economic and social modernization of the Republic of Korea*. Council on East Asian Studies. Cambridge: Harvard University Press.

Morgan Guaranty Trust. 1984. Korea: Adjustment model for the 1980s. *World Financial Markets* (March).

Nam, S. W. 1984. Korea's stabilization efforts since the late 1970s. Korea Development Institute Working Paper no. 8405, Seoul, Korea.

Park, Y. C. 1985a Korea's experience with external debt management. In *International Debt and the Developing Countries*, ed. G. W. Smith and J. T. Cuddington. Washington, D.C.: World Bank.

Park, Y. C. 1985b. Economic stabilization and liberalization in Korea, 1980–84. In *Monetary Policy in a Changing Financial Environment*, Bank of Korea, Seoul, Korea.

World Bank. 1984. *Korea: Development in a global context*, Washington, D.C.: World Bank.

———. 1986. *World Development Report*, Washington, D.C.: World Bank.

———. 1987. *Korea: Managing the industrial transition*. Washington, D.C.: World Bank.

7   Mexico 1958–86: From Stabilizing Development to the Debt Crisis

Edward F. Buffie, with the assistance
of Allen Sangines Krause

7.1 Introduction

The purpose of this chapter is to critically examine macroeconomic policy in Mexico during the period 1958–86. This period is of special interest as it embodies two distinct, sharply contrasting phases. Between 1958 and 1972, the inflation rate never exceeded 6 percent while annual output growth averaged 6.7 percent. The period since 1972, by contrast, has been marked by a succession of increasingly severe macroeconomic crises. At the end of 1986, Mexico was saddled with a huge foreign debt, triple digit inflation and had suffered a 13.5 percent decrease in real per capita income in the preceding five years.

Sections 7.2 through 7.5 analyze economic performance during the era of Stabilizing Development and the Echeverria, Lopez Portillo and De La Madrid administrations. In these sections we track the evolution of economic policy and the major macroeconomic variables of interest such as real wages, the foreign debt, capital flight, the fiscal deficit (broken down according to the deficits of the parastatal sector, financial intermediaries, and the rest of the government) and different measures of financial intermediation. The final section evaluates the post-1982 adjustment record.

7.2 The Record of Stabilizing Development

After the devaluation of the peso in 1954, the Mexican economy entered a phase of high growth and low inflation that would last until

Edward F. Buffie is an associate professor of economics at Vanderbilt University.
Allen Sangines Krause is a lecturer at the Instituto Technologico Autonomo de Mexico.

the end of the 1960s. This period has since come to be known as the era of Stabilizing Development (SD). The main objectives of economic policy during SD were to increase private sector savings and capital accumulation, maintain price stability and a fixed parity with the dollar, and increase real wages. These goals were largely achieved, leading observers to speak of a "Mexican miracle." The exchange rate was kept fixed at 12.5 pesos per dollar and the annual inflation rate averaged 3.8 percent. Real output grew at an average rate of 6.7 percent and the share of gross fixed investment in GDP rose (at 1960 prices) from 16.2 percent in 1958 to 20.8 percent in 1970. The real manufacturing sector wage inclusive of fringe benefits grew at an annual average rate of approximately 4 percent.[1]

Economic policy during this period was consistent and well defined. To promote private capital accumulation, profits were taxed at a low rate and public sector investment was directed toward projects complementary to private investment (mostly social infrastructure). A substantial increase in financial intermediation also played an important role in stimulating private investment. The supply of bank funds and private sector credit grew rapidly in response to a policy of maintaining real deposit rates at positive levels competitive with those offered in the United States. In real terms, bank credit to the private sector grew at an average annual rate of 14.8 percent.

Fiscal and monetary policies were coordinated with a view to preserving a fixed exchange rate and overall price stability. The growth rate of the monetary base was strictly controlled and it was well understood that if the fiscal deficit exceeded the level consistent with the planned rate of monetary emission, expenditures were to be lowered until the gap was eliminated. The main source of funds for financing the fiscal deficit was not the printing press but rather forced "loans" extracted from the commercial banking system through the imposition of high reserve ratios ($\approx$34 percent). Since bank deposits grew at a rapid pace, this provided a considerable margin for noninflationary financing of the fiscal deficit.

The conventional view holds that the SD program was inherently flawed and that starting sometime around the mid-1960s the economy was besieged by a host of intractable problems:

1. *Inadequate employment growth.*[2] Underemployment is alleged to have worsened as a result of policies aimed at stimulating investment, which made capital relatively cheap and encouraged firms to use less labor-intensive technologies, and the protectionist trade regime, which promoted the capital-intensive, import-substituting industrial sector at the expense of the labor-intensive agricultural sector.

2. *A worsening distribution of income.*[3] Neglect of agriculture and inadequate employment growth meant that the poorest groups gained little in the growth achieved under SD.

3. *Progressive loss of fiscal control.*[4] Concern about the deteriorating distribution of income created pressure to increase social welfare expenditures, leading to a sharp increase in overall public sector spending in the last half of the 1960s. Because of an earlier failure to achieve any significant tax reform, revenue growth could not keep pace and the fiscal deficit started rising, climbing from 0.9 percent of GDP in 1965 to 3.8 percent in 1970. The larger fiscal deficits, in turn, caused the payments balance to deteriorate and by 1970 the current account deficit had reached the unprecedented figure of $1.19 billion.

4. *Diminishing growth potential.*[5] It is often claimed that the economy began to lose steam after 1965 when growth in agricultural output declined steeply and the opportunities for "easy" and efficient import-substitution had been largely exhausted.

We are unable to find much support for the above critique. There is little hard evidence that either underemployment or the distribution of income worsened during the SD era. Claims that underemployment worsened are quite tenuous given the numerous, serious problems with the employment data in the 1960 and 1970 populations censuses.[6] Estimates of employment growth differ widely depending on the nature of the adjustment made to correct flaws in the data. Although the quality of the data is problematic, on balance, the evidence lends greater support to the view that the SD policies succeeded in greatly reducing the extent of underemployment. For the industrial sector, even pessimistic estimates show growth rates of employment well above that of the labor force.[7] Nor does it seem that high employment growth in the industrial sector was achieved at the expense of employment growth elsewhere in the economy. Gregory (1986) reviews the data on wages and productivity in the informal sector and concludes that they strongly contradict the hypothesis that the large shift of labor out of agriculture depressed informal sector incomes. During the 1960s real wages and labor productivity increased substantially across establishments of all sizes in industry, commerce and services.[8]

Utilizing data from various household expenditure surveys, numerous studies have been made of how the distribution of income has evolved since the early 1950s. These studies generally conclude that the distribution of income worsened during SD. This conclusion, however, is open to question in view of problems in the comparability of the data across surveys and possible biases in the summary measures of the income distribution. Moreover, there is some evidence which suggests that, regardless of how the overall distribution may have changed, the poor benefitted substantially in absolute terms from the high rate of economic growth. According to van Ginneken (1980), the percentage of families living in poverty declined from 45 percent in 1958 to 30 percent in 1969.[9]

The claim that the economy's growth momentum began to decline after the mid-1960s appears to be similarly weak. The high rates of growth of agricultural output between 1945 and 1965 were based on the development of large scale irrigation schemes in the northwest that improved existing lands and brought vast amounts of new land under cultivation. By 1965, this source of growth had been largely exhausted.[10] Agricultural growth fell off sharply after 1965 because of political constraints on land redistribution that prevented investment that would develop the more populous rain-fed agricultural areas, not because SD entailed "neglect of the agricultural sector." Furthermore, despite the deceleration in agricultural growth, overall growth remained satisfactory thanks to the strong performance of the industrial sector. The share of investment in GDP rose from 18.7 percent to 20.8 percent and total output grew at an annual average rate of 6.9 percent over 1966–70.

Finally, we also disagree with the view that fiscal discipline began to break down during the Diaz Ordaz administration. The increase in the fiscal deficit from 0.9 percent of GDP in 1965 to 3.8 percent in 1970 reflected merely the normal workings of a very well-defined political expenditure cycle. Table 7.1 displays the results of regressing the detrended values of current, capital, and total government expenditures for the period 1965–85 on six dummy variables (D1–D6) corresponding to the six years making up the presidential term.[11] It is clear that fiscal policy follows a very distinct cycle. The expenditure cycle seems to stem both from the perceived political advantages of increasing expenditures shortly before elections and from the incongruity between the natural gestation period of investment projects and the fixed, six-year term (*sexenio*) of each administration (reelection is not allowed). Fiscal expansion invariably occurs in the two years preceding the upcoming election. Capital spending increases strongly in the fifth year in a rush to complete investment projects before the term of the existing administration expires. In the following year, spending surges again as current expenditures rise in the campaign to strengthen political support just before the election. Immediately after the election, spending falls sharply as capital expenditures temporarily decline while a new set of investment projects are being designed and the new administration strives to reduce the fiscal deficit. Fiscal control then prevails until the fifth year when the cycle starts to repeat itself.

Returning to the issue of fiscal discipline in the latter part of the SD period, since 1965 was the first year of the Diaz Ordaz *sexenio*, the

Table 7.1   **The Political Business Cycle**

	Total Public Sector Expenditure	Current Expenditure	Capital Expenditure
D1	−.076	−.026	−.19
	(2.32)	(.63)	(4.24)
D2	−.063	−.067	−.04
	(1.93)	(1.61)	(.90)
D3	−.151	−.038	.043
	(.46)	(.92)	(.96)
D4	−.016	−.002	−.025
	(.15)	(.04)	(.046)
D5	.12	.082	.218
	(2.98)	(1.62)	(3.96)
D6	.079	.091	.059
	(2.40)	(2.18)	(1.32)
R^2	.71	.70	.80
R^2	.56	.47	.65
Durbin-Watson statistic	1.22	1.47	1.81

increase in the fiscal deficit between 1965 and 1970 was not at all out of the ordinary. The relevant comparison is between the fiscal deficits of 1964 and 1970. This comparison does not support the notion of mounting fiscal problems. In both years, the deficit was approximately 4 percent of GDP.

7.3   The Echeverria Administration: Shared Development

Economic policy changed radically with the accession of Luis Echeverria to the presidency. After contractionary measures were temporarily imposed in 1971 to reduce the payments deficit, an enormous fiscal expansion took place. In the succeeding five years, general government employment doubled and the share of total public sector spending in GDP jumped from 20.5 percent to 30 percent. Much of the increased spending took place in the parastatal sector. Between 1971 and 1975, real current expenditure by public sector enterprises grew at an average annual rate of 18 percent; capital outlays rose at an even faster rate of 29.3 percent.

Another attempt at tax reform failed in 1972. Consequently, the fiscal deficit soared, climbing to 10 percent of GDP in 1975 and 1976. Unlike in the preceding Diaz Ordaz administration, a large portion of the deficit was financed by borrowing from the Central Bank. The growth rate of the monetary base accelerated from 19.8 percent in 1972 to 33.8 percent in 1975 and the share of seignorage in GDP rose to triple the average level of the 1960s.

A second important shift in monetary policy concerned the management of interest rates. Whereas real deposit rates were maintained at positive levels throughout SD, after 1972 this policy was allowed to lapse. Nominal interest rates were not adjusted upward in step with increases in inflation, and as real rates turned negative the "financial miracle" terminated abruptly. The total stock of real bank funds fell 13.3 percent from 1973 to 1976. Financial disintermediation, in turn, by reducing the growth of demand for bank reserves—much the largest component of the monetary base—made it far more difficult to prevent excessive growth in the high-powered money supply. The government reacted by raising the reserve ratio from .313 in 1970 to .511 in 1976. Nonetheless, real bank reserves grew at an annual rate of only 5.7 percent over 1973–76, a figure far below that (9.8 percent) recorded during the preceding Diaz Ordaz administration.

For a couple of years, expansionary demand policies were successful in stimulating strong output growth. However, problems soon began to appear. After 1972, when recovery from the 1971 recession was complete and excess capacity had largely disappeared, inflation accelerated, rising above 20 percent in 1973 and 1974. Furthermore, while aggregate growth was high from 1972–74, much of the growth was concentrated in the public sector. Private investment weakened, dropping from 14 percent of GDP (at 1970 prices) in 1971 to 12.7 percent in 1975. Government financial policies seem to have been at least partly responsible for the slump in private investment; negative real deposit rates, slowing the growth of bank funds, and higher reserve requirements caused the supply of credit to the private sector to diminish sharply.

More threatening than either the acceleration in inflation or the decline in private investment was the deterioration in the payments balance. As the nominal exchange rate remained pegged at 12.5 pesos per dollar, the real exchange rate fell rapidly and the current account deficit deteriorated until it reached the alarming level of $4.4 billion in 1975, a figure equivalent to 5.1 percent of GDP. The reluctance to raise domestic interest rates in the face of higher inflation and a clearly overvalued peso caused the overall payments balance to deteriorate to an even greater extent. Capital flight commenced on a large scale, withdrawing $3.6 billion dollars from the country in 1975 and 1976 (Zedillo 1987, 177).

The large payments deficits were mirrored in a fast-mounting level of foreign indebtedness. From a figure of $6.3 billion at the start of 1971, the total foreign debt more than quadrupled to $27.9 billion by the end of 1976. Almost all of this debt was taken out by the public sector from the commercial banks.

In 1976, the economic program of the Echeverria administration collapsed under extreme balance of payments pressures. Extensive import controls were imposed and parastatal expenditures were sharply curtailed, but little was done to check spending by other branches of the government or to curb monetary expansion. As a result, though the burden of debt service was not exceptionally high (35 percent of current account income if short-term debts could be rolled over), the current account deficit remained sizeable ($3.7 billion for the year), capital flight persisted and the Central Bank's stock of foreign exchange reserves became severely depleted. On 31 August, the peso was devalued nearly 100 percent and the economy went into a severe tailspin. During the last four months of the year, manufacturing sector employment declined 4.2 percent, the inflation rate surged to 60 percent, and there were frequent threats of bank runs. Shortly before Lopez Portillo's inauguration, negotiations began on the terms for a standby agreement with the IMF.

7.4 The Lopez Portillo Administration

The Lopez Portillo administration soon reached an agreement with the IMF on a stabilization program to be implemented in stages over three years. The program called for the usual mix of trade liberalization and monetary and fiscal austerity. In its first year, the program was fairly successful. The fiscal deficit was lowered from 9.9 percent to 6.7 percent of GDP, the inflation rate declined from 27.2 percent to 20.7 percent, and the current account deficit fell by over two billion dollars in 1977. GDP growth slowed further to 3.4 percent, but the decline was far less severe than anticipated. (GDP had been forecasted to remain constant).

When it became widely known that Mexico's oil wealth was far greater than formerly thought, the Fund program was dropped in favor of a "new," more expansionary policy package. The new development plan entailed large, sustained increases in real government expenditures. In this respect, the plan appeared to continue the discredited Public Expenditure—Led Growth strategy of the Echeverria administration. It was argued, however, that an economic base expanded and strengthened by oil wealth could support a much enlarged role for the public sector. Furthermore, strong fiscal stimulus was to be only one part of a comprehensive reform package that would avoid the main policy errors of the Echeverria administration.

In the ensuing four years, the Mexican economy recorded some impressive accomplishments (see tables 7.2a and 7.2b). Over the 1978–81 period, real GDP growth ranged between 8.0 and 9.1 percent and employment in the high-wage manufacturing sector and the public sector increased 27.2 percent and 41.4 percent. respectively. Both private

Table 7.2a   Macroeconomic Aggregates (% change)[1]

	1976	1977	1978	1979	1980	1981	1982
Real GDP	4.2	3.4	8.3	9.1	8.3	8.0	−0.5
Manufacturing	5.0	3.6	9.8	10.6	7.2	7.0	−2.9
Agricultural and fisheries	1.0	7.5	6.0	−2.1	7.1	6.1	−0.6
Inflation[2]	27.2	20.7	16.2	20.0	29.8	28.7	98.9
Manufacturing sector employment[3]	−0.06	1.9	7.9	6.7	7.2	2.9	− 8.5
General government employment	9.8	5.7	7.5	9.9	10.8	9.6	5.3
Public sector employment	9.1	5.5	7.3	9.2	10.4	9.3	5.9
Real investment	0.4	−6.7	15.2	20.2	14.9	14.7	−15.9
Private	6.1	−6.7	5.1	22.7	13.7	14.0	−17.3
Public	−7.6	−6.7	31.6	17.1	16.7	15.8	−14.2

Table 7.2b   Composition of Output (% of GDP)[4]

	1976	1977	1978	1979	1980	1981	1982
Private consumption	69.9	69.0	68.9	68.7	68.2	67.9	69.0
Government consumption	9.0	8.6	8.8	8.8	8.9	9.1	9.3
Gross fixed capital formation	20.9	18.9	20.0	22.1	23.5	24.9	21.0
Private	12.9	11.7	11.3	12.7	13.4	14.1	11.7
Public	8.0	7.2	8.7	9.4	10.1	10.8	9.3
Change in inventories	2.3	3.5	3.0	2.8	4.6	5.1	0.5
Exports	7.9	8.8	9.1	9.3	9.1	9.0	10.2
Imports	10.1	8.8	9.9	11.7	14.3	15.9	10.1

Sources: Sistema de Cuentas Nacionales de Mexico: Cuentas de Produccion del Sector Publico 1975–1983 for government employment data. The manufacturing sector employment series is from Indicadores Economicos. All other data is from the National Income Accounts of INEGI (Instituto Nacional de Estadistica Geografia e Informatica).
[1]Real variables are expressed in terms of 1970 prices.
[2]December to December change in the CPI.
[3]December to December change.
[4]Output shares at 1970 prices.

and public sector investment spending increased greatly. The share of public sector investment in GDP rose (at 1970 prices) from 7.2 to 10.8 percent and that of the private sector increased from 11.7 to 14.1 percent. The inflation rate began creeping upward after 1978 but never exceeded 30 percent.

Despite the substantial increase in the economy's investment rate, the acceleration in growth after the 1977 recession was not sustainable. In retrospect, it is clear that little, if any, policy reform took place and that the oil bonanza simply resulted in the policy mistakes of the Echeverria administration being repeated on a larger scale. Both current and capital expenditures of the public sector grew more rapidly than projected and got completely out of hand after 1980. Total real public sector expenditure increased by 97.7 percent in the space of four years, climbing from 29.5 percent of GDP in 1977 to 41.3 percent in 1981, a figure some nine percentage points above the peak value recorded during the Echeverria administration (see table 7.3). This massive increase in expenditure led to large fiscal deficits as it was not matched by a similar buildup in revenues. After declining to 6.7 percent of GDP in 1977, the overall fiscal deficit grew steadily and then skyrocketed to 14.7 percent in 1981 when real public sector spending (net of interest payments on the external debt) rose an astounding 28.6 percent.

The breakdown in the overall deficit shown in table 7.4 points to stagnation of nonoil revenues, in addition to rapid expenditure growth, as an important factor in the rising deficits. PEMEX initially registered a small surplus, but after 1978, when petroleum exports commenced on a large scale, the surplus rose rapidly, reaching 6.3 percent of GDP in 1980 and then falling back to 4.1 percent in 1981. This sizeable revenue windfall was offset to a large extent by slow revenue growth elsewhere in the public sector. Between 1978 and 1981, the deficit of the non-PEMEX parastatal sector increased from 2.8 percent of GNP to 5.1 percent, with more than half of the increment owing to the decline in the sector's revenue share. The revenue share of the nonparastatal sector declined to an even greater extent, dropping from 10.5 percent of GDP in 1978 to 8.3 percent in 1981. Moreover, part of current expenditures of the Federal government probably reflects expenditures induced by revenue shortfalls in the nonparastatal sector. In the detailed fiscal accounts of SHCP (Secretaria de Hacienda y Credito

Table 7.3   **Public Sector Expenditures and Revenues (% of GDP)**

	1977	1978	1979	1980	1981	1982
Expenditure	29.5	31.0	32.2	34.6	41.3	46.4
Current	22.0	22.3	22.6	24.9	28.0	36.0
Interest payments on the foreign debt	1.9	2.0	2.1	2.1	2.3	5.1
Other	20.1	20.3	20.5	22.8	25.7	30.7
Capital	7.5	8.7	9.6	9.7	13.3	10.6
Revenues	24.2	25.5	26.2	27.8	27.7	30.1
Economic deficit	5.4	5.5	6.0	6.8	13.6	16.3
Deficit on financial intermediation[1]	1.4	1.2	1.4	1.0	1.2	1.4
Monetary deficit	6.7	6.7	7.4	7.9	14.7	17.6

Source: Estadisticas Hacendarias del Sector Publico: Cifras Anuales 1965–1982 (SHCP).
[1]Deficit of La Banca de Desarrollo.

Table 7.4   Deficit Breakdown (% of GDP)

	1977	1978	1979	1980	1981	1982
PEMEX						
Expenditure	3.9	4.8	5.5	5.8	7.5	7.5
Current[1]	2.0	2.1	2.5	2.9	3.6	4.5
Capital[2]	1.9	2.7	3.0	3.0	3.9	3.0
Revenues[3]	4.9	5.8	7.4	12.1	11.6	15.8
Deficit	−1.0	−1.0	−1.9	−6.3	−4.1	−8.3
Non-PEMEX parastatals						
Expenditure	12.0	12.0	11.5	12.0	13.0	12.5
Current[1]	9.8	9.5	8.9	9.0	9.9	9.9
Capital[2]	2.3	2.5	2.7	3.1	3.1	2.6
Revenues[3]	9.0	9.2	8.7	8.2	7.9	8.1
Deficit	3.0	2.8	2.8	3.9	5.1	4.4
Other[4]						
Expenditure	13.6	14.2	15.2	16.7	20.8	26.5
Current	10.3	10.7	11.2	13.0	14.5	21.5
Capital	3.3	3.5	4.0	3.7	6.3	5.0
Revenues	10.2	10.5	10.1	7.5	8.3	6.2
Deficit	3.3	3.7	4.9	9.2	12.5	20.2

Source: Estadisticas Hacendarias del Sector Publico: Cifras Anuales 1965–1982 (SHCP).
[1]Gasto de operacion plus ajenas de gasto (Operating expenditure plus "outside account" expenditure).
[2]Physical investment only (excludes financial investment).
[3]The sum of current income, capital income, taxes paid, and *ajenas de ingreso* ("outside account" income).
[4]Includes DDF (Department of the Federal District).

Publico), it is not possible to trace the majority of transfer payments by the federal government. These unaccounted for transfers increased steadily throughout the Lopez Portillo *sexenio* and reflect mostly expenditures to cover the losses of various price support schemes, local "development institutions" and firms in which the government has a minority interest.[12] If such transfers are treated as a negative revenue item (i.e., as "induced" subsidies), the revenue share in GDP of the non-PEMEX public sector fell by 5.8 percentage points over 1978–81, implying, remarkably, a three percentage point *decrease* in the sum of non-PEMEX revenues and the PEMEX surplus.

The large decrease in the share of nonoil revenues was due principally to a reluctance to raise public sector prices. The failure to maintain real public sector prices, moreover, also greatly diminished the size of the PEMEX surplus. Domestic energy prices changed very little as world petroleum prices shot upward after 1973 so that by 1980 the average internal price of petroleum products was less than a quarter of the world market price. The revenue loss from the implicit subsidy on domestic consumption of PEMEX products amounted to 6.2 percent of GDP in 1980, a figure almost as large as the entire public sector economic deficit that year.[13]

As earlier in the Echeverria administration, the large fiscal deficits gave rise to unsustainably large balance of payments deficits which ultimately proved to be the undoing of the Public Expenditure–Led Growth strategy. Trade liberalization combined with real exchange rate appreciation lowered the real price of imported goods approximately 28 percent from 1977 to 1981, provoking a stupendous, across-the-board increase in demand. Between 1978 and 1980, real imports of capital goods and intermediate inputs increased by more than 100 percent. As the relaxation of quotas favored consumption goods more than other types of imports, the volume of imported consumer goods increased even more strongly, rising by over 200 percent in the same three-year period. On the export side, oil sales became very sizeable after 1978. From 1978 to 1981, dollar earnings generated by petroleum exports increased 682 percent. Overall export earnings, however, rose at a considerably slower rate as nonoil exports suffered both from an appreciating real exchange rate and the dismantling of the CEDIS system of subsidies. After jumping to a decade-high level in 1977, the real price of manufactured exports plummeted, declining more than 40 percent in the next four years. Predictably, the volume of manufactured exports slowed sharply in 1979 and then turned negative in 1980 and 1981.

The financial counterpart to the large current account deficits was a fast growing level of external indebtedness. The total foreign debt increased almost threefold to $81 billion at the end of 1981.[14] This figure, however, considerably overstates the increase in *net* foreign debt. Table 7.5 gathers together various estimates of capital flight during this period. The wide variation in the estimates arises from different data bases.[15] According to the Cumby and Levich estimate, capital flight siphoned off 46 percent of the extra debt accumulated between 1977 and 1981. A problem with their estimate is that the net inflow of external resources is calculated from World Bank data on the change in gross external indebtedness. But as Zedillo points out (1987, 175–76), this is not an accurate measure of net new indebtedness because in certain years some of the increment in the reported debt figures simply reflects more extensive coverage of the government's debt-reporting systems. Zedillo uses the Bank of Mexico's balance of payments data to measure the change in net indebtedness (a much more accurate measure), but also makes the odd adjustment of subtracting from the official current account data imputed interest payments on identified Mexican deposits abroad. (For some reason, reinvested interest income from foreign assets is not treated as capital flight.) In the column labeled "Modified Zedillo" we remove this latter adjustment. This gives a figure for capital

Table 7.5   Capital Flight[1] ($ billion)

	Cumby and Levich	Zedillo	Modified Zedillo[2]	Gulati-Adjusted		
				CL[3]	Z[4]	MZ[5]
1977	4.99	0.69	0.98	5.61	1.31	1.60
1978	1.76	0.07	0.60	1.17	−0.52	0.01
1979	2.37	0.23	1.06	1.52	−0.62	0.25
1980	6.75	−0.68	3.89	3.72	−3.71	0.86
1981	8.56	9.73	14.03	6.15	7.32	11.62
1982	7.24	8.23	9.03	6.60	7.59	8.39
1983	11.71	2.42	3.39	6.88	−2.41	−1.44
1984	6.02	2.33	3.67	−0.66	−4.35	−3.01
1985	—	1.92	3.75	—	−0.68	1.15
Cumulative total 1977–82	31.67	18.27	29.59	24.77	11.37	22.69
Cumulative total 1977–85	—	24.94	40.40	—	10.83	26.29

Sources: Cumby and Levich (1987, 58); Gulati (1987, 73); and Zedillo (1987, 177).
[1]The Morgan Guaranty definition of capital flight: change in the foreign debt plus net foreign direct investment plus the current account surplus minus the change in short-term foreign assets of the banking system minus change in foreign exchange reserves. The Zedillo estimates also subtract the change in other official external assets.
[2]Estimate obtained using Zedillo's data and the official figures for the current account deficit.
[3]Cumby-Levich estimate with current account data adjusted by Gulati's estimate of net trade invoice faking.
[4]Zedillo estimate with current account data adjusted by Gulati's estimate of trade-invoice faking.
[5]Modified Zedillo estimate with current account data adjusted by Gulati's estimate of net trade-invoice faking.   \

flight that is $3.9 billion less than that of Cumby and Levich (for 1977–81). Finally, in the fourth column, the previous three estimates are corrected using Gulati's estimates (1987, 73) of net capital flight effected through trade-invoice faking. In Mexico *underinvoicing* of imports exceeded underinvoicing of exports during this period, so that estimated capital flight is reduced. The Gulati adjustment suggests that approximately one-third of the increase in total gross debt may have ended up financing capital flight.[16]

Nearly all of the new debt was contracted by the public sector; the private sector debt tripled during the 1978–81 period but still stood at only $21.9 billion in 1981. Most of the $53 billion of debt held by the public sector took the form of medium- or long-term commercial loans extended to different parastatal firms (PEMEX alone had contracted $15.7 billion of foreign debt by 1981), but the short-term debt also grew rapidly and by the end of 1981 accounted for 20.3 percent of the total public sector debt. Since over half of private sector borrowing was short-term, for the aggregate debt the corresponding figure is a much higher 27.7 percent. By contrast, just three years earlier the share of short-term debt stood at only 13.5 percent.

Despite the large windfall conferred by oil discoveries and the high rates of GDP growth achieved between 1978 and 1981, it seems safe to say that an increase in the foreign debt of this magnitude was excessive. Table 7.6 shows how the standard debt burden measures evolved.[17] The net debt service measures take account of the fact that the private and public sectors hold income earning foreign assets as well as foreign debts. In these figures, the net debt is calculated, crudely, as the cumulative value of past (official) current account deficits starting from 1951.

While all of the debt burden measures decreased sharply after 1980 when oil exports increased by $6.5 billion, it is also evident that the heavy binge of short-term borrowing in the immediately preceding years had placed the country in a financially precarious position. Even in 1981, debt service inclusive of short-term amortization claimed nearly 80 percent of total current account income. If short-term amortization is excluded (which gives a better sense of the medium-run debt service profile), the debt service burden was not particularly onerous in 1980 or 1981 judged by the usual standards. Observe, however, that just one year later and notwithstanding a 13 percent increase in the dollar value of oil exports, a much less sanguine picture emerges. In 1982, debt service exclusive of short-term amortization absorbed 62.2 percent of total current account income and 10.6 percent of GDP.[18] The corresponding figures for net debt service are smaller but still quite large.

When the inevitable reversal in net foreign lending occurred in 1982, the inconsistencies in policy immediately drove the economy into deep stagflation. The strong growth in notional supply that had checked inflationary pressures in previous years was reversed as extremely restrictive quotas and a series of large real devaluations of the peso forced a 36.2 percent reduction in imports of intermediate inputs. Contraction on the supply side coupled with expansionary fiscal policy sent the inflation rate soaring to 99 percent while, for the first time since 1932, real output fell. Despite the reduction in real output and the large currency devaluations, the current account deficit remained huge and capital flight assumed massive proportions. It became increasingly clear that Mexico would not be able to adhere to the existing repayments schedule. On 1 September, 1982 the government reacted by nationalizing the banking system and imposing comprehensive exchange controls. In the last four months of the year, a de facto moratorium on debt service existed; all payments on the private sector debt ceased as did most payments on the principal of the public sector debt.

Table 7.6   Debt Burden Measures

	1976	1977	1978	1979	1980	1981	1982
Total debt ($ billion)	27.9	30.3	35.1	42.4	54.4	81.0	87.6
Total debt/GDP[1]	31.4	37.0	34.2	31.5	29.2	33.8	53.4
Public sector debt service[2]	2.5	3.8	6.3	10.2	7.7	10.3	14.9
($ billion)							
% of merchandise exports	67.7	82.5	103.7	115.4	50.8	52.9	70.0
% of current account income	29.9	41.8	54.0	62.6	30.8	33.4	53.0
% of GDP[1]	2.8	4.7	6.1	7.6	4.1	4.3	9.1
Total debt service[3] ($ billion)	2.9	4.3	6.8	11.0	9.2	13.2	17.4
% of merchandise exports	78.8	91.8	112.7	124.7	60.8	67.9	82.1
% of current account income	34.8	46.5	58.7	67.6	36.9	42.8	62.2
% of GDP[1]	3.2	5.2	6.6	8.2	4.9	5.5	10.6
Total debt service #2[4]	—	10.9	12.5	15.7	15.5	24.3	39.9
($ billion)							
% of merchandise exports	—	235.1	206.2	178.6	102.7	125.0	187.8
% of current account income	—	119.1	107.2	96.8	62.3	78.8	142.4
% of GDP[1]	—	13.4	12.2	11.7	8.3	10.1	24.3
Net debt[5] ($ billion)	19.0	22.7	24.3	27.0	31.9	39.1	51.6
Net debt service[6] ($ billion)	2.3	3.8	6.0	9.6	6.9	8.9	12.4
% of merchandise exports	63.8	81.2	99.7	109.4	45.8	45.6	58.5
% of current account income	28.2	41.1	51.9	59.3	27.8	28.7	44.3
% of GDP[1]	2.6	4.6	5.9	7.2	3.7	3.7	7.6
Net debt service #2[7]	—	10.4	11.7	14.4	13.3	19.9	34.9
($ billion)							
% of merchandise exports	—	224.5	193.2	163.3	87.7	102.7	164.2
% of current account income	—	113.8	100.5	88.5	53.2	64.7	124.5
% of GDP[1]	—	12.7	11.4	10.7	7.1	8.3	21.3

Sources: Mexican Economic Outlook (CIEMEX-WHARTON) for data on the total debt and short-term public and private sector debt. All other data comes from Indicadores Economicos.

[1]Calculated by dividing nominal GNP by the period average controlled exchange rate to get GDP measured in dollars. There is *no* correction for deviations of the actual exchange rate from the equilibrium exchange rate.

[2]Public sector interest payments and amortization of the medium- and long-term debt.

[3]Public sector debt service plus private sector interest payments.

[4]The sum of public and private sector interest payments, public sector amortization of the short-, medium-, and long-term debt, and amortization of the short-term private sector debt. Amortization of the short-term debt is assumed to equal the previous period's short-term debt.

[5]Calculated as the cumulated value of official current account deficits starting from 1951.

[6]Calculated by scaling total interest payments by the public and private sectors by the ratio of net debt to total debt. No attempt is made to adjust for the fact that the interest rate on private sector foreign assets differs from the rates charged for foreign loans to the public and private sectors.

[7]Calculated as the sum of public sector amortization of the short-, medium-, and long-term payments. Net interest payments are total interest payments by the public and private sectors scaled down by the ratio of net debt to total debt. Amortization of the short-term debt is assumed to equal the previous period's short-term debt.

The 1982 debt crisis came, ironically, at the end of a period in which the Mexican economy had been presented an exceptional opportunity to embark upon an era of high and stable growth. During the 1977–82 period, Mexico enjoyed very favorable terms of trade and was blessed by the discovery of enormous oil wealth. The Lopez Portillo administration freely spent these windfalls in a sustained and extraordinary increase in fiscal expenditure. Foreign lending was undoubtedly an important permissive factor, particularly in 1981, and 1982.

The overly rapid accumulation of foreign debt by the Lopez Portillo administration would not have inflicted lasting damage on the economy had the funds been used to finance efficient investment projects. Unfortunately, this did not happen. According to the various estimates discussed earlier, between 38 percent and 53 percent of the debt accumulated during this period financed capital flight. A large portion of the remainder financed higher public sector consumption and investment. It is difficult to believe that the increase in current expenditures did much to enhance the economy's productive capacity, particularly as the share of human capital–related expenditures remained small. And though little hard data exists on the productivity of state-owned enterprises, there is little doubt that many of the public sector investments undertaken in this period were fundamentally unsound and have subsequently yielded very low social returns.

After making due allowance for capital flight, the splurge in government consumption and inefficient investments by the parastatal sector, it is difficult to escape the conclusion that Mexico obtained remarkably little for the $59.7 billion of debt taken out during the Lopez Portillo years. Perhaps the best evidence in support of this conclusion is provided by the extreme hardship the economy has subsequently suffered in servicing the debt.

7.5   The De La Madrid Administration and the Present Crisis

The De La Madrid administration began with a two-year respite from large scale debt service payments. On 10 December 1982, an agreement was reached with the commercial banks to reschedule $23 billion of capital payments on the public sector debt coming due between 23 August 1982 and 31 December 1984.

During the same period in which the restructuring of the external debt was negotiated, a wide-ranging stabilization–with–structural reform program was agreed upon with the IMF. Fiscal discipline was rigidly enforced and the consolidated public sector deficit relative to the GDP was halved from 17.6 percent to 8.9 percent (tables 7.7 and 7.8). Stringent monetary policy accompanied fiscal austerity. The real

Table 7.7   Public Sector Revenues and Expenditures (% of GNP)

	1982	1983	1984	1985	1986ᴾ
Expenditure	46.4	42.8	40.3	40.9	45.7
Current	35.8	35.0	33.4	34.6	40.1
interest on foreign debt	5.1	5.1	3.0	2.6	4.4
other	30.7	29.9	30.4	32.0	35.7
Capital	10.6	7.8	6.9	6.3	5.6
Revenues	30.1	34.3	33.0	32.6	31.0
Economic deficit	16.3	8.5	7.3	8.4	15.2¹
Deficit on financial intermediation²	1.4	0.5	1.4	1.6	1.1
Monetary deficit	17.6	8.9	8.7	10.0	16.3

Sources: Data for 1982–85 are from SHCP. The 1986 figure for capital expenditure is from the Bank of Mexico's Informe Anual. All other data for 1986 are from Indicadores Economicos. Currrent expenditure is calculated residually by subtracting capital expenditures from total expenditure.

ᴾPreliminary figures.

¹There is an inexplicable discrepancy of 474.2 billion pesos between the revenue and expenditure calculation of the deficit and the sources of funds measure of the economic deficit.

²Deficit of La Banca de Desarrollo.

monetary base fell 12.5 percent and real credit extended to the public sector declined 15.5 percent.

In order to meet debt service obligations claiming more than 60 percent of total current account earnings (table 7.9), strict import controls were employed to force a 43 percent reduction in the volume of total imports. The private sector bore the brunt of the adjustment: the ratio of private to public sector imports fell from to 1.67 to .99, exceeding the previous post–World War II low (which occurred in 1981) by some 66 percentage points. Even after adjusting for the unusually high level of imports in 1981, this represents an extraordinary degree of import compression. The huge curtailment in imports in 1983 combined with the 1982 reduction of 39 percent brought the private sector import volume 25 percent below its *1970* level.

The price exacted for improvement in the external accounts and the public sector finances was deepening stagflation (see tables 7.10a and 7.10b). Notwithstanding stiff monetary and fiscal contraction and wage restraint sufficient to produce cuts of 17 percent in the real minimum wage and 21 percent in the overall real manufacturing sector wage, the inflation rate declined only slightly from 98 percent to 81 percent. While inflation remained high, real GDP declined 5.9 percent and aggregate underemployment increased substantially. The greatest decline in economic activity occurred in the manufacturing sector, where output decreased 7.3 percent and employment fell 6 percent.

Table 7.8   **Deficit Breakdown**

	1982	1983	1984	1985	1986P
PEMEX					
Expenditure	7.5	6.2	5.7	5.1	5.4
Current	4.5	4.2	4.0	3.8	4.2
Capital	3.0	2.0	1.6	1.3	1.2
Revenues	15.8	21.5	19.3	18.1	13.0
Deficit	−8.3	−15.3	−13.6	−13.0	−7.6
Non-PEMEX parastatals[1]					
Expenditure	12.5	14.1	13.8	14.4	13.6
Current	9.9	11.2	10.9	11.7	11.0
Capital	2.7	2.9	2.9	2.7	2.6
Revenues	8.1	7.8	8.5	9.1	9.4
Deficit	4.4	6.3	5.3	5.3	4.2
Other[2]					
Expenditure	26.5	22.5	20.8	21.4	26.8
Current	21.5	19.6	18.4	19.1	25.0
Capital	5.0	2.9	2.4	2.3	1.8
Revenues	6.2	5.0	5.2	5.4	8.6
Deficit	20.2	17.5	15.6	16.1	18.2

Sources: 1982 and 1983–86 figures are not fully comparable. For 1982, data are from Estadisticas Hacendarias del Sector Publico: Cifras Anuales 1965–1982 (SHCP). For the parastatal sector, current expenditure is calculated as operating expenditures plus *ajenas de gasto* (outside account expenditure) and total revenue is the sum of current income, capital income, taxes paid, and *ajenas de ingreso* (outside account income). Data for 1983–86 are from Indicadores Economicos. Current expenditure is operating expenditure plus *variacion de cuentas ajenas* (change in outside accounts). Total revenue is income (net of transfers) plus taxes paid.

+Preliminary figures.

[1]Includes expenditures and revenues of DDF (Department of the Federal District) after 1982. In 1982, DDF expenditures and revenues are in "Other."

[2]Does not include DDF expenditures and revenues after 1982. The "out-of-budget" deficit is treated as part of current expenditures.

The second straight year of severe stagflation also brought an enormous contraction in aggregate investment spending (−27.9 percent), jeopardizing the future growth prospects of the economy. Given the high rate of inflation that prevailed throughout 1983, it is improbable that demand contraction induced the collapse in private sector investment spending. Rather, the main explanatory factors appear to lie elsewhere. Financial disintermediation and the abrupt cutoff in foreign lending led to a sharp reduction in bank credit: Total real lending to the private sector dropped to 66 percent of its 1981 level.[19] Large upward jumps in the real prices for capital goods and complementary inputs sharply diminished profit margins, reinforcing the contractionary effect of the credit squeeze. The real price of imports rose approximately 29 percent while the real domestic price of energy inputs

Table 7.9   Debt Burden Measures

	1983	1984	1985	1986
Total debt ($ billion)	93.8	96.6	97.3	98.3
Total debt/GDP[1]	65.8	56.4	55.1	77.3
Public sector debt service[2] ($ billion)	12.3	11.7	11.1	9.6
% of merchandise exports	55.0	48.3	51.3	59.7
% of current account income	42.4	35.5	36.1	39.5
% of GDP[1]	8.6	6.8	6.3	7.5
Total debt service[3] ($ billion)	14.6	14.1	13.0	11.1
% of merchandise exports	65.4	58.1	60.1	69.5
% of current account income	50.4	42.8	42.3	45.9
% of GDP[1]	10.2	8.2	7.4	8.8
Total debt service #2[4] ($ billion)	30.5	27.9	17.5	15.0
% of merchandise exports	136.8	115.5	80.8	93.4
% of current account income	105.5	84.9	56.9	61.7
% of GDP[1]	21.4	16.3	9.9	11.8
Net debt[5] ($ billion)	57.9	52.4	48.2	47.0
Net debt service[6] ($ billion)	10.7	8.7	7.9	6.8
% of merchandise exports	48.0	36.0	36.4	42.3
% of current account income	37.0	26.5	25.6	28.0
% of GDP[1]	7.5	5.1	4.5	5.3
Net debt service #2[7] ($ billion)	26.7	22.6	12.4	10.6
% of merchandise exports	119.5	93.4	57.1	66.2
% of current account income	92.1	68.7	40.2	43.8
% of GDP[1]	18.7	13.2	7.0	8.3

Sources: Mexican Economic Outlook for data on the total debt and short-term public and private sector debt. All other data comes from Indicadores Economicos.

[1]Calculated by dividing nominal GNP by the period average controlled exchange rate to get GNP measured in dollars. There is *no* correction for deviations of the actual exchange rate from the equilibrium exchange rate.

[2]Public sector interest payments and amortization of the medium- and long-term debt.

[3]Public sector debt service plus private sector interest payments.

[4]The sum of public and private sector interest payments, public sector amortization of the short-, medium-, and long-term debt, and amortization of the short-term private sector debt. Amortization of the short-term debt is assumed to equal the previous period's short-term debt.

[5]Calculated as the cumulated value of official current account deficits starting from 1951.

[6]Calculated by scaling total interest payments by the public and private sectors by the ratio of net debt to total debt. No attempt is made to adjust for the fact that the interest rate on private sector foreign assets differs from the rates charged for foreign loans to the public and private sectors.

[7]Calculated as the sum of public sector amortization of the short-, medium-, and long-term debt, amortization of the short-term private sector debt, and net interest payments. Net interest payments are total interest payments by the public and private sectors scaled down by the ratio of net debt to total debt. Amortization of the short-term debt is assumed to equal the previous period's short-term debt.

Table 7.10a   Macroeconomic Aggregates (% change)[1]

	1982	1983	1984	1985	1986P
Real GDP	−0.5	−5.3	3.7	2.8	−3.8
Manufacturing	−2.9	−7.3	4.8	5.8	−5.6
Agriculture and fisheries	−0.6	2.8	2.5	3.8	−2.1
Inflation[2]	98.9	80.8	59.2	63.7	105.7
Manufacturing employment[3]	−8.5	−6.0	2.3	0.2	−6.7
Real investment	−15.9	−27.9	5.5	6.4	−12.2
Private	−17.3	−24.2	9.0	13.4	−9.8
Public	−14.2	−32.5	0.6	−4.4	−16.5

Table 7.10b   Composition of Output (% of GDP[4])

	1982	1983	1984	1985	1986
Private consumption	69.0	67.3	66.6	66.1	66.2
Government consumption	9.3	9.7	10.0	9.9	10.1
Gross fixed capital formation	21.0	16.1	16.3	16.9	15.4
Private	11.7	9.4	9.9	10.9	10.2
Public	9.3	6.6	6.4	6.0	5.2
Change in inventories	0.5	1.0	1.4	2.7	2.2
Exports	10.2	12.1	12.9	12.2	13.0
Imports	10.1	6.2	7.2	7.7	6.9

Sources: The manufacturing sector employment series is from Indicadores Economicos. All other data is from the National Income Accounts of INEGI.
PPreliminary figures.
[1]Real variables are measured at 1970 prices.
[2]December to December change in the CPI.
[3]December to December change.
[4]Output shares at 1970 prices.

increased 52 percent. The high real import prices led to huge reductions of 62.2 percent and 31 percent, respectively, in the volumes of imported capital goods and intermediate inputs.

In 1984 and the first part of 1985, a number of reflationary demand- and supply-side measures produced a modest recovery (from deep recession to mild recession). Real public sector investment declined another 10.4 percent in 1984, but real current expenditures net of interest payments on the foreign debt rose 5.1 percent and fiscal incentives were introduced to encourage private investment spending. Most important, the favorable payments balance recorded in 1983 allowed import controls to be greatly relaxed: Real private sector imports of intermediate inputs and capital goods rose 48.2 percent in 1984 and 35.4 percent in 1985.[20]

Disquietingly, the modest recovery was not accompanied by progress in lowering the fiscal deficit. The overall deficit declined from 8.9 percent to 8.7 percent of GDP in 1984 and then jumped up to 10 percent in 1985 as revenues fell short of, and expenditures far exceeded, their targeted values.[21] Declining oil prices lowered PEMEX's surplus, but other factors contributed as well to the growth in the deficit. While higher public sector prices raised income of the non-PEMEX parastatals, the deficit on financial intermediation worsened considerably and general tax revenues continued to stagnate (see table 7.11). Clearly, despite avowals to the contrary, no substantive effort has been made to enlarge the overall tax base. Remarkably, the share of income taxes was allowed to decline 1.6 percentage points over the 1981–85 period, pulling down the general tax take by an almost equal amount. Only part of this decline can be attributed to the depressed level of corporate profits; since 1982, the lower yield from personal income taxes accounts for nearly all of the reduction in the income tax share.

The impact of the mounting fiscal deficit was felt most strongly in financial markets. To lessen inflationary pressures, strict control over the growth rate of the monetary base was maintained. Consequently, a large part of the deficit had to be financed by the sale of government bonds (CETES) to the banking system and the public. In early 1985 the decision was made to place 250 billion pesos of CETES with Banca Multiple. After October, lending to the private sector was frozen and virtually all excess bank funds were diverted to purchases of various government issued assets (CETES, petrobonds, etc.).[22]

Table 7.11   Public Sector Prices and Revenues[1]

	1981	1982	1983	1984	1985	1986
Real public sector prices[2]	100	108.5	131.3	139.1	133.1	—
Revenues of non-PEMEX parastatals[3]	7.9	8.1	7.8	8.5	9.1	9.4
General tax revenues	10.8	9.0	9.0	9.0	9.3	9.4
Income taxes	5.8	4.9	4.2	4.2	4.2	4.3
Personal	2.6	2.6	2.0	1.9	2.0	2.0
Indirect taxes[4]	5.0	4.1	4.8	4.8	5.0	5.1
Foreign trade	1.1	0.90	0.50	0.50	0.67	0.87

Source: Indicadores Economicos.
[1]Revenues are expressed as a percentage of GDP.
[2]Period average price deflated by the period average CPI.
[3]Sum of revenues (exclusive of any transfers received) plus taxes paid.
[4]Sum of value added taxes, taxes on production and services, taxes on foreign trade, and "other" taxes. Does *not* include gasoline taxes (which we classify as revenues of PEMEX).

Financing the deficit in this fashion led to generally rising interest rates and a strong contraction in lending to the private sector. Whereas the inflation rate (December to December) rose slightly from 59.2 to 63.7 percent, the average cost of bank funds increased each month, rising from 47.5 percent in December 1984 to 65.7 percent in December 1985. During the same period the yield on three-month CETES jumped from 49.2 percent to 74.1 percent. The increased interest rate spread between CETES and bank funds provoked a new wave of financial disintermediation, reversing the gains made in 1984. While real credit to the public sector increased 12.6 percent in 1985, the real stock of bank funds fell 12.9 percent and (real) credit to the private sector contracted slightly.

The severe credit squeeze imposed on the private sector, falling oil prices, and the catastropic earthquake in September pushed the economy back into recession. In the second half of 1985, real GDP growth turned negative as private investment spending and manufacturing sector output contracted sharply. Overall GDP growth for the year amounted to just 2.7 percent.

At the start of 1986, the economy was sent reeling by the collapse in world market oil prices. By July, Mexican crude was fetching only $8.45 per barrel. Prices recovered somewhat thereafter, but the average price for the year still came to only $11.45, 53 percent below the 1985 average ($25.35).[23] The dollar value of oil exports declined $8.5 billion, a loss equivalent to 6.7 percent of the 1985 GDP.[24] Following previous declines, this brought the country's terms of trade to its lowest level in more than thirty years (see table 7.12). Adjusted for changes in world market interest rates, Mexico's terms of trade in 1986 stood 43.4 percent below their level in 1970 at the end of the era of Stabilizing Development. Between 1981 and 1986, the terms of trade deteriorated nearly 60 percent.

The De La Madrid administration responded to the oil price shock by digging its heels in deeper. Essentially, the pre-shock policy course was continued but with an extra measure of austerity. To blunt the impact on the trade balance, the rate of depreciation of the peso was accelerated strongly in 1986, producing, by the year's end, a 35 percent increase in the real exchange rate. Aggressive devaluation has been supplemented by limited fiscal adjustment and extremely contractionary monetary policy. Some new expenditure cuts and tax increases were introduced, but these measures fell far short of neutralizing the impact of the oil price drop, and the overall public sector deficit soared to 16.3 percent of GNP in 1986.

As in previous years, the fiscal deficit was financed largely by depriving the private sector of credit. The real monetary base fell 11.7

Table 7.12   Terms of Trade Indices

	Unadjusted	Adjusted for Changes in International Interest Rates
1960	87.8	87.2
1961	89.6	88.3
1962	83.9	82.0
1963	89.1	87.3
1964	85.7	84.8
1965	84.1	83.5
1966	85.2	85.1
1967	83.9	84.1
1968	89.0	90.4
1969	88.0	92.2
1970	96.7	100.0
1971	100.0	100.0
1972	103.3	100.7
1973	115.2	121.2
1974	100.1	116.4
1975	97.8	96.1
1976	113.0	119.2
1977	113.0	121.9
1978	104.1	115.6
1979	113.1	110.4
1980	127.6	123.5
1981	124.3	127.4
1982	108.2	94.5
1983	98.8	77.4
1984	97.1	66.5
1985	91.9	71.5
1986	65.6	54.6

Source: Informe Anual 1986.

percent while the stock of real government debt (issued by the federal government) held by the public rose 23 percent.[25] Even though nearly all marginal bank credit (77–92 percent) remained reserved for the public sector, the large increase in bond supply could not be absorbed without inducing a strong rise in real interest rates. The real (compounded, annual equivalent) interest rate paid by three-month CETES averaged 19.54 percent in 1986. Bank rates followed suit. The average cost of real bank funds was 6.3 percent and the real nonpreferential loan rate fluctuated between 13 percent and 18.2 percent.

Renewed austerity coming on top of the terms-of-trade loss brought the weak 1984–85 recovery to a grinding halt: Real output declined 3.8 percent, real investment 12.7 percent and manufacturing sector employment 6.7 percent at the same time as the inflation rate jumped from 63.2 percent to 105.7 percent. Despite the introduction of quarterly wage adjustments, the real (minimum) wage fell (8.4 percent) for the fifth consecutive year.

7.6 Post-1982 Economic Policy: An Evaluation

Judged against almost any set of economic criteria, the post-1982 adjustment record has been a dismal failure. At the end of 1986, real output stood slightly below its 1982 level and the inflation rate had accelerated to over 100 percent. In per capita terms, real income fell 11 percent during this four-year period, with labor bearing the brunt of the decline: Since 1982, real wages have decreased approximately 30 percent, falling far below (32 percent for the real minimum wage) the levels that prevailed at the end of the Stabilizing Development era (see table 7.13). Nor do the prospects for recovery look particularly promising. Both private and public sector investment remain heavily depressed, and while large current account surpluses were achieved in 1983 and 1984, by early 1986 balance-of-payments problems had emerged once again.

Adverse external shocks and the burden of servicing the debt made some deterioration in the economy's performance inevitable. Over the 1983–86 period, Mexico's terms of trade (adjusted for changes in world market interest rates) declined 42.2 percent, the most severe blow coming in 1986 with the collapse of world market oil prices. The worsening terms of trade coupled with debt service claiming 40–50 percent of total current account income have forced an extraordinary degree of import compression upon the private sector. Contrary to textbook models, import compression is almost certain to be strongly stagflationary. The reason for this is simply that in Mexico, as in most LDCs, intermediate inputs and capital goods account for over 90 percent of total imports. On the normal assumption that factors of production are gross complements, a reduction in imports, whether imposed directly by import controls or induced by a real devaluation, exerts a powerful contractionary effect upon economic activity. Cutbacks in imported intermediates lower labor demand at a given real wage and discourage investment by reducing the productivity of capital. Restrictions on capital goods imports further depress investment by raising the supply price of capital. As most imported machinery lacks close domestic substitutes, there is little, if any, demand stimulus created by expenditure switching; instead, the construction sector goes into a slump as investment orders fall off sharply.

Table 7.14 shows how the private sector import volume has evolved since 1970. Clearly import compression has gone far beyond simply offsetting the rapid growth of the oil boom years. Between 1981 and 1983, real private sector imports were cut 73 percent; even after two

Table 7.13   Real Wages (1970 = 100)[1]

	Average Minimum Wage[2]	Manufacturing Sector Overall[3]	Manufacturing Sector Blue Collar
1964	76.4	—	—
1965	74.8	—	—
1966	85.7	—	—
1967	83.3	—	—
1968	94.7	—	97.9
1969	91.0	—	99.5
1970	100.0	100.0	100.0
1971	95.0	101.2	100.7
1972	107.6	106.7	106.6
1973	101.1	104.3	103.9
1974	110.8	104.5	106.6
1975	112.1	107.8	110.8
1976	124.7	116.7	123.2
1977	123.9	118.5	125.3
1978	119.7	116.2	121.9
1979	117.2	114.5	119.9
1980	109.0	111.2	114.8
1981	110.8	115.1	116.1
1982	97.9	114.1	116.9
1983	81.4	90.3	87.0
1984	75.9	84.0	83.5
1985	74.9	85.2	—
1986	68.6	—	—

Sources: Minimum wage data are from INEGI. The blue-collar and overall wage series for the manufacturing sector are from the Bank of Mexico's Encuesta Industrial Mensual as reported in Indices de Precios (February 1986, pp. 86–87).
[1]Period average wage index deflated by the period average CPI.
[2]The minimum wage index is a weighted average of minimum wages in different regions, where the weights are given by the region's share in the total salaried population of the nation. In years in which there was more than one wage adjustment, the period average figure is generated by weighting the wage in each subperiod by the fraction of the year over which it prevailed.
[3]Composite index for manufacturing sector wages and salaries inclusive of fringe benefits.

years of "recovery," the import volume in 1985 barely exceeded its 1978 level.

But while the terms-of-trade shock and the burden of debt service made some contraction inevitable, errant policy must also shoulder a good portion of the blame for the post-1982 debacle. The excessive use of quantitative restrictions and massive real devaluations to regulate the current account has caused import compression to be deeper and more prolonged than necessary. In view of the complementary nature of domestic factors and imports, a policy directed far more toward promoting manufacturing and agricultural exports would have minimized the impact of debt service on import flows.

Table 7.14   Private Sector Import Volume[1] (1970 = 100)

1970	100.0	1979	184.6
1971	98.3	1980	236.0
1972	104.0	1981	275.7
1973	114.4	1982	166.7
1974	133.9	1983	74.8
1975	125.5	1984	105.1
1976	112.8	1985	143.2
1977	103.1	1986[2]	133.3
1978	131.7		

Sources: Indicadores Economicos for dollar import values and the National Income Accounts for the aggregate import volume.

[1]Estimated as the aggregate import volume multiplied by the ratio of the dollar value of private sector merchandise imports to total merchandise imports.

[2]The 1986 import volume is estimated by deflating the dollar value of total merchandise imports by the dollar price index for imports and then splicing to the National Income Accounts index for the aggregate import volume.

Fiscal and interest rate policy have intensified the contractionary blow delivered against the private sector by import compression. The De La Madrid administration did not offset higher debt service payments and lower oil prices with adequate fiscal adjustment for many years. Instead, limited tax increases and cuts in current expenditures were supplemented by a variety of other policies aimed at restraining the inflationary pressures created by the large fiscal deficits.

Notes

1. This figure comes from the Bank of Mexico's survey of large firms in the manufacturing sector.
2. Tello (1979, chap. 1), Reynolds (1970), Solis (1981, 7–8), Clavijo and Valdivieso (1983), Rizzo (1984, 101, 122), Aspe and Sigmund (1984), Newell and Rubio (1984).
3. See, for example, Tello (1979, chap. 1), Solis (1981), Villareal (1983, 382, 386) and Aspe and Beristain (1984, 23).
4. See Camancho (1977) or Solis (1981).
5. Bueno (1972), Camancho (1977), Tello (1979, chap. 1), Looney (1985, chap. 2), Villareal (1983).
6. The original 1960 census was marred by gross processing errors and the corrected version still appears to greatly overenumerate the size of the agricultural labor force. Classification schemes also differ between the two censuses and in the 1970 census a large number of labor force participants were not assigned to any category.
7. Unikel (1978) estimates that the average annual growth rate of industrial sector employment during the 1960s was 3 percent while labor force growth averaged 1.4 percent. Altimir (1974), on the other hand, estimates that industrial sector employment grew at an annual average rate of 5.2 percent.

8. Gregory (1986, 232, 238–39).

9. van Ginneken classified families with incomes below 10,000 pesos in 1970 prices (close to the 1970 minimum wage) as living in poverty.

10. See World Bank (1979, 28–33) and Solis (1981).

11. Serial correlation was tested for using the limits for the Durbin-Watson statistic developed by Fairbrother for regression equations without a constant term. In those cases where the Durbin-Watson value fell in the indeterminant range, Bartlett's test was then applied as a second check for serial correlation. In none of the regressions was there evidence of first-order serial correlation.

12. Expenditures to cover revenue shortfalls in four broad areas account for the bulk of these transfers: (1) the DIF, an institute for aiding the homeless and poor children (headed by Lopez Portillo's wife); (2) the National University; (3) unregistered subsidiaries of CONASUPO; and (4) *chiquilleria* (small stuff), a category comprised mostly of companies in which the government has a minority interest, educational institutions other than the National University, and local development centers.

For reasons we do not fully understand, Jorge Hierro was kind enough to take the better part of one month out of his life (shortly before getting married) to unravel this mystery. We are greatedly indebted to him.

13. Rizzo (1984, 122) has calculated the cost of the gross subsidy. The figure in the text is obtained by multiplying Rizzo's figure by the share of private sector investment and consumption in GDP, where the latter is taken to be a rough approximation of the private sector share in total energy consumption.

14. The debt data here and in subsequent sections is taken from *Mexican Economic Outlook,* (CIEMEX-WHARTON), various issues. Data on the short-term debt is of poor quality.

15. All of the estimates in table 7.5 employ the Morgan Guaranty definition of capital flight. Cuddington (1986) has pointed out that the Morgan Guaranty definition of capital flight treats "normal" capital flows (foreign assets acquired for purposes of ordinary business activity, for portfolio diversification, etc.) as capital flight. Given that our interest is in how the net foreign debt evolved, this is the appropriate definition of capital flight. For estimates that attempt to distinguish between flight capital (or speculative capital flows) and normal capital flows, and for a discussion of the conceptual difficulties this entails, see Cuddington (1986) and Cumby and Levich (1987).

The data bases differ in several other ways besides those discussed in the text. For reasons that are not clear, the IMF data used by Cumby and Levich on the current account deficit and the change in reserves differ a great deal from the Bank of Mexico data as reported in Indicadores Economicos.

16. The extent to which capital flight estimates should be adjusted for discrepancies between home and partner country trade data is open to dispute. Partner and home country data may differ for reasons other than illegal trade. (See Cumby and Levich 1987 on this point.)

17. The figures for the ratios of debt and debt service to GNP do not contain a correction for departures of the real exchange rate from its long-run equilibrium value. As the peso was heavily overvalued between 1979 and 1981, the figures for these years are undoubtedly underestimates of the true values.

18. These are the figures for debt service implied by adherence to the existing repayments schedule. In the last four months of 1982, Mexico suspended all payments on the private sector debt and most payments on principal of the public sector debt. The suspension of debt service appears in the Mexican balance-of-payments accounts with a positive sign under the category *ingreso*

virtual (virtual income) and a matching negative sign under the category *egreso virtual* (virtual expenditures).

19. Total credit to the private sector is the sum of credit extended by the Central Bank (which is negligible), the development banks and commercial banks.

20. These real import figures are calculated by deflating dollar import aggregates by the dollar price index for total imports found in the Bank of Mexico's Informe Anual 1985 (201).

21. To a substantial extent, the large fiscal deficits since 1982 reflect an inflated level of current expenditures associated with the inflationary component of interest payments on the internal debt. We are skeptical, however, of the argument that a small value for the inflation-adjusted deficit indicates that inflation is purely inertial and that no further fiscal adjustment is necessary. Furthermore, the true size of the inflation-adjusted deficit in Mexico is still very much an unsettled question. There is some doubt about the accuracy of the figures reported by SHCP. It seems, for example, that double counting is a problem. Apparently, foreign loans contracted by NAFINSA (the principal development bank) and relent in pesos are counted twice, as part of the external and internal debt of the public sector. (See Perez 1986, 17.)

22. Loans for low-income housing, agricultural development, and export promotion were exempted from the credit squeeze.

23. Informe Anual 1986.

24. Ibid.

25. Published figures overstate the true decrease in the real monetary base in 1985. Much of the decrease reflected on administrative sleight of hand. In January, 1985 the legal reserve ratio was lowered from 48 percent to 10 percent. (For commercial banks, the 10 percent rate applied to deposits exceeding the December 1984 level while for La Banca de Desarrollo it applied to deposit balances above the highest balance registered in 1984.) At the same time, however, all banks were required to use 35 percent of their deposits to purchase federal government debt instruments and the commercial banks were also required to place 3 percent of their funds at the disposal of La Banca de Desarrollo (Informe Anual 1985, 119–20). In effect, a large part of bank reserves were simply reclassified as government debt. The figure stated in the text is calculated on the assumption that the ratio of bank reserves to M4 in 1986 was the same as in 1984.

References

Altimir, O. 1974. La medicion de la poblacion economicamente activa de Mexico. *Demografia y Economia* 8:50–83.

Aspe, P., and J. Beristain. 1984. The evolution of income distribution policies during the post-revolutionary period in Mexico. In *The political economy of income distribution in Mexico,* ed. P. Aspe and P. Sigmund. New York: Holmes and Meir Publishers.

Aspe, P., and P. Sigmund. 1984. Introduction. In *The political economy of income distribution in Mexico,* ed. P. Aspe and P. Sigmund. New York: Holmes and Meir Publishers.

168   Edward F. Buffie/Allen Sangines Krause

Bueno, G. 1971. The structure of protection in Mexico. In *The structure of protection in developing countries,* ed. B. Balassa. Baltimore: The Johns Hopkins University Press.

Camancho, M. 1977. Los nudos historicos del sistema political mexicano. In *Las crises en el sistema politico Mexicano,* ed. L. Meyer et al. Mexico, D.F.: El Colegio de Mexico.

Clavijo, F., and S. Valdivieso. 1983. La creacion de empleos mediante el comercio exterior: el caso de Mexico. *El Trimestre Economico* 50:873–916.

Cuddington, J. 1986. Capital flight: estimates, issues and explanations. *Princeton Studies in International Finance* no. 58. Princeton, N.J.: International Finance Section, Department of Economics, Princeton University.

Cumby, R., and R. Levich. 1987. On the definition and magnitude of recent capital flight. In *Capital flight and Third World debt,* ed. D. R. Lessard and J. Williamson. Washington, D.C.: Institute for International Economics.

Gregory, P. 1986. *The myth of market failure: Employment and the labor market in Mexico.* Baltimore: Johns Hopkins University Press.

Gulati, S. 1987. A note on trade misinvoicing. In *Capital flight and Third World debt,* ed. D. R. Lessard and J. Williamson. Washington, D.C.: Institute for International Economics.

Looney, R. 1985. *Economic policymaking in Mexico: Factors underlying the 1982 crisis.* Durham: Duke University Press.

Newell, R., and L. Rubio. 1984. *Mexico's dilemma: The political origins of economic crisis.* Boulder and London: Westview Press.

Perez, J. 1986. El deficit operacional. In *Diagnostico Economico* (CIEMEX-WHARTON) 1:11–25.

Reynolds, C. 1970. *The Mexican economy: Twentieth-century structure and growth.* New Haven: Yale University Press.

Rizzo, S. 1984. Generation and allocation of oil economic surpluses. In *The political economy of income distribution in Mexico,* ed. P. Aspe and P. Sigmund. New York: Holmes and Meir Publishers.

Solis, L. 1981. *Economic policy reform in Mexico: A case study for developing countries.* New York: Pergamon Press.

Tello, C. 1979. *La politica economica en Mexico: 1970–1976.* Mexico, D.F.: Siglo Veintiuno Editores, sa de cv.

Unikel, L. 1978. *El desarrollo urbano de Mexico.* Mexico, D.F.: El Colegio de Mexico.

van Ginneken, W. 1980. *Socioeconomic groups and income distribution in Mexico.* London: International Labour Organization.

Villareal, S. 1983. Perspectivas de la economia mexicana. *El Trimestre Economico* 50: 377–401.

World Bank. 1979. Special study of the Mexican economy: Major policy issues and prospects. World Bank Report no. 2307-ME.

Zedillo, E. 1987. Mexico. In *Capital flight and Third World debt,* ed. D. R. Lessard and J. Williamson. Washington, D.C.: Institute for International Economics.

8　Debt Crisis and Adjustment in the Philippines

Robert S. Dohner and Ponciano Intal, Jr.

8.1　Introduction

The last four years have been the most tumultuous period in the postwar history of the Philippines. In August 1983, Benigno Aquino, a popular opposition figure, was assassinated on his return from exile in the United States. That October, the Philippines declared the first of what was to be a series of 90-day moratoriums on principal repayments on its external debt. The rescheduling negotiations were difficult, and it was not until May 1985 that an agreement was signed with the country's private creditors.

In the interim the Philippines carried out a stringent IMF adjustment program which eliminated the current account deficit and restored the rate of inflation to near zero. But the output cost was substantial; between 1983 and 1986 real per capita income fell by 18 percent. In some sections of the country, particularly the sugar growing area of Negros, there was widespread malnutrition. The growing economic plight, along with rising middle class and business opposition to the government, contributed to the February 1986 overthrow of Ferdinand Marcos, a ruler who had been entrenched in the Philippines for 20 years.

Robert S. Dohner is an associate professor of international economics at the Fletcher School of Law and Diplomacy, Tufts University. Ponciano Intal, Jr. is an assistant professor and chairman, Department of Economics, University of the Philippines at Los Banos.

The opinions expressed in this chapter are those of the authors, and not necessarily those of the National Bureau of Economic Research or any other sponsoring institution. Financial support from the United States Agency for International Development is gratefully acknowledged.

The fledgling democracy led by Corazon Aquino, the wife of the slain opposition leader, started with much goodwill, but severe economic problems, including a debt service burden amounting to almost half of exports. The Philippines, the sole Asian country to declare a moratorium, is often overlooked in discussions of the current less developed country (LDC) debt crisis. Also overlooked is the fact that the country was once widely viewed as one of the successor generation of East Asian tigers. What is remarkable in retrospect is not the debt buildup that took place, nor the fact that the Philippines had to reschedule. Rather it is that what appeared to be rapid economic growth and structural transformation could unravel so quickly during the 1980s, even before the Aquino assassination, the cutoff of external funding, and the adjustment program. Although foreign borrowing pumped the economy up, it failed to establish self-sustaining growth. At the same time, the excesses of the Marcos government weakened the private business sector, leaving the country vulnerable to the shocks of the 1980s.

8.2 Debt Buildup

Ironically, the Philippines began the 1970s with debt rescheduling and an IMF-sponsored stabilization program, the product of fiscal expansion and short-term borrowing during Marcos's first administration. The early 1970s was a period of economic recovery, aided by rising world commodity prices. But the political environment deteriorated at the same time, with increasing protests, kidnappings, and other violence. To restore order, and to prolong his own hold on office beyond the constitutional limit, Marcos declared martial law in September 1972.

Although security threats, some real and some faked, provided the rationale for declaring martial law, the justification for maintaining it quickly became the promise of higher economic growth and greater equality. Marcos initiated a series of reforms, including land reform, and launched a greatly expanded public development investment program. Between 1972 and 1976 public-sector fixed investment rose from 2 percent of GNP to 6.5 percent of GNP. Private investment also grew in this period, as total gross domestic capital formation rose from 22 to 31 percent of GNP (see table 8.1).

Although the oil price shock of 1974 and the subsequent fall in world commodity prices hit the Philippines severely, policymakers maintained their investment strategy. There was ready external financing. The United States supported the Marcos government, and aid flows increased sharply after martial law. The country also began to tap multilateral lending sources, and funds were available from commercial banks. For the remainder of the decade the Philippines maintained a domestic growth rate of 6.5 percent per year, and a current account deficit of about 5 percent of GNP.

Table 8.1   Philippine Macroeconomic Indicators (percentage of GNP)

	1972	1973	1974	1975	1976	1977	1978	1979	1980	1981	1982	1983	1984	1985	1986
Real GNP (% change)	5.4	9.3	5.6	5.8	7.4	6.3	5.8	6.9	5.0	3.4	1.9	1.1	-6.8	-3.8	1.5
Investment share GNP	21.6	21.9	26.7	30.6	31.3	29.0	29.1	31.0	30.7	30.7	28.8	27.5	19.2	16.3	14.0
government fixed investment	2.1	2.3	3.4	4.3	6.6	6.9	7.2	7.3	6.9	8.0	7.2	6.1	4.1	3.7	n.a.
National Government budget															
Expenditure	14.4	14.3	11.7	16.0	15.2	14.9	14.8	13.7	14.4	15.8	15.7	14.0	12.7	13.5	17.8
Revenue	12.5	13.2	12.2	14.7	13.5	13.0	13.6	13.5	13.1	11.8	11.4	12.0	10.8	11.6	13.1
Surplus/(deficit)	-2.0	-1.2	0.5	-1.2	-1.8	-1.9	-1.2	-0.2	-1.3	-4.0	-4.3	-2.0	-1.9	-1.9	-4.7
Current account balance	0.1	5.0	-1.2	-5.6	-5.8	-3.6	-4.6	-5.1	-5.4	-5.4	-8.1	-8.1	-3.5	-0.2	3.3
M1 (% change)	24.9	12.3	24.0	14.5	17.1	23.7	13.4	11.2	19.6	4.4	-0.1	38.3	3.5	6.5	19.2
Inflation rate (CPI)	16.6	16.5	34.2	6.8	9.2	9.9	7.3	16.5	17.6	12.4	10.4	10.0	50.3	24.9	0.7

n.a. = not available.

With the rise in the current account deficit the country's foreign debt grew rapidly, nearly tripling between 1974 and 1978 (table 8.2). The public sector did most of the borrowing, and held over 70 percent of the foreign debt of the nonbanking sector by the end of the decade. The Philippines borrowed increasingly from banks, and in the form of loans with floating interest rates. But this was true of all LDC borrowers during the 1970s, and the shifts towards commercial terms and floating rates were less pronounced in the Philippines than in most borrowers. The country's policymakers managed the debt carefully during the 1970s, lengthening maturities, and refinancing when better terms were available. As a result, the debt service ratio (interest and amortization payments as a percentage of exports) increased only slightly, reaching 21 percent by 1980.

In a shift of policy from that of previous postwar governments, the Marcos administration actively encouraged foreign direct investment. But even though direct investment inflows increased sharply after 1972, they played a minor role in total external finance, averaging only 8.6 percent of external borrowing during the 1970s.

In the other direction, capital outflow by Philippine residents, or capital flight, has long been a feature of the economy. A comparison of the total inflow of funds with the financing needs for the current account deficit and reserve accumulation indicates an outflow of about $3.6 billion from 1971 to 1980, or roughly one-third of the increase in total external indebtedness.[1] Capital flight in the Philippines was not nearly so large as in Argentina or Mexico, but was much larger than in Korea or Brazil. Thus foreign direct investment did not add appreciably to the inflow of capital, while capital flight was a substantial drain.

Still, at the end of the 1970s the Philippines was hardly a problem debtor. The country had significantly increased its external indebtedness, but had also raised its export and GNP growth rates. At the end of 1979, the Philippines had a debt/GNP ratio comparable to that of Korea. Its debt service ratio was higher, but was well below that of most Latin American borrowers.

The Philippine economic situation deteriorated rapidly after the second oil price shock in 1980. The government tried to counter the growing domestic recession by raising expenditure, and announced an ambitious program of energy and industrial investment. As a result, the public sector deficit rose sharply, from 2 percent of GNP to 5.5 percent, and the current account deficit widened to 8 percent of GNP (table 8.1, and table 8.5 below).

In contrast to neighboring countries, and to its own experience after the first oil shock, the Philippine economy did not recover under the impetus of increased investment spending. Growth rates dropped each year after 1979 (table 8.1, and table 8.10 below). The dollar value of

Table 8.2   Philippine External Debt (millions of US $)

	1970	1974	1978	1980	1982	1983	1984	1985	1986
Total external debt	2,297	3,755	10,694	17,252	24,677	24,816	25,418	26,252	28,186
Nonmonetary debt	2,088	2,726	8,189	12,318	17,601	19,468	20,211	21,270	25,598
Medium- and long-term	1,779	2,395	6,932	9,770	13,141	15,412	15,926	17,679	22,808
Short-term	309	331	1,257	2,548	4,460	4,056	4,285	3,591	2,790
Monetary sector debt	159	1,029	2,505	4,934	7,076	5,348	5,207	4,982	2,588
Memorandum items									
Debt/GNP (percent)	33.2	25.5	44.5	49.0	62.8	72.7	80.6	82.2	95.2
Debt/exports goods, services	174	106	218	215	308	305	317	332	32.8
Debt service ratio total external debt[a]	29.2	14.6	20.1	20.8	38.1	38.2	43.5	33[b]	33[b]
Short-term as % of total external debt	22.6	36.2	35.2	43.4	46.7	37.9	37.3	32.7	19.1

Sources: Philippine Central Bank, Management of External Debt and Investment Accounts Department (MEDIAD), and Central Bank, Financial Plan Data Center. Unpublished data.

[a]Total interest payments plus amortization of medium- and long-term debt as percentage of exports of goods and services.

[b]After rescheduling.

Philippine exports hit a peak in 1980, and then fell at an average rate of almost 5 percent per year through 1983, the result not only of weak international prices, but also falling commodity export volumes.[2] Slower domestic growth and higher world real interest rates severely affected major domestic firms, many of them highly leveraged. A domestic financial crisis in 1981 brought about the failure of several large firms, many of which were bailed out by the government. Industrial failures continued to proliferate, leaving the Philippine government, and particularly the two major state banks, with nonperforming assets with a book value in the billions of dollars.

Philippine external borrowing accelerated in the early 1980s, and total foreign debt nearly doubled between 1979 and 1982. Borrowing increased under the pressure of a swollen current account deficit, but capital flight also accelerated sharply in the early 1980s, averaging 4.8 percent of GNP in 1981 and 1982. Net foreign direct investment inflows slowed to a trickle, as growing disinvestment offset direct investment inflows.

The cautious borrowing policy of the 1970s disappeared in the early 1980s. The most abrupt change was the increasing use of short-term borrowing. This was particularly true of the public sector, which accounted for two-thirds of the increase in short-term debt outside the monetary sector.[3] Much of the increased borrowing was also done through the monetary sector. The Central Bank borrowed heavily between 1980 and 1982, and encouraged banks to do so by providing swap arrangements.[4] Despite its borrowing, Central Bank reserves fell by $2 billion (two-thirds) from the end of 1980 to mid-1983.[5] As a result, the monetary sector went from a net external asset position at the end of 1979, to a $2.7 billion net liability position by 1982. By 1982 the share of short-term debt, including monetary sector debt, in total debt rose to 47 percent, a much higher share than in other LDC debtors. The Philippines first considered declaring a moratorium in late 1982. When it finally did so in October 1983, its foreign exchange reserves were nearly exhausted.

8.3 The Role of External Shocks

The Philippines's real income position, and its ability to sustain its level of foreign indebtedness, were diminished by the two oil price shocks and the accompanying industrial country recessions. The commodity price increases of 1973 and 1974 temporarily raised Philippine incomes, but between 1972 and 1976 the terms of trade fell by 22 percent, equivalent to an income loss of 4.3 percent of GNP.[6]

The second oil price shock period, 1979 to 1982, had a much more severe effect. The income loss from the change in the terms of trade was larger, equivalent to 6.9 percent of GNP. This time, the terms of trade deterioration was coupled with a rise in real interest rates of almost 12 percentage points, adding another 3.5 percent of GNP to the income loss.[7] Thus the external shock totaled about 10 percent of GNP, which was among the largest for major LDC debtors.

The Philippines faced an additional external problem not shared by other debtors. The terms of trade deterioration was not just a product of the two shock periods, but was more secular in nature. Between 1967 and 1979 (the predebt shock peak), Philippine terms of trade fell by 35 percent. The deterioration was quite steady, interrupted only in 1973–74, and 1977–79; even at the 1974 commodity price peak, Philippine terms of trade were below their 1970 level. It is of course difficult to say what was anticipated and what was unexpected about these movements in the terms of trade, but the required adjustments for the Philippine economy were large.

8.4   Philippine Policy and the Debt Crisis

The Philippines was hit more severely by external shocks than most debtor countries. Yet at the same time, the debt crisis that occurred in the Philippines was not simply a result of the second oil price shock and the rise in world real interest rates. The Philippines had developed a borrowing momentum that could not be sustained, and the country would have eventually come to an external crisis even if the shocks of the 1980s had not been there to hurry the process along.

There were two fundamental economic difficulties. First, the Philippines failed to develop self-sustaining growth that would have eased the burden of servicing its external debt. Second, the country failed to shift resources towards the traded goods sector, as was required both by its increasing debt burden and by its declining terms of trade. In more concrete terms, the problems were poor returns from investments, difficulties in mobilizing domestic resources to fund investment, and the maintenance of a trade regime that did not sufficiently encourage exports. In addition, the Marcos government created a political-economic environment that discouraged independent investment, led to capital flight, and eventually crippled much of the productive economy.

8.4.1   Investment

The post-1974 period in the Philippines has been described as one of "debt-driven" growth. Indeed, the economy depended on expanding investment to generate Keynesian output growth. Of the total increment in GDP in the rapid growth period 1974–79, 42 percent came from increased investment expenditure, 28 percent from construction expenditure alone.[8] Despite the rapid rise in investment, and the apparently high levels of capital formation, the Philippines was not successful in translating these additions to the capital stock into economic growth.[9] In comparison to neighboring countries, the Philippines invested more to grow less, and as table 8.3 indicates, this was particularly true during the martial law period. The situation had become much worse by the early 1980s; between 1980 and 1983 the share of investment in GDP averaged over 29 percent, but GDP grew by only 2.6 percent per year.

There is no single explanation for the low return on investment expenditures. In part this was due to a shift towards infrastructure investments with longer gestation and payout periods. The expansion of investment had a particularly large construction component, much of it in public or quasi-public facilities: luxury hotels, cultural centers, and some of the notorious projects of Imelda Marcos such as the villa built entirely of coconut products or the University of Life.

Other investments were hurt by changes in world demand and prices. These include major investments in copper refining, sugar mills, and arguably, the nuclear power plant that the Philippines built.

But more fundamental causes were involved. In the latter half of the 1970s, investment and output growth shifted towards capital-intensive industries, particularly intermediate goods, industries which by definition required large investments per unit of output. This shift was the result of the high degree of tariff protection given to the domestic manufacturing industry coupled with the rapid growth of construction and other investment expenditures. Capital-intensive industries, and capital-intensive methods within industries, were encouraged by an industrial incentive system that greatly cheapened capital, by low real interest rates in the 1970s, and by credit rationing that channeled low

Table 8.3   Comparative Investment/Growth Rates

	Investment Rate[a]		GDP Growth Rate		Ratio (ICOR[b])	
	1967–72	1974–80	1967–72	1974–80	1967–72	1974–80
Philippines	20.5	29.5	5.27	6.46	3.88	4.57
Indonesia	12.8	20.0	8.20	7.42	1.56	2.70
Malaysia	18.2	25.8	n.a.	7.26	n.a.	3.55
Thailand	24.3	26.1	6.46	7.48	3.77	3.48
Korea	25.2	29.8	10.0	7.67	2.53	3.89

Sources: Philippines: National Economic and Development Authority (NEDA), The national income accounts CY 1946–75, National income series no. 5 (Manila: NEDA, 1978); and Philippine statistical yearbook 1987. Others: IMF International Financial Statistics.
[a]Gross domestic capital formation as percentage of GDP.
[b]Incremental capital-output ratio.
n.a. = not available.

cost funds to approved investments. The rapid growth of these industries was responsible for much of the low output response and low employment generation of investment in the Philippines, and for the apparent fall in manufacturing productivity over the decade.[10] And, limited by their high cost to the domestic market, these industries suffered when the investment and construction boom faded in the 1980s.

Favoritism in allocation of loans and government projects and profit skimming on imported capital equipment also reduced the profitability of investment. The Philippines paid more for imported capital equipment than other LDCs, and stories of kickbacks paid by equipment suppliers have begun to emerge.[11] In many of these projects the returns were made simply by the project going forward, and not by the profitable operation of the resulting installation.

The investments made in the 1970s proved particularly vulnerable to the economic slowdown and higher interest rates of the 1980s. Many of the investments ended up in receivership, in the hands of the two state banks and the National Development Company. These nonperforming assets, and their accompanying debt service obligations, form the most difficult fiscal problem the new government faces.

8.4.2   Resource Mobilization

The second weakness of Philippine economic policy was the continued dependence on foreign borrowing to fund domestic investment. To maintain economic growth in the face of external recession, the Philippines increased government expenditure and borrowed abroad in 1975. But the current account deficit never narrowed, and was still about 5 percent of GNP in 1979. By 1982, after the second oil shock, the deficit had risen to over 8 percent of GNP. The current account has both a macroeconomic side, and a microeconomic/resource-allocation side. We discuss the first here, the inability to generate sufficient domestic resources to fund the higher level of investment.

Table 8.4 breaks down investment and savings into public and private components. Private savings rose briefly during the mid-1970s as the economic growth rate accelerated, but trailed off by the end of the decade, leaving a private-sector gap of about 2 percent of GNP.

Public-sector revenue generation might have had the most promise, since the level of taxation in the Philippines has historically been very low in comparison to other LDCs. And, shortly after martial law was declared, there was a significant increase in the national government's revenue share of GNP, due to increased tax compliance, as well as premium duties levied on international trade. However, despite repeated commitments to raise government revenue, and a series of annual tax measures, the revenue share remained about 13 percent for the rest of the decade.[12] The Philippines ran hard just to stay in place.

Table 8.4   Savings/Investment Balances (percentage of GNP)

	1976	1978	1980	1982	1983	1984	1985
Private sector							
Investment	24.73	21.88	23.73	21.61	21.43	15.05	12.57
Savings	23.56	20.77	20.75	18.02	16.57	12.33	13.95
Personal	10.88	8.44	5.98	3.25	1.97	−0.80	−0.53
Corporate[a]	3.09	2.87	5.49	4.44	4.27	2.67	3.50
Depreciation[b]	9.59	9.47	9.28	10.33	10.33	10.46	10.98
Surplus (deficit)	−1.17	−1.12	−2.99	−3.59	−4.87	−2.72	1.38
Public sector							
Investment	6.56	7.20	6.94	7.16	6.09	4.11	3.69
Savings	1.82	3.93	4.98	3.20	4.00	4.02	3.37
Surplus (deficit)	−4.73	−3.27	−1.96	−3.96	−2.09	−0.08	−0.33
Net foreign resources/ current account	5.90	4.31	4.95	7.55	6.96	2.75	−1.05

Source: Philippines, NEDA, National Accounts section.
[a]Includes saving by government-owned corporations.
[b]Includes statistical discrepancy.

The country depended heavily on indirect taxes and taxes on international trade, taxes which had low elasticity. Some of the rise in the revenue share had been transitory, particularly additional export taxes levied on windfall prices that disappeared after 1975. Finally, the government eroded the corporate tax base during the decade by granting a large number of incentives and exemptions. The Marcos government, which needed to solidify its position by granting tax exemptions, was not strong enough politically to increase overall tax rates and collections.

The domestic recession lowered the government's tax collections in the early 1980s. In addition, changes in the way taxes were calculated reduced income tax collections, as did increasing evasion. As a result, the share of national government revenue in GNP fell by 2 percent between 1979 and 1982. This occurred at the same time that the national government and publicly owned corporations increased their investment to offset the recession, and the consolidated public-sector deficit rose sharply to over 5 percent of GNP by 1982 (table 8.5). Private savings slumped in 1982, the product of falling per capita income and expectations of a future exchange rate depreciation. So in spite of a fall in private-sector investment, the resource gap of the private sector also increased.

8.4.3   Trade Policy and Exchange Regime

As described above, the two oil price shocks were dramatic episodes in what has been a pronounced secular deterioration in the Philippine terms of trade. At the same time, the debt service obligations of the Philippines steadily rose as a result of the increased use of foreign

Table 8.5   Public-Sector Balances (percentage of GNP)

	1980	1981	1982	1983	1984	1985	1986
National government							
Revenue	13.1	11.8	11.4	12.0	10.8	11.6	13.0
Expenditure	14.4	15.8	15.7	14.0	12.7	13.5	17.6
Current	9.3	8.7	9.2	9.1	8.1	9.3	10.9
Capital	5.1	7.1	6.4	4.9	4.5	4.2	6.7
equity, net lending	2.0	3.0	3.5	2.1	2.7	2.7	4.5
Surplus (deficit)	−1.3	−4.0	−4.3	−2.0	−1.9	−1.9	−4.6
Local government							
Surplus (deficit)	0.0	0.1	0.1	0.1	0.0	0.0	0.0
Social security							
Surplus (deficit)	0.8	0.8	0.9	0.8	0.6	0.8	0.8
Government corporations							
Investment	4.5	5.4	5.0	4.9	3.1	2.7	1.5[b]
Cash generation	0.1	0.0	−0.1	0.7	0.5	0.7	0.0[b]
Transfers from national government	2.0	2.8	3.0	2.1	1.1	0.9	1.9[b]
Surplus (deficit)[a]	−2.5	−2.7	−2.1	−2.1	−1.5	−1.1	0.9[b]
Consolidated non-financial public Sector							
Investment	8.2	10.4	9.0	8.2	6.9	6.6	n.a.
Surplus (deficit)	−3.0	−5.7	−5.4	−3.2	−2.8	−2.2	−3.7

[a]After transfers from the national government.
[b]Figures for 1986 refer to 14 major nonfinancial government corporations.
n.a. = not available.

capital. Both of these required a shift in Philippine productive resources towards traded goods industries. This did not occur during the period leading up to the debt crisis. Despite the rapid growth in nontraditional manufactures exports, and the transformation in the Philippine export mix, the share of exports in total output increased only modestly and arguably fell on a net basis.

Relative price movements signal resource shifts, and table 8.6 presents several measures relevant to the traded goods sector in the Philippines. Despite some variation, the price measures tell much the same story. The real depreciation that took place during the 1970 stabilization program was sustained until the middle of the decade. After that point there was a gradual but persistent fall in the relative price of tradable goods and a decline in Philippine export competitiveness. This is most clearly seen in the relative price of tradable to nontradable goods, which declined by about 9 percent from its level at the beginning of the decade. The real exchange rate (Philippine prices relative to those of its trading partners) varies over a wider range, but shows a decline from the mid-1970s.[13] The one competitiveness measure that shows a continued improvement is the real wage rate, which was an important factor in

Table 8.6   Philippines Relative Price Indexes

	(1) PTraded/ PNonTraded	(2) REER	(3) Terms of Trade	(4) PExports/ PGDP	(5) Manufacturing Real Wage
1967	85	73	127	94	
1968	88	73	123	95	108
1969	92	74	121	90	107
1970	97	109	119	118	103
1971	100	107	111	109	105
1972	100	100	100	100	100
1973	110	108	113	125	87
1974	115	96	115	159	77
1975	112	104	88	125	86
1976	107	102	78	102	81
1977	105	101	71	95	86
1978	102	108	79	98	85
1979	101	101	87	105	85
1980	97	99	69	96	91
1981	93	96	60	90	n.a.
1982	91	91	59	74	n.a.
1983	93	109	61	91	n.a.
1984	103	109	60	101	n.a.
1985	101	96	56	83	n.a.
1986	93	117	65	87	n.a.

Notes:

1. Traded goods prices are a weighted average of gross value-added (GVA) deflators for agriculture and forestry, mining, and tradable manufactures. Nontraded prices are a weighted average of GVA deflators for construction, electricity and gas, and services. Weights are 1972 value addeds.

2. Dollar wholesale prices in major Philippine markets divided by dollar prices in the Philippines. Markets are the United States, Japan, Germany, the Netherlands, and Korea. An increase in the index is a real depreciation.

3. Export unit value divided by import unit value.

4. GVA deflators from national accounts.

5. Basic manufacturing wage divided by GDP deflator. Wage series discontinued in 1981. n.a. = not available.

the growth of manufactures exports from the Philippines during the decade.

Philippine trade and industrial performance have been determined by a system of protection initiated in 1950. To deal with external imbalance, the Philippine government began licensing imports, in amounts determined by essentiality of the product. The incentives created for domestic production of these goods led to rapid industrialization and growth during much of the decade, but the growth rate had slowed appreciably by 1959.

The Philippines carried out a liberalization program in 1960–62, depreciating the exchange rate and removing import controls. However the intention was never to alter the protective system, and tariffs were raised to counteract the effect of ending import licensing. The liberalization did not succeed in producing more rapid growth, nor in developing manufactures exports. Modest import controls were reintroduced at the end of the 1960s as the balance of payments worsened, and were extended further during the 1970s.

The disappointing economic performance of the 1960s blunted the challenge to the structure of import protection. Policy turned toward industrial promotion through incentives legislation (1967) and narrow export promotion through investment incentives and duty free imported inputs (1970.) As a result, three streams of trade policy developed in the 1970s. First, import-substituting manufacturing continued to have heavy tariff protection. This was supplemented with non-tariff barriers and industrial incentives in the latter part of the decade.

Second, manufactures exports, especially apparel, footwear, and electronic components, grew rapidly in the 1970s under the impetus of the 1970 depreciation, falling real wages, and duty free imports of materials. However no provision was made to compensate exporters for the high cost of domestic procurement. As a result almost all inputs were imported, margins of domestic value added were very thin, and export growth was heavily dependent on export processing zones and bonded warehouses.

Third, the Philippines increased the taxation of traditional export commodities, particularly agricultural commodities. Temporary export taxes were introduced after the devaluation in 1970, but were later made permanent, and supplemented with windfall duties in 1974. The two most important export crops, coconuts and sugar, were monopolized under government sanction, and a substantial levy was placed on coconut (copra) producers.[14] As a result of the increasing effective taxation, traditional exports stagnated during the 1970s and then fell during the early 1980s.

Philippine export performance is highly mixed. Nontraditional manufactures exports grew rapidly, and increased their share of total exports from 6 percent in 1970 to 60 percent by 1980. But the overall growth of exports was insufficient given the high investment, high foreign-borrowing strategy the country pursued. The share of merchandise exports in GDP was nearly the same at the end of the decade as it was at the beginning (table 8.7.) This was in sharp contrast to neighboring countries, where significant increases in exports took place.

Furthermore, the export/GDP share overstates the Philippine position. The very rapid growth of nontraditional exports shifted the structure of Philippine exports towards goods with higher import requirements

Table 8.7   Export Shares in GDP

	1970	1974	1976	1978	1980	1982	1984
Percentage shares merchandise exports to GDP							
Philippines	15.1	18.6	14.2	14.2	16.4	12.6	16.7
Malaysia	41.3	43.8	47.5	46.7	54.0	44.6	48.3
Thailand	10.5	18.1	17.9	17.5	19.3	18.6	20.2
Philippines memo items							
Exports net of	15.1	17.7	12.6	12.4	14.0	10.3	12.5
consignment imports							
Service exports[a]	2.6	3.5	3.0	4.6	4.7	5.9	6.3

Sources: Philippines: Central Bank, *Annual report: Statistical bulletin,* 1985, table 6.55, and unpublished balance-of-payments data. Others: Asian Development Bank, *Key Indicators of Developing Member Countries,* 1986.
[a]Net of interest receipts and U.S. base rental.

and lower domestic value added. The result was to increase the import component of the country's exports, lowering the net foreign exchange generation of the traded goods sector. A rough correction for this effect is shown in table 8.7 where consignment imports for the garment and semiconductor industries are netted out of Philippine exports. The result is a narrowing export/GDP ratio over the decade.[15]

The structure of protection bears much of the responsibility for the slow rate of output growth and low returns on investment described above, as well as the insufficient growth of exports. Despite the rapid growth of labor-intensive exports, Philippine manufacturing remained capital intensive, with low productivity growth *and* low employment generation.[16] What the Philippines did in the 1970s, through investment incentives and import protection, amounted in fact to a strategy of secondary import substitution concentrating on intermediate goods. This strategy saw some success, particularly under the impetus of increased domestic investment and construction, but by 1978 had reached its zenith. The manufacturing growth rate declined continuously starting in that year, and the industries promoted in the 1970s suffered huge output declines in the 1980s (table 8.8).

The major break in trade policy came in 1981, when the Philippines started an import decontrol and tariff reduction program under a World Bank Structural Adjustment Loan. This came at a time when what the Philippines desperately needed was a substantial devaluation and expenditure reduction. The program was soon superceded by import controls adopted during the crisis in 1983, although it reduced revenue collections, and probably increased the output declines that took place in domestic manufacturing.

Table 8.8   **Real GDP by Industrial Origin (percentage change)**

	1983–85	1986
GDP market prices	−9.6	1.1
Agriculture	5.6	3.7
Industry	−19.9	−2.7
Mining	−10.1	−11.9
Manufacturing	−14.2	0.8
Construction	−44.8	−20.6
Services	−9.8	2.3
Total manufacturing	−14.2	0.8
Misc. manufactures	32.0	0.2
Basic metals	13.8	−4.9
Publishing	7.3	10.5
Beverages	3.7	−7.9
Leather	1.5	−11.6
Footwear	−0.5	13.6
Electrical machinery	−4.0	19.6
Food	−6.9	0.9
Rubber	−13.0	3.2
Tobacco	−15.5	−23.0
Petroleum products	−17.2	0.3
Furniture	−23.2	10.1
Wood and cork	−23.9	−27.6
Paper	−26.0	8.9
Chemicals	−26.7	−7.0
Textiles	−29.5	21.4
Nonmetal minerals	−35.3	0.5
Metal products	−35.5	−2.8
Nonelectrical machinery	−50.1	4.9
Transport equipment	−81.9	−4.4

Source: Philippines, NEDA, "The national income accounts of the Philippines," mimeo (August 1987).

8.4.4   The Martial Law Business Environment: "Crony Capitalism"

The last contributor to the debt crisis in the Philippines was a more general change in the business environment that occurred under martial law. The change had its roots in the Philippine political system, and the challenge that martial law presented.

Politics in the Philippines has traditionally been dominated by a group of wealthy families, who exercised political control in local areas and competed among themselves for the presidency. Although from a well-to-do family, Marcos was not really of this group. When Marcos declared martial law in 1972, suspended the Constitution, and dissolved Congress, he put himself directly in opposition to the traditional oligarchs. In order to solidify the position of the martial law regime Marcos did two things. The first was to centralize political power and government functions in the national government in Manila, and greatly expand the national government and military role. The second response was to create a countervailing elite: his own family, his wife's, and a group of Marcos associates, or, as they were called, cronies.

To do so, Marcos used the power of the state to dispense and accumulate wealth. Public works contracts, government procurement, industrial incentives, and inexpensive credit were all channeled to Marcos supporters, including the military, to cement loyalty, and through kickbacks, to enrich Marcos himself. None of this, except the inclusion of the military, was unusual in Philippine politics; "What are we here for?" asked one former Philippine president when questioned about graft in his administration. What was unusual was the scale on which this took place under martial law. This was made possible by the greatly expanded level of public investment in the 1970s, financed by foreign borrowing. It was also supported by the preference of external creditors for public guarantees, which further concentrated the flow of financial resources through the state.

But Marcos's use of state power went beyond simple graft. The most important part of the wealth accumulation was done through the creation of monopolies, either through direct intervention to control an industry, or through the grant of exemptions or exclusive privileges to favored individuals. The government intervened directly in food marketing, the fertilizer industry, labor export, gambling, and, through the Cultural Center of the Philippines, in pornographic film distribution. Monopolies were created in the two most important export crops, sugar and coconuts. Run by two Marcos cronies, these generated billions of pesos of revenue. In addition, presidential decrees gave tariff and tax exemptions or exclusive import rights to particular firms, granting effective monopolies. Among the industries affected were livestock and television imports, peroxide, sugar milling equipment, and cigarette filter production.

Outright expropriation was done only at the outset of martial law. Later, less visible pressure was brought to bear on profitable firms to sell out to Marcos family members, or to cronies. The cronies built business empires, based on very high financial leveraging. They were willing to take large financial risks due to their implicit government backing, an assumption that proved correct in the 1980s when the government rescued many crony firms.

These actions took a significant toll on the behavior of the private sector not associated with the Marcos government. Businessmen became less willing to invest and expand in the Philippines for fear of attracting attention, and instead moved their money outside the country. In order to protect themselves from the cronies and from their own government, firms invited foreign joint venture participation, reasoning that Marcos or his associates would be reluctant to move against a firm with foreign ownership. Political opposition among the business class began to surface in 1980, grew after the corporate bailouts of 1981, and became widespread after the Aquino assassination.

By the end of the 1970s, corruption in the Philippines was large enough to have macroeconomic consequences. The effects went beyond the drain of funds through corruption. Increasing government interventions, monopolization, and grants of exclusive privilege sapped the efficiency of the economy, lowered the profitability of investments that were undertaken, and increased the vulnerability of the Philippines to the financial crises of the early 1980s. Crony capitalism provides much of the explanation for the deterioration of economic growth and asset portfolios in the 1980s, and was the first thing that the new Aquino government sought to diminish.

Power and wealth were mixed motives for Marcos's actions from the beginning. Furthermore, there were some successes of the martial law administration; not all of its actions can be characterized as plunder and theft. But, in the latter part of the 1970s the balance began to tilt, and the accumulation of wealth became the predominant motive. And this in turn severely limited the willingness and ability of the government to react to the approaching economic crisis.

8.4.5 Crisis and Adjustment

The Marcos government first tried to counter the domestic recession, but it came under increasing pressure from its external creditors, including the IMF and World Bank, from its own statutory limitation on external debt, and from its increasing difficulty in generating counterpart funds to match foreign project inflows. The Philippines changed its policy course during 1982, cutting national government expenditure and dramatically slowing the growth of the money supply. But by this time the drain on reserves and the drying up of short-term capital had already begun, and the moratorium, finally declared on 15 October 1983, had become inevitable.

Three things had a critical effect on the adjustment period that followed. First, the Philippines had almost exhausted its foreign exchange reserves when the moratorium was declared. The severe liquidity constraint decisively influenced the trade and exchange rate policy the country adopted during the crisis. The second factor was a massive increase in base money that occurred in the last half of 1983, which largely accommodated the devaluations that took place in June and October.[17] By the beginning of 1984 the inflation rate was over 60 percent. The final factor was the almost complete dissembling of the portfolios of the state-owned financial institutions. By 1984 and 1985, government aid to these institutions absorbed almost 2 percent of GNP.

Under pressure from the severe shortage of foreign exchange, the Philippine government reverted to trade and exchange rate policy which had characterized much of the postwar period. Banks were required to surrender foreign exchange holdings to the Central Bank, which in turn allocated the supply to priority uses. Taxes on traditional exports were raised, and the fall in their export volume continued. The government effectively created a multiple exchange rate system by allowing importers to obtain foreign currency on the black market. This greatly increased the import premium, and meant a continuing shortage of foreign exchange at the Central Bank, even for priority allocations. Non-traditional manufactures exports increased, but not by enough to prevent an overall decline in export volumes. The current account deficit was reduced, but this was brought about by a dramatic fall in imports, particularly capital goods imports.

Under IMF pressure, the Philippines devalued further in 1984, reduced export taxes, and abandoned the exchange surrender requirement, unifying the exchange rate. But the Fund was further concerned with inflation, and the huge growth in the money supply that had taken place. In a highly unusual step, the IMF demanded a reduction in the *level* of the money supply as a precondition for an agreement, and the program that the Philippines and the Fund finally agreed on had stringent monetary growth restrictions. The Central Bank met the precondition, and met most of the monetary targets, primarily through the sale of Central Bank bills, with interest rates at times over 40 percent.

Evaluating monetary policy during this period is difficult. Reported interest rates lagged behind the inflation rate, so that real interest rates only turned positive in 1985. However, the real money supply fell by 30 percent during 1984, to the lowest level of the decade. In addition, there was a decisive shift of what bank credit there was to the public sector; real credit to the private sector fell by 49 percent between 1983 and 1985.

The program was highly successful at meeting the external targets and in reducing the rate of inflation. The Philippines eliminated all payments arrears by the end of 1985, and had virtually eliminated the current account deficit. The noninterest current account balance increased by nearly 10 percent of GNP in a three-year period (table 8.9).

The inflation rate fell as rapidly as it had risen. Although six-month changes in the CPI remained at rates above 50 percent for all of 1984, by May 1985 the inflation rate was below 10 percent per year. For all of 1985 (December–December) the rate was below 6 percent, the lowest since the 1960s, and prices actually declined slightly in 1986.

Table 8.9   **Philippine Noninterest Current Account ($ million)**

	1982	1983	1984	1985	1986
Balance	− 1575	− 1139	741	1875	1892
% of GNP	− 4.0	− 3.3	2.4	5.9	6.4

Source: Philippine Central Bank.

The output cost of the stabilization was high. Per capita incomes fell by 15 percent from 1983 to 1985, with a further 3 percent fall in 1986. Total investment expenditure fell by 50 percent. The manufacturing sector was particularly hard hit, with the largest losses posted by the industries that had been protected during the 1970s (see table 8.8). The credit squeeze had a drastic effect, forcing many firms to the wall. It was this reduction of output and the attendant compression of imports that was responsible for achieving external balance so quickly. Over the course of the program there was little change in the balance of incentives for traded goods, and a 4 percent reduction in the volume of exports.

A substantial output cost was also paid for reducing inflation so quickly, and the emphasis in the IMF program on reducing monetary growth appears misplaced. Reducing inflation in the Philippines has never been as difficult as in many Latin American countries, for the Philippines lacks the institutional features that give inflation momentum. Unionization is very low, and indexation virtually absent. The Philippines has repeatedly exhibited substantial real wage declines after devaluations and the same occurred between 1983 and 1986. But the credit stringency that was imposed by the monetary policy, and the shift in credit towards the public sector to support the losses of the two state banks, had a severe effect on domestic business and financial institutions. The Philippines has been traumatized by six years of financial upheaval, and it will take some time to restore confidence.

Despite the high output cost, the Philippines did achieve a successful and rapid stabilization between 1983 and 1985, and the new government started with the considerable advantage that those stabilization costs had already been paid. Arguably, the program was instrumental in bringing about the change in government, and the end to the abuses of the crony period. And yet, stabilization has not been the real problem for the Philippines; the Philippine economy is relatively easy to stabilize. It is the achievement of sustained economic growth that has proved more elusive, and the problems here are more microeconomic and resource allocational than they are macroeconomic in nature.

In the end, the Philippine debt crisis is largely a microeconomic story. Foreign debt and the domestic investment it funded were used to mask the problems of a sluggish and overprotected manufacturing sector, increasing taxation of agricultural exports, and the vitiation of the domestic economy through cronyism. It is true that the second oil shock and the following interest rate shock accelerated the Philippine crisis. In addition, Philippine policymakers made their own problems worse by failing to respond to the external shock, by betting heavily against devaluation through the issuance of swap and forward contracts, and by waiting so long to declare a moratorium. But the fundamental difficulties would not have been avoided through a more favorable external environment or better short-run macro management. By failing to make fundamental resource allocation adjustments when external financing was available, the Philippines made its problems far more difficult in the 1980s.

8.5 The Aquino Government

The popular revulsion against the excesses of the Marcos administration has placed the Aquino government in a unique position. The new government has dismantled the monopolies in coconuts and sugar, and has committed itself to less market interference and equal application of the law. While it is unrealistic to suppose that corruption will disappear from Philippine political life, it is likely to be drastically reduced in scale; Mrs. Aquino has already dismissed two cabinet members for graft, despite their close association with her husband. The government has also enacted a comprehensive tax reform that reduces exceptions and will increase the responsiveness of the tax system.

The Aquino government faces the problem that has plagued the Philippines since independence: how to achieve self-sustaining output, wage, and employment growth. The new government has continued the trade liberalization program that was interrupted by the debt crisis, although against heavy domestic opposition. And it has encouraged activity in the rural sector and reduced the discrimination against traditional export goods.

But the world economy is far less hospitable than it was in the 1960s and 1970s, and the debt accumulation and array of nonperforming assets are a heavy burden of the past. Economic recovery and growth in the Philippines will require a high degree of political determination, as well as a fraction of the external funds that were available to build the martial law regime.

Appendix

Table 8.10   Real GNP by Expenditure Shares and by Industrial Origin (percentage changes)

	1973	1974	1975	1976	1977	1978	1979	1980	1981	1982	1983	1984	1985	1986
Personal consumption	5.8	4.9	4.8	5.0	5.3	5.2	4.8	4.5	4.0	3.1	2.9	1.0	0.2	0.9
Government consumption	11.8	14.7	7.7	2.1	0.9	3.0	3.7	3.7	3.7	6.4	-3.9	-6.1	-0.6	4.2
Gross domestic investment	10.9	22.9	23.5	15.4	-0.1	8.6	11.2	4.4	2.3	-3.5	-4.7	-36.7	-20.7	-8.3
Fixed investment	3.4	19.2	31.6	15.0	1.9	8.4	11.7	6.9	3.5	0.6	-2.8	-28.1	-23.1	-14.8
Exports	14.2	-10.7	1.5	18.6	16.5	3.8	6.8	13.4	1.2	-2.6	6.9	11.6	-7.2	21.8
Less: imports	4.0	16.3	6.2	1.0	6.4	12.9	16.4	3.3	-2.7	3.5	-1.6	-5.3	-23.0	25.4
GDP	8.5	5.0	6.4	8.0	6.1	5.5	6.3	5.2	3.9	2.9	0.9	-5.7	-4.0	1.1
GNP	9.3	5.6	5.8	7.4	6.3	5.8	6.9	5.0	3.4	1.9	1.1	-6.8	-3.8	1.5
GDP by industrial origin														
Agriculture	6.1	2.6	4.3	8.0	5.0	4.1	4.5	4.7	4.0	3.1	-2.1	2.3	3.2	3.7
Industry	12.4	5.6	8.7	10.4	8.4	6.1	8.0	4.7	4.5	2.1	0.7	-10.5	-10.5	-2.7
Mining	4.0	0.2	3.0	3.2	16.8	3.8	18.0	4.8	-2.7	-7.3	-2.5	-10.7	0.7	-11.9
Manufacturing	14.0	4.7	3.5	5.7	7.5	7.3	5.4	4.2	3.4	2.4	2.3	-7.1	-7.6	0.8
Construction	8.6	12.8	44.2	33.3	9.6	2.8	13.7	5.6	9.7	3.2	-4.8	-23.7	-27.6	-20.6
Services	7.0	6.2	5.9	6.0	4.9	5.9	5.8	6.2	3.4	3.5	3.6	-6.7	-3.3	2.3

Source: Philippines, NEDA, "The national income accounts of the Philippines," various issues.

Notes

1. This does not cover capital flight through export underinvoicing or import overinvoicing, which has also characterized the Philippines.

2. In contrast to other countries in this study, exports of services make up a significant part (one-third) of total Philippine exports. These include not only the rental on U.S. military bases, but also the supply of overseas workers, and construction services as well. Dollar earnings from exports of goods and services stayed roughly constant from 1980 to 1984.

3. Short-term debt was not covered in IMF programs, nor were revolving credits (the vast majority of short-term debt) included in the Philippine statutory debt limitation.

4. In a swap arrangement a bank would borrow abroad in foreign currency, and then exchange the proceeds with the Central Bank for pesos. The Central Bank agreed to sell foreign currency to the bank at a set exchange rate in the future, so the bank could pay back the loan.

5. This was unknown at the time, for the Central Bank was systematically overstating its reserves, by amounts of as much as a billion dollars.

6. Throughout, we measure terms of trade effects as the amount of additional exports needed to maintain an import level. Import prices rose 28.7 percent relative to export prices. This, times an import share in GNP of 15.0 percent, equals 4.3 percent. The terms of trade income loss in this case excludes the transitory income gain of 1973 and 1974.

7. The starting point for the terms of trade calculation was the year 1978. Between 1978 and 1982 import prices rose 33.1 percent relative to Philippine export prices; this times the 1979 import share of GNP of 20.8 percent equals 6.89 percent. The average interest rate paid on Philippine external debt rose from 5.21 percent in 1979 to 8.73 percent in 1982. Rates of export price inflation used to calculate the real interest rate were 5.20 percent (the 1975–79 average) and −2.96 percent (the 1979–85 average). The change in the real interest rate was multiplied by the share of gross external debt, less foreign assets of the monetary system, in the average 1979–80 GNP. These types of calculations are highly sensitive to the endpoints. The endpoints were chosen as reasonable approximations, and produce neither the highest nor the lowest income changes possible.

8. Net exports added a negative 3 percent to the GDP increment over the same period.

9. There is some question about the true level of capital formation and savings in the Philippines, in part engendered by the low resultant growth rate. Studies of the World Bank's International Comparisons Project indicate a significantly lower value for the Philippine investment share.

10. Richard Hooley (1985) has estimated a decline in total factor productivity of Philippine manufacturing of 2 percent per year in the latter half of the 1970s. Factor productivity improved within most industries, but interindustry shifts were responsible for the overall decline.

11. A particularly egregious example is the Bataan nuclear power plant, built by Westinghouse, at a cost three times that of a similar plant built by Westinghouse in Pusan, Korea.

12. A rise in government revenue was a major goal of the IMF's Extended Finance Facility for the Philippines (1976–79). A revenue share of 17 percent was also part of the Philippines' 1974–77 Development Plan.

13. The Philippines had what amounted to a de facto real peg against the dollar until 1983, riding the dollar down in 1978 and then up between 1980 and 1982.

14. Two further developments affected the supply of traditional exports. Conservation legislation reduced the legal exports of logs, which had accounted for 27 percent of exports in 1970, to near zero by the end of the decade, and the suspension of U.S. sugar quotas in 1974 deprived the Philippines of a highly lucrative market. The increasing taxation of export agriculture was to some degree offset by substantial investments in irrigation for domestic grain, and the Philippines briefly became a rice exporter during the 1970s.

15. One area where the Philippines did have considerable export success was in the service sector. Philippine overseas construction and contract labor services grew substantially during the decade, boosting the service export share from 2.5 to 6 percent of GDP. Ironically, this is an indication that Philippine factors of production, particularly labor, were more productive outside the country than within.

16. The peak share of manufacturing in employment was reached in 1956.

17. A major source of the monetary expansion was losses that the Central Bank suffered on a large volume of outstanding forward contracts and swap agreements. These had been issued as a form of patronage, and as a way of borrowing reserves.

Reference

Hooley, Richard. 1985. *Productivity growth in Philippine manufacturing: Retrospect and prospects*. Monograph no. 9. Manila: Philippine Institute for Development Studies.

9 Turkish Experience with Debt: Macroeconomic Policy and Performance

Merih Celâsun and Dani Rodrik

9.1 Policy Phases and Adjustment Patterns

Turkey was the first major developing country (LDC) debtor to face a payments crisis after 1973. Turkey's debt debacle began in mid-1977, before the second oil shock of the late 1970s. Indeed, Turkey's debt reschedulings prior to 1982 were the largest ever undertaken, and accounted for nearly 70 percent of the total volume of debt renegotiated by all LDCs in the 1978–80 period. Despite this massive restructuring of debt, Turkey experienced an agonizing foreign exchange crisis from 1978 to 1980. In early 1980, in an unexpectedly bold fashion, Turkey launched an outward-oriented adjustment program which produced an export-led recovery and an acceptable degree of creditworthiness by 1982–83, just as the LDC debt crisis started to dominate the headlines.

Against the backdrop of such anomalous characteristics, Turkey has been informally referred to as "the Baker Plan country before the Baker Plan." The Baker Plan (in October 1985) called for intensive, market-based micro-level domestic adjustments in return for expanded international lending to the problem debtors. In recent years, the multilateral lending institutions have increasingly stressed trade and financial liberalization in their programs for LDCs with debt-servicing difficulties. Together with the well-known cases of the export-oriented East Asian economies, Turkey's recent adjustment experience is often cited by the international financial community as a successful reference case for the approach currently promoted in the management of the LDC crisis.

Merih Celâsun is a professor of economics at the Middle East Technical University in Ankara, Turkey. Dani Rodrik is an assistant professor of public policy at the John F. Kennedy School of Government, Harvard University, and a faculty research fellow at the National Bureau of Economic Research.

In the design of adjustment programs for major debtors, a set of common questions arise as to the appropriate timing and magnitude of external financing, the proper mix and sequencing of domestic policies, and the nature of social costs likely to be faced in the transition process. Our forthcoming monograph on the Turkish experience (see the country studies volumes of this project), on which the present chapter draws, aims to provide a balanced account, intended for generalized assessments as well as for policy evaluations specific to Turkey.

Our approach is essentially ex post and empirical, and we do not offer economic projections or explicit recommendations for future policy actions. The underlying objective of the study is to contribute to an improved understanding of foreign borrowing and of policy-performance linkages in the Turkish economy in the face of the external disturbances of the post-1973 period.

9.1.1 Background

In its recent history, Turkey faced foreign exchange stringency at three junctures: in 1957–58, 1969–70, and 1978–80. Each episode involved IMF-supported programs involving stabilization with devaluation. Domestic political difficulties and unrest were heightened at each instance, paving the way for military interventions in 1960, 1971, and 1980, mainly on grounds of restoring law and order. The payments difficulties were relatively mild in 1969–70, as was the partial military intervention in 1971, which did not result in the dissolution of the existing Parliament. The military takeovers of 1960 and 1980 were more complete, however, resulting in the adoption of new constitutions (in 1961 and 1982). At each stage, the military interventions were transitional and brief. They were terminated with multiparty parliamentary elections and the formation of civilian governments.

With the institutionalization of formal planning in the early 1960s, Turkey pursued its development efforts in the context of five-year plans, which gradually lost their policy effectiveness in the post-1973 period. During the initial two plans (1963–67 and 1968–72), GNP growth averaged around 6.8 percent per year with relative price stability and moderate reliance on external assistance (amounting to about 1.5 percent of GNP per year). The planning techniques in this period made heavy use of a restrictive trade regime, state enterprise investments, and financial repression as key institutional tools in achieving the import-substituting industrialization objectives.

9.1.2 The 1970s: Debt Crisis and Lack of Adjustment

For the Turkish economy, the 1970s were the best of times and the worst of times. The decade witnessed an unprecedented spurt of investment and growth until about 1977, accompanied by what looked like a steady improvement in income distribution. This was followed by a crash that was equally unprecedented. From mid-1977 on, Turkey found itself in a monumental debt crisis which took several years of intricate negotiations with creditors and a long series of rescheduling agreements to resolve. Growth suffered heavily, with two years of real contraction at the end of the decade; income distribution began to turn against urban workers and the peasantry.

With hindsight, it is not too difficult to provide a broad interpretation of the Turkish experience prior to 1977. The early years of the decade had been a time of great optimism as the perennial external constraint appeared to have been permanently relaxed, thanks largely to a rapid rise in workers' remittances. As table 9.1 shows, the current account was actually in surplus for two years in a row in 1972 and 1973. Partly as a consequence, the public sector went on an investment binge shortly thereafter, and encouraged the private sector to follow suit. As the share of investment rose from 18.1 percent of GDP (in 1973) to 25.0 percent (in 1977), the real growth rate of the economy reached its zenith at 8.9 percent (in 1975 and 1976).

There were two problems, however. First, all of this was taking place in the context of the fourfold rise in world oil prices. Second, the government succumbed to all of the usual policy pitfalls: price distortions including overvalued exchange rates, large public sector deficits, and an accommodating monetary stance. These helped swing the current account sharply into deficit, moving it from a surplus of $534 million in 1973 to a deficit of $3,431 million in 1977. The current deficits were financed by external borrowing, much of it short term.

Table 9.1   Macroeconomic Performance of Turkey During the 1970s

	Real GDP Growth (%)	Inflation Rate (WPI) (%)	Current Account Balance ($ mill.)	Investment (% of GDP)
1972	6.0	18.0	47	20.1
1973	4.1	20.5	534	18.1
1974	8.8	29.9	−662	20.7
1975	8.9	10.1	−1,889	22.5
1976	8.9	15.6	−2,286	24.7
1977	4.9	24.1	−3,431	25.0
1974–77	7.3	19.9	−2,067	23.2
1978	4.3	52.6	−1,595	18.5
1979	−0.6	63.9	−1,203	18.3
1980	−1.0	107.2	−3,304	21.4
1978–80	0.9	74.6	−2,034	19.4

Sources: State Institute of Statistics, State Planning Organization, and the Central Bank.

As foreign lenders started getting jittery at the beginning of 1977, the stage was set for a debt crisis. New flows slowed down to a trickle, and the Central Bank's depleted reserves forced it into arrears on payments to foreign banks, governments, and export suppliers. The consequent foreign exchange shortages led to a forced reduction of the current account deficit by administrative means, the collapse of investment and growth, and an upsurge of inflation (see table 9.1). The next few years witnessed a series of debt renegotiations with creditors.

What were the sources of this debt debacle? Conventional wisdom stresses the adverse external environment, misguided exchange rate and fiscal policies, and the short-term nature of the liabilities incurred during the 1973–77 period. But there must have been more at work. Until the debt crisis of 1982, Turkey's debt problems were among the most severe experienced by the postwar international system. Unlike practically all of the other newly industrializing countries experiencing debt difficulties, Turkey got into trouble after the first oil shock, rather than the second one. This suggests, prima facie, that the usual explanations of the crisis—in terms of a combination of external shocks with a number of key inappropriate domestic policies such as overvalued exchange rates and a lax monetary and fiscal stance—at best will go only part of the way in explaining its origins. In comparative perspective, the external shocks experienced by Turkey were not particularly severe; nor were the Turkish macroeconomic policies excessively distorted. It is likely that these policies would have gotten Turkey into trouble eventually. But we have to look for additional reasons why Turkey's crisis occurred sooner rather than later.

The precocious nature of Turkey's debt crisis is best explained by reference to the borrowing "strategy" in place. Between 1975 and 1977 Turkey relied on a form of foreign borrowing with intrinsically destabilizing features. To attract capital inflows, the authorities depended disproportionately on the so-called convertible Turkish lira deposit (CTLD) scheme, whose key feature was that it protected domestic borrowers from all exchange risk. This exchange guarantee acted as a subsidy on foreign borrowing by the private sector, as the domestic currency was already perceived to be overvalued by the beginning of 1975. More important, it rendered the implicit subsidy an increasing function of the expected depreciation of the Turkish lira.

The resulting borrowing was heavily biased toward the "strong" currencies (predominantly the deutsche-mark and the Swiss franc) with low nominal interest rates. As borrowing increased and the current account deteriorated, there was increased anticipation of further depreciation of the domestic currency. That in turn raised the implicit subsidy on foreign borrowing, giving rise to even greater incentives to borrow. Hence the CTLD scheme had the fatal flaw of engendering an ever-expanding spiral of over-borrowing by the private sector. According to our calculations, the marginal cost of foreign funds (denominated in D-marks) was at least 20–25 percent towards the end of 1976, implying a real interest-rate burden of around 16–21 percent. Borrowing went on, since domestic borrowers paid only a fraction of this cost, with the rest effectively socialized under the exchange guarantee.

Consequently, even though the counterpart to the current deficits of the period was, in an accounting sense, an investment boom by the public sector (see table 9.2), it is hard to envisage that this could have justified foreign borrowing at such terms. The boom was sustainable only to the extent that foreign banks were willing to increase their exposure to Turkey at an ever-increasing pace. Once foreign banks slowed their lending, the edifice collapsed.

The crisis developing in mid-1977 threw Turkey into a period of forced adjustment. As foreign exchange sources dried up, external balance for the first time in many years became a genuinely binding constraint, requiring an adjustment in the relationship between income and absorption in the economy. How was this adjustment achieved? Policy itself was of little help. The IMF was called on to administer a series of stabilization programs, and two sets of adjustment measures were announced, one in early 1978 and the other in 1979. But both

Table 9.2   **Investment-Saving Balance and Growth of Real Expenditures, 1973–77**

	1973	1974	1975	1976	1977
	(percent of GNP)				
Investment	18.1	20.7	22.5	24.7	25.0
Private	11.1	10.0	10.3	13.1	11.9
Public	7.0	10.8	12.2	11.6	13.1
Domestic Savings	20.3	18.4	17.4	19.3	18.0
Private	11.6	11.0	8.5	11.2	11.7
Public	8.8	7.4	9.0	8.1	6.4
Foreign Savings	2.2	2.3	5.0	5.4	6.9
Sectoral savings – Investment balances					
Private	0.5	1.0	−1.8	−1.9	−0.2
Public	1.8	−3.4	−3.2	−3.5	−6.7
Total	2.3	−2.4	−5.0	−5.4	−6.9
	(percent)				
Growth of real expenditures[a]					
Private	3.7	7.3	7.4	9.6	2.7
Public	7.4	10.3	20.2	12.5	9.0
Total	4.5	7.9	10.0	10.2	4.2

Sources: State Planning Organization.
[a]Excluding expenditures on inventories.

programs, as well as the two corresponding IMF standby arrangements, proved unsuccessful. Until January 1980, the various adjustment measures undertaken by the authorities can be described as "too little, too late." The reduction in government spending was only half-hearted, and exchange rate policy, albeit more active, lagged behind rising inflation. The policymakers were too conscious of political support to administer radical shock treatment, and too divided to implement any feasible alternative.

The burden of achieving the requisite adjustment fell on investment and inflation (see table 9.1). Between mid-1977 and early 1980, a collapse in investment and an inflationary spiral were the key mechanisms for ensuring that the external constraint was met. In the absence of sufficient reduction in nominal expenditures, and of real exchange rate depreciations, absorption could be brought in line with the available resources only by engineering inflation. It was inflation that equilibrated the open-economy income identity by closing the gap between ex ante demand and supply.

9.1.3   The 1980s: Adjustment Policies and Stabilization

In conjunction with inner-oriented expansionary macroeconomic policies, the largely unnoticed buildup of price distortions in 1973–77 had produced not only a stagnation in exports, but also a rapid rise in the intensity of imports in production, resulting in a negative import-substitution as a source of growth at the aggregate level. Against the background of import and output contraction, commodity shortages and hoarding, and strained relations with the international financial community during 1978–79, the newly installed minority government of Süleyman Demirel was persuaded to introduce a comprehensive package of policy measures in January 1980. The policy package was unexpectedly bold in terms of its anti-inflationary measures as well as its qualitative aspects, which gave clear signals of a greater export- and market-orientation in the development strategy.

As shown in table 9.3, the macroeconomic and trade performance has been quite remarkable since then, especially in a generally unfavorable world economic environment. Following the contraction of output in the first year of the policy package, GNP growth has averaged around 4.6 percent per year (in 1981–85), accompanied by sharp rises in trade ratios. In value terms, merchandise exports have increased from around $2.3 billion in 1979 to $8.3 billion in 1985 with the share of manufactured products going from 35 to 75 percent in the same period.

The reduction in the rate of inflation from about 105 percent in 1980 to 28 percent in 1983 was a substantial one, even though inflationary pressures intensified in 1984–85. After declining 20 percent in 1977–

Table 9.3   Macroeconomic Performance, 1980–86

	1980	1981	1982	1983	1984	1985	1986[a]
A. % Annual Increase							
1. Real value added GNP	-1.1	4.1	4.5	3.3	5.9	5.1	7.8
Agriculture	1.7	0.1	6.4	-0.1	3.5	2.4	7.1
Manufacturing	-6.4	9.5	5.4	8.7	10.2	5.5	10.2
2. Real expenditure[b]							
Private	-6.3	-0.3	4.3	4.7	5.9	4.0	8.4
Public	2.0	5.2	2.1	1.5	2.3	8.9	9.0
Total	-4.7	0.8	3.8	4.0	5.2	5.0	8.6
3. Employment	-0.1	0.9	0.9	0.7	1.3	1.1	2.1
4. GNP deflator	103.9	41.9	27.4	28.0	49.8	43.6	32.8
5. Terms of foreign trade ($)	-22.8	-9.4	-4.6	-1.4	12.9	1.1	
B. Trade Ratios							
(% of GNP, current prices)							
1. Exports of goods (fob)[c]	5.0	8.0	11.0	11.6	14.7	15.6	12.9
2. Exports of goods and services (XGS)[d]	6.3	10.2	14.8	15.6	19.4	21.5	18.4
3. Imports of goods (cif)	13.6	15.2	16.5	18.1	21.4	21.9	19.1
Oil	6.6	6.6	7.0	7.2	7.3	6.8	3.9
Nonoil	7.0	8.6	9.5	10.9	14.1	15.1	15.2
4. Current deficit (after debt relief)	5.5	3.5	2.2	4.1	2.8	1.9	2.2
C. Monetary Parameters							
M1/MB (money base)	1.5	1.2	1.1	1.2	0.8	0.7	
M2/MB	1.8	2.0	2.2	2.1	1.9	1.9	
GNP/MB	9.3	8.0	7.4	7.3	6.7	6.4	
GNP/M1	6.3	6.7	6.5	5.9	8.1	8.6	
GNP/M2	5.0	4.0	3.4	3.5	3.5	3.4	
M2/Domestic credits	0.7	0.8	1.0	1.0	1.2	1.2	

(*continued*)

Table 9.3 (continued)

	1980	1981	1982	1983	1984	1985	1986[a]
D. Domestic Credits (%)[e]		100	100	100	100	100	100
by: Deposit money banks		59	64	66	70	72	77
Investment banks		13	12	13	13	11	8
Central bank		28	24	21	17	17	15
to: Public sector		48	40	37	32	28	29
Treasury		14	13	12	10	12	11
Public enterprises		34	27	25	22	16	18
Private sector		52	60	63	68	72	71
E. External Debt							
Debt stock ($ billion)		16.9	17.9	18.4	21.3	25.3	31.2
Of which short-term		2.2	1.8	2.3	3.2	4.8	6.9
Debt/GNP		0.29	0.33	0.36	0.42	0.48	0.53
Debt/XGS		2.80	2.22	2.31	2.18	2.22	2.79
Debt service/XGS		0.30	0.31	0.32	0.28	0.32	0.38
Net resource transfer/GNP		0.01	-0.007	0.003	-0.007	-0.02	-0.007

Sources: State Planning Organization and Central Bank of Turkey.
[a]Provisional estimates (March 1987).
[b]Real domestic final expenditures, excluding inventory changes.
[c]Includes transit trade.
[d]Excludes workers' remittances.
[e]Net of Central Bank advances to the banks.

79, private fixed investment further dropped around 26 percent in real terms during 1980–1982. Thus, the output increase came essentially from the existing productive capacity, which responded to the increased availability of the imported inputs, and from expenditure-switching policies of the new program.

A number of special factors have played an important role in Turkey's economic recovery since 1980. Among these, the most salient ones were (i) the transitional military rule from 1980 to 1983, which provided continuity and added political clout in the policy process; (ii) sizable debt relief and new lending; (iii) special market conditions in the Middle East affected by the Iran-Iraq conflict in the Persian Gulf; and (iv) substantial downward flexibility of real wages and agricultural prices, which made it possible to attain a new set of equilibrium prices and conditions more compatible with macroeconomic stability and increased trade-orientation in the economy. As shown in table 9.4, debt relief and new external credits were very sizable, obviating the need to generate surpluses in the noninterest current account in the earlier years of the program (unlike the situations faced by the Latin American debtors in the post-1982 period). An effective policy dialogue with the IMF (initially involving a three-year standby agreement of SDR 1,200 million) and the World Bank (providing five SAL's totaling $1.6 billion in addition to regular project lending) facilitated debt relief agreements, concessional bilateral lending, and all-around creditor support during the 1980–85 period.

Policy Sequence

The adjustment program of the 1980s proceeded in discernible stages. The immediate policy objectives of the first stage (1980–81) were to restore an acceptable degree of macroeconomic stability, to relieve shortages of essential commodities, and to induce an export-oriented recovery in output. Regaining public confidence by eliminating hoarding and parallel markets was perceived as a prerequisite for the subsequent structural components of the program.

The initial policy package of January 1980 contained a steep devaluation (exceeding IMF expectations), deregulation of private-sector industrial prices, and huge price hikes for the state economic enterprise (SEE) products and services (ranging from 45 percent for gasoline to 300 percent for paper and 400 percent for fertilizer against the backdrop of 70 percent inflation). The package contained supplementary incentives for export promotion and simplified administrative procedures for imports. The first significant but still partial change in the import regime came in January 1981 with the elimination of the quota list (with all items not shown in the liberalized lists for imports remaining prohibited). In June 1980, bank interest rates were substantially

Table 9.4 Financing the Current Account, 1980–86 ($ million)

	1980	1981	1982	1983	1984	1985	1986 (provisional)	1980–85 ($ billion)	%
Part A: After Debt Relief									
Interest payments	−668	−1,184	−1,465	−1,441	−1,586	−1,753	−2,134	−8.1	
Noninterest current account	−2,270	−485	630	−387	179	740	606	−1.6	
Current account balance	−2,938	−1,669	−835	−1,828	−1,407	−1,013	−1,528	−9.7	
Part B: Before Debt Relief									
Current account balance	−3,408	−1,919	−935	−1,898	−1,407	−1,013	−1,528	−10.6	−100.0
Nondebt financing	−475	−100	−229	−62	150	298	−169	−0.4	−4.0
Direct foreign investment	18	95	55	46	113	95	125	0.4	4.0
Changes in reserves	−512	−263	−297	−269	208	−20	−545	−1.2	−10.9
Counterpart to valuation changes	19	68	13	161	−171	223	251	0.3	3.0
Net foreign borrowing	3,883	2,019	1,164	1,960	1,257	715	1,697	11.0	104.0
Long-term (LT)	2,194	1,165	1,030	303	1,046	−20	525	5.7	54.1
Debt relief (interest + principal)	1,450	850	750	1,000	580			4.6	43.8
Other LT (net)	744	315	280	−697	466	−20	525	1.1	10.3
IMF (net use)	422	268	129	117	−142	−103	−241	0.7	6.5
Implied short-term	1,267	586	5	1,540	353	838	1,413	4.6	43.4
Memo items									
Debt repayment (LT, after relief)	−586	−620	−952	−1,066	−1,104	−1,858	−2,145	−6.2	
Debt service (after relief)	−1,254	−1,804	−2,417	−2,507	−2,690	−3,611	−4,279	−14.3	
Net resource transfer	2,745	577	−401	139	−329	−1,038	−437	1.7	

Sources: Central Bank of Turkey, IMF, and OECD. The present data partly reflect the latest available figures provided in the 1986 Annual Report of the Central Bank.

Note: Based on the revised presentation of the balance of payments.

deregulated, resulting in sharp rises in rates for time deposits and nonpreferential credit to borrowers. A firm signal for the maintenance of a realistic exchange rate policy was given initially through frequent mini-devaluations, and from May 1981 on by daily adjustments. By the end of 1981, an export-driven output recovery had begun, accompanied by a substantially depreciated currency and a sizable reduction in the rate of domestic inflation.

The second stage of the program (in 1982–83) strove to consolidate the conditions for macroeconomic stability, and to maintain the relative price realignment as of the end of 1981. During this stage of policy consolidation, no major moves were made towards the further liberalization of domestic and external markets. Institutional measures produced some helpful results in areas such as external debt management, establishment of a new framework for the small and ineffective securities market, and income tax changes aiming at supply-side responses. However, the tax reform resulted in the reduction of the tax/GNP ratio from 19 percent in 1981 to 17 percent in 1983 as it offset the bracket creep of the previous inflationary period.

The financial liberalization process initiated by the flexible interest rate policy was not followed up with sufficient care and expertise. Turkey faced a major crisis in mid-1982 with the collapse of brokerage firms that had been involved in highly risky credit transactions and corporate bond trading. The crisis led to the replacement of the top economic team, a relaxed monetary stance, and a somewhat reduced official enthusiasm for outward orientation.

The third stage (from November 1983 on), under the civilian government of Turgut Ozal, featured a deeper liberalization of the current and capital accounts of the balance of payments. Although far from being a neutral trade regime, the new trade policy framework provides an unprecedented openness to the Turkish economy on merchandise trade and invisible transactions. A novel feature of the import component of the new trade regime is the presence of a negative list, which explicitly indicates the prohibited import items. The pre-1984 import regimes had contained only positive lists (subject to varying degrees of liberalization), beyond which all imported items were prohibited. Thus, the removal of the quantitative restrictions (QRs) was significant in the trade reform moves of early 1984. Tariffs and other levies on imports have also been reduced, but they have been subject to frequent revisions by the authorities.

The post-1983 government introduced additional policy changes, mainly in the area of fiscal management. Further measures also have been taken to strengthen the bank supervision system and to allow foreign commercial banks to enter Turkey's financial market. Following the reactivation of syndicated borrowing from the international market in 1982, local commercial banks have been increasingly allowed by the authorities to utilize short-term credits and foreign exchange deposits in their trade-financing operations. The external debt stock has climbed from $18 billion in 1983 to $31 billion in 1986, reflecting in part the appreciation of the major European currencies against the U.S. dollar since early 1985. As a result, and with the termination of debt relief in 1984, Turkey's debt servicing burden has increased substantially in the last few years (see section E in table 9.3)

Interpreting the Post-1980 Adjustment

How do we interpret the relatively successful adjustment of the Turkish economy in the post-1980 period? It seems clear that the radical changes in the structure of relative prices, and the attendant shifts in patterns of income distribution, were the key internal mechanism for reducing inflation and initiating export-led recovery. Figure 9.1 displays the drastic transformation in the relative price structure after 1978. While the prereform period (1978–79) had already set some of these changes in motion, particularly the decline in real wages and in agriculture's terms of trade, the policies of the 1980s consolidated and accentuated them. The net effect was a substantial increase in the profitability of the traded manufactures sector, and a sharp reduction in labor and farmers' incomes. On the whole, these also implied an improvement in the terms of trade of the public sector vis-à-vis the private sector, which proved to be the key to the reduction of real private expenditures. Hence, these relative price changes not only

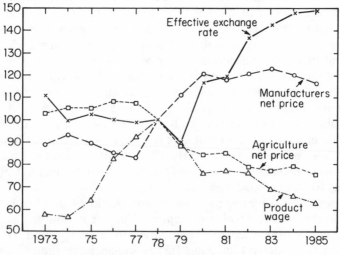

Fig. 9.1   Selected real prices (1978 = 100)

resulted in expenditure switching, in the conventional manner, but were also instrumental in reducing absorption.

In combination with wage repression and lower support prices for agriculture, these relative price changes have been engineered mainly by SEE price increases, exchange rate depreciation, and switching to positive rates on bank deposits. The restructured price system sharply favored the public sector, increased the share of SEEs in public savings, and lowered the dependence on Central Bank financing. In turn, the share of private disposable income in GNP declined at constant prices. Besides promoting expenditure-switching towards exports, the relative price and income shifts thus contributed to reductions in current absorption and public sector deficits, particularly during the 1980–82 period. In the absence of a significant additional tax effort, the burden of adjustment in the public sector fell mainly on subsidies, employee salaries, and current social expenditures as the government strove to sustain public employment and fixed investments in infrastructure sectors.

With the adoption of the policy of positive real rates on time deposits, the income velocity of broad money (M2) was gradually lowered from 5.0 in 1980 to 3.4 in 1985. Besides favorably affecting the expansion of financial intermediation in the economy, the positive deposit rates have served to increase the availability of bank credit to finance working capital, albeit at sharply increased bank-loan risks and real user costs. In the presence of reduced but still large public sector deficits, the high interest rates have contributed to private net savings mainly through lower private business investment rather than through higher savings rates in the private sector.

That these sharp changes in relative prices could be maintained is in no small measure due to the special political circumstances of the period. The military regime of 1980–83 was in the comparatively rare position of enjoying broad popular support as it restored law and order, which had been severely lacking before September 1980. In addition, debt relief and capital inflows reduced the magnitude of the requisite fiscal retrenchment.

9.2   Aspects of Debt and Adjustment

9.2.1   External Borrowing, Wage Flexibility, and Trade-Liberalizing Devaluations: A General Equilibrium Analysis (1978–83)

A comparative study of the Turkish adjustment efforts in 1978–79 and 1980–83 brings out the important roles of the trade adjustment mechanism and of the macroeconomic context in a semi-industrial country facing disturbances from the external environment. The 1978–

79 episode reveals that import compression by means of quantity rationing (serving as the trade adjustment mechanism) has a limited effectiveness in maintaining a modicum of growth in a heavily import-dependent and structurally rigid economy, especially under lax demand management.

In turn, the post-1980 experience shows the feasibility of resuming outward-oriented expansion under a gradually liberalized trade regime supported by timely external assistance, an improved macroeconomic setting, and adequate shifts in relative prices and incomes. The Turkish case also suggests, however, that the required changes in relative prices and income distribution may be quite pronounced in an economy characterized by structural rigidities and distortions. In the context of such policy concerns and research issues, our longer monograph summarizes the findings of a general equilibrium analysis with a computable multisectoral model calibrated to observed 1978–83 data.

Our counterfactual simulations explore the economy-wide effects of trade-liberalizing devaluations (which aim at reduced levels of quantity rationing of nonoil imports) under varying sets of urban wage policies and predetermined limits on external borrowing. The simulations demonstrate and quantify the high marginal productivity of external borrowing and the growth-supporting role of the downward flexibility of real wages under the economic conditions of Turkey prevailing in the early 1980s.

9.2.2 Trade Regime and Export Performance

It is possible to recast the Turkish experience with external debt in terms of a narrative exclusively involving trade flows. In such a case, the rapid accumulation of debt in 1973–77 would be seen as the consequence of rising imports with stagnant exports. In 1978–79, the economy could be seen as in a tailspin with imports collapsing. The recovery after 1980 would be the result of a phenomenal increase in exports, which allowed a revival in imports. To be sure, such a perspective is seriously misleading, since it focuses on trade alone. The accumulation of external debt and its servicing are both clearly macroeconomic phenomena. These two are fundamentally linked to the relationship between aggregate expenditures and national income. As such, the various microeconomic measures comprising a country's trade regime play a somewhat secondary role. Nonetheless, Turkey's case demonstrates that the kind of import dependence and structural rigidity fostered by import-substitution policies render adjustment to a payments crisis much more painful. The extent to which an economy is export oriented makes a big difference to the ease with which a given stock of foreign debt can be serviced, and is therefore an important indicator of creditworthiness. Here too, the post-1980 Turkish experience is exemplary.

In view of the rather miraculous export performance since 1980, it is important to gauge the relative contributions of the various factors at work. A rough statistical decomposition of the increase in the volume of exports between 1979 and 1984 yields some interesting results. The bulk of the increase turns out to be accounted for by a dummy variable for 1981:II, which alone "explains" 58 percent of the difference between the actual and counterfactual levels of exports in 1984. The real exchange rate depreciations since 1979 "explain" 30 percent of the increase in exports, and the reduction in exchange rate volatility another 7 percent, bringing the total contribution of exchange rate policy to 37 percent. The slowdown in industrial countries, on the other hand, has made a negative contribution of 12 percent.

It is rather surprising that exchange rate policy has played such a moderate role in view of the vast real depreciations achieved since 1980. Also, the predominant role of the dummy variable points to a significant upwards shift in export supply or export demand (or both) during 1981. It is tempting to ascribe this effect to the Iran-Iraq war, as a boom in exports to these two countries started during 1981. In addition, a non-negligible share of the increase in exports after 1980 turns out to have been the result of a statistical fiction: To take advantage of generous export subsidies, domestic entrepreneurs appear to have changed their invoicing practices from mild underinvoicing to substantial overinvoicing (at an average rate of 13 percent during 1981–85 in exports to the OECD). Finally, the depressed state of private investment throughout the first half of the 1980s suggests that very little export-oriented structural change has taken place in fact, with the bulk of exports coming from increased capacity utilization.

9.2.3 Public-Sector Financial Management

In comparative perspective, two aspects of Turkish fiscal policy stand out. First, as argued above, large fiscal deficits were not the ultimate cause of the debt crisis of 1977. In an accounting sense, of course, the growing current account deficits had their counterpart in a deteriorating fiscal balance. Whatever danger that may have implied over the longer run, the timing of the crisis was determined instead by the dynamics of debt itself. Under the convertible lira scheme, the capital account was set on an unsustainable course of ever-increasing foreign borrowing. Hence, the Turkish case may represent one instance where it may make sense to reverse the usual causality, and to ascribe the fiscal deficits to increasing debt rather than the reverse. The public sector acted as a vacuum; foreign inflows kept coming in.

The second important aspect is that fiscal policy has played only a moderate role in the adjustment process of the 1980s. While the reform in pricing policies in agriculture and state enterprises has served to enhance public savings, foreign official assistance in the early years of the recovery obviated the need for a dramatic retrenchment. Indeed, the public sector borrowing requirement (PSBR) stood at 10 percent in the first year of the adjustment program (1980), not too far from its level at the height of the crisis in 1977 (see figure 9.2). Since 1980, the public sector borrowing requirement has averaged around 5 percent of GNP, a large number in new of the growing debt-servicing burden and the consequent need to maintain the current account deficits at reasonable levels.

The continuing burden of fiscal deficits has produced two crucial dilemmas. First, it has increased the cost of maintaining external competitiveness, as real exchange rate depreciations tend to increase the debt-servicing burden on the budget. Second, it has forced the government to rely increasingly on short-term domestic borrowing at real interest rates far exceeding the rate of growth of the economy, raising severe questions about longer-term stability.

9.2.4 External Financial Relations and Debt Management

Turkey's important geopolitical role in the Middle East and as a NATO member bordering on the Soviet Union was critical after 1979 in mobilizing Western support—in terms of both debt relief and new flows—of a magnitude not experienced in any other recent case. A widespread feeling around official circles, as expressed in a *New York Times* editorial on 3 January 1979, was that "[t]he strategic importance of Turkey . . . is too great for Ankara's fate to be left to the [International] Monetary Fund and commercial banks abroad." Official lenders' enthusiasm has also affected the policies of the IMF and the World Bank which showered Turkey with generous amounts of program lending. During the first four years after the crisis of 1977 (1978–81), ex-

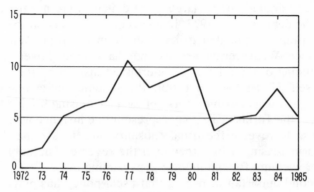

Fig. 9.2   Evolution of the PSBR, 1972–85 (percent of GNP)

ternal flows allowed the Turkish economy to run an average current account deficit of 3.4 percent (of GNP), and an average noninterest current account deficit of 2.3 percent. In fact, net resource transfers to Turkey turned negative for the first time only in 1982, a comfortable five years after the original crisis. The contrast with the post-1982 experience of other heavily-indebted countries could not be starker.

The absence of an intense squeeze on the current account, as was the case in most other countries, has greatly facilitated the implementation of the reforms after 1980, as well as setting the stage for a recovery. It is largely because of capital inflows that the Turkish stabilization took place *alongside* an economic expansion. In this key respect, Turkey's adjustment experience provides an obvious lesson for the current strategy in the global debt crisis.

Since 1982, Turkey's reliance on official inflows has diminished. Such inflows have been replaced by syndicated loans, and, to a much greater extent, by renewed short-term borrowing on the part of domestic banks and the Central Bank. The borrowing experience of the last few years has brought to the fore the recurring penchant of policymakers for rather exotic borrowing arrangements with relatively short-term maturities and high premia over international rates (e.g., the CTLDs in the 1970s, the Dresdner Bank scheme in the 1980s). These have not served Turkey well in the past, and there are some questions as to whether they will do so in the future.

9.3 Conclusions and Prospects

Turkey has managed to transform itself from the problem country of the 1970s to the model debtor of the 1980s. Our account stresses the role both of the domestic policy changes and of the external environment in this accomplishment. While a remarkable amount of adjustment has clearly taken place, some problem areas continue to cloud the horizon.

First, the problems of fiscal adjustment are, if anything, likely to become accentuated in an era of growing debt-service burden. The fiscal retrenchment that has taken place since 1980 has not been a remarkable one, and the public-sector budget remains the Achilles' heel of the Turkish macroeconomy. Second, the Turkish economy still lacks a well-founded "debt strategy." Ever since the mid-1970s, the debt accumulation process has been marked by recourse to rather exotic arrangements whose long-term stability is problematic. Third, the extent to which the real economy and growth process have adjusted to the changes in the structure of relative prices since 1980 is unclear. Most disappointing in this respect is the apparent lack of buoyancy of private investment in tradables. Finally, the Turkish economy continues to be plagued by the consequences for income distribution of the debt crisis of the late 1970s. Any attempt to reverse these consequences will likely put strains on macro balances that are already somewhat shaky.

Appendix

Table 9.5   External Debt, 1978–86

(mill. US $)	1978	1979	1980	1981	1982	1983	1984	1985	1986
Total external debt	14,399	14,223	16,315	16,861	17,619	18,391	21,288	25,012	31,228
Medium and long-term debt	7,223	10,667	13,835	14,667	15,455	15,352	16,782	18,395	21,837
Multilateral organizations (incl. IMF)	2,168	2,474	3,398	3,857	4,531	4,916	5,434	6,103	6,588
Bilateral credits[a]	4,212	4,370	5,983	6,712	7,115	6,566	7,305	8,013	10,187
OECD	3,871	3,976	5,253	5,901	6,146	5,613	6,168	6,776	8,270
Commercial Banks[b]	487	3,464	3,436	3,257	3,229	3,262	3,693	4,014	4,833
Private lenders	356	359	1,018	841	580	608	350	265	229
Short-term Debt	7,176	3,556	2,480	2,194	2,164	3,039	4,506	6,617	9,391
Public sector[a]	1,894	1,104	1,448	1,161	1,104	1,737	2,663	3,755	5,406
Dresdner Bank[c]	363	344	365	473	817	1,251	1,778	2,678	3,788
Bankers' credits	333	18	10	—	—	65	195	432	944
overdrafts	341	244	254	69	48	164	417	376	77
Private Sector[a]	5,282	2,452	1,032	1,033	1,060	1,302	1,843	2,862	3,985
CTLDs[d]	2,860	617	543	473	585	647	61	18	6
Suppliers' Credits (cash against goods)	1,560	1,400	—	—	—	—	—	—	—
Acceptance credits	862	435	377	230	276	318	703	1,093	1,061
Pre-Export financing	—	—	112	330	199	254	414	609	629
FX deposit accounts	—	—	—	—	—	83	544	724	1,250

Source: Central Bank.

[a] The subcategory or subcategories shown represent only a partial list of this kind of debt, with the exception of the years 1978–83 in the private sector in which the list of subcategories is complete.

[b] Includes rescheduled convertible Turkish lira deposits (CTLDs) from 1979 on.

[c] These include deposits with maturity longer than one year.

[d] Nonrescheduled CTLDs.

Remarks on Country Studies

Miguel Urrutia
Anne O. Krueger

Miguel Urrutia

I found the papers analyzing the origins of overindebtedness in a group of Latin American countries both interesting and original. I read them without the feeling of "déjà vu," which now seems inevitable when facing publications on the debt problem.

A reading of the Latin American case studies and Jeffrey Sachs's overview chapter leads one to the conclusion that an understanding of the political economy of fiscal policy may be a key to understanding both the origins of the debt crisis and the policies needed for overcoming it. The problem of fiscal policy-making in the region is therefore the issue I would like to deal with in these comments.

Concentrating on that issue, which addresses the area of national policy-making, does not mean, however, that I include myself in the camp of those who blame the debt crisis exclusively on the policy mistakes of the debtor countries. We are all aware that the best solution to the debt problem is rapid growth in the OECD countries and enhanced access for Latin American exports to the industrialized economies.

I can even imagine countries conditioning the payment of interest on their debt to certain market-opening measures or increases in import quotas. Such a bargaining strategy would require broadening the debt bargaining process to include not only developed country bankers, the multilateral financial institutions, and ministers of finance from debtor countries, but also trade ministers from indebted and industrialized countries. I should imagine that the issue of who sits at the debt bar-

Miguel Urrutia is the manager of the Economic and Social Development Department of the Inter-American Development Bank.

gaining table will be argued with ever greater emphasis by the developing countries in the following months.

Because the relationship between trade and debt is well known, and the inconsistency between protectionism and the servicing of the debt has been thoroughly explored elsewhere, I would like to concentrate on the analysis of national policy responses to the debt crisis.

The Origins of the Debt Crisis in Latin America

The Brazilian case study suggests that even before the second oil shock, "there were signs of an accumulating domestic disequilibrium as the ambitious investment plan was followed. Government expenditures outran its finance. . . ." The study shows, therefore, that the accumulation of debt was in good part caused by the fiscal deficit. But Cardoso and Fishlow also blame the fiscal deficit for the failure of the stabilization attempts, including the Cruzado Plan. "The budget deficit is central not only to the failure of the Cruzado Plan, but to the acceleration of inflation and high real interest rates of the 1981–84 stabilization period."

The Mexican crisis has even clearer fiscal origins. As Buffie and Krause point out, during the 1977–82 period, Mexico enjoyed very favorable terms of trade and was blessed by the discovery of enormous oil wealth. The Lopez Portillo administration simply matched those windfalls by an extraordinary increase in government spending. Fiscal statistics support their claim. Total real public-sector expenditure increased by 94.4 percent in four years, climbing from 31.0 percent of GDP in 1978 to 41.3 percent in 1981.

The cause of the Mexican crisis of the 1980s was largely fiscal, and the difficulties experienced with the economic adjustment process had the same cause. The authors conclude that

> [t]he De La Madrid administration has not offset higher debt service payments and lower oil prices with adequate fiscal adjustment. Instead, limited tax increases and cuts in current expenditure have been supplemented by a variety of other policies aimed at restraining the inflationary pressures created by the large fiscal deficits. . . . In imposing high reserve ratios, in requiring banks to allocate a large share of their portfolio to the purchase of various government issued assets, in financing a greater part of the fiscal deficit through bond sales, and in reducing expenditures to augment the stock of infrastructure capital, a series of devastating blows have been dealt to the profitability of private investment.

One wonders why governments can do anything except tax reform. The other measures affect profits, as would taxes, but taxation seems politically impossible. Why? We can receive some enlightenment by looking at the extreme policy disasters of Bolivia.

I found the paper by Morales and Sachs particularly interesting. The only quibble I have with it is that they start their story after the 1952 revolution. I am not an expert on Bolivian history, but I understand that the Revolution of 1952 was truly a revolution, and that it destroyed a feudal social order. The land reform was radical and effective. The depth of the transformation may explain part of the postrevolutionary political instability. In Europe the revolutionary replacement of the feudal order by a bourgeois state was also often followed by substantial political instability and frequent military governments.

The post-1952 story, however, rightly emphasizes the pervasiveness of an ideology that assigns the state a leading role in development policy, in a political context where governments do not have the power and organization to tax income and wealth. The contradiction between the role assigned to government in the development process and the political impossibility of producing income for the government through taxation meant that governments of both right and left continuously tried to finance a large modernizing state either through foreign debt or inflation.

The interesting question to ask is why in Bolivia, and in other Latin American nations, taxation was never really tried as a source of finance for the kind of state that the dominant ideology demanded.

Some Hypothesis on the Political Economy of Fiscal Policy

Morales and Sachs relate how in Bolivia governments on the left sought redistribution through higher wages and a larger role for public-sector workers, while governments on the right sought instead to bolster favored segments of the private sector through generous government subsidies. What appears to happen is that the middle class political and military elites pressure for increased government expediture and never consider the possibility of taxing themselves.

When the power base of a regime is exclusively middle class, taxation is unattractive because the easiest group to tax in developing countries is employees of the formal sector. Latin American middle-class ideologues, therefore, are not fanatics of the income tax or of sales taxes. Middle class governments also do not have sufficient bureaucratic control of the countryside to tax land directly, so they attempt to do it through import tariffs and price controls. But short of stalinist agricultural price controls, agricultural price policy is not easily translated into central government tax revenues.

The more traditional politicians, with a rural landlord base of support, do not want to tax land since this would mean taxing themselves. They cannot, on the other hand, tax the middle class because the army and organized labor can be mobilized to pressure the regime against urban taxes through urban violence (general strikes or threats of a coup). In summary, regimes whose only base of support is the middle class may be unable to tax. Is that the nature of political regimes in Bolivia since 1952?

It should be pointed out that if the middle class is defined as the 7th–9th income decile, it includes the military, organized labor, and the bureaucracy. All of these groups are interested in a large state and low income and consumption taxes. This is the worst possible environment for fiscal policy. It may indeed be that in Bolivia, as in Colombia and Venezuela in the 19th century, the object of politics, as the authors point out, has been "the battle of the 'ins' versus the 'outs' ". The state is then viewed as an instrument of redistribution of income *within* the middle class.

In Mexico, before Echeverria, maybe the political base was broader. Certainly the PRI had strong peasant support, which allowed it to maintain legitimacy without having to deliver large state benefits to the urban classes. The PRI could not achieve a large proportion of tax revenues to GDP, but it could maintain fiscal equilibrium by not overspending. As Mexico urbanized, the peasant base became less important and internal politics within the PRI became very dependent on the distribution of benefits within the state bureaucracy itself. This pressured government expenditure without creating a constituency for tax reforms. Also, institutionally, the chances of fiscal equilibrium diminished when the function of spending was separated from the Secretaría de Hacienda, responsible for revenues, and given to the Secretaría de Presupuesto, only responsible for spending. Significantly, the best way to get elected presidential candidate of the PRI has been to become head of the spending agency.

The military governments of Argentina also seem to have had a very narrow middle-class base. The Peronistas, dominated by the public-sector unions, simply represented another faction of the middle class.

The Colombia Case Study

There was one case in Latin America of a country that did not increase its debt excessively in the 1970s—Colombia. It also carried out at least two wide-ranging tax reforms, and maintained a low budget deficit.

Politics in Colombia have some interesting characteristics, and this may explain the country's uncommon fiscal policies. It is a formal democracy and the political process was more participatory in the 1970s than in other nations. In this, Costa Rica, Venezuela, and some of the Caribbean countries have greater similarity to Colombia than to the countries studied in the NBER project. In Colombia, the political parties (in power for 140 years) are multiclass, and rural and urban informal sectors are influential in the parties. Finally, the government in 1974–

78 had a large rural base of support, and the president had developed a strong commitment to promoting development in the rural sector and dismantling the import substitution model of development. He was against subsidizing organized labor and industrialists, was antibureaucracy, and had his urban support among the unorganized who suffered most from inflation. In summary, the political base of the government was not middle class, and not suprisingly middle class income grew less rapidly than the income of the poor and the rich in the 1970s.

The main objective of the government in power between 1974 and 1978 was to control inflation, and, with this objective, it carried out a tax reform in 1974, and, also to control inflation, the government did not increase the foreign debt. In contrast, in the early 1980s another government, whose political base was largely the bureaucracy, increased debt and government expenditure rapidly. That policy created a minor debt crisis in 1983–84, but Colombia was the only country in Latin America that adjusted successfully after 1982. It did it by almost wiping out the fiscal deficit in 1984–85, not only by decreasing expenditures, but also by increasing taxation.

The president in 1984–85 had his political base largely among the unorganized urban masses. He had little support from the army or the upper middle class, and substantial support from a political class whose source of income is politics and not industry or large landholdings.

In summary, fiscal responsibility may only emerge in the region as the basis of support for Latin American governments is diversified. Narrow middle class governments may be incompatible with fiscal equilibrium.

Conclusions

The optimistic conclusion of the previous analysis is that the deepening of democracy that has occurred in the 1980s may facilitate in the future a more rational fiscal policy. The lesson, on the other hand, is that adjustment policies must be designed keeping in mind the high political cost of policies that affect negatively primarily the politically strong middle class.

The point is not that policies unpopular with the middle class should not be adopted. Quite the contrary. The objective should be to design components of the adjustment policy that must include tax reform, but, at the same time to take measures which will create political support for the government from other groups in society. This means the design of social investment projects and social safety nets which will develop political support from nonmiddle class constituencies.

It is not prudent to limit adjustment programs to wage restraints, liberalization of labor legislation, decreases in government employment, and elimination of urban subsidies, for all of these measures negatively affect the politically powerful middle class. Some of the democracies in Latin America have shown that tax reform is viable within an adjustment program that generates employment and improves the prospects of the very poor or marginal groups in society. It may be that a good criterion for judging an adjustment package is to examine whether it includes tax reform *and* measures which make tax reform politically viable.

Anne O. Krueger

To provide an overview of the country studies presented is a real challenge. To focus the discussion, I shall concentrate my remarks on two main issues: the origins of the debt problems of the developing countries in the 1980s, and the political-economic assumptions that seem implicitly to underlie much of our thinking on policy issues such as foreign borrowing and debt.

Origins of the Debt Problems

There is no doubt that the worldwide recession of the early 1980s, coupled with falling commodity prices and rising nominal interest rates, exacerbated the difficulties of all debtor countries. However, some countries (e.g., Turkey) were unable to maintain debt-service even before 1980, and some (e.g., Mexico) clearly did not encounter difficulties because of external circumstances. There is no point in asking whether domestic policies or worldwide conditions led to the problems. In each country the debt problem had a magnitude, and both domestic and external factors contributed. The precise quantitative contribution of each varied from country to country.

In a sense, the fundamental question is: When a country borrows to finance current-account imbalances[1] on a continuing basis, is that borrowing path sustainable? From economic theory, we know that the current account deficit equals the excess of investment over savings. When borrowing finances additional investment with a rate of return greater than or equal to the rate of interest at which borrowing takes place, and barring serious mismatches between the timing of debt-servicing obligations and the stream of earning from the additional investment, a current account deficit should be associated with additional earning sufficient to finance debt-service obligations.

This simple framework permits development of a taxonomy with which to analyze the origins of the debt difficulties of developing

Anne O. Krueger is the Arts and Sciences Professor of Economics at Duke University and a research associate of the National Bureau of Economic Research.

countries. We note that investment can exceed savings either because investment is "high" compared to "normal" domestic savings (relative to a country's per capita income level) or because investment is "normal" and domestic savings are low.[2]

Case 1: Investment "high" and in excess of savings; the real rate of return on investment exceeds the real interest rate. In this case, debt-servicing obligations should be readily met, except perhaps for transitory difficulties associated with jumps in the real interest rate (on variable-rate debt) or with worldwide recession. This is the "textbook" case of self-financing debt. Among the countries covered in the NBER project, Korea seems to fit here: the real rate of return on investment was high (estimated to be in excess of 30 percent); and capital inflows permitted a higher rate of investment, and therefore, economic growth, given Korean savings (which do not appear to have been low relative to per capita income, at least after the mid-1960s when borrowing started). Indonesia may also be in the group.

Case 2: Investment high, savings "normal," but a low and possibly even negative real rate of return on investments. In this circumstance, borrowing would not be indefinitely sustainable. Earnings from debt-financed projects would increasingly fall short of debt-servicing obligations and, at some point, further borrowing along this path would be unsustainable. A rise in the world real interest rate on variable rate debt would certainly accelerate the time at which unsustainability became evident, if it did not itself precipitate a cessation of voluntary lending and an inability to meet debt-servicing obligation.

Among the countries in the NBER project, Argentina, Mexico, and the Philippines arguably fall into this category. A high fraction of domestic investments had relatively low rates of return, for reasons discussed further below.

Case 3: Investment normal, but savings "low" and/or a low real rate of return on investment. Low savings could result either because incentives failed to reflect changing conditions, as in Turkey where domestic petroleum prices were not increased significantly after the oil price increase of 1973 (so that the private consumption share was unaltered at domestic prices but increased at world prices), or because of public-sector behavior, discussed further below. Brazil, as well as Turkey prior to 1979, appears to fall in this category.

Case 4: Investment equals saving. Here there are three subcases.[3]

a. Savings and investment are approximately normal relative to income, and the real rate of return is reasonably high. In this circumstance (Colombia in the 1970s) the growth rate is satisfactory and could have been augmented by borrowing.

b. Savings and investment are "normal," but the rate of return is low. Growth is therefore slow, but again, no debt problems emerge. India probably falls in this category.

c. Savings and investment are "low" with either a normal or a low real rate of return on investments. In this case, growth is sluggish, but again, debt is not a problem. Burma and Haiti, among others, may fall into this category.

As these cases indicate, a country can fail to have a debt problem and nonetheless have poor economic performance. Conversely an apparently satisfactory rate of growth may be possible only because of borrowing, which may mask difficulties either with resource accumulation or resource allocation.

Case 5: Everything that can go wrong does. In addition to low domestic savings and a low real rate of return, the terms of trade deteriorate sharply enough (or crops fail badly enough) so that imports cannot be reduced as quickly as export earnings fall. In this case, debt mounts sharply and no corresponding income streams are generated.

Among the countries in the NBER project, Bolivia seems to belong here. It may simply be an extreme example of case 3, but seems to have encountered sufficiently bad fortunes to deserve a special category. Some African countries not included in the NBER project also undoubtedly belong in this group. Given earlier economic policies and low rates of return, adverse shifts in the terms of trade have been large enough to render the problem qualitatively, as well as quantitatively, different from those of other heavily indebted countries.

This taxonomy is, of course, rough, and only suggestive. It may, nonetheless, provide an organizing framework for diagnosis. To complete it, however, it is necessary to analyze the sources of low rates of return and/or savings and investment rates.

Consider low or negative real rates of return first. How can these come about? While there are obviously any number of possibilities, two sources appear to have figured prominently: (1) a trade and payments regime that provided distorted incentives of private-sector investment[4] and (2) inefficient public-sector investment programs.

That a highly restrictive trade and payments regime can lead to privately profitable investment opportunities with a low or negative social rate of return has been documented in both theory (see Bhagwati and Srinivasan 1978) and practice (see Krueger 1978). Further, Brecher and Díaz-Alejandro (1977) have shown that capital inflows in these circumstances can have negative real returns to the economy as a whole. Cumulatively, one would expect debt-servicing difficulties to mount in these circumstances, and one suspects that the trade regime was a major contributory factor to the debt-servicing difficulties of Turkey in 1979.

Likewise, public-sector investments can be highly inefficient. The Philippines study cites a nuclear power plant never put into operation, and that may be less inefficient than continuing to operate some white elephants. Loss-making investments are not infrequent. Mexico's and Brazil's low rates of return on investment appear to be largely attributable to this factor.

As to determinants of the savings rate, a significant factor in the 1970s was the failure of some governments, possibly most notably Turkey, and to a lesser extent Brazil, to let the domestic price of petroleum reflect the altered international terms of trade after 1974. The result was that consumption as a percentage of GNP remained relatively constant at domestic prices but rose in international prices by 2 to 3 percentage points. The borrowing that offset the current account deficit clearly did not generate any earning streams to service the debt.

Public consumption also rose sharply in a number of countries, and was not offset by tax increases. In these circumstances increased public consumption absorbed public and/or private savings. Debt accumulation permitted the maintenance of investment levels in the short term, but cumulatively, earnings streams were not generated to service them.[5]

Political Economy of Government Policy

In any discussion of debt, the role of government and governmental decision features prominently. An important question that arises in this connection is the assumptions to be made about governmental behavior. Are all actions taken by governments rational? Do governments, like individuals, decide rationally? Are choices deliberate outcomes of rational processes?

In discussions of the debt problem and needed reforms, implicit assumptions about these issues appear. Were exchange rate distortions the result of policies deliberately chosen with a full understanding of the future consequences? Or, instead, were ideas of the day with respect to the infant industry argument and the allegedly low costs of protection an important factor? This is not the occasion on which to develop a full-blown theory of government behavior. But a few comments seem to me to be in order, inspired by the implicit theories that are present in some of the papers and today's discussion.

First, what is politically infeasible today may not be tomorrow, and ideas influence both the range of choice and the feasibility of change. It was "politically impossible" to abandon a highly restrictionist trade regime in Turkey in much of the 1970s, but it was done starting in 1979 and the architect of the economic reform has won several elections based largely on his economic policies.

Second, markets respond to government policies and those responses often induce political reactions. Thus, smuggling may persuade policymakers to tighten controls or to alter the exchange rate and reduce incentives for smuggling. Either way, people respond to perceived problems based on their understanding of the consequences of alternative responses. Politicians may fear change, be uninformed as to the benefits of change, and thus resist. Within governments there are normally competing ideas and interests. But again, the professional knowledge of the economist can be important in affecting thinking.

In this regard, it is important to ask whether government policies "cause" outcomes. It is true, for example, that the Korean government "targeted" exports. But it is also true that those targets were set in consultation with exporters whose plans, in turn, were in part determined by the real exchange rate and other components of the incentive system. Were "targets" responsible for exports, or was there a process whereby the desire to increase export earnings (and the realistic exchange rate that accompanied it) set in motion a selection process to induce economically efficient exporters? If the latter, the government could still have "targeted," but the interpretation is quite different.

More generally, however, policies which have with hindsight turned out to be ill advised were often buttressed with justifications such as "infant industry," or "import substitution," or other ideas of the day. While particular interests might in any event have held sway, it is nonetheless important to bear in mind that governments are not monolithic, and that decisions are often the result of a process in which conflicting claims are resolved. In this context, the "legitimacy" of ideas is important. If there are bases on which it can be demonstrated that, e.g., the costs of an overvalued exchange rate are higher than the opponents of change assert, the likelihood that action will be taken increases.

There has been learning in the past thirty years. It has come partly out of experience, and especially from the contrast between countries whose policies were outer-oriented and those whose policies were inner-oriented. It has also come partly out of research results. It is all too easy to forget that the "climate of professional opinion" twenty years ago was much more forgiving of the policies that have been so condemned in discussions today. The role of economists in sanctioning, or at least not condemning, policy mistakes should not be ignored. Ironically, the power of ideas is often most underestimated by those whose stock in trade it is!

Evidence such as that coming out of the NBER project should further the progress of ideas. There is fear of policy reform, beyond that which would appear warranted based on the experience of past reform efforts. The gains are usually underestimated and the losses overestimated. In the Korean case, the benefits came very quickly. As other reforms, such as the Turkish, prove less injurious and more beneficial than expected, it is to be hoped that knowledge will once again facilitate the adoption of policies leading to higher levels of economic *and* political welfare.

Notes

1. For expository simplicity, I ignore other techniques of financing current account deficits such as running down foreign exchange reserves (because that path is unsustainable in the longer term) and direct foreign investment (because it was not a major factor in the debt difficulties of the 1980s).
2. It could, of course, be that investment was high and savings low. Among the countries covered in the NBER project this does not seem to have been the case.
3. Ignore the case where savings and investment are "high" and the real rate of return on investment is high. This is probably the Japanese case and Korea may have entered this group in 1986.
4. It should be noted that one cannot necessarily identify the source of the problem with the category (private or public) of the borrower. Any government confronting a fiscal deficit can either borrow abroad or it can borrow domestically. If it does the latter and drives up the domestic rate of interest, private firms will be induced to borrow abroad. This mechanism seems to have been deliberately employed in Brazil, on the theory that lenders would provide more favorable terms to private than to public borrowers.
5. Note that there are two transfer problems associated with public-sector debt servicing: raising revenue domestically and buying foreign exchange. The revenue problem is apparently more acute in countries where fiscal deficits were financed with foreign borrowing, while the foreign exchange problem has probably been more acute in instances where the foreign trade regime led to low rates of return on investments.

References

Bhagwati, Jagdish N., and T. N. Srinivasan. 1978. Shadow prices for project selection in the presence of distortion: Effective rates of protection and domestic resource costs. *Journal of Political Economy* 86(11):97–116.
Brecher, Richard A., and Carlos S. Díaz-Alejandro. 1977. Tariffs, foreign capital and immiserizing growth. *Journal of International Economics* 7(4):317–22.
Krueger, Anne O. 1978 *Foreign trade regimes and economic development: Liberalization attempts and consequences.* Cambridge, Mass.: Ballinger Publishing.

II   Special Topics

10   How Sovereign Debt Has Worked

Peter H. Lindert and Peter J. Morton

10.1 Introduction

The international financial community has often preferred to repeat the past rather than study it. Since 1974 international lending has passed through another cycle of enthusiasm followed by nonrepayment and creditor revulsion, repeating a pattern that has recurred several times since the 18th century.

The process is costly. Relative to ordinary private lending, lending to sovereign foreign debtors brings costs to either side or both sides, and often to third parties. The unenforceability of debt service obligations sooner or later breeds lasting creditor distrust and cuts the supply of capital to countries where its marginal product is generally high. The debtors' macroeconomies are destabilized by the borrowing boom and later bust, especially when the bust brings unforeseen austerity.

Those caught in the current lingering debt crisis cannot blame their innocence on an absence of historical literature. That literature was vast even before the crisis broke in 1982, and in this chapter we extend it in two directions. Section 10.2 discusses creditors' returns and the treatment of defaulters since 1850. Past lending to foreign goverments has brought high private returns in the aggregate, but with curious patterns. Investors seem to have paid little attention to the past repayment record of the borrowing governments. They may or may not have been wise in ignoring the past. Their inattention, at any rate,

Peter H. Lindert is a professor of economics and the director of the Agricultural History Center at the University of California at Davis. Peter J. Morton is an assistant professor of economics at Hofstra University.

reveals that they do not punish governments with a prior default history, undercutting the belief in a penalty that compels faithful repayment.

Section 10.3 turns to historical experience with the different policy options available in the wake of a major debt crisis. Noting the necessary imperfections in any policy approach, we discuss some arguments in favor of the older bond-era direct confrontation between problem debtors and their creditors, an approach that usually led to partial default. The more recent approach of bringing the IMF and the World Bank into tripartite debt-crisis negotiations has brought extra costs relating to moral hazard, delays, and macroeconomic adjustment.

10.2 Sovereign Debt Repayment Since the Early 19th Century

If there were no third-party rescuer, no International Monetary Fund, how would soverign debt work? How well would creditors and debtors be likely to fare? How far below the ex ante contracted rates of return were the rates eventually realized by the whole chain of debtholders? Were the returns either so excessive or so low that they suggest a case for special policy intervention in defense of either debtors or creditors? While the future need not match past patterns, there is a long and varied history to tap in forming guesses.

10.2.1 Background

Fresh lending to foreign governments followed the same wave-like pattern as other international lending in the 19th century and early 20th centuries. There was a post-Napoleonic wave in the 1820s, including loans to most of the newly independent nations of Latin America, followed by widespread default. Gross lending to governments, like international lending in general, returned to high tide in the 1850s, in the late 1860s–early 1870s, in the late 1880s, in 1904–14, and again in the late 1920s. The wave of lending to foreign governments in the late 1920s, like that of 1974–82, exceeded any before World War I in real absolute value and even as a share of lender-country GNP. Each wave ended with at least some occurrence of repayments breakdown, sometimes because of international trade depression, sometimes because of government budget crises, and sometimes because of revelation of financial abuses.

Who defaulted, and when? Soon after the lending wave of the 1820s most Latin American governments defaulted to some degree. Several southern states in the United States defaulted in the 1830s–40s and again in the Reconstruction era. Latin America and the Eastern Mediterranean (Greece, Turkey and, momentarily, Egypt) figured prominently in the default waves of the mid-19th century. The end of the late-1880s lending wave featured relatively few defaults, the most notable being Argentina's partial nonrepayment (on which more later) and lingering difficulties with Colombia's debt service. Brazil's good record was finally compromised with repayment lapses necessitating refunding loans in 1898 and 1914. The 1910s brought wholesale defaults in the Mexican Revolution, the Russian Revolution, and the fall of the Ottoman Empire. The broadest wave, however, came in the early 1930s (Eichengreen and Portes 1986; Eichengreen, chap. 11 in this volume) in which essentially all of Latin America, most of Eastern Europe, Turkey, and China defaulted. In the early postwar years, with bond finance dried up and most of the trickle of loans coming from governments or with their guarantees, outright default was replaced with a murmur of repeated concessionary refundings for problem governments, notably Turkey, Latin America, and some newly independent nations. The list of countries needing concessionary refundings in the 1970s and 1980s is more extensive but similar, still featuring Latin America, Eastern Europe and now much of Africa.

Other areas always repaid. One was Western Europe outside of Germany and Spain. Another consisted of the sovereign Arab nations, with only slight exceptions. Asia east of the Persian Gulf consistently repaid, except for China in the 1930s, Japan between 1941 and 1952, and the independent Philippines. So did the white Commonwealth nations.

To judge debtors' repayment behavior or to judge the lenders' behavior, one needs a careful accounting of their borrowings and debt-service outflows. We began with the bonds outstanding in 1850, and those floated between 1850 and about 1970, following them all the way to settlement or to the end of 1983. We follow the experiences of ten borrowing governments: Argentina, Australia, Brazil, Canada, Chile, Egypt, Japan, Mexico, Russia and Turkey. We follow their foreign bond debt, drawing on bondholder annuals, periodic compendia of foreign investments (Fenn, Fitch, Kimber, Dominick and Dominick, etc.), and country studies. We concentrate on bond lending, with separate later treatment of the brief bank-loan wave of 1974–82.

10.2.2 Choosing Summary Measures

Summarizing the flows of real resources between creditors and debtors calls for three related measures. One is the internal rate of return on the loans, with all flows converted into real consumable resources in the lending countries.

The second measure is the real rate of return on an alternative asset, used for comparison with the real (and realized) internal rate on foreign sovereign debt. The main quantitative results all compare sovereign foreign debt with home-country (U.K. and U.S.) bonds. The third summary measure is a net present value of the foreign sovereign debt vis-à-vis home country debt.

Table 10.1 sets the stage by introducing national average ex ante returns and capitalized values contracted at the time of bond issue. In the bond era, investors asked for premia ($v - \bar{\rho}$) on foreign government bonds that were usually between 1.5 and 2.6 percent. These premia will serve as a yardstick for several comparisons to follow. We will find, first, that the real realized returns were well below these ex ante premia. Virtually all of the shortfall in real realized returns was due

Table 10.1   Contracted Nominal Returns on Bond Lending to Ten Foreign Governments, All Marketed Bonds, 1850–1970 with Payments through 1983

Borrowing Nation	n	Rates of Return(%)			(Millions of $)		Risk-Neutral Expected % of Capital loss
		v	$\bar{\rho}$	$v - \bar{\rho}$	NPV	L_0	
Argentina	181	5.92	3.47	2.45	561.4	2,476.6	2.31
Brazil	129	6.19	3.64	2.55	572.3	1,517.4	2.40
Chile	60	6.89	3.94	2.95	274.5	637.5	2.76
Mexico	48	5.83	3.11	2.72	376.8	843.8	2.57
Four Latins	418	6.09	3.52	2.57	1,785.0	5,475.4	2.43
Australia	439	5.60	4.52	1.09	1,358.7	9,836.9	1.03
Canada	488	4.51	2.82	1.69	925.9	1,635.6	1.61
Egypt	20	6.71	3.29	3.43	222.9	513.9	3.21
Japan	60	5.75	3.51	2.24	525.1	1,682.4	2.11
Russia	48	4.94	2.92	2.01	1,952.2	3,456.4	1.92
Turkey	46	5.86	3.33	2.53	744.9	1,300.1	2.39
These six	1,101	5.44	3.86	1.59	5,729.7	18,425.3	1.50
All ten	1,519	5.59	3.78	1.81	7,514.7	23,900.6	1.72

Notes:

n = the number of bonds covered here.

v = the internal rate of return implied by the bond issue price and repayment terms.

$\bar{\rho}$ = the rate of interest on bond lending to the home government (U.K. consol rate or U.S. Treasury long-term bond rate, depending on the place of issue).

NPV = net present value, defined in the following special way: the amount investors were able to save by buying the same promised repayment stream from a foreign government at higher interest instead of from the British or U.S. government.

L_0 = the gross value initially lent to the foreign government.

The "risk-neutral expected % of capital loss" = $(v - \bar{\rho})/(1 + v)$ is a suggestive hypothetical measure used here as in Feder and Just (1984). If bond purchasers were risk-neutral, the coexistence of the two rates of return, v and $\bar{\rho}$, would imply the stated percentage of expected nonrepayment on the higher-yielding foreign bonds. To the extent that purchasers are risk-averse, $(v - \bar{\rho})/(1 + v)$ overstates their expectation of capital losses and instead reflects their aversion to the asset with the higher contracted yield.

Our sample excluded bonds issued in the 1970s and 1980s, except for those issued by Australia. We sought to follow all external bond issues up to about 1970. Specifically, our bond populations stopped with bonds issued in the following final years: Argentina, 1968; Australia, 1978; Brazil and Chile, 1930; Canada, 1967; Egypt, Japan and Turkey, 1965; Mexico, 1966; and Russia, 1916. All subsequent flows were followed through 1983, after which the remaining small balances were assumed to be paid off.

to defaults, not to ex post inflation, which affected both home-bond and foreign-bond returns similarly. Second, the ex ante rates in table 10.1 did not differ across countries in any way that consistently foretold the international differences in ex post returns. The wide differences in realized returns were either poorly predicted or, as seems more likely, simply impossible to predict.

Real realized returns are summarized in table 10.2, with values in sterling at 1913 prices converted into 1913-price dollars at $4.86. Leaving the details in individual-country experience to the fuller version of this study, we examine the global returns.

10.2.3 Global Returns to Lenders, in the Bond Era and since 1973

Combining the ten countries' diverse experiences, table 10.2 shows that investors made more on bond lending to foreign governments than on safer home governments, despite the revolutions and the Great Depression. Foreign bondholders got a net return premium of 0.44 percent per annum on all bonds outstanding anytime between 1850 and about 1970 (with payments carry-over traced through 1983). Curiously enough, the bonds issued in the troubled years between 1915 and 1945

Table 10.2   **Realized Real Returns on Bond Lending to Ten Foreign Governments, 1850–1970, with Payments through 1983**

Borrowing Nation	n	Rates of Return(%)			($ mill. at 1913 prices)	
		ν	$\bar{\rho}$	$\nu - \bar{\rho}$	NPV	L_0
Argentina	187	3.52	1.56	1.96	405.9	1,943.4
Brazil	143	2.97	2.14	0.83	156.5	1,278.5
Chile	60	1.66	1.88	−0.22	−3.9	501.3
Mexico	52	−0.21	1.72	−1.92	−140.1	564.6
Four Latins	442	2.65	1.75	0.86	418.4	4,287.7
Australia	439	3.00	1.97	1.03	669.6	4,873.6
Canada	488	1.91	0.35	1.56	512.3	969.1
Egypt	21	6.21	3.68	2.53	219.5	408.8
Japan	60	2.90	1.33	1.58	290.3	1,346.5
Russia	48	1.31	2.94	−1.63	−691.1	3,340.9
Turkey	54	1.29	2.58	−1.29	−174.0	919.1
These six	1,110	2.40	2.14	0.26	826.6	11,858.0
All ten	1,552	2.47	2.05	0.42	1,245.0	16,145.8

Notes: The algebraic symbols are defined as in table 10.1, except that real rates replace nominal. The rates of return, ν and $\bar{\rho}$, now contain subtractions for the ex post rate of consumer-price inflation in the lending country, and every flow is deflated by a lending-country consumer price index.

The present figures are based on a larger set of bonds than in table 10.1. Conversion bonds, aimed at reviving payments on previous problem bonds, are now included. In some cases these were attached to the records of the previous problem bonds, while in other cases they were entered as separate bonds.

fared better (for creditors) than those issued back in the prewar golden age. The bonds issued between 1850 and 1914 barely broke even with home-government bonds in the ex post measures used here, while those from 1915 to 1945 realized a premium of 1.21 percent.

Have creditors fared better or worse on loans to foreign governments since 1973? Like their bond-era predecessors in table 10.1 above, they charged roughly a 2 percent interest premium in ex ante nominal terms. So far, up to the landmark Brazilian suspension of payments in February 1987, virtually the full debt service was honored. The flurry of reschedulings in the period 1982–86 had little effect on realized rates of interest, offering debtors little relief. To be sure, financial markets have come to *expect* a breakdown of debt service. The informal secondary market for banks' loans to problem debtors has discounted Third World loans by about a third. Top U.S. banks have posted over $16 billion in reserve-addition loss, a significant part of it an expected loss on foreign debt. Yet these market expectations of banks' losses greatly exceed the shortfall of realized debt service. As of the end of 1986, creditors could afford a write-down of 9.2 percent and still receive the same ex post return they would have received from U.S. government bonds of the same maturities as the loans to the third World. By taking a 4.0 percent loss, alternatively, they could have reaped the same 0.42 percent premium over U.S. bonds that their bond-era predecessors received. Or they could suffer major losses if the pessimism of the secondary loan market is correct. The jury is still out.

10.2.4 Past Problem Debtors Have Become Problem Debtors

There is a curious tendency toward historical consistency in the identities of the defaulters. The set of borrowing countries defaulting (wholly or partially) before World War I had a higher probability of default in the 1930s than did other countries receiving loans in the 1920s. Again, the set of borrowing countries defaulting either before 1930 or in the 1930s had a higher probability of needing concessionary "rescheduling" of loans since World War II.

Table 10.3 summarizes the historical consistency in the identities of the defaulters and reschedulers. The shares of countries falling into problem-debtor status (default, arrears, or, in the 1980s, signing rescheduling agreements) are contrasted between two kinds of countries: those with and those without such status in an earlier period. We chose periods long enough so that a worldwide wave of defaults had time to abate, allowing a renewal of worldwide lending. There is a striking pattern of statistical significance. In either worldwide lending crisis (the 1930s and 1980–86), the problem debtors tended to be those who had had problems earlier. The pattern holds whether one looks across all countries or just across large samples of developing countries. We can

Table 10.3   **Historical Rates of Transition into Problem-Debtor Status, among Five Periods, 1820–1986**

Earlier period →	Later period	Among Earlier Full Repayers		Among Earlier Problem Debtors		Difference in Transition rates	
		n	δ_r	n	δ_d	$\delta_d - \delta_r$	(signif.)
A. All debtors							
1820–79 →	1880–1929	19	.105	23	.696	.591	* *
1880–1929 →	1930s	32	.313	20	.800	.487	* *
1820–79 →	1930s	23	.217	26	.692	.475	* *
1930s →	1940–79	22	.182	22	.364	.182	
1940–79 →	1980–86	118	.237	21	.666	.429	* *
1820–1929 →	1980–86	24	.167	25	.640	.473	* *
1930s →	1980–86	25	.200	24	.625	.425	* *
B. Developing-country debtors only							
1820–79 →	1880–1929	9	.222	23	.696	.473	*
1880–1929 →	1930s	22	.409	20	.800	.391	*
1820–1929 →	1930s	14	.357	26	.692	.335	*
1930s →	1940–79	11	.364	20	.350	.014	
1940–79 →	1980–86	96	.292	20	.700	.408	* *
1820–1929 →	1980–86	8	.500	23	.696	.196	
1930s →	1980–86	9	.556	22	.682	.126	

Notes:
n = number of countries covered.
δ = share of sovereign debtor governments becoming problem debtors in the later period.
* = difference is significant at the 5% level with a two-tailed test.
* * = difference is significant at the 1% level with a two-tailed test.
"Sovereign debtor governments" are national or local governments in those countries whose national government was recognized as sovereign in budget setting and contract law in both the earlier and the later period, and which actually received foreign loans within both periods. Excluded (as nondebtors) are four usually-creditor nations: U.S., U.K., France, Germany. "Problem debtors" are those whose national or local governmetns did not repay contracted external debt in full, whether through repudiation or through recorded arrears lasting more than a year or (1980–86 only) signing rescheduling agreements with creditors.

reject the notion that repayments breakdown in crises is uncorrelated with the same nation's distant debt history.

10.2.5   Were Defaulters Punished?

A clear result from the history of rates of return on sovereign debt relates to the ex post treatment of those who fell into arrears: The only ones punished were a few countries defaulting in isolation before 1918. The majority of nonrepayers "escaped" punishment during global crises. In the 1930s, debtors may have seemed to suffer credit cutoffs and trade retaliation, but the impression misleads. In that crisis and its long early-postwar aftermath, the United States and other creditors were indiscriminate in their denial of fresh credits: Almost *no* governments in less developed countries got fresh loans, whether they were repaying old ones or not. Even trade policy, which had the chance to discriminate in the bilateralism of the 1930s, was not used to discriminate against defaulters or in favor of faithful repayers. Protectionism was too sweeping.

In the enthusiastic lending of the 1974–82 wave, lenders paid no attention to past histories of default. Between 1976 and 1979, for example, the same interest premia were charged to those Third World countries that had repaid faithfully in the past and those who had not.

In the 1980s, the signs of discrimination against problem debtors remain weak. Bond lending has virtually dried up, and the revival of bank lending has been very meager, for countries who have repaid faithfully as well as for those demanding repeated rescheduling. Whatever the private wisdom of the pervasiveness of creditor pessimism, the external cost of repayments breakdown seems as evident in the 1980s as in the 1930s: Some faithful repayers (e.g., Colombia, Egypt) have suffered credit contraction along with problem debtors.

Thus the seeming irrelevance of repayments history in creditors' eyes is itself a lesson of history. It predicts that borrowers will not suffer much by following the lead of Peru and Bolivia in 1984 and Brazil and Ecuador in 1987 in cutting repayments and demanding partial write-downs of debt, at least if they do so collectively.

10.3 Options for Handling Debt Crises: Some Suggestions from History and Theory

A combination of history and theory offers tentative lessons on dealing with a repayments crisis once it has already occurred. What is special about the lingering crisis of the 1980s is official third-party intervention, led by the IMF.

To understand what difference the third-party option makes in a debt crisis, we start with an analytical framework developed elsewhere (Lindert 1986). The framework derives much of its power from the definition of a debt crisis: A debt crisis exists *if, in the absence of a better offer, the debtor would rather impose unilateral nonrepayment than repay fully.* By definition, simple full repayment by the debtor, with no outside help, is ruled out. Further, the definition of a debt crisis makes it virtually a situation of revealed overlending, so that merely lending more on the same terms cannot erase the default incentive except under implausible conditions. The alternatives to destructive default reduce to two: either (1) write-downs of part of the debt (either unilaterally or through bilateral negotiation), or (2) third-party rescue packages (sometimes involving relending by the original creditors). Either option brings gains in world wealth by avoiding destructive penalties by the creditors, the damage value of which would not be fully recaptured by them. And either accelerates the renewal of fresh lending, relative to doing nothing about the crisis. But they differ in other important respects.

10.3.1   Two-Party (or Unilateral) Debt Write-Downs

Partial debt write-downs can work, and have worked, in a variety of ways. They can be imposed unilaterally by debtors, in the knowledge that the creditors cannot inflict sufficient damage to dissuade them. In this unilateral case, the debtor calculates the share of write-down that would push marginal benefits down to the marginal cost (direct penalties and loss of borrower surplus on later credit) of extra repudiation. Creditors then decide whether to take the imposed settlement or to hold out indefinitely. The unilateral variant was imposed by Brazil in 1943, and by the end of the decade most creditors had taken what Brazil offered. Credit to Brazil was slow to revive thereafter, but probably no slower than it was for better-repaying Third World countries.

A smoother and more bilateral process is one in which the debtor, in announcing a plan for partial write-down, chooses terms that are more likely to win quick acquiescence by creditors, possibly in consultation with creditors. Two excellent illustrations were the Mexican decrees under Porfirio Diaz in 1885 and Argentina's Romero Plan of 1893. In both cases, creditors soon gave their collective approval, and repayments and fresh lending promptly followed.

Still more bilateral are cases in which the two sides work out a compromise from the start. This is easiest in cases where the debtor is willing to write down very little, i.e., cases closer to pure rescheduling with no change in capitalized contractual value. The Brazilian refunding loans of 1898 and 1914, worked out with the help of the Rothchilds, serve as examples. These refunding loans, incidentally, were accompanied by conditionality, with Brazil restricting her money supply as part of the bargain.

The two-party (and unilateral) write-downs were not always prompt or tidy. In some cases delays were involved, and in others no solution was reached. Massive total default was the outcome of the Mexican, Russian, and Turkish Revolutions and in many cases of default during the 1930s. History, like existing game theory, has no way of assuring a smooth outcome of international debt conflict. But the mechanisms of direct bargaining and write-downs are traditional and simple, and free of the special complications arising from the remaining alternative, third-party intervention.

10.3.2   The Three-Party Approach

Postwar international debt settlements have been shaped by the intervention of such third parties as the IMF, the Paris Club, and the World Bank. The period of most intense activity, the attempts to reschedule and renegotiate debt since the crisis became acute in 1982, has revealed special problems with the three-party approach, both in practice and as a stylized ideal type.

In practice, third-party intervention has brought delays and temporizing rollovers. The rescheduling agreements have basically just postponed and capitalized debt service, without any real concessionary terms. They have also become addictive: Almost every country involved in rescheduling since 1978 has been covered by new agreements ever since. The lingering uncertainty over the shape of the ultimate settlement is, we suspect, a major force depressing capital formation throughout the Third World since 1982.

The stylized three-party approach would involve a relending rescue not yet evident in actual practice. The third party would give new concessionary loans, bailing out the original creditors and granting a capital gain (a partial default) to the debtors, at the expense of distant taxpayers. If such genuine concessions were forthcoming, they would replace the problems of existing practice with two new problems. One is the difficulty of prescribing the right amount of austerity to the debtor as part of the settlement, given that the amount of debt outstanding competes with the macroeconomic need for austerity as a yardstick for gaining concessions. More basic is the familiar problem of moral hazard: Any concession is a reward for testing the limits of prudence, inviting more unstable lending in the future, with greater disruption to world investment. To become a superior alternative to two-party debt adjustments, the three-party approach would have to provide new solutions for these basic problems.

10.4 Summary

A closer look at the history of international lending has furthered our understanding of the debt-crisis dynamic on two fronts. First, the workings of the process in the absence of international agencies like the IMF has been illuminated with historical measures of ex ante and ex post returns. Defaults notwithstanding, investors between 1850 and about 1970 earned sizeable premia on the overall portfolio of loans to the ten top borrowing governments. Chile, Mexico, Russia, and Turkey were exceptions, bringing foreign creditors lower returns than domestic bonds. Since 1974, creditors have received sufficient service that they could now withstand significant partial defaults and still earn the historical premia over lending to their home governments. Countries that had defaulted in the past were significantly more likely to become problem debtors again. Yet defaulting governments have seldom been punished, either with direct sanctions or with discriminatory denial of later credit.

Second, policy options for debt-crisis management can be appraised by contrasting the recent debt negotiations under IMF—World Bank tutelage with the more direct bargaining approach of the bond era. The assistance of the international agencies has raised several problems avoided by the older bilateral mechanism. Partial debt write-downs, imposed by the borrowers with creditor acquiescence, might dominate all other policy options.

References

Dominick and Dominick. 1934–37. *Dollar bonds issued in the United States.* New York: Dominick and Dominick.

Eichengreen, Barry, and Richard Portes. 1986. Debt and default in the 1930s: Causes and consequences, *European Economic Review* 30 (June): 559–640.

Fenn's compendium of the English and foreign funds and *Fenn on the funds.* 1874–1898. Various editions, London.

The Fitch record of government finances. 1918. 3rd. ed. New York: Fitch Publishing.

Kimber, Albert W., ed. 1925. *Kimber's record of government debts and other foreign securities, 1925.* 9th annual ed. New York: Exporter's Encyclopedia Corp.

Kimber, Albert W., and Alfred Nagel, ed. 1933. *Kimber's record of government debts, 1932–33.* New York: Overseas Statistics, Inc.

Lindert, Peter H. 1986. Relending to sovereign debtors. Working Paper (September). University of California, Davis, Institute for Governmental Affairs.

11 The U.S. Capital Market and Foreign Lending, 1920–1955

Barry Eichengreen

11.1 Introduction

In the last 15 years, U.S. portfolio lending abroad has passed through a series of stages. After 1970 a period of inactivity first gave way to a surge of bank lending, followed by the development of debt-servicing difficulties and finally the curtailment of foreign lending. To a surprising extent, the recent rise and retreat of foreign lending resembles previous historical episodes in which surges of foreign lending were abruptly terminated by waves of default, only to start up again after a lull of several decades. This chapter studies the last such complete episode— the "debt cycle" through which the U.S. economy passed in the four decades following World War I—to see what light it sheds on recent developments in international capital markets.

11.2 The Debt Cycle of the 1920s

The forces underlying the debt cycle of the 1920s were set in motion by World War I. The war transformed the United States from a net debtor to a creditor nation: between 1914 and 1919, largely as a result of loans floated on behalf of the French and British governments, America's net debtor position was extinguished and replaced by a net creditor position of comparable magnitude (see table 11.1). There followed a

Barry Eichengreen is a professor of economics at the University of California at Berkeley and a research associate of the National Bureau of Economic Research.

The work reported here draws on research conducted jointly with Richard Portes and supported by a World Bank research grant on LDC debt. Opinions expressed are the author's alone. I thank seminar participants at Tel Aviv University, where an earlier version of this paper was presented, and Stanley Fischer and Peter Lindert for helpful comments.

Table 11.1   International Investment Position of the United States 1897–1939 (Excluding War Debts) ($ billions)

Item	End of 1897	1 July 1914	1919	End of Year 1930	End of Year 1933	End of Year 1939
United States investments abroad (private account)						
Long-term:						
Direct	0.6	2.7	3.9	8.0	7.8	7.0
Portfolio	0.1	0.9	2.6	7.2	6.0	3.8
Total long-term	0.7	3.5	6.5	15.2	13.8	10.8
Total short-term	—	—	0.5	2.0	1.1	0.6
Total long- and short-term	0.7	3.5	7.0	17.2	14.9	11.4
Foreign investments in the United States						
Long-term:						
Direct	{3.1	1.3	0.9	1.4[a]	1.8[b]	2.0
Portfolio[c]		5.4	1.6	4.3[a]	3.1[b]	4.3
Total long-term	3.1	6.8	2.5	5.7	4.9	6.3
Total short-term	0.3	0.5	0.8	2.7	0.5	3.3
Total long- and short-term	3.4	7.2	3.3	8.4	5.4	9.6
Net creditor position of the United States						
On long-term account	−2.4	−3.3	4.0	9.5	8.9	4.5
On short-term account	−0.3	−0.5	−0.3[d]	−0.7[d]	0.6	−2.7[d]
On long- and short-term account	−2.7	−3.8	3.7	8.8	9.5	1.8
U.S. wholesale prices (1897 = 100)	100	146.7	299.6	185.8	141.7	165.8

Sources: Lewis (1938), Lary (1943), U.S. Department of Commerce, *Historical Statistics of the United States* (1976).

Note: All data for 1919 and data for 1929 on foreign long-term investments in the United States are unofficial estimates; other data are as estimated by the Department of Commerce.

[a]1929 data. [c]Includes miscellaneous investments.

[b]1934 data. [d]Net debtor position.

surge in peacetime lending, mainly by the United States, matched previously only by the United Kingdom in the period 1900–13. That lending reflected a combination of factors: continued rapid growth of the U.S. economy, the wartime rise in saving, and the demand for capital to reconstruct the devastated European economies.

Yet in the immediate aftermath of World War I, the international capital market remained becalmed. It is true that changing rates of return played some role in the reignition of U.S. foreign lending; figure 11.1 shows how, compared to domestic medium-grade bonds, the return on foreign medium-grade bonds rose steadily from the early 1920s until 1928. But rates of return by themselves account for little of the variation in the volume of foreign lending. The role of other factors, specifically risk, is especially evident before 1924, when U.S. investors were virtually unwilling to lend to foreigners at any price. The risks of lending were most evident in the case of Central Europe. So long as the value of their reparations obligations remained uncertain, it was not clear that the nations of this region possessed the resources to service additional external debt. So long as their financial systems remained in disarray, it was not clear that they were capable of mobilizing those resources they possessed. The initiation of lending required League of Nations intervention in the form of stabilization loans and assistance in carrying out fiscal and monetary reform.

Yet the perception that foreign lending was risky was not limited to Central Europe. At the beginning of the 1920s, lending to Latin America also remained depressed (table 11.2). Here the dominant factor was the depressed level of world trade and uncertain prospects for its recovery, which cast doubt over the capacity of foreign debtors to generate export revenues. The initiation of lending required substantial steps to reconstruct international trade and international financial

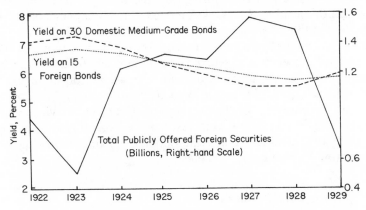

Fig. 11.1   Relative interest rates and foreign issues, 1922–1929

Table 11.2   Distribution of American Foreign Security Issues, 1919–29
(percentages of total, total in millions)

Year	Europe (%)	Canada (%)	Latin America (%)	Asia (%)	Total ($m)	Total in Constant 1929 Prices ($m real)
1919	60.3	30.4	8.9	0.2	377.5	259.6
1920	51.5	38.2	10.1	0.0	480.4	334.4
1921	26.2	32.5	38.6	2.5	594.7	580.5
1922	29.5	23.5	31.2	15.6	715.8	704.3
1923	26.1	29.0	27.7	17.0	413.3	391.0
1924	54.7	15.7	19.4	9.9	961.3	934.7
1925	58.9	12.8	14.8	13.2	1,067.1	983.0
1926	43.5	20.3	33.1	2.8	1,110.2	1,056.4
1927	44.2	18.1	26.0	11.5	1,304.6	1,299.3
1928	48.0	14.8	26.5	10.5	1,243.7	1,221.3
1929	21.5	44.0	26.5	7.8	658.2	658.2

Source: Computed from U.S. Dept. of Commerce, *American Underwriting of Foreign Securities* (various issues). The final column deflates the current price total by U.S. wholesale prices, from U.S. Department of Commerce, *Historical Statistics of the United States* (1976).

Note: Percentages may not sum to 100 because of rounding.

arrangements. If a lesson is to be drawn from the initiation of this earlier debt cycle, it is that an existing debt overhang and threats to an open trading system can dam the flow of resources to potential borrowers, and that outside intervention by governments or international institutions may be required to restart it.

In the 1920s as in the 1970s, the surge in foreign lending was greatly stimulated by financial innovation. American investors acquired familiarity with the merits of foreign bonds through the Liberty Loan campaign of World War I. Banks enlisted in that campaign established or expanded their bond departments. Still others established security affiliates to engage in the entire range of bond market activities. Once the Federal Reserve Act relaxed restrictions on foreign branching, member banks began to move abroad. The growth of the investment trust enabled the small investor to participate in the market. Together, the rapid development of retailing and underwriting activities and the proliferation of investment vehicles provided organizations and individuals both the incentive and the opportunity to increase their participation in foreign bond markets.

11.3   Pricing Foreign Bonds

How did foreign lending operate once it was again underway? A standard criticism of the international capital market in the 1920s is that it failed to discriminate adequately among borrowers. This same criticism has been leveled at U.S. lenders in the 1970s, providing the motivation for studies of the pricing of foreign bonds (Guttentag and Herring 1985). These modern studies provide a benchmark for comparison with my analysis of the bond market in the 1920s. I analyze the determinants of the yield to maturity on a pooled time series–cross section of some 200 categories of foreign bonds issued in the United States between 1920 and 1929. (Complete results are reported in Eichengreen, vol. 1, chap. 3 of this project.) I find a positively sloped yield curve and a relatively high risk premium on foreign corporate bonds. While both results are consistent with standard models, interestingly they contrast with the findings of other investigators for the 1970s (Edwards 1986). I also find that the lowest risk premia were consistently charged to Scandinavian countries, members of the British Commonwealth, small Western European countries, and small Central American republics economically or politically dependent on the United States, confirming that national reputation and political considerations played a role in the pricing of foreign bonds. But there is little evidence that lenders took into account current economic policies in borrowing countries, or that they charged higher premia for larger loans. It would seem that reputation more than current economic developments influenced bond market participants.

This analysis provides some evidence that lenders discriminated among potential borrowers on the basis of reputation and political factors that conveyed information about the probability of default. But did they discriminate adequately? To address this issue I specify a simple model of ex ante and ex post returns. The expected rate of return on risky loans, i_r, should exceed the risk-free rate, i_f, by a risk premium:

$$(1) \qquad i_r = i_f + \delta\sigma$$

where σ is default risk so $\delta\sigma$ is the premium on risky loans. Ex ante (of default) the return on risky loans exceeds that required:

$$(2) \qquad i_{ex\ ante} = i_r + \beta\sigma$$

where $i_{ex\ ante}$ is the ex ante rate of return. The ex post return differs from that required by investors by their expectational error, ϵ.

$$(3) \qquad i_{ex\ post} = i_r + \epsilon.$$

Substituting and solving for the ex post return gives

$$(4) \qquad i_{ex\ post} = \frac{\beta/\delta}{1 + \beta/\delta} i_f + \frac{\delta + \beta}{\delta} i_{ex\ ante} + \epsilon.$$

If investors' expectational errors have mean zero, in a regression of ex post on ex ante returns the constant term

$$\left(\frac{\beta/\delta}{1 + \beta/\delta} \, i_f\right)$$

should be positive and the coefficient on $i_{ex \; ante}$ should be greater than unity.

Using the ex ante and ex post rates of return calculated by Eichengreen and Portes (1986) for a sample of 50 dollar bonds (national, provincial, municipal, and corporate) issued in the United States between 1924 and 1930, equation (4) can be estimated, yielding

$$(5) \qquad i_{ex \; post} = 9.00 - 120.59 \, i_{ex \; ante}$$
$$(0.94) \qquad (0.89)$$

$$N = 50 \qquad R^2 = 0.016$$

with t-statistics in parentheses. Although the constant term is positive, the coefficient on $i_{ex \; post}$ is less than unity, which is inconsistent with the joint hypothesis of rational expectations and market efficiency. That coefficient can be interpreted to mean that investors systematically underestimated the cost of default on those bonds most at risk, incompletely incorporating differential default risk into the spreads they demand of foreign borrowers.

If default risk was imperfectly perceived at time of issue, bondholders still could have recognized and acted upon it subsequently. I therefore examine the pricing of these same foreign bonds after 1931. Naturally, the suspension of service is reflected in the prices of defaulting bonds. But in addition it is evident in the prices of continuously serviced bonds, as illustrated by the implicit expected capital losses (probability of default times capital loss in the event) on three Scandinavian bonds considered in figure 11.2. This suggests that default carried negative externalities creating doubt about the creditworthiness even of countries maintaining service on their external debts.

11.4   Default and Market Access

Approximately two-thirds of foreign securities held by American investors fell into default over the course of the Depression decade. Contemporaries were convinced that the experience had a lingering impact on the attitudes of American investors. One way to approach this issue is to compare U.S. foreign lending in the ten years immediately succeeding World Wars I and II. Clearly, the second half of the 1940s and the first half of the 1950s constitute a special period in the history of the world economy, following as they do a global war. But the years 1919–28 are an equally special period for many of the same reasons, rendering the comparison apposite. The comparison reveals

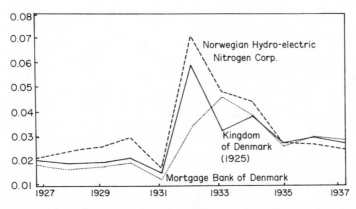

Fig. 11.2   Implicit expected capital losses: Scandinavian bonds

that U.S. capital exports actually were larger in the second postwar decade than in the first (table 11.3). The difference is due, however, almost entirely to unilateral transfers by government, notably the Marshall Plan. Moreover, the real value of portfolio lending fell dramatically between the decades following World Wars I and II, by more than 80 percent. This is precisely what one would expect had purchasers been deterred by interwar experience with default.

This decline in portfolio lending could reflect either a general disenchantment with foreign loans or a special inability to borrow by countries with a recent history of default. While consistent country data on the extent of total foreign borrowing after World War II are notoriously difficult to obtain, reasonably consistent data on stocks of debt in 1945, 1950 and 1955 are available courtesy of Avramovic (1958). In the raw data, no relationship between default in the 1930s and borrowing after 1945 is apparent. But reputational effects are only a subset of the factors affecting a government's willingness and ability to borrow abroad. Standard borrowing models advance country size, the share of imports in domestic consumption, and export variability as additional determinants of foreign borrowing. My analysis of the role of these factors and of past debt-servicing records in the extent of borrowing in the post-World War II decade builds on the Avramovic data as supplemented by United Nations and International Monetary Fund documents and annual reports of bondholders' protective committees. Table 11.4 reports cross-section regressions for 32 countries, of which 18 are Latin American. The dependent variable is terminal stock of debt of the public authorities. Indebtedness is positively related to GNP, the import share, and the initial stock of debt, as anticipated. But there is no evidence that the severity of interwar default, as measured by the share of debt in default in 1935, was negatively related to ability

Table 11.3   U.S. Foreign Lending in the Two Postwar Decades, 1919–28 and 1946–55 (In millions of current dollars for 1919–28 and in 1919–28 average prices for 1946–55.)

	1919	1920	1921	1922	1923	1924	1925	1926	1927	1928	Decade Average
Public, long- and short-term	2,328	175	-30	-31	-91	-28	-27	-30	-46	-49	217
Private											
Direct, long-term	94	154	111	153	148	182	268	351	351	558	237
Other, long-term	75	400	477	669	235	703	603	470	636	752	502
Short-term	n.a.	n.a.	n.a.	n.a.	82	109	46	36	349	231	142
Unilateral transfers											
Private	832	634	450	314	328	339	373	361	355	346	433
Government	212	45	59	38	37	25	30	20	2	19	49

	1946	1947	1948	1949	1950	1951	1952	1953	1954	1955	Decade Average
Public, long- and short-term	2,705	3,079	690	462	106	96	265	139	-59	197	682
Private											
Direct, long-term	206	546	486	468	424	311	537	469	425	523	444
Other, long-term	-114	36	47	57	338	268	135	-118	204	153	107
Short-term	278	137	78	-133	102	63	59	-107	404	121	97
Unilateral transfers											
Private	603	497	470	377	310	258	279	321	321	290	368
Government	2,015	1,416	2,580	3,620	2,430	1,904	1,315	1,262	1,131	1,299	1,871

Source: U.S. Department of Commerce, *Historical Statistics of the United States* (1976, 198–201, 866–67).

Notes: n.a. indicates not available. Decade average short-term capital flow for the twenties is for the years 1923–28 only.

Table 11.4   **Determinants of the Stock of Debt, 1955 (Dependent variable is in millions of U.S. dollars.)**

	(1) Log of Debt	(2) Level of Debt	(3) Log of Debt	(4) Level of Debt
Constant	−2.15 (1.25)	−1254.12 (3.78)	−2.65 (1.78)	−1,169.87 (3.88)
Share of debt in default, 1935	0.65 (1.27)	613.40 (2.89)	0.75 (1.56)	557.65 (2.90)
Log GNP	0.75 (4.21)	—	0.81 (5.50)	—
GNP	—	0.08 (7.04)	—	0.07 (10.34)
Import/GNP ratio	0.85 (0.31)	3,723.12 (3.12)	1.01 (0.38)	3,497.55 (3.10)
Log debt in 1945	0.16 (3.52)	—	0.17 (3.56)	—
Debt in 1945	—	0.67 (2.91)	—	0.68 (2.99)
Export variability	0.01 (0.62)	−0.01 (0.64)	—	—
Number of observations	32	32	32	32
R^2	0.74	0.88	0.74	0.88
F	15.16	37.39	19.29	47.67

Source: See text.
Note: t-statistics in parentheses.

to borrow between 1945 and 1955. There is no evidence that countries which defaulted in the interwar period found it more difficult to borrow in the immediate post–World War II years.

While the Avramovic data have the virtue of consistency, they have the problem of combining all external debt of governments, whether extended by international agencies, creditor country governments, or private investors. It would be advisable to analyze private portfolio lending (to both public and private sectors) separately from lending by public agencies before concluding that no trace of interwar defaults can be discerned in the geographical distribution of postwar lending. This can be done for private portfolio lending to the Latin American countries, for which the United Nations (1965) has published estimates. Table 11.5 reports a regression analysis of these data. The bivariate relationship between postwar portfolio borrowing and interwar default, shown in the first column, is positive but statistically insignificant. Once

Table 11.5   Determinants of Private Portfolio Capital Inflow to Latin American Countries, 1946–55 (The dependent variable is in millions of U.S. dollars.)

	(1)	(2)	(3)
Constant	−3.59 (0.18)	−3.14 (0.12)	7.11 (0.18)
Share of debt in default, 1935	17.75 (0.76)	−14.31 (−0.81)	−17.63 (0.86)
GNP	—	0.01 (4.64)	0.01 (4.31)
Import/GNP ratio	—	46.00 (0.38)	5.63 (0.03)
Debt in 1945	—	—	−0.013 (0.35)
Export variability	—	−0.005 (3.22)	−0.005 (3.13)
Number of observations	18	18	18
R^2	.04	.68	.69
F	0.58	7.01	7.15

Source: See text.
Note: t-statistics in parentheses.

other correlates of the demand for debt are added to the equation, the coefficient on interwar debt turns negative, as the reputational hypothesis would predict, although it is statistically indistinguishable from zero at standard confidence levels. Once again, it is impossible to reject the null hypothesis that variations across countries in the severity of interwar default had essentially no impact on access to private portfolio capital during the postwar years.

The finding of a much reduced volume of private portfolio lending and the finding of no greater difficulty of borrowing for countries that defaulted previously are not difficult to reconcile with one another. Recall that interwar default translated into expectations of significant capital losses on the bonds of even those countries which continued to service their debts. This suggests that some effects of interwar defaults were external to the initiating country, consistent with the conclusion that the main legacy of interwar debt default was to depress the volume of private portfolio lending generally, not to divert it to faithful servicers from countries which lapsed into default.

11.5 Conclusion

What picture of the capital market emerges from this study of the United States' first 35 years as a creditor nation? It is impossible to characterize the market as either perfectly rational or wholly irrational. Advocates of a return to the bond market as a panacea for recent difficulties with sovereign lending should take note of these conclusions. While switching from bank loans to the bond market may divert some of the risk shouldered by creditor-country banking systems (Eichengreen and Portes 1987), bond market participants have shown no greater facility than have bank loan officers historically in distinguishing good credit risks from bad. Nor were bond markets any more successful in smoothing the flow of capital to developing-country debtors.

What picture of the legacy of default for the subsequent behavior of the capital market emerges from this study of the last complete debt cycle? Recent theoretical studies of sovereign lending in the presence of potential default (Eaton and Gersovitz 1981) have posited the existence of a default penalty, usually interpreted as the costs of reduced capital market access. The finding that, compared to countries which maintained debt service throughout, countries which lapsed into default in the 1930s were no less able to borrow in the 1940s and 1950s, is difficult to reconcile with this simple view. If there were costs of default, they did not take the form of differential credit-market access in the first postwar decade. But this does not imply that default was costless. Evidence from bond prices in the 1930s and from the volume and composition of lending in the 1940s and 1950s suggests that at least some of the costs of default spilled over among debtor countries. These costs took the form of reduced access to private portfolio capital flows for defaulting and nondefaulting countries alike.

References

Avramovic, Dragoslav. 1958. *Debt-servicing capacity and postwar growth in international indebtedness.* Baltimore, Md.: Johns Hopkins University Press.

Eaton, Jonathan, and Mark Gersovitz. 1981. Debt with potential repudiation: Theoretical and empirical analysis. *Review of Economic Studies* 48: 289–309.

Edwards, Sebastian. 1986. The pricing of bonds and bank loans in international markets: An empirical analysis of developing countries' foreign borrowing. *European Economic Review* 30: 565–89.

Eichengreen, Barry, and Richard Portes. 1986. Debt and default in the 1930s: Causes and consequences. *European Economic Review* 30: 599–640.

————. 1987. The anatomy of financial crises. In *Threats to International Financial Stability,* ed. Richard Portes and Alexander Swoboda, 10–58. Cambridge: Cambridge University Press.

Guttentag, Jack, and Richard Herring. 1985. *The Current Crisis in International Lending,* Washington, D.C.: The Brookings Institution.

Lary, Hal B. et al. 1943. *The United States in the world economy.* Washington, D.C.: Government Printing Office.

Lewis, Cleona. 1938. *America's stake in international investments.* Washington, D.C.: The Brookings Institution.

United Nations. 1965. *External financing in Latin America.* Department of Economic and Social Affairs, Economic Commission for Latin America. New York: United Nations.

United States Department of Commerce. Various years. *American underwriting of foreign securities.* Washington, D.C.: Government Printing Office.

————. 1976. *Historical statistics of the United States: Colonial times to 1970.* Washington, D.C.: Government Printing Office.

12   Structural Adjustment Policies in Highly Indebted Countries

Sebastian Edwards

12.1 Introduction

Five years after the eruption of the debt crisis most countries of the developing world are still struggling to get back on their feet. Although the collapse of the world financial system predicted by some overly pessimistic observers has not materalized, the debt crisis is far from over. In fact, when traditional creditworthiness indicators, such as debt-exports or debt-service ratios are analyzed, the highly indebted countries are now (late 1987) in an even weaker position than in 1982 (see Edwards 1987a). It has now become apparent that a long-term resolution of the debt problems will be a painful and protracted process, that will still require major additional adjustment efforts by the indebted countries, as well as extensive negotiations between debtor governments, creditor governments, the multilateral institutions, and the banks.

The adjustment approaches followed until now by most of the highly indebted countries can best be described as *emergency stabilization programs* geared towards generating very large trade balance surpluses in very short periods of time. Given the sudden halt in external financing after 1982, these countries had little choice but to use every possible tool at their disposal to achieve the needed turnabout in their current

Sebastian Edwards is a professor of economics at the University of California, Los Angeles, and a research associate of the National Bureau of Economic Research.

This is a summary of a paper presented at the National Bureau of Economic Research Conference on Developing Countries Debt; Washington, D.C., 21–23 September 1987. I have benefited from discussions with Marcelo Selowsky. I am grateful to Alejandra Cox-Edwards, Edgardo Barandiaran, Pari Kasliwal, Miguel Savastano, Jeff Sachs, and to the participants of the pre-conference meeting held in Cambridge in May 1987 for helpful comments. Financial support from UCLA's Academic Senate and from the National Science Foundation is gratefully acknowledged.

accounts. As a consequence the adjustment process has been quite costly, generating drastic declines in real income and important increases in unemployment. In fact, in a number of Latin American countries in 1986 real per capita GDP was below its 1970 level (Edwards 1987a)! A long-run solution to the debt crisis problem would entail: (1) the regaining of creditworthiness by these countries, and thus the resumption of voluntary lending by the international financial community; and (2) the resumption of sustained growth.

The purpose of this chapter is to analyze a number of issues related to structural adjustment in the highly indebted developing countries. The chapter begins with a review of the main features of the adjustment process followed during 1982–87; it is noted that in almost every case this has been a period of recessionary adjustment based on investment and import cuts. Then, the potential role of trade liberalization reforms in the resumption of sustained growth in these countries is examined. The analysis deals with (1) the relation between outward orientation, export promotion, and growth; (2) appropriate sequencing of trade liberalization and stabilization programs; (3) tariff reform and unemployment; (4) credibility and structural reforms; and (5) the role of devaluations in structural reform programs.

12.2   The Nature of the Adjustment, 1982–87

12.2.1   Origins of the Crisis

During the second half of the 1970s and the early 1980s most of the developing nations embarked on a foreign borrowing binge. Between 1975 and 1982 the developing world's long-term foreign debt more than tripled, growing from $162.5 billion to $551.2 billion. Naturally, this huge increase in indebtedness was made possible by the liberal way in which, after the first oil shock in 1973, the international financial community and in particular the banks, provided funds to these countries. There is no doubt that the pace at which the developing countries were accumulating debt in the late 1970s and early 1980s—at a rate exceeding 20 percent per year—was not sustainable in the medium to longer run; some type of adjustment was bound to take place. The world, however, was shocked by the severity of the crisis; instead of there being an orderly and slow reduction of the flow of borrowing, a major crisis that brought capital flows to a virtual halt took place.[1]

The behavior of the world economy during the early 1980s, and in particular the increase of interest rates, the decline in commodity prices, and the sluggish growth of the industrial countries, played an important role in determining the magnitude and timing of the crisis. Also, in many cases macroeconomic mismanagement in the borrowing countries contributed greatly to the crisis. In particular, lax fiscal policies and inadequate exchange rate policies that resulted in acute overvaluations greatly weakened the external sector in many of the highly indebted countries. Perhaps one of the most devasting effects of the generalized tendency towards real exchange rate overvaluation is that it fueled massive capital flight out of the developing world. In country after country, as it became increasingly apparent that the overvaluation was unsustainable in the longer run, the public began to speculate heavily against the central bank by acquiring foreign exchange and moving it abroad. In fact, in a recent empirical study Cuddington (1986) has found that there is a significant relation between overvaluation and capital flight.

12.2.2   The Adjustment

In August of 1982, immediately following Mexico's announcement that it was facing serious financial difficulties, the international financial community greatly reduced the amount of funds intermediated to the developing world. For the developing countries as a whole external financing was reduced by almost 40 percent between 1981 and 1983. Moreover, the major debtors were forced to fully close a current account deficit that by 1982 had exceeded $50 billion in less than 3 years. By 1985 the aggregate current account had reached virtual equilibrium (– $0.1 billion) (see table 12.1). These very rapid adjustments were achieved entirely by reductions in imports and in investment. Moreover, for the IMF's category of "15 highly indebted countries," the

Table 12.1   Selected Indicators for Major Debtors, 1979–88[a]

Year	Trade Balance (U.S. $ billions)	Current Account (U.S. $ billions)	Rate of Change of Per Capita Real GDP	Ratio of Gross Capital Formation to GDP	Central Government Deficit as Percentage of GDP	Average % Change Consumer Price Index
1979	– 1.9	– 24.6	3.6	24.9	0.8	40.8
1980	4.4	29.5	2.6	24.7	0.8	47.4
1981	– 7.5	– 50.3	– 1.6	24.5	3.7	53.2
1982	3.2	– 50.6	– 2.7	22.3	5.4	57.7
1983	28.3	– 15.2	– 5.5	18.2	5.2	90.8
1984	43.2	– 0.6	– 0.1	17.4	3.1	116.4
1985	40.8	– 0.1	0.9	16.5	2.7	126.9
1986	22.9	– 11.0	1.4	16.8	4.5	76.2
1987	18.8	– 14.0	1.2	17.6	3.6	86.3
1988	22.3	– 10.5	2.4	n.a.	n.a.	87.2

[a]These data refer to the IMF's highly indebted countries: Argentina, Bolivia, Brazil, Chile, Colombia, Ivory Coast, Ecuador, Mexico, Morocco, Nigeria, Peru, Philippines, Uruguay, Venezuela, Yugoslavia. These data have been obtained from IMF, *World Economic Outlook,* 1987.
n.a. = not available.

dollar value of exports was lower in 1986 than in 1980, with the magnitude of this decline exceeding 15 percent. This drop was basically the result of a decline in the prices of these countries' exports of almost 25 percent between 1980 and 1986.

For the major debtors as a group, investment declined from an average of 26 percent of GDP in 1973–77 to an average of 17.2 percent in 1983–86. In most cases public investment and investment in the construction sector were the components most severely curtailed. Naturally, this decline in investment has serious consequences for the prospects of renewed growth.

Most countries faced the need to reverse the direction of the net transfers by resorting to a combination of expenditure-reducing and expenditure-switching policies, including devaluation, the imposition of capital controls, and import quotas. The adjustment required both a significant increase in real interest rates as well as major relative price changes or real devaluations. In most cases the selection of policy packages was based on the perceived "effectiveness" of these policies in the short run, rather than on efficiency, income distribution, or welfare considerations. As a result of the efforts made to implement rapidly effective policies a number of trade-offs between different objectives, including improvement in the current account and inflation, emerged during the process (Edwards 1987a).

In spite of the relatively successful efforts to reduce public expenditures, fiscal deficits increased in relation to the precrisis period in the major debtors as a group. In many of these countries total tax revenues were negatively affected by the recessions that followed the crisis. As a consequence of this decline, the reliance on inflationary financing increased substantially (see table 12.1).

The restraint of wage increases was, in most countries, another major component of the expenditure-reducing package. In most countries the adjustment also relied on higher real interest rates, which helped keep expenditure, and in particular investment, in check.

After August 1982 most countries also relied on expenditure-switching policies; these consisted in most cases of a combination of nominal devaluations and, at least initially, of a major escalation in the degree of trade restrictions. The extent of the devaluations varied from country to country, being particularly severe in Latin America. In an effort to assure that the effects of the nominal devaluations on the real exchange rate did not erode via inflation, most countries adopted some kind of active exchange rate management where the exchange rate continued to be adjusted after the initial parity change. In fact, as of July 1986, out of the 15 major debtors 12 had some sort of crawling peg regime consisting of periodical adjustments of the nominal rate somewhat related to the differential between internal and external inflation (Edwards 1987a).

Another important feature of the exchange rate policy followed by many countries was the adoption of multiple exchange rates. Immediately following the crisis in many (but not all) of the major debtors the devaluation policies were supplemented by the imposition of trade restrictions. In some countries the extent of trade restrictions has recently been somewhat relaxed, while others have announced some easing up in the near future.

In spite of the significant efforts to adjust made by most of these countries, and of the costs incurred in the process, the magnitude of their trade surpluses has systematically fallen short of their interest payments. In Latin America, for example, in 1986 the interest bill amounted to 5.3 percent of GDP while the trade surplus reached 2.3 percent of GDP. In most countries up to this point this financing gap has been closed, usually after long and protracted negotiations, by packages of funds provided by the banks and the multilateral institutions.

In sum, in spite of the involvement of the IMF in this first phase of the adjustment process, the actual policy packages implemented by most of the debt-troubled countries differed markedly from what we can describe as an orthodox IMF-type stabilization program. Generally speaking, the current adjustment process has been inflationary with high and persistent fiscal deficits, and with increasingly distorted external sectors, with a profusion of quantitative restrictions (QRs) and multiple exchange rates.

12.3 Trade Liberalization and Adjustment with Growth

The emergency packages implemented until now have succeeded in averting what some considered to be an almost sure collapse of the world financial system. This has been achieved, however, at a significant cost for the major debtors in terms of decline in employment, income, and standard of living. The key question now is how to move from the current situation towards what we can call phase 2 of the adjustment process, a phase characterized by adjustment and growth. A number of authors—and indeed the supporters of the Baker plan, as well as the IMF—believe that a rapid trade liberalization, coupled with devaluation, privatization, and financial reform, is the most reasonable strategy for achieving these objectives. For example, Balassa et al. (1986, 88) have recommended that, among other things, the developing nations should eliminate all QRs and reduce, during a period of five years, imports tariffs to a uniform 15 to 20 percent; these tariff reforms should be coupled with significant devaluations, in order not to "deprotect" the tradable goods sectors. In this section we analyze the potential role of trade liberalization in the next phase of the adjustment process in the developing countries. We emphasize the relation between trade liberalization and export promotion, the employment effects of liberalization, and the relation between liberalization and anti-inflationary policies.

12.3.1   Outward Orientation, Export Promotion, and Trade Liberalization

There is little doubt that a longer-run solution of the debt crisis will require the adoption of policies that rely more heavily than in the past on export growth.[2] Even ECLA/CEPAL, the former champion of import substitution development, has recommended outward-oriented policies for the troubled Latin American nations (Bianchi et al. 1987).

Outward orientation and export promotion require some kind of trade liberalization and tariff reduction, especially of imported inputs and capital goods. Indeed, the historical evidence clearly shows that those countries that have successfully pursued export promotion (i.e., the East Asian nations), have had a trade regime substantially more liberal than those countries that have followed indiscriminatory import substitution based on protectionism (Edwards 1987a). Although outward orientation requires *some* trade liberalization, there are no reasons, either theoretical or empirical, that suggest that the "optimal" degree of liberalization implies zero, or even very low, tariffs coupled with no government intervention in any sphere of the development process. Indeed the rich historical lessons emanating from the Southern Cone suggest that this kind of extremely liberal reform may backfire at an immensely high cost in terms of output and employment (Edwards and Cox-Edwards 1987). The successful experiences with export-led growth in the East Asian countries also support this view; although in these countries trade regimes have been significantly liberal, government intervention in promoting exports has been important and tariffs have never been anything close to a very low uniform level (Edwards 1987a).[3]

Although it is not possible to make broad generalizations, the evidence suggests that at the present time in the majority of the highly indebted countries the trade regime is still not sufficiently liberalized. In order to take advantage of more rapid growth based on the external sector, most of these countries will need to go through some type of rationalization and liberalization of their imports sector (Edwards 1987a).

12.3.2   Trade Liberalization with a Government Budget Constraint

An important policy question is whether the trade liberalization component of an outward-oriented strategy should be attempted at the same time as a country is embarked on a severe stabilization and anti-inflationary program. Not surprisingly, the answer depends on the intensity of the trade reform and of the ongoing inflation.

Historically, there has been a close link between *mild* trade liberalizations and stabilization programs.[4] It is important to notice that most successful liberalization accompanied by anti-inflationary policies have seldom consisted of the complete elimination of QRs and major tariff reductions of the kind now recommended for the indebted countries. The Chilean episode with liberalization and stabilization between 1975 and 1983 illustrates very vividly one of the most serious trade-offs that emerges when a substantial liberalization reform is undertaken at the same time as a major anti-inflation program. As in most successful stabilization programs, in the last phase of the Chilean stabilization effort, when inflation was reduced from 40 percent to 9 percent per annum, there was a significant real exchange rate appreciation that reduced the degree of competitiveness of the tradables sector at a time when, because of the trade reform among other factors, the *equilibrium* real exchange rates had significantly depreciated. In the Chilean case this real appreciation was partially the result of the active use of exchange rate management to bring down inflation; in mid-1979 the nominal exchange rate was fixed relative to the dollar. As is well known by now this real appreciation played an important role in the disappointing outcome of the Chilean episode; it seriously deprotected the tradables sector, it generated perverse expectations of devaluation and, ultimately, it conspired with the high real interest rates to provoke the worst financial debacle of Chilean history (Corbo de Melo, and Tybout 1986; Edwards and Cox-Edwards, 1987).

A crucial objective of any stabilization program—and, indeed of those undertaken by the major debtors—is to reduce the magnitude of the fiscal deficit. Many times there will be an important trade-off between a trade liberalization that reduces import tariffs and the achievement of this fiscal objective. Surprisingly, the policy and theoretical literatures on trade liberalization policies have most times tended to ignore the fiscal role of tariffs in the developing nations. However, in many of the poorer countries governments use tariff proceeds extensively to finance their expenditure. Table 12.2, for example, contains data on the fiscal importance of taxes on international trade for eight countries. As may be seen, in some cases taxes on trade are as high as one-third of total revenue of the central government.

As long as tariff rates are below the maximum revenue level there will be a trade-off between trade liberalization and the generation of the government surplus required to finance debt servicing. Then, short of reducing government expenditures, what is required is to replace trade restrictions by less distortive taxes that can generate the same (or a higher) amount of revenue. This, of course, means that major reforms of the tax system (i.e., the adoption of VATs) would be required in most countries. Tax reforms are not only politically difficult to have approved, but from an administrative perspective it is many times very difficult to get them going (see Conrad and Gillis 1984). This, of course, imposes some fiscal restrictions on the speed at which tariffs can be reduced.

Table 12.2   **Taxes on International Trade as a Percentage of Government Revenue: Selected Developing Countries, 1984**

	$\left(\dfrac{\text{Import Tariffs}}{\text{Total Tax Revenue}}\right)^{a}$	$\left(\dfrac{\text{Taxes on Trade}}{\text{Total Revenue}}\right)^{a}$
Argentina	4.9%	13.3%
Bolivia	25.6	30.0
Chile	13.4	10.8
Indonesia	3.5	3.3
Korea	16.1	14.0
Mexico	3.0	2.7
Peru	10.2	n.a.
Philippines	22.1	23.7

Source: Constructed from raw data from the International Monetary Fund's *Government Finances Statistics Yearbook.*
[a]Refers to central government.
n.a. = not available.

Although in most cases the implementation of a major tax reform will take a substantial amount of time, there are some policies conducive both towards improved efficiency and higher revenues in the short run. The most obvious one is the replacement of QRs, (i.e., licenses, prohibitions, and so on) by import tariffs (Edwards 1987a).

In terms of the sequencing of reform, then, an important principle is to make sure that tariff reduction reforms should only be undertaken once the fiscal deficit is under control. In many cases this will mean that the tax system has to be reformed and other sources of revenue have been found. Replacing QRs by tariffs, or devising a QR auctioning system are measures that can be implemented without producing fiscal costs, while at the same time they improve efficiency. Also, by solving the fiscal imbalance first, the probability of a dangerous real exchange rate overvaluation is reduced.

12.3.3   Tariff Reform and Unemployment

The effects of trade reform on employment are a key consideration when evaluating the short-run effects of these policies. This is particularly the case under the current conditions, when the highly indebted countries are already experiencing very high levels of unemployment. Moreover, from a political economy perspective the unemployment effects of any policy are crucial; democratic governments—and even those not so democratic, but in a weakened position—will try not to generate massive unemployment: The costs of employment are recognized in the short run, while the benefits of the structural policies that provoked it usually are reaped in the medium run, when a different government is in office.

Models of adjustment in an open economy discussed in Edwards (1988) suggest that, contrary to the most simplistic textbook view, as long as it takes time to reallocate capital from one sector to the other and (real) wages exhibit some inflexibility, a tariff reduction reform may very well result in large unemployment in the short run. A first-best solution to this problem is to (fully) eliminate the source of real wage rigidity; with complete flexibility wages will, in the short run, go down until all the labor force is absorbed. In the longer run, however, as capital is reallocated, real wages will increase and surpass their prereform level. If for political or other reasons real wages cannot fall sufficiently in the short run, a second-best solution is to proceed slowly with the trade reform; tariffs should be reduced gradually in a preannounced fashion. In theory, in this way capital owners will have time to reallocate capital, avoiding the short-run unemployment effects of the trade reform (see Edwards 1988). A crucial point, however, for this solution to work is that capital allocation in fact responds to the *announcement* of reform; that is, the reform should be *credible*.

The limited existing evidence on the short-run aggregate employment consequences of trade liberalization indicates that in the case of mild reforms there have not been significant aggregate unemployment effects. This, indeed, would seem to be one of the preliminary conclusions of the exhaustive cross-country study undertaken at the World Bank and directed by Papageorgiou, Michaely, and Choksi (1986). In terms of substantial trade reforms the Chilean experience, with its textbook-type policies, is educational. Between 1974 and 1979 Chile underwent one of the most, if not the most, ambitious trade liberalization of the modern time: Quantitative restrictions were fully eliminated, a multiple exchange rate system consisting of up to 15 different exchange rates was unified, and tariffs were slashed to a uniform 10 percent. Edwards (1985), for example, calculated than an upper bound for the unemployment effects of the trade reform was 3.5 percentage points of the labor force, or 129,000 people, with the bulk of this unemployment located in the food, beverages, tobacco, textiles and leather products subsectors (57,000 people). More recently, de la Cuadra and Hachette (1986) have calculated that the trade reform generated a reduction of employment in the manufacturing sector of approximately 50,000 workers. Even though these are not negligible numbers, they clearly indicate that an explanation for the bulk of the Chilean unemployment should be sought elsewhere (Edwards and Cox-Edwards 1987).

In sum, a gradual lowering of tariffs offers a number of attractive features for economies such as the debt-ridden countries. First, this strategy is likely to reduce the short-run unemployment consequences of the trade reform. Second, there will likely be positive effects on savings helping growth prospects.[5] Third, it will tend to improve the current account. And finally, a gradual reduction of tariffs will have positive effects on the government budget. On the negative side a gradual trade reform may lack credibility, in which case it may even induce perverse responses (see section 12.3.5).

12.3.4 Structural Adjustment and Devaluation

Nominal devaluations are an important component of most stabilization programs, and they have played a central role in the adjustment efforts following the debt crisis. The purpose of these nominal devaluations is to generate a *real* exchange rate adjustment, that would reverse the real appreciation that usually precedes the balance of payments crisis.

Until quite recently most traditional structural adjustment programs in the developing nations have contemplated discrete nominal devaluations, where the official nominal exchange rate is abruptly adjusted by a fairly large percentage. More recently, however, more and more countries are opting for the adoption of some sort of crawling peg after the devaluation. In a recent study on 18 devaluation episodes in Latin America, Edwards (1987b) found that those countries that had adopted a crawling peg had been significantly more successful in sustaining a real depreciation than the discrete devaluers. This study indicates that among the Latin American crawlers in Bolivia (1982), Peru (1975), and Mexico (1982) the higher real exchange rate was sustained at the cost of substantial permanent increase in rate of inflation.

In spite of the prominent role of devaluations in conventional adjustment programs, very little work has investigated empirically the effects of devaluations on the real level of economic activity or on income distribution. A study by Edwards (1986) suggests that in the short run devaluation has led to a slight fall in output in the developing countries. A 10 percent depreciation leads to a one-time loss of almost 1 percent of GNP. In the second year, the economy returns to trend. To the extent that more rapid trade liberalizations require larger devaluations, these results provide new arguments in favor of gradual reforms.

12.3.5 Credibility, Sustainability, and Reversibility of Trade Reforms

Credibility is a fundamental ingredient of successful structural reforms. If the public attaches a nontrivial probability to policy reversal, it will try to anticipate this event, generally introducing strong destabilizing forces into the structural adjustment process. Latin America's history is replete with frustrated economic reforms that have failed because of the lack of credibility. (See Rodriguez 1983 for an analysis of the Argentine experience under Martinez de Hoz.)

The inability to establish consistency between fiscal and exchange rate policies has many times been at the heart of the trade reform credibility crisis in Latin America. For example, in most cases where (mild) trade reforms have been reversed, the public early on perceived that the inflation tax required to finance the fiscal deficit was inconsistent with maintaining a predetermined nominal exchange rate. Under these circumstances expectations of overvaluation, speculative attacks, exchange controls, and future devaluations developed. In trying to anticipate these events the optimizing private sector will usually take steps—such as diversifying its portfolio internationally (i.e., "capital flight")—that will sometimes move the economy in the opposite direction from that intended by the reform. Edwards (1987b) has found that more than 80 percent of reversals of trade liberalizations in Latin America can be traced to inconsistent fiscal policies.

An important question is whether a gradual (i.e., slow) trade reform will be more or less credible than an abrupt one. Theoretical models of credibility of economic policy are only now being developed, and have not yet reached a level that enables us to answer this question with enough precision. In principle, it is possible to argue that gradualism has characteristics that work in both directions, at the same time enhancing and compromising credibility. On one hand—by reducing the unemployment effect and by allowing for a firmer fiscal equilibrium—a gradual trade reform will tend to be more credible; on the other hand, a slow reform will allow those groups negatively affected by it (i.e., the import substitution manufacturing sector) to organize and lobby against the policies. At the end, as is so often the case in economics, whether gradualism will enhance credibility will depend on factors specific to each country. What is clear, however, is that policymakers should always pay special attention to the establishment of credibility when pursuing important long-term structural changes.

Although at this point, given our knowledge of the policymaking process and its interaction with the private sector, it is not possible to derive a precise theorem, the arguments presented in this section—including unemployment, fiscal, and other considerations—suggest that, in general, it would be more prudent to implement the trade reform component of an outward-orientation policy in a gradual way.

12.4 Conclusion

The adjustment packages of 1982–87 sought "effectiveness." On some grounds, and especially in terms of the turnarounds of the current accounts, the results have been quite impressive. The costs, however, have been high. Not only did real income decline, but real wages declined in most countries, and unemployment soared. There is little doubt that this is not a sustainable adjustment path. A successful adjustment means that debtor countries will have to bring down their debt-to-GDP ratios to a level consistent with the reestablishment of creditworthiness, while recovering their growth of output and consumption. The first objective means that the country has to transfer a given discounted value of resources to the rest of the world. The second means that the country has to increase its rate of capital formation and the efficiency of resource use. The problem faced by the highly indebted nations can be posed as follows: how to minimize the present value of the consumption costs associated with making a transfer of a specific discounted value? The problem then has two dimensions: how to minimize the cost of the transfer at each moment of time, including its distributive aspect, and what should be the flow of transfers over time consistent with a given present value of the flow?

A sustained increase in the indebted countries exports, which is, of course, a prerequisite for a long-term solution to the crisis, will not only require an efficient tradables sector and a "realistic" real exchange rate but, more important, that the current protectionist trend in the industrial countries and in particular in the United States be reversed. Data presented in Edwards (1987c) indicate that at this time the extent of nontariff barriers as a form of protection in the industrial countries is very significant. Moreover, the data show that these trade impediments are particularly important for goods originating in the developing nations, and that their tariff equivalents are in many cases very significant. Asking the highly indebted developing countries to pay their debts and at the same time impeding their exports from reaching the industrialized markets is not only unfair, but also politically unwise.

Notes

1. The cause behind the spectacular growth in borrowing during the 1974–82 period varied from country to country. See Edwards (1987a) for a detailed discussion.

2. There is now a vast literature that clearly suggests that outward-oriented countries have greatly outperformed those nations that have followed discriminatory import substitution policies. See, for example, the World Bank 1987 *World Development Report* and the literature cited therein. On CEPAL see, for example, Bianchi, Devlin, and Ramos (1987).

3. The case of Korea, for example, is highly educational. In 1985, 90 percent of Korean imports were subject to automatic approval (i.e., were not subject to any form of licensing) and the average tariff was only 26 percent.

4. See, for example, Krueger (1978) and Little (1982).

5. This will take place by means of the change in the consumption rate of interest (Edwards 1987a).

References

Balassa, B., G. M. Bueno, P. P. Kuczynski, and M. H. Simeonsen. 1986. *Toward renewed economic growth in Latin America.* Washington, D.C.: Institute of International Economics.

Bhagwati, J. 1978. *Anatomy and consequences of exchange control regimes.* Cambridge, Mass.: Ballinger Publishing Co.

Bianchi, A., R. Devlin, and J. Ramos. 1987. The adjustment process in Latin America, 1981–1986. Paper presented at World Bank–IMF symposium, on Growth-Oriented Adjustment Programs in Washington, D.C.

CEPAL. 1986. *Panorama economico de America Latina.* Santiago, Chile.

Conrad, R., and M. Gillis. 1984. The Indonesian tax reform of 1983. Harvard Institute for International Development, Discussion Paper no. 162. Cambridge: Harvard University.

Corbo, V., J. de Melo, and J. Tybout. 1986. What went wrong in the Southern Cone. *Economic Development and Cultural Change* 34 (3): 511–34.

Cuddington, J. 1986. *Capital flight: Estimates, issues, and explanations.* Princeton, N.J.: Princeton Studies in International Finance.

de la Cuadra, S., and D. Hachette. 1986. The timing and sequencing of trade liberalization policy: The case of Chile. Unpublished ms, World Bank.

Dornbusch, R. 1988. Our LDC Debts. *The U.S. in the world economy,* ed. M. Feldstein. Chicago: University of Chicago Press.

Edwards, S. 1985. Stabilization with liberalization: An evaluation of the years of Chile's experience with free-market policies, 1973–1983. *Economic Development and Cultural Change* 33 (2): 223–54.

———. 1986. Are devaluations contractionary? *Review of Economics and Statistics* 68 (3): 501–8.

———. 1987a. Structural adjustment policies in highly indebted countries. Paper presented at NBER Conference on Developing Countries Debt in Washington, D.C. In *Developing Country Debt and Economic Performance,* vol. 1, ed. J. Sachs. Chicago: University of Chicago Press, forthcoming, 1989.

———. 1987b. Exchange controls, devaluations, and real exchange rates: The Latin American experience. Paper presented at Conference on Exchange Controls in June in Bogota, Colombia.

———. 1987c. The U.S. and foreign competition in Latin America. NBER Working Paper no. 2544. Also in *The U.S. in the world economy,* ed. M. Feldstein. Chicago: University of Chicago Press, 1988.

———. 1988. Terms of trade, exchange rates, and labor market adjustments in developing countries. *The World Bank Economic Review* 2 (2): 165–85.

Edwards, S. and A. Cox-Edwards. 1987. *Monetarism and liberalization: The Chilean experiment.* Cambridge, Mass.: Ballinger Publishing Co.

International Monetary Fund. 1987. *World Economic Outlook.*

Krueger, A. O. 1978. *Foreign trade regimes and economic development: Liberalization attempts and consequences.* Cambridge, Mass.: Ballinger Publishing Co.

Little, Ian M.D. 1982. *Economic Development.* New York: Basic Books.

Papageorgiou, D., M. Michaely, and A. Choksi. 1986. The phasing of a trade liberalization policy: Preliminary evidence. Paper presented at AEA meeting in New Orleans.

Rodriguez, C. A. 1983. Politicas de estabilización en la economía Argentina 1978–1982. *Cuadernos de Economía* 20 (59): 21–42.
Sachs, J. 1987. Trade and exchange rate policies in growth-oriented Adjustment Programs. NBER Working Paper no. 2226. Cambridge, Mass. National Bureau of Economic Research.
World Bank. 1987. *World Development Report.*

13   The Politics of Stabilization and Structural Adjustment

Stephan Haggard and Robert Kaufman

13.1   Introduction

A major theme of the country studies in this volume is the relationship between policy choice and economic performance. What policies contributed to debt crises in the first place and what corrective measures have been most successful in managing them? This chapter, by contrast, examines the way political processes, both international and domestic, influence developing country stabilization and adjustment efforts. Of course, economic circumstance defines the policy agenda and is a powerful constraint on the range of policy options. But states that are similarly situated in economic terms have adopted different adjustment strategies and external bargaining positions because of domestic political constraints. Programs that succeed in one context are therefore difficult to implement in others. We review a range of different hypotheses about the politics of adjustment and build some contingent generalizations around the country cases included in this volume. While we cannot provide ironclad political laws, such analysis is important both in understanding the past and in generating realistic and sustainable programs in the future.

13.2   The International Politics of the Debt Crisis

One of the most notable features of the crisis period that began in August 1982 with the emergency rescheduling of the Mexican debt has

Stephan Haggard is associate professor of government and an associate at the Center for International Affairs, Harvard University. Robert Kaufman is a professor of political science at Rutgers University.
We have benefitted from comments by Werner Baer, Jeff Frieden, Joan Nelson, Dani Rodrik, and Jeffrey Sachs.

been the politicization of international credit issues. Although the Reagan administration initially hoped to maintain a distance from the negotiations between debtors, banks, and the IMF that have characterized the postcrisis period, concerns about the stability of the international financial system impelled treasury and central bank officials from the creditor countries to become actively involved in the process. In the case of certain strategically important countries, such as Mexico, Turkey, and Egypt, traditional foreign policy concerns also came into play.

Notwithstanding calls for more comprehensive solutions, rescheduling remains the central mechanism for managing the debt crisis, which suggests that international credit flows to developing countries must be analyzed in a bargaining framework. Despite some marginal innovations, three features of the international bargaining structure have remained more or less constant. First has been the assumption—or the fiction—that all obligations are to be met in full. Until recently, relief had not been on the agenda, despite the development of a secondary market in which developing country debt traded at fairly deep discounts. Second, was the assumption that the burden of policy changes should fall primarily on the debtors rather than the creditors. Developing countries have failed in their political efforts to link the debt issue with developed country fiscal and trade policies, interest-rate management, or the reform of international commodity trade, and have had very uneven success in securing additional concessional aid flows. Finally, all negotiations have been handled on a case-by-case basis. Each debtor is expected to confront its creditors alone, rather than in collaboration with other debtor countries facing similar problems. Whatever practical arguments may be advanced in favor of this system over a more comprehensive one—and there are many (Cooper 1986)— it is clearly a bargaining structure that tends *eo ipso* to favor the creditors.

There are three resources that developing countries can bring to bear in these negotiations: size, political-strategic significance, and the availability of nonconditional resources.

13.2.1 Size

Evidence from recent rescheduling exercises suggests that larger debtors do better than smaller ones in the rates, maturities, and grace periods they receive (see table 13.1). They have also been more successful in securing additional forms of relief, including the concerted lending agreements (Sachs and Huizinga 1987). Larger debtors have also pioneered more unorthodox rescheduling agreements and adjustment packages. Mexico was the first country to negotiate a multi-year rescheduling agreement (MYRA), and Argentina was able to win IMF acceptance of the unorthodox price freeze and currency plan known as the Plan Austral.

Table 13.1 **Average Terms of Bank Debt Reschedulings, By Group of Countries (1978-June 1985)**

	Grace Period	Maturity	Interest Rates (spread over LIBOR)
Large Debtors (> $25 billion, Jan. 1, 1985)	3.25 years	11.31 years	1.41%
Medium-sized Debtors ($10 to $25 billion)	4.36 years	8.28 years	1.69%
Small Debtors (<$10 billion)	2.61 years	7.26 years	1.82%

(Note: Average terms for rescheduling of medium- and long-term bank debt, both public and private. Excludes restructuring of short-term debt, arrears and terms of trade facilities. Debtors are classified on basis of total external liabilities of banks and non-banks to banks end-December 1985. "Large" debtors are Brazil, Mexico, Argentina and Venezuela; "medium-sized" debtors reaching rescheduling agreements during the period are Chile, Philippines, Yugoslavia and Poland. Source: Watson, et. al. 1986.

An exception to this rule concerns the likelihood of repudiation. Until Brazil's suspension of payments in February 1987, large countries had been content to exercise the tacit *threat* of repudiation; the smaller and weaker countries—Bolivia, Peru, Ecuador, Costa Rica, the Dominican Republic, Honduras, the Ivory Coast, Zaire and Zambia—actually exercised the option. Small debtors may be more tempted to "free ride," particularly in a setting where increasing numbers of other countries are doing so. The reason for small country repudiation may also have to do with bank strategy and reputational concerns. Banks may prefer to allow small states to repudiate rather than to concede to the financing required to keep loans performing.

13.2.2 Strategic Significance

Size is not the only variable of significance in determining bargaining outcomes, however. A number of smaller states, including Zaire, have manipulated their strategic position or concern about domestic political instability to gain additional assistance. Turkey probably provides the clearest example of how geo-strategic concerns influence official assistance. Of $9.8 billion of debt that Turkey restructured between 1978 and 1987, $5.5 billion was negotiated through a consortium of OECD governments. The OECD did link its 1979 offer of concessional finance to acceptance of an IMF program, but the amount of additional assistance totalled $3 billion over the next three years despite the fact that the 1979 program was not particularly successful. The OECD commitments were followed by unusual levels of assistance from the World Bank and IMF, including five consecutive structural adjustment loans and a three-year standby agreement in 1980 that brought Turkey's total IMF commitments to 870 percent of quota, the largest multiple awarded to any country up until that time.

More generally, central banks of the Group of Five have played an important role in managing particular crises through the organization of rescue packages and the provision of bridging loans. Informal conventions have divided these international lender of last resort responsibilities along lines of regional and political influence. Germany played a leading role in Turkey and Poland; the United States in Mexico; France in Francophone Africa (Wellons 1987, chap. 7). This decentralized pattern of leadership includes the provision and orchestration of concessional assistance, which, as is well known, also follows lines of political interest.

13.2.3 Nonconditional Resources

A final factor influencing debt negotiations, particularly with the IMF, is the availability of nonconditional resources. These resources naturally shift bargaining power toward the debtors and make them less likely to accept Fund conditionality. This tendency is particularly clear among the capital-importing oil exporters, including Venezuela, Nigeria, Mexico, Ecuador, and Indonesia prior to the Pertamina crisis. The stylized facts are as follows. Commodity booms make governments more dependent on commodity-based revenue because of the relative ease politically of taxing commodity exports as opposed to income. The income from commodity exports also provides the basis for additional foreign borrowing. This double windfall has three political consequences. First, it reduces the political incentives to undertake any adjustments that have distributional consequences. Second, it increases the range of political claims on state-controlled resources, not only from rent- and revenue-seeking groups in society, but from spending constituencies within the government itself. Finally, the windfalls provide governments with resources that can be used for political ends, whether through corruption and the "financing" of elections, pork-barrel expenditures on particular projects that cement geographical bases of support, or the expansion of subsidies and entitlements.

It is thus common to see increased government revenues from commodity booms mark the beginning of a cycle of increased borrowing, widening fiscal deficits and, ultimately, a return of balance of payments crises. Mexico provides an example. In 1978 when the country began to experience a boom as the result of increased oil revenues, it repaid its obligations to the IMF and abandoned the terms of a standby reached in 1976. A new cycle of borrowing began, purportedly to finance investment in the oil sector itself. By early 1982, voices within the government and the international financial community were urging caution.

Yet there was a political decision not to stop the country's growth prior to elections. Central to the fiscal problems the country faced was a rapid expansion of subsidies to food and domestic energy consumption designed to cement the ruling party's support among the urban working and middle classes.

13.2.4   Cooperation among Debtors

In addition to the possibility of operating within the prevailing case-by-case bargaining structure, debtors may conceivably seek to alter the rules of the game through cooperative behavior. Up until now, the barriers to collective action among debtors have been greater than those facing the relatively small group of money-center banks. Banks have thus been able to discourage a debtor cartel by isolating and punishing recalcitrant debtors, while rewarding others, such as Mexico, for good behavior. The debtors with real power have therefore preferred the advantages of striking their own separate deals to the risks of cartel leadership.

The barriers to collective action among debtors should not be overestimated though. LDC debt is also heavily concentrated on the borrower side. Given this concentration, the defection of one large debtor would be enough to change the system substantially, even with the assumption of free riding. There can be little doubt that the negotiations surrounding Brazil's February 1987 suspension of interest payments will have a profound effect on future reschedulings. Learning among debtor governments increases the possibility that concessions granted in one case will become the basis for demands by other countries even in the absence of overt collaboration.

13.3   The Domestic Politics of Stabilization and Adjustment

The international and domestic politics of stabilization and adjustment are closely linked. Since no debtor government can deflect all of the costs of adjustment, each must also bargain with domestic actors over how to allocate burdens on the home front. The central political dilemma is that stabilization and adjustment policies, no matter how beneficial they may be for the country as a whole, entail the imposition of short-term costs and have distributional implications. Two questions are of importance: Why do governments choose the policy packages they do—the question of program *design*—and what are the political conditions under which they will be sustained, the problem of *implementation*. We focus on the influence of three clusters of variables: the power of different interest groups; the nature of central government institutions, including the bureaucracy; and the influence of short-term political calculations, including those associated both with elections and with other, less institutionalized, political transitions.

13.3.1   Interest Groups: Business, Labor, and the Urban-Rural
Balance

Business-Government Relations

The central problem confronting any government in its relations with
the private sector is in establishing a credible and predictable policy
environment. Confidence in government policy is a major factor in
determining time horizons and willingness to take risk, and thus affects
levels of investment and capital flight. Other things being equal, leftist
governments and political systems with a history of populist attacks
on business and property rights will face greater difficulties establishing
the credibility of policy, regardless of their stated intentions. Perhaps
the sharpest contrast among the countries included in this project is
between Argentina and Korea. Argentine politics in the postwar period
has been deeply polarized between populist and antipopulist forces. A
close relationship exists between political cycles and the broad swings
in the country's macroeconomy. The Korean political system under
Park Chung Hee (1964–79), by contrast, while not without periods of
unrest, was based on a firm business-government alliance. Populist and
leftist forces were excluded, if not repressed. Policy was coherent and
credible, contributing to a high level of investor confidence.

It is important to note, however, that segments of business may have
reason to oppose orthodox stabilization and structural adjustment measures; much depends on their sectoral position and international finance
and trade links. Firms with strong international financial ties and export-
oriented industries are more likely to support orthodoxy. Even where
they are not *politically* organized, liquid asset holders constitute a
constraint on governments of both the left and right through the threat
of capital flight (Frieden forthcoming). Those without dependence on
international financial markets, by contrast, will have less reason to
back a conciliatory policy toward international creditors, and may positively oppose credit restraint and the removal of various sectoral supports. While export-oriented firms will support more liberal trade and
exchange rate policies, firms in import-substituting sectors that have
been heavily subsidized and protected will present an obstacle to market-
oriented reforms, including import liberalization. The longer such policies have been in place, the more politically difficult it is to make the
transition to outward-oriented policies. These types of cleavages among
different segments of business are particularly visible in the large, Latin
American countries, including Brazil and Mexico.

The Political Role of Labor

The urban informal sector has operated as a constraint on government policy in a number of countries. The lifting of food subsidies, in

particular, has frequently resulted in spontaneous rioting (Bienen and Gersovitz 1985). In general, however, the organized workers of the modern sector, both public and private, are best positioned to act politically against stabilization and devaluation, with their anticipated consequences for employment and real wages. Other things being equal, one would expect the degree of unionization and the likelihood of adopting and sustaining orthodox stabilization and structural adjustment measures to be inversely correlated. Those governments relying heavily on labor support are more likely to tolerate inflation, experiment with heterodox programs, and adopt tough bargaining postures with external creditors.

This expectation is not necessarily borne out, however. As with the private sector, the political behavior of labor depends on sectoral position. Equally important, however, is the institutional context within which labor operates. Where strategic labor sectors are weak and penetrated, the burdens of stabilization policies are easy to impose, although the economic program, and the government itself, may encounter long-term costs in the form of decreased legitimacy. Weak or controlled labor movements in the Philippines and Korea granted the government greater leeway in imposing the costs of stabilization, at least initially. Labor control was also a central feature of the stabilization programs of the "bureaucratic authoritarian" governments of Argentina, Brazil, Chile, and Uruguay over the 1960s and 1970s.

Literature on the advanced industrial states suggests that where labor is organized in peak associations with a secure place in the political process, it may be easier to induce them to trade short-term wage restraint for longer-term gains. This holds true even under leftist governments (Goldthorpe 1984). None of the developing countries have developed the kind of corporatist arrangements linking business, government, and labor that are found in the small European democracies. Nonetheless, Venezuela and Mexico suggest that the integration of labor into multiclass parties may affect the government's ability to negotiate compensatory agreements that ease the adjustment process.

The greatest difficulty comes in intermediate cases where labor is capable of defensive mobilization, but uncertain about its longer-term place in the political system. This situation is typical of a number of developing countries making the transition to democracy, including Brazil, where labor movements have previously been under strong government control.

The Role of the Rural Sector

For some policy reforms, including devaluation and food pricing policy, the balance of power between rural and urban interests may be the most salient cleavage. In general, countries in which political elites are forced to be attentive to the countryside should pursue policies favorable to agricultural and rural interests, including realistic exchange rate policies (Sachs 1985). This, in turn, is likely to occur where political parties have rural roots or where the peasantry is available for revolutionary mobilization. Indonesian macroeconomic policy following the rural uprisings of the mid-1960s provides a particularly clear example.

Several caveats are in order, however. First, predictions are difficult to make on the basis of simple proxies of the urban-rural balance alone. A large unorganized rural sector can easily be offset by concentrated urban interests, as is the case in a number of African countries. Second, it is not clear that the turn to outward-oriented growth in the East Asian NICs can be linked to a concern with rural interests. Fears of insurgency and rural unrest were behind the land reforms in Korea and Taiwan in the fifties, but the turn to export-led growth is more clearly traced to a decline in aid flows and the structural problems associated with import-substitution. It can be argued, however, that these structural problems were partly a function of the *absence* of natural resource exports that could finance continued import-substitution. In Latin America, by contrast, the availability of such resources allowed import-substitution to continue for longer than it might have otherwise.

13.3.2   The Role of Political Institutions

As the foregoing discussion should make clear, policy choice is not only a function of the distribution of interests, but of the institutional context in which they operate. The major debate on stabilization among political scientists concerns whether authoritarian or elected governments are more "successful" at stabilization (Haggard 1986; Kaufman 1985; Remmer 1986; Ames 1987, chap. 5). Cross-national studies do not yield conclusive results, but this probably has to do with the crudeness of the authoritarian-democratic dichotomy. A distinction must be made between "strong" and "weak" authoritarian governments. "Strong" authoritarian governments possess a number of organizational resources that make them more successful in imposing the costs of stabilization, at least in the short run. These include a relatively insulated decision-making process, weak legislatures, and corporatist organization, or control, of interests. Korea's ability to adjust swiftly during the early 1980s, for example, can be traced in part to a tightly controlled budgetary process and controls on labor.

Many "authoritarian" governments, however, are in fact quite weak, characterized by extensive patron-client networks, a low degree of insulation from the political demands of society, extensive interference in even routine economic decision making by political elites and a high degree of instability. At the extreme, some "authoritarian" regimes are little more than personal autocracies in which the lines between public and private finances are blurred. The succession of Bolivian military juntas in the late 1970s and early 1980s is representative of a system in which central political institutions are extremely weak. Such systems are likely to have more difficulties than "strong" authoritarian regimes in imposing costs, and will probably fare worse than many democracies.

This is particularly true where democracies have evolved stable patterns of interest group representation and consultation; just like "authoritarian" governments, democracies constitute a heterogenous category. A distinction is possible between those plebiscitary democratic systems, such as Peru, that rest on broad, mass appeals and those with more institutionalized systems of representation, usually involving stronger party systems, such as Colombia. Such institutional mechanisms aggregate broader interests, and can thus act as a check both on the disruptive impact of plebiscitary appeals as well as on particularistic rent seeking.

Analysis of institutional capacity must be extended to the bureaucracy itself. The attention given to policy reform among economists has not, in general, been matched by adequate attention to the administrative requirements of successful policy implementation. Quite obviously, the administrative capacity of government is a crucial determinant of the success of a number of policy measures, particularly those structural adjustment measures demanding government support. The transition to export-led growth in Korea, for example, involved not only reforms in the broad system of incentives, but a complex system of *organizational* supports to exporters, including the provision of market information and technical assistance, a complex drawback system, and subsidized credit. All of these policies rested on an efficient bureaucracy (Haggard, Kim, and Moon 1987).

The characteristics of the bureaucracy likely to affect its performance include patterns of recruitment, particularly the extent to which they are meritocratic or not, and the degree of coordination among different ministries and between ministries and state-owned enterprises. This last issue is particularly salient for the analysis of the debt crisis. In all of the cases included in this project, state-owned enterprises were crucial in the expansion of foreign debt. Obligations were frequently incurred without central government or ministerial approval, and even without the monitoring that would give central bank and finance ministry officials an adequate picture of debt aggregates.

While it should be clear that bureaucratic capabilities matter, several amendments are required. First, the ability of bureaucracies to act, even highly competent ones, is dependent on the larger political context. In Mexico over the last two decades, for example, the influence of the treasury and central bank has changed directly with the broader political strategy of successive administrations. Second, bureaucracies can easily become overdeveloped or wedded to organizational routines that impede, rather than facilitate adjustment. While central government guidance was important in earlier phases of export-led growth in Korea, Taiwan, and Singapore, dirigiste traditions may now present barriers to more rapid growth. The dogmatic course pursued by entrenched laissez-faire technocrats in Argentina and Chile in the late 1970s provides another example of bureaucratic rigidity.

The bureaucracy must also be viewed not only as an administrative structure, but as an interest group in its own right. Civil servants are politically significant actors in a number of countries, particularly small, low-income states where they play an important role in urban coalitions. Establishing control over the expansion of the government itself is one of the most difficult tasks associated with stabilization and adjustment. Brazil's difficulties in reining in its sprawling state-owned enterprise sector provides an example.

13.3.3 Political Cycles and Transitions

The broad analysis of interest groups and institutions is useful in drawing some cross-national comparisons, but we also want to know what political forces influence policy changes over time *within* particular countries. This demands closer attention to the short-term survival strategies of politicians (Ames 1987). One important hypothesis centers on electoral cycles. Incumbent governments will manipulate macroeconomic policy to maximize their short-term electoral chances, tolerating higher levels of inflation in order to achieve lower levels of unemployment, for example. Adjustment programs are more likely to be abandoned prior to elections, while post-election periods, particularly where incumbents have been returned, are more conducive to stabilization.

The evidence for the business cycle claim is weak in the advanced industrial states and its analytic underpinnings have also been challenged. Brian Barry (1985, 300) notes, for example, that it assumes "a collection of rogues competing for the favors of a larger collection of dupes." Some of the factors mitigating the electoral cycle in the advanced industrial states are likely to be absent in the developing countries, however. Policy-making institutions are weaker and less insulated and publics less informed. Lower levels of income and extensive poverty are likely to make instrumental appeals more powerful. The one, thorough cross-national study done on the cycle for a group of developing countries finds strong evidence for politically motivated fiscal policy (Ames 1987). Individual country studies included in this project, such as those for Mexico (chap. 7 in this volume) and the Philippines (chap. 8), also suggest the existence of political cycles of spending.

The political cycle model must be extended to cover noninstitutionalized transitions between democratic and authoritarian regimes. Given the uncertainty surrounding such transitions, new democratic governments are likely to pursue expansionist policies early in office, a pattern exactly the opposite of that predicted for institutionalized democracies. The expansionist phases of the Cruzado and Austral plans in Brazil and Argentina reflect this pattern. New authoritarian regimes, by contrast, frequently come to power amidst political-economic crises precisely to impose "discipline." This was true, though under differing circumstances, in Brazil (1964), Argentina (1966 and 1976), Turkey (1971 and 1980), Indonesia (1966), Bolivia (1971), and Korea (1980). Authoritarian governments will pursue more politically motivated policies only as they face opposition and attempt to make the transition to constitutional rule (Ames 1987, chap. 5).

13.4 Conclusions

Drawing conclusions for policy from political analysis may, at first, seem difficult, since a number of variables that are relevant are not manipulable. In fact, there is probably more room for political maneuver and persuasion than is frequently recognized. The reform process is not merely a technical, policy-making exercise, but demands the building of political coalitions of support. This can be facilitated by campaigns of information targeted at groups that stand to gain. Imposing costs is, of course, more difficult, but groups will be more likely to acquiesce to short-term costs if they are consulted and sense that their position in the political system is secure. In a number of policy areas, compensation to potential losers may be less costly than an effort to force through policies that are likely to fail politically. The timing of the introduction of reform measures is also at least partly manipulable, and can affect the likelihood of program success. In some cases, it may be wiser simply not to initiate a program at all, rather than to introduce measures that are doomed to failure. Political analysis also suggests the importance of a range of longer-term reforms that affect the capacity of governments over time. These include administrative reform and training, which have been given inadequate weight in Fund programs to date. In the end, however, there is no substitute for a nuanced understanding of the political and social setting into which economic programs are introduced.

References

In addition to the references cited here, we have also drawn on the country studies done for this project: Juan Antonio Morales and Jeffrey Sachs, Bolivia;

Eliana Cardoso and Albert Fishlow, Brazil; Rudiger Dornbusch and Juan Carlos
de Pablo, Argentina; Edward Buffie, with the assistance of Allen Sangines
Krause, Mexico; Wing Thye Woo and Anwar Nasution, Indonesia; Susan Collins and Won-Am Park, Korea; Merih Celâsun and Dani Rodrik, Turkey; Robert
Dohner and Ponciano Intal, Jr., the Philippines.

Ames, Barry. 1987. *Political survival: Politicians and public policy in Latin
America.* Berkeley: University of California Press.
Barry, Brian. 1985. Does democracy cause inflation? Political ideas of some
economists. In *The politics of inflation and economic stagnation,* ed. Leon
N. Lindberg and Charles S. Maier. Washington, D.C.: The Brookings
Institution.
Bienen, Henry S., and Mark Gersovitz. 1985. Economic stabilization, condi-
tionality, and political stability. *International Organization* 39, no. 4: 729–
54.
Cooper, Richard. 1986. The lingering problem of LDC debt. *The Marcus Wal-
lenberg Papers on International Finance.* vol. 1, no. 5. Washington D.C.:
International Law Institute and School of Foreign Service, Georgetown
University.
Frieden, Jeffrey. n.d. Debt, development and democracy in Latin America:
Classes, sectors and the international financial relations of Mexico, Brazil,
Argentina, Venezuela and Chile. *Comparative Politics,* forthcoming.
Goldthorpe, John H., ed. 1984. *Order and conflict in contemporary capitalism.*
Oxford: Clarendon Press.
Haggard, Stephan. 1986. The politics of adjustment: Lessons from the IMF's
extended fund facility. In *The politics of international debt,* ed. Miles Kahler.
Ithaca, N.Y.: Cornell University Press.
Haggard, Stephan, Byung-kook Kim, and Chung-in Moon. 1987. The transition
to export-led growth in Korea, 1954–1966. Unpublished ms., Harvard
University.
Kaufman, Robert. 1985. Democratic and authoritarian responses to the debt
issue: Argentina, Brazil, and Mexico. In *The politics of international debt,*
ed. Miles Kahler. Ithaca, N.Y.: Cornell University Press.
Nelson, Joan. 1984. The political economy of stabilization: Commitment, ca-
pacity and public response. *World Development* 12, no. 10 (October): 983–
1006.
Remmer, Karen. 1986. The politics of economic stabilization: IMF standby
programs in Latin America, 1954–1984. *Comparative Politics* (October).
Sachs, Jeffrey D. 1985. External debt and macroeconomic performance in Latin
America and East Asia. *Brookings Papers on Economic Activity,* 2: 523–73.
Sachs, Jeffrey D., and H. Huizinga. 1987. U.S. commercial banks and the
developing country debt crisis. *Brookings Papers on Economic Activity* 2:
555–601.
Wellons, Philip. 1987. *Passing the buck: Banks, governments, and Third World
debt.* Boston: Harvard Business School Press.

14   Conditionality, Debt Relief, and the Developing Country Debt Crisis

Jeffrey D. Sachs

14.1 Introduction

This chapter examines the role of high-conditionality lending by the International Monetary Fund and the World Bank as a part of the overall management of the debt crisis. High-conditionality lending refers to the process in which the international institutions make loans based on the promise of the borrowing countries to pursue a specified set of policies. High-conditionality lending by both institutions has played a key role in the management of the crisis since 1982, though the results of such lending have rarely lived up to the advertised hopes. One major theme of this paper is that the role for high-conditionality lending is more restricted than generally believed, since the efficacy of conditionality is inherently limited.

A related theme is that many programs involving high-conditionality lending could be made more effective by including commercial bank debt relief as a component of such programs. I shall argue that such debt relief can be to the benefit of the creditor banks as well as the debtors, by enhancing the likelihood that the debtor governments will adhere to the conditionality terms of the IMF and World Bank loans, and thereby raise their long-term capacity to service their debts.

Almost by definition, countries in debt crisis that appeal to the Fund or the Bank for new loans have already been judged to be uncreditworthy by normal market criteria. In such treacherous circumstances, it is appropriate to ask why the IMF or the World Bank should be extending new loans. As an alternative, for example, the international institutions could allow the creditors and debtors to renegotiate new

Jeffrey D. Sachs is a professor of economics at Harvard University and a research associate of the National Bureau of Economic Research.

terms on the old loans without any official involvement. Such two-party negotiations between creditors and debtors characterized earlier debt crises, before the IMF and World Bank existed (see Lindert and Morton, chap. 10 in this volume, for a discussion of the earlier history).

In principle, continued lending by the international institutions could be justified by several nonmarket criteria: as a form of aid, as an investment by the creditor governments that finance the IMF and World Bank in political and economic stability of the debtor country (see Von Furstenberg 1985a, 1985b, for such a view); as an extension of the foreign policy interests of the major creditor governments; as a defense of the international financial system, etc. Loans are not usually defended on these grounds, though in fact such considerations are frequently important. Of course, these criteria are valid to an extent, but also extremely difficult to specify with precision as a basis for IMF–World Bank lending.

Another defense of lending, also with considerable merit in some circumstances, is that the IMF (and World Bank to a far lesser extent), can act as a "lender of last resort," analogous to a central bank fighting a banking panic in a domestic economy. The argument holds that the private commercial bank lenders to a country might panic, and all decide to withdraw their funds from the country even though the country is a fundamentally sound credit risk in the longer term (see Sachs 1984, for such a model). In this case, lending by the IMF can eliminate the liquidity squeeze on the country, and thereby help both the creditors and the debtors. As in the case of a domestic banking panic, the IMF helps to overcome a well-defined market failure.

This argument was part of the basis of the original IMF intervention into the debt crisis in the early 1980s. The argument following the Mexican crisis in mid-1982 was that countries were suffering from a liquidity crisis, made acute by the simultaneous rise in world interest rates and the sudden cessation of commercial bank lending. It seemed at the time that the crisis could be quickly resolved (as argued, for example, by Cline 1984), since it represented merely a liquidity squeeze.

The liquidity arguments are no doubt true in some cases, but most observers now doubt that the developing country debt crisis represents merely a problem of liquidity. Six years after the onset of the crisis, almost no countries have returned to normal borrowing from the international capital markets, and the secondary-market value of bank loans to the debtor countries reflect very deep discounts in valuation. For many countries at least, the crisis represents more fundamental problems of solvency and longer-term willingness to pay on the part of the debtor nations.

In these circumstances, other justifications (that can be in addition to the liquidity argument) have been advanced for the large role of the

IMF and World Bank lending. By far the most important argument is that *strict conditionality* attached to IMF–World Bank loans can make such loans sensible on normal market terms. The assumption is that the international institutions are better than the banks at enforcing the good behavior of the debtor country governments, and therefore have more scope for lending.

The importance of conditionality in justifying IMF–World Bank lending is certainly well placed. Nonetheless, the role for high-conditionality lending is overstated, especially in the case of countries in a deep debt crisis. In practice, the compliance of debtor countries with conditionality is rather weak, and this compliance problem has gotten worse in recent years, since a large stock of debt can itself be an important disincentive to "good behavior." In other words, the debt overhang itself makes it less likely that conditionality will prove successful.

The reason is straightforward. Why should a country adjust if that adjustment produces income for foreign banks rather than for its own citizenry? since deeply indebted countries recognize that much of each extra dollar of export earnings gets gobbled up in debt servicing, a very large stock of debt acts like a high marginal tax on successful adjustment. Therefore, two counterintuitive propositions could be true when a country is deeply indebted: "Good behavior" (such as a higher investment rate) can actually reduce national welfare, by increasing the transfer of income from the debtor country to creditors; and explicit debt relief by the creditors can increase the amounts of actual debt repayment, by improving the incentive of the debtor country to take the necessary adjustments.

14.2   High-Conditionality Lending by the IMF and World Bank

The argument for high-conditionality lending is that the IMF and the World Bank can compel countries to undertake stabilizing actions in return for loans, thereby making the loans prudent even when the private capital markets have declared the country to be in uncreditworthy. A full theory of conditionality would have to explain three things. First, if the actions being recommended to the country are really "desirable" for the country, why is it that the country must be compelled to undertake the policy? Second, if the country must indeed be compelled to undertake the actions, what types of force or sanctions can be used to guarantee compliance? And third, why is it that international institutions are better able to impose conditionality than are the private capital markets?

One solution to the conundrum of why countries must be compelled to accept conditionality is the problem of "time consistency": A debtor government accepts ex ante the need for a policy adjustment as the quid pro quo for a loan, but the government has a strong incentive to avoid the policy change once the loan is arranged. In this case, the role of conditionality is to bind the country to a course of future actions, actions which make sense today but which will look unattractive in the future. In other words, the goal of conditionality is to make the ex ante and ex post incentives for adjustment the same (where ex ante and ex post are with respect to the receipt of the loan).

The question of enforcement of conditionality agreements is in many ways tougher than the question of why conditionality is needed. The justification for IMF–World Bank lending rests on two propositions regarding enforcement: (1) that the enforcement of IMF–World Bank conditionality is sufficiently powerful to result in an "acceptable" rate of compliance with IMF–World Bank programs; and (2) that the official institutions have an advantage over the commercial banks in enforcing conditionality. Both assumptions are problematic.

For both the international institutions and the commercial banks, the legal bases of conditionality are weak. In the domestic capital markets, bond covenants are legally binding restrictions on the behavior of debtors, and can generally be enforced with only modest transactions costs. In the international arena, particularly for loans to sovereign governments, the transaction costs for enforcing loan agreements are extremely high. As most writers have recognized recently, the main method of enforcement for lenders (whether official or private) involve the threat of cutoffs of *new* loans to misbehaving borrowers. Such a cutoff in lending can of course be extremely disruptive and costly to a borrower.

Theoretical work and empirical evidence both establish that the threat of a lending cutoff is a credible, but inherently limited sanction. Thus, conditionality, whether by the IMF and World Bank, or by the commercial banks themselves, cannot, on an a priori basis, be expected to have the same force as a binding bond convenant in a domestic loan. From the beginning, we should appreciate the inherent limitations of the enforcement mechanisms in conditionality on international lending.

Conditionality is limited in effectiveness not only because of enforcement difficulties, but also because of the complexity of negotiating with a sovereign borrower. In the case of a bond convenant, there is a clear legal responsibility on the borrower to carry out the conditions of the covenant. When a government is the debtor, however, there is likely to be a considerable diffusion of power within the government, to the extent that the individual parts of the government negotiating the conditionality agreement may well lack the *authority* to implement the agreement.

14.2.1 The Debt Overhang and the Weakness of Conditionality

What must also be appreciated is the fact that the current *overhang of external debt to private creditors* can greatly hinder the effectiveness of IMF conditionality, at least under the prevailing design of IMF programs. Virtually all IMF programs to date have been designed under the assumption that the debtor country *can and will* service its external debts in the long run on a normal market basis. The programs are constructed under the maintained assumption of such normal debt servicing. (For example, in the technical calculations in Fund programs, interest rates on the existing debt are assumed to be at market rates; the country is assumed to clear all arrears on a reasonable timetable, etc.)

Contrary to this assumption, however, it might easily be the case that a country is better off defaulting on a portion of its debts than it would be with timely debt servicing, if such is possible (a dozen or more countries have indeed taken such unilateral action by 1987). There may simply exist no IMF high-conditionality program based on full debt servicing, that if followed, actually makes the country better off than it would be without the program but with a partial suspension of debt payments. In other words, the IMF program might simply be too tight relative to the available options of the debtor governments.

In such circumstances, four things could happen. The best outcome, I will suggest below, would be for the IMF to design a program that is actually based on partial and explicit debt relief. So far, the IMF has avoided this rather obvious approach, partly because it has underestimated the possible efficiency gains for all parties (creditor, debtors, and the Fund) that might result. The second possibility is that the IMF and the debtor government would fail to sign a program, and the country would simply suspend payments on part of its private sector debts. This has been the case with Peru during 1985–87, and Brazil in 1987. The third possibility, and indeed the typical case in recent years, is that the Fund and the country would sign a program based on full debt servicing, even though both parties *fully expect* that the agreement will breakdown in due course. Either the conditionality would be allowed to fall by the wayside and the country would continue to borrow from the Fund but without living up to earlier commitments, or the IMF program would eventually be suspended.

A fourth possibility that deserves important consideration, would be for the IMF and World Bank to approve programs with debtor countries that allow for a buildup of arrears (i.e., nonpayments) to the commercial bank creditors, in well-defined circumstances. These circumstances would include (1) a large overhang of debt that is deemed to be highly inimical to the stabilization efforts of the country; and (2) the unwillingness of the commercial creditors either to grant relief or significant new financing. By allowing for the buildup of arrears to private creditors, the IMF could design more realistic programs without the need to press the private creditors for specific amounts of debt relief. The debt relief would instead emerge in the bilateral bargaining of the debtor and the creditors.

14.3   The Recent Experience with Conditionality

Multicountry analyses of IMF conditionality generally arrive at a fairly pessimistic assessment of IMF loan practices. In particular, the evidence suggests that IMF programs are very frequently, if not typically, unsuccessful in restoring stability and growth in countries beset with balance of payments and inflation problems. As an example, in a review of Fund programs supported by standby arrangements in upper-credit tranches during 1969–78, Beveridge and Kelley (1980) found that fiscal targets were achieved in about half the cases, but "[b]y 1977 and 1978, expenditures were contained as planned in less than 20 percent of the programs, compared with over 50 percent in 1969 and 1970" (p. 213). Also, Beveridge and Kelley found that governments were not generally successful in meeting targets with respect to the composition of expenditure between current and capital outlays.

Stephan Haggard's (1985) recent review of IMF programs under the Extended Fund Facility (EFF) is no more heartening. According to Haggard's count, "of the thirty adjustment programs launched under the auspices of the Extended Fund Facility, twenty-four were renegotiated, or had payments interrupted, or were quietly allowed to lapse. Of these twenty-four, sixteen were formally cancelled by the IMF, virtually all for noncompliance" (pp. 505–6).

Haggard's bleak conclusions are echoed in a recent study by Remmer (1986) of IMF programs during 1954–84. It is worth quoting Remmer at length on the question of IMF conditionality:

Unsuccessful implementation of IMF recipes has been the norm in Latin America, not the exception. A high proportion of standby programs have failed to push key indicators of government finance and domestic credit even in the right direction. Moreover, examining IMF standby programs on a before and after basis shows that changes in key indicators are more readily attributable to chance than to the operation of IMF stabilization programs. The obvious conclusion is that the economic, social, and political impact of IMF programs has been overstated. To describe the IMF as a "poverty broker," as does the title of a recent book, or to charge the Fund with undermining democracy is to engage in hyperbole. The power of the IMF remains a useful myth for governments seeking a scapegoat to explain difficult economic conditions associated with severe balance of payments disequilibria, but the ability of the IMF to impose programs from the outside is distinctly limited (p. 21).

14.4   External Debt and Conditionality

The theme of this section is that high external indebtedness can reduce the incentives for a country to undertake necessary macroeconomic adjustments, and thus further reduce the chance that the terms of a conditionality agreement will be fulfilled. Indeed, for very high levels of indebtedness, it may be useful for creditors to forgive some of the debt as an incentive for better performance, recognizing that such an incentive could actually *raise* the repayments to creditors in the long run.

There are really two linkages between a debt overhang and the effectiveness of conditionality, one obvious and the other a bit more subtle. The obvious linkage has already been made: In the absence of debt relief, a country may have no incentive to honor a conditionality agreement, and to carry through on an economic reform program. The foreign debt acts like a tax on adjustment. The debt relief removes the tax, and encourages the country to undertake efficient reforms.

The second linkage occurs when debt relief is a *necessary but not sufficient* condition for inducing the country to undertake needed reforms. It may be, for example, that a prerequisite of new investment spending requires *both* new external financing and debt relief, and the external financing itself requires conditionality, since the creditors understand that the country would prefer to borrow abroad and then not undertake the investment.

14.5   Some Implications for the Pace and Phasing of Adjustment Programs

The postwar history of stabilization, liberalization, and conditionality can make a pessimist of the most tenacious optimist. Few stabilization and liberalization plans meet their initial objectives, and many fail miserably. We have seen that conditionality is inherently limited in its capacity to effect adjustment in the debtor countries, and that the limitations are even more severe in the presence of a debt overhang. In many cases, debt relief might have to be combined with conditionality to improve the likelihood of success of IMF and World Bank programs.

Given these limitations, it is important to make the objectives of conditionality consistent with the limited efficacy of conditionality.

Programs of the IMF and World Bank should be tailored according to a realistic assessment of the possible accomplishments. One of the most important issues in this regard is the balancing of the demands of stabilization with those of longer-term structural reform. Since the major debtor countries suffer from acute macroeconomic disequilibria (with inflation rates in Argentina, Brazil, and Mexico well exceeding 100 percent per year in 1987), a crucial issue is the balancing of macroeconomic stabilization with other types of structural reform.

The main theme of this section is that structural reform (especially a shift towards greater outward orientation and trade liberalization) is a very difficult process that takes many years to bring to fruition. The process is so difficult economically and politically that it is likely to fail under the best of macroeconomic circumstances, and is in general greatly jeopardized by a concurrent macroeconomic stabilization crisis. The historical record suggests that stabilization should be given temporal priority in the design of adjustment programs, with structural reforms proceeding gradually and mostly *after* macroeconomic balance has been restored.

The historical record (e.g., as contained in the important studies of Krueger 1978 and Bhagwati 1978) suggests that most attempts at liberalization fail. Moreover, a high inflation rate seems to be a serious hindrance in successful liberalization, since in most cases in which liberalization was attempted with an inflation rate above 30 percent, the experiment failed. There are several reasons for this adverse linkage, including the fact that fear of accelerating inflation may induce governments to undertake inadequate devaluations at the start of a liberalization exercise, and then to fail to keep the exchange rate adjusting downward in correction for a domestic inflation rate in excess of the world rate.

Other research, by Killick et al. (1984) and Ching-yuan Lin (1985), agree with the proposition that the simultaneous application of stabilization and widespread liberalization is unlikely to be sustainable and successful. Killick notes that a degree of liberalization was sought alongside stabilization in at least 8 of 23 standby arrangements in 1978–79, with meagre results. He concludes, "It does not seem that the means available to, or employed by, the Fund are strong enough to achieve its liberalisation objective in more than rare cases" (p. 238). Lin has made a persuasive case, this time based on a comparative economic history of East Asia and Latin America, that a reduction in inflation should take precedence over all other targets, including liberalization, when inflation rates are high and prone to rise. In a detailed comparison of the stabilization experiences of Latin American and East Asian countries, Lin argues that the success of the Asian cases was built on a reduction of inflation that preceded the liberalization attempts by 5 years or more:

In both Chile and Argentina, the control of hyperinflation and the liberalization of the economy occurred at the same time [in the mid-1970s]. This greatly compounded the difficulties of the domestic industries by forcing them to cope with both the depressive effects of the stabilization policies and the increased competition of foreign producers at the same time. This contrasts sharply with the situation in Taiwan and South Korea, where the control of hyperinflation preceded intensive trade policy reforms by several years (chap. 4, p. 8).

Lin also points out at some length that inflation control was supported by a worsening rather than an improvement of the trade balance, since foreign funds were used to support the governments of Taiwan and Korea after the resort to money creation was brought under control:

> In all of the cases mentioned, the eventual contraction of the inflationary process required the restoration of political stability and productive capacity, with the injection of massive foreign aid and the restriction of deficit financing by the central bank playing important roles (ibid.).

14.6   Conclusions: Toward an Improved Use of Conditionality

We have noted that the efficacy of conditionality is inherently limited, and that the current overhang of debt greatly complicates the situation. In cases of extreme indebtedness, the debt itself might set up incentives that are adverse to significant adjustment or liberalization. In such a case, partial debt forgiveness can actually raise the expected repayments to the creditors, while at the same time giving greater incentive to the country for favorable adjustment. To be most successful, debt relief should almost surely be combined with IMF–World Bank conditionality, to enhance the likelihood that the debt relief actually turns into economic reform.

The historical experiences with liberalization alone, and with stabilization alone, are not very encouraging. The difficulties of combining the two policy initiatives are formidable. The historical record suggests that it is virtually impossible to bring inflation under control, while simultaneously trying to liberalize the economy. One is hard pressed to fund an example of an economy which stabilized, liberalized, and improved the external position all at the same time. Only South Korea, Brazil, and Indonesia seem to provide examples of implementing the first two measures, and in those cases the programs were supported by a strong military government that substantially reduced real wages (at least in Brazil and South Korea) at the outset of the programs, and by favorable world conditions, including growing world trade, and after a few years, access to foreign borrowing in significant amounts.

These findings suggest the following list of guidelines for improving the use of conditionality in future lending by the IMF and the World Bank. Most important, the IMF and World Bank should recognize the limited efficacy of conditionality, and act accordingly:

1. Approve fewer programs.
2. Require more prior actions in cases where the efficacy of the conditionality is doubtful.
3. Encourage governments to enlist the necessary range of political support behind the terms of a high-conditionality program before the program is made final.
4. Approve programs which allow a buildup of arrears to private creditors in cases where the private creditors (a) fail to grant debt relief and (b) fail to provide sufficient amounts of new financing.
5. Encourage the use of debt relief schemes as a way to enhance the likely adherence to conditionality terms.
6. Narrow the goals of conditionality: Make macroeconomic stabilization the preeminent aim, with structural reform to be implemented only as macroeconomic stability is restored.

References

Beveridge, W. A., and M. R. Kelley. 1980. Fiscal content of financial programs supported by stand-by arrangements in the upper-credit tranches, 1969–78. *IMF Staff Papers* 27(2): 205–49.
Bhagwati, J. 1978. *Anatomy and consequences of exchange control regimes.* Cambridge, Mass.: Ballinger Publishing Company.
Cline, W. 1984. *International debt.* Washington, D.C.: Institute for International Economics.
Hagard, S. 1985. The politics of adjustment. *International Organization* 39(3): 505–34.
Killick, T., with G. Bird, J. Sharpley, and M. Sutton. 1984. *The quest for economic stabilization.* London: Overseas Development Institute.
Krueger, A. 1978. *Foreign trade regimes and economic development: Liberalization attempts and consequences.* Cambridge, Mass.: Ballinger Publishing Company.
Lin, C. 1985. Latin America and East Asia: A comparative development perspective. Unpublished manuscript, International Monetary Fund.
Remmer, K. 1986. The politics of economic stabilization: IMF standby program in Latin America, 1954–1984. *Comparative Politics* (October): 1–24.
Sachs, J. 1984. Theoretical issues in international borrowing. *Princeton Studies in International Finance* no. 54 (July). Princeton, N.J.: Princeton University.
Von Furstenberg, G. M. 1985a. Adjustment with IMF lending. *Journal of International Money and Finance* (June): 209–22.
———1985b. The IMF as marketmaker for official business between nations. Indiana University, processed

15 Private Capital Flows to Problem Debtors

Paul Krugman

15.1 Introduction

One of the key elements of the approach to the debt problem that has dominated official thinking since 1982 has been an effort to mobilize private flows of capital to countries with debt-servicing problems. Bank lending in particular was expected to provide most of the capital flow under the debt strategy as it first emerged in 1983, and was supposed to play a major role under the Baker initiative of 1985. Yet in fact private capital flows to problem debtors have consistently fallen far short of expectations. To a first approximation the debtors have made resource transfers equal to interest less official inflows. Since official inflows themselves have been fairly small, the end result has been that debtors have been forced to run massive trade surpluses.

The purpose of this chapter is to reexamine the prospects for private capital flows to problem debtors. The central question is whether it is possible to induce sufficient capital inflows to aid substantially in the servicing of debt.

The chapter is in three parts. Section 15.2 reviews the rationale for new private capital flows to countries that are having difficulty servicing their current debt. Section 15.3 asks why this seemingly solid rationale has not so far been matched by an equally solid flow of financing in practice. Section 15.4 then considers whether private capital can be attracted through innovative mechanisms, such as debt-equity conversions, instead of through the concerted bank lending that has been the basis of private capital flows so far.

Paul Krugman is a professor of economics at the Massachusetts Institute of Technology and a research associate of the National Bureau of Economic Research.

15.2   The Rationale for Private Capital Inflows

To a man from Mars, or *The Wall Street Journal,* the proposition that new lending is essential to deal with the debt crisis seems extremely strange—a proposal to throw good money after bad. Yet private capital inflow has been a centerpiece of the official strategy for dealing with the debt crisis. Its rationale rests on two points: the possibility that a country may have growing debt yet be growing more creditworthy over time, and the possibility that lending at a loss may be in the interest of the creditors if it defends the value of existing claims.

15.2.1   The Analytics of Debt Growth and Creditworthiness

Consider the following numerical example. A country has a GNP of $200 billion, and an external debt of $100 billion (slightly above the average debt to GNP ratio for the IMF's category of "fifteen heavily indebted countries"). It must pay an interest rate of 9 percent on the debt. The world inflation rate is 4 percent, and the country's real GNP is expected to grow at an annual rate of 3 percent.

If the country were obliged to pay all interest out of current income, then even if all principal were rescheduled it would be obliged to run a surplus on noninterest current account of $9 billion, or 4.5 percent of GNP. While such a surplus is not impossible to run, it is sufficiently large to impose substantial strains on the economic and political situation in debtor countries.

Suppose, however, that the country is able to attract $4 billion of new money. Then it will need to run a noninterest surplus of only $5 billion, or 2.5 percent of GNP—a more tolerable number. It might at first seem that this simply puts the country even deeper into debt—which in a literal sense it does, since the debt grows by 4 percent. The country's real GNP, however, we have assumed will grow at 3 percent, which together with the price increase of 4 percent will imply 7 percent growth in money GNP. Thus the ratio of debt to GNP will fall, and the country will be in a more favorable position, not a less favorable one, at the start of the next year.

In fact, if the country were merely seeking to stabilize its ratio of debt to GNP, it could borrow $7 billion, and make net payments of only $2 billion, or 1 percent of GNP. If it were able to borrow this much, and willing to devote 1 percent of GNP to net interest payments indefinitely, it could honor all its debt commitments. If the real interest rate were lower, or the growth rate higher, the necessary resource transfer (noninterest current account) would be even smaller. Calculations of this kind underlay the optimism of many economists about the debt of LDCs in the 1970s, and continue to be the basis of optimistic assessments now.

Despite this favorable long-term arithmetic, claims on many heavily indebted countries continue to be viewed as highly risky, and sell at well below par on the secondary market. The reason for this is presumably that the favorable arithmetic depends on countries' willingness to continue moderate resource transfer for very extended periods. With debt equal to half of GNP, growth at 3 percent, and real interest rate of 5 percent, resource transfer at the rate of 2.5 percent of GNP would have to continue for 25 years to work off all the debt. If "debtor fatigue" were to set in before that, preventing further resource transfer, the debt would be worth less than par, even if the country were willing to run surpluses for quite a while. For example, even ten years of resource transfer would provide a present value of resource transfer equal to only 45 percent of the value of the debt.

Doubt over whether debtors will be willing to run the trade surpluses needed to honor their debts for the very extended periods thus envisaged underlies the unwillingness of banks or other lenders to provide new money to the problem debtors. However, there remains a case for new lending by existing creditors to defend the value of their claims. This case for "involuntary," or perhaps more accurately, defensive lending, underlies the concept and rhetoric of the US-IMF debt strategy.

15.2.2   The Case for Defensive Lending

When does it make sense to lend more money to a country already having trouble servicing its debt? The issue is often framed as one of liquidity versus solvency: The country is *illiquid,* that is, short of cash to pay its debt service, but it is *solvent,* that is, given time it will be able and (more important) willing to make resource transfers to its creditors equal in present value to its debt. However, it is quickly apparent upon reflection that this cannot be quite right; if a country were known to be merely illiquid, not insolvent, it would be able to attract voluntary lending to deal with its liquidity problem. It is only the possibility of a solvency problem that creates the liquidity problem.

The right way to think about the situation is as one of uncertainty in which defensive lending by existing creditors buys an option to collect on their claims in the future if the situation improves. Suppose that it is fairly likely that a country will fail to pay its debt in full even if it is able to avoid an immediate crisis; but that it is virtually certain that the country will repudiate an important part of its obligations if its creditors attempt to collect full interest immediately. Then new lending that reduces the interest burden, although a losing proposition in isolation, may be worthwhile because it improves the expected value of the initial debt.

Even under very adverse circumstances this defensive lending argument can justify quite substantial increases in creditor exposure. To see why, consider the basic algebra of the situation. Let D be a country's outstanding debt, and d be the subjective discount that creditors place on that debt (which may be inferred from the secondary market price if that market is sufficiently well developed). Suppose that by relending part of the interest, and thus averting an immediate liquidity crisis, creditors can reduce the discount to some smaller amount, d'. Such a program will have a cost—the expected loss on the new lending—and a benefit—the increase in the value of existing claims. The cost will be $d'L$, where L is the value of new lending; while the benefit will be $(d - d')D$. Thus a program of defensive lending will be worth undertaking as long as

$$d'L < (d - d')D,$$

or

$$L/D < (d - d')/d'.$$

Now suppose that in the absence of a program of defensive lending the discount on claims would be 50 percent, while even with such a program the discount would be reduced only to 40 percent. Even with these fairly dismal numbers, it would be worthwhile for creditors to expand their exposure by 25 percent to protect their original investment.

The orthodox view of the debt problem was that this incentive for defensive lending could be used to mobilize new bank lending on a sufficient scale that, combined with adjustment efforts by the countries and an improving external environment, problem debtors could be returned to normal capital market access after a few years. It was recognized from the beginning, however, that there were serious obstacles to mobilization of capital flows from existing creditors; these obstacles now look more serious than was realized in 1983.

15.3 Bank Lending to Problem Debtors Since 1982

15.3.1 The Magnitude of Bank Lending

Table 15.1 presents a first overview of the lending of banks from the opening of the debt strategy at the end of 1982 to the end of 1986. The essential impression conveyed by the table is that the mobilization of private capital flows to debtors that was a central element of the debt strategy took place to a very limited extent in 1983 and 1984 and basically not at all since. Whether one looks at the broader aggregate of problem debtors or the narrower aggregate of Latin America, one sees that since 1982, and especially since 1984, debtor countries have run noninterest surpluses large enough to cover the bulk of their interest due, with a small contribution from official sources and very little from

Table 15.1   **Indicators of Bank Lending to Problem Debtors**

	1982	1983	1984	1985	1986
15 debtors					
Private debt	336.9	337.3	347.0	341.8	342.0
(growth rate)	—	0.1	2.8	-1.5	0.1
Current account	-50.6	-15.2	-0.6	-0.1	-11.8
Resource transfer	-12.8	21.0	38.3	37.4	21.1
Debt/GDP	41.7	47.0	46.8	46.3	48.4
Debt/exports	269.8	289.7	272.1	284.2	337.9
Latin America					
Private debt	291.9	292.1	303.2	303.8	308.0
(growth rate)	—	0.0	3.8	0.2	1.4
Bank debt (growth)	6.1	3.1	-0.1	2.7	0.9
Current account	-42.4	-10.9	-2.6	-4.7	-16.1
Resource transfer	-8.1	21.7	32.1	28.3	12.4
Debt/GDP	42.9	47.3	47.6	46.8	48.5
Debt/ exports	273.8	290.3	277.1	295.5	354.7

Source: International Monetary Fund (1987) and UNCTAD (1987).

private new money. Only in 1986 was there a move toward current account deficit, which must have had capital inflows as its counterpart; more on this turn of events later.

Admittedly, this aggregative picture is somewhat misleading, for two reasons. First, it conceals differences among countries. While banks were on net withdrawing from some troubled but still relatively liquid debtors (e.g., Venezuela), they were significantly expanding their exposure in others. Second, the flow of funds reveals disbursements, but it is at least equally important to look at commitments, especially given the role of "concerted" lending for defensive purposes. Tables 15.2 and 15.3 provide some information on these issues. They show that while the details are more complex than aggregates convey, the essential point remains that there has not been much bank lending to problem debtors, especially after 1983–84. The central question is why the seemingly forceful case for defensive lending generated only a brief, modest injection of new money.

15.3.2   Debtor Performance and the Supply of Funds

The bankers themselves prefer to ascribe their limited willingness to lend to the failure of the countries to show adequate progress in economic policy. However, there are good reasons to discount this view. For one thing, the criticism seems unreasonable. Debtor countries have achieved trade surpluses greater than anyone believed possible in 1983. Admittedly this is the inevitable counterpart of the absence of new money, but it still means that in the most direct issue of performance,

Table 15.2   Bank Lending to Selected Countries (billions of dollars)

	1983	1984	1985	1985 1st half	1986 1st half
15 Heavily Indebted Countries	11.1	5.4	−1.9	−1.2	−3.4
Argentina	2.3	0.3	0.6	0.7	0.1
Brazil	5.2	5.2	−2.9	−1.0	−1.0
Korea	2.2	3.5	2.3	1.4	−0.2
Mexico	2.8	1.2	0.7	0.1	−0.8
Venezuela	−1.3	−2.2	0.4	−0.1	−0.3

Source: M. Watson, R. Kincaid, C. Atkinson, E. Kalter, and D. Folkerts-Landau, *International Capital Markets: Developments and Prospects*, International Monetary Fund, December 1986.

Table 15.3   LDC Lending Commitments (billions of dollars)

	1981	1982	1983	1984	1985	1984:1	1984:2	1985[a]	1986[a]
All capital importers	47.0	42.6	32.6	29.9	16.1	17.6	12.3	13.2	18.7
Latin America									
Total	25.2	23.0	15.3	15.4	2.5	11.4	4.0	2.4	7.9
Spontaneous	25.2	23.0	2.0	0.6	0.1	0.3	0.1	0.1	0.2
Concerted			13.3	14.8	2.4	11.1	3.7	2.3	7.7

Source: See table 15.2.
[a]First 3 quarters

the ability and willingness to generate foreign exchange with which to service debt, the countries have delivered more, not less, than was expected of them.

More fundamentally, the asserted link between debtor performance and the availability of new money confuses defensive lending with free-market transactions. For a country that is borrowing from voluntary lenders on the open market, the ability to borrow does indeed depend on confidence in the country's management and prospects. Once problem debtor status has been achieved, however, the new money provided through concerted action is not governed by the same motives. Provided that they are able to act cooperatively, creditors will lend as much as they have to in order to protect their investment, not as much as the country has earned or as much as it can be expected to service. If anything, good economic policies, by reducing the need for new capital, may weaken a country's bargaining position and lead to a *reduction* of the supply of new money and a worsening of its terms.

A perverse relationship between performance and the supply of new money is evident in the case of Mexico. When Mexico was apparently able to run massive trade surpluses while resuming modest growth, it received no new money. When oil prices collapsed, the first new-money package in more than two years was negotiated.

15.3.3   The Free-Rider Problem

One prospect that raised fears in the early stages of the debt problem was that defensive lending by creditors would be paralyzed by the problem of getting collective action. There is an inherent free-rider problem in defensive lending: The *collective* lending of existing creditors raises the expected value of their *collective* claims, but for any *individual* creditor it would be preferable to opt out. In effect, the call for defensive lending from creditors asks that lenders, whom we suppose act competitively under normal circumstances, suddenly begin to act collusively once the country is in debt trouble.

Data on U.S. banks does show evidence of a free-rider problem. The small regional banks have consistently either reduced their LDC exposure more or expanded it less than either the money center banks or the middle-sized banks. However, the concentration of debt in the hands of larger banks is sufficient that this has been only a minor drag on net bank lending. Put differently, even if all banks had increased their exposure as rapidly as the money center banks, there would still have been a very modest flow of bank lending to problem debtors. And as long as defensive lending remains worthwhile, free riding should have led to *faster,* not slower growth in the exposure of the core banks.

15.3.4   Bargaining Power

The simplest explanation for low bank lending is that the banks did not lend because they did not have to: They found themselves in a strong enough bargaining position to extract full interest from the countries without a quid pro quo of new money. Defensive lending failed to take place because it was unnecessary. The corollary to this view is that the failure of the banks to come up with new money in 1984–86 does not show that they can never be induced to do so; the banks did not fail to act in their own interest.

The principal evidence for the view that banks were simply striking a hard bargain with the debtors is negative. There is no indication that banks were disappointed in the performance of debtors in 1984–85, leading to unwillingness to lend (and in any case we have already argued that there is if anything a perverse connection between performance and defensive lending). There were no cases of new-money packages scuttled by attempts of small banks to free ride. Most important, until 1986 there was no indication that the failure to provide new money was pushing countries to the edge of refusal to pay interest.

In a sense the question should be put the other way. It is not very puzzling that banks lent so little, since they seem to have judged correctly that they could do so without adverse consequences. The question is why the countries were so willing to acquiesce.

One point that may help explain the acquiescence of the countries is the cynical but unfortunately apparently valid political observation that only the recent rate of change of the economic situation, not the level, matters for political purposes. By this criterion the debtors were, in 1984 and 1985, doing acceptably well; although their incomes had taken a severe beating in 1981–83, in 1984–85 Mexico achieved modest growth and Brazil rapid growth, despite the need to run very large trade surpluses. Again, the impression one gets is that the countries felt they were doing well enough to be unwilling to press their case with the bankers and set in motion unknown risks.

Another important element in debtors' willingness to accept an unfavorable bargain has probably been the political pressure from creditor country governments, especially the United States, carrying the implicit message that sanctions of a nonfinancial kind will be imposed on debtors that fail to service their debt.

15.3.5 Implications

The failure of the commercial banks to provide new money on the scale envisaged in 1983 has been seen by many observers, including myself, as a sign of the unworkability of the strategy of relying on concerted lending by existing creditors. This interpretation would be correct if the lack of new money essentially reflected an inability of the creditors to undertake collective action. The discussion here suggests, however, that this was not the case; that creditors *were* acting in a collectively rational fashion, and that they lent so little because that was the strategy that made sense in their own interest. If this alternative explanation is correct, then a change in the situation can lead to a very different response from the banks. If the countries become tougher bargainers, or the banks less tough, then bank lending can still be provided, as the Mexican package illustrates.

15.4 Debt Conversion Schemes as an Alternative to Bank Lending

A number of analysts have suggested that the answer to the debt problem lies to a significant degree in encouraging other forms of capital inflow to substitute for bank financing. In particular, financial industry experts have pressed strongly for the conversion of foreign debt into equity claims. Thus our discussion of bank lending must be supplemented by a discussion of this alternative.

Advocates of these swaps at first seemed to be claiming that such conversions would simultaneously reduce countries' external obligations and generate an inflow of direct foreign investment. Some cooling of enthusiasm has occurred as careful analysis has shown that a debt-equity conversion in fact does neither. The advantages of debt-equity swaps are in fact fairly subtle, and there are potentially serious disadvantages.

Debt-equity swaps are actually part of a broader array of schemes in which investors who have acquired some of a country's external debt at a discount on the secondary market are permitted to redeem that debt for some kind of domestic asset. In the largest program of debt conversion to date, that in Chile, more than half of the debt conversion has actually taken the form of sales of debt to the debtors, without any requirement that the proceeds be invested in equity.

Investments made by means of debt conversion schemes in no case contribute to net capital inflow; the whole point is that they allow investors to acquire claims on a country through a transaction with the country's creditors rather than its residents. The potential benefits lie instead in the future effect on a country's stream of net investment income. First, debt, which carries with it an obligation to make a flat stream of nominal payments over time, may be replaced with other liabilities whose payment stream rises over time with growth and inflation. This services the same aim of shifting the time profile of payments that defensive lending was supposed to accomplish. Second, in some circumstances debt conversion may serve as a backdoor route to debt forgiveness; investors may be induced to acquire assets with an expected present value less than the face value of the converted debt.

Against these potential benefits must be set two possible costs. First is that a debt conversion scheme may divert capital inflow that would otherwise have taken place through other channels; since at best debt conversion makes no contribution to net capital inflow, *any* such diversion represents a net capital outflow. Second is the possibility that debt conversion schemes will have an adverse fiscal impact.

Although many debt conversion schemes are possible, the essential advantages and disadvantages may be understood by making two key distinctions. On one side is the distinction between debt-equity swaps, in which debt must be converted into equity and held in that form, and "debt-peso" swaps, in which debt is converted into cash without a restriction on how that cash is to be invested. On the other side is the distinction between conversions involving private debt, which have no fiscal impact, and those involving public or publicly-guaranteed debt.

15.4.1 Conversions of Private Debt to Equity

The most favorable kind of debt conversion is one in which the debt of private firms is exchanged for equity (not necessarily of the same firms). Since dividends can be expected to rise over time with inflation and economic growth, this serves the desirable aim of tilting the time profile of a country's payments to foreign creditors in the direction of the time profile of its ability to pay. A secondary advantage is that to the extent that earnings on equity are related to the economic state of the country this conversion shifts the country to a more equitable sharing of risk.

Even this most favorable form of debt conversion, however, can aggravate a country's foreign exchange constraint in the short run. To the extent that a purchase of equity through debt conversion substitutes for a purchase that would have taken place in any case—that is, to the extent that there is anything less than 100% additionality—the conversion reduces net capital inflows. Since some substitution of debt-equity swaps for capital inflows is surely unavoidable, even this best case of debt conversion represents a trade-off of a worsened capital account now for a more favorable investment income profile in the future.

15.4.2 Conversions of Private Debt to Cash

A sale of external debt back to the creditor, without a requirement that the proceeds be invested in equity, differs from a debt-equity swap both in being less likely to have favorable effects on the profile of future investment payments, and in running greater risks of worsening the capital account in the short run.

The best case of a "debt-peso" swap would be one in which domestic residents are induced to repatriate external assets that they would otherwise have retained outside the country. The initial capital account impact of this transaction would be zero. Future payments of interest and principal would be reduced. However, because the owners of the repatriated capital would presumably invest the funds domestically, they would in future substitute the income from these investments for additional repatriations. Thus the overall effect on the stream of resource transfers that the country must make to the rest of the world is uncertain; it depends on the planned domestic consumption of the investors.

The concern with debt conversions not tied to equity investment is that they offer greater opportunity than debt-equity swaps for actions that worsen the capital account. Most extreme would be the case where debt is converted into domestic currency, and this currency is then converted (legally or illegally) into foreign exchange and exported again.

Such "round-tripping" would turn debt conversions into a device for facilitating capital flight. Less dramatically but equally harmful in its effect on the capital account is the use of debt conversions as a substitute channel for repatriation of earnings on overseas assets; the effect of this substitution is to reduce net capital inflows one-for-one.

The main justification that one might offer for unrestricted conversions of debt is that they may serve as an indirect way for a country to buy back its own debt at a discount; more on this below.

15.4.3 Conversion of Public Debt

Conversion of public debt, whether into equity or unrestricted, has the same effects as conversion of private debt, with an additional fiscal impact.

The conversion of external public debt into local currency, if not sterilized, will be inflationary. Thus it must be offset by an issue of domestic debt, which turns it from the point of view of the government into a swap of foreign for local currency debt. From a fiscal point of view, this is a definite *disadvantage*. The reason is that in problem debtors real interest rates on internal debt are far higher than on external debt. This in turn reflects the fact that the credibility of government promises to repay, both internal and external, is uncertain. In the case of external debt, however, rescheduling agreements have frozen creditors into holding claims at an interest rate well below what they would require to hold those claims voluntarily. A debt conversion unfreezes these claims and converts them into new, short-term claims on which the government must pay a high enough interest rate to compensate for risk of nonpayment. Thus a debt conversion involving public debt, even if it is structured so as not to worsen the capital account, trades off the benefit of an improved composition of external liabilities for the cost of worsened fiscal situation.

15.4.4 Summary

This review of the effects of debt conversions does not convey a favorable impression. However, there is one other potential advantage of debt conversions that may be an important motivation: they offer an end run around some of the legal and institutional obstacles to debt forgiveness. Given the substantial discounts on secondary market sales of problem debtors' obligations, some governments may regard it as a worthwhile investment to buy back their own national debt. However, direct buyback at a discount raises legal problems. By inducing third parties to buy the debt, and then collecting some fee for the process, governments can achieve approximately the same result. Thus Chile has auctioned off rights to "debt-peso" conversions (though not debt-equity swaps), which in effect allows the government to buy back the debt at a discount equal to the auction premium. Other countries may achieve the same aim by specifying a different exchange rate for debt conversions than for other transactions.

At least so far, however, the debt forgiveness aspect has been limited. In the Chilean case the auction prices on debt-peso conversions have been much smaller than the secondary market discounts, presumably reflecting the fact that within Chile, with capital exports controlled, the shadow price of foreign exchange is higher than its official price. And debt-equity swaps are not auctioned off.

In summary, the idea of using debt-equity conversion as an alternative to defensive lending has been heavily oversold. Such conversions not only cannot eliminate the need for debt-creating capital inflows, they may easily increase rather than decrease the necessity for new borrowing.

15.5 Outlook for Capital Flows

Direct foreign investment cannot be counted on to provide the financing that banks have failed to provide, and schemes like debt-equity swaps are much more problematic than their sponsors seem to have appreciated. The desirability of debt relief is still controversial, and in any case it poses operational difficulties that none of the actors in the debt situation seem at this point ready to take the lead in resolving. Thus the central question regarding financing for problem debtors is whether involuntary lending by banks can be restarted. This depends crucially on the interpretation of the problems with mobilizing lending so far. If the stalling of lending during 1984–86 really reflected an inability of the banks to act in their own interests, prospects are bleak. If it represented collectively rational behavior on the part of the banks, then the limits on bank lending tell us only that the banks chose not to, not that they will not.

The argument made here is that the evidence is most consistent with the view that low bank lending was the outcome of a bargaining process in which, for a variety of reasons, creditors had very high bargaining power compared with debtors. A shift in that bargaining process will produce a different result. Specifically, the bargain will shift if debtor countries come to realize that a return to normal market access is not imminent, that the internal political costs of continuing full debt service are high, that the external cost from a failure to reach agreement with the banks is low, and, perhaps, that the U.S. government will not take political revenge on deadbeats. Given a situation of this kind, creditors will prefer to negotiate some combination of de facto capitalization of interest and reduced rates rather than fail to reach any agreement.

What about the possibility of debt moratoria and sanctions against the debtors? If all parties were fully informed about each others' motives and opportunities, we would expect everyone immediately to reach a bargain that reflected the ability of the players to mete out and receive punishment, without any necessity for the actions actually to take place. However, given the uncertainty involved, it will probably be necessary for players to demonstrate their resolve by announcing debt moratoria, seizing assets, and so on. Ideally third parties would be able to mediate and avoid such open confrontations, which have real costs, although less than is often supposed. However, the important point if confrontations cannot be avoided—which will sometimes be the case—is to realize that periods in which debtors and creditors fail to reach agreement are a part of the game, not the end of it.

Thus the outlook, if this analysis is correct, is in fact for a revival of bank financing to the debtors. This financing may for a while take the form of arrearages, until the debtors and creditors reach agreement. Eventually it will be formalized in a new agreement. There will be new bank lending because the countries will need it; the moral of this chapter has been that the supply of capital to problem debtors is, in the end, driven by the demand.

References

Bulow, J., and K. Rogoff. A constant recontracting model of sovereign debt. Unpublished ms., Stanford University.

Cline, W. 1983. *International debt and the stability of the world economy.* Washington, D.C.: Institute for International Economics.

Dooley, M., 1986. An analysis of the debt crisis. IMF Working Paper, WP/86/14. Washington, D.C.: International Monetary Fund.

Dornbusch, Rudiger. 1987. Our LDC debts. NBER Working Paper no. 2138. Cambridge, Mass.: National Bureau of Economic Research.

Eaton, J. and M. Gersovitz. 1981. Debt with potential repudiation. *Review of Economic Studies* 48: 289–309.

Feldstein, M. 1986. International debt service and economic growth: Some simple analytics. NBER Working Paper no. 2076. Cambridge, Mass.: National Bureau of Economic Research.

Feldstein, M., H. de Carmoy, P. Krugman, and K. Narusawa. 1987. Restoring growth in the debt-laden Third World. Prepared for the Trilateral Commission, New York.

International Monetary Fund. 1987. *World Economic Outlook* (April).

Kaletsky, A. 1985. *The costs of default.* New York: Priority Press.

Krugman, P. 1985. International debt strategies in an uncertain world. In *International debt and the developing countries,* ed. G. Smith and J. Cuddington. Washington, D.C.: World Bank.

Larrain, F. 1986. Market-based debt reduction schemes in Chile: A macroeconomic perspective. Catholic University, Santiago, Chile. Mimeo.
Morgan Guaranty Trust. 1986. *World Financial Markets* (September).
Rubinstein, A. 1982. Perfect equilibrium in a bargaining model. *Econometrica*
50:97–109.
Sachs, J. 1984. *Theoretical issues in international borrowing.* Princeton Studies
in International Finance No. 54. Princeton, N.J.: Princeton University Press.
———. 1986. The debt overhang problem of developing countries. Paper presented at the conference in memorial to Carlos Díaz-Alejandro August 1986
at Helsinki, Finland.
UNCTAD. 1987. *Trade and Development Report.* United Nations Conference
on Trade and Development.
Watson, M., D. Mathieson, R. Kincaid, and E. Kalter. 1986. *International
Capital Markets: Developments and Prospects,* IMF Occasional Paper #43.
Washington, D.C.: International Monetary Fund.
Watson, M., R. Kincaid, C. Atkinson, E. Kalter, and D. Folkerts-Landau.
1986. *International Capital Markets: Developments and Prospects,* IMF Eco-
nomic and Financial Surveys (December) Washington, D.C.: International
Monetary Fund.
World Bank. 1986. *World Development Report.*

16 Debt Problems and the World Macroeconomy

Rudiger Dornbusch

16.1 Introduction

In this chapter I discuss the role world macroeconomic factors—interest rates, commodity prices, and industrial countries' growth—have played in bringing the debt crisis about and how they either facilitated or made more difficult the first five years of adjustment. I also ask whether and how the world macroeconomy is likely to contribute to the solution of the debt problem in the years ahead.

16.2 External Debt and Debt Crisis

I first set out a conceptual framework to discuss debt problems and the macroeconomic background to the debt crisis in 1979–82.

16.2.1 A Conceptual Framework

Debt service difficulties may either take the form of an inability to pay the principal of a maturing debt, as is the case for Colombia or Venezuela today, or an inability to pay both interest and principal. I focus here on debt difficulties of the more serious kind, where interest cannot be paid. The reason is that difficulties in paying principal, when interest is regularly paid, should not present any problem since rolling over is a routine operation. The only reason difficulties with principal can become debt problems is if creditors wish to limit their regional exposure and hence insist on payment of principal even from those countries who are good debtors.

Rudiger Dornbusch is Ford International Professor of Economics at the Massachusetts Institute of Technology and a research associate of the National Bureau of Economic Research

Focusing on interest payments, the current account of the balance of payments can be separated into two components: the noninterest current account (NICA) which includes trade in goods and in all services except interest payments on the external debt on the one hand, and interest payments on the other. Interest payments in turn can be financed by noninterest surpluses or by net capital inflows:

(1)   Interest Payments = NICA + Net Capital Inflows

"Net Capital Inflows" includes four categories: reserve decumulation, direct foreign investment inflows, long-term portfolio inflows, and short- or medium-term borrowing abroad which is often called "new money." In the debt problems of the interwar period or the period preceding 1914, new money took the form of a "funding loan." Today it is concerted or involuntary lending by the commercial bank creditors and multilateral institutions.

Table 16.1 shows these current account components for problem debtor countries in the 1978–87 period.[1] In the period up to 1982 both interest payments and the noninterest deficit need financing and hence are reflected in a rapidly rising debt. Since 1983 a large part of interest is paid by noninterest surpluses and hence the increase in debt is limited. But even so, debt is still rising, reflecting the financing of the remaining interest payments not met by the surplus, and the financing of capital flight and reserve build-up.

A noninterest deficit is often called the net *inward* resource transfer since it measures the net imports of goods and services (other than interest) over which a country acquires command. Noninterest deficits

Table 16.1   The Current Account Deficit and External Debt: Countries with Recent Debt-Servicing Difficulties ($ billion)

	Noninterest Current Account Deficit (Resource Transfer)	Interest Payments	Current Account Deficit	External Debt
1978	17.1	14.8	31.9	242
1979	10.1	21.8	31.9	292
1980	5.0	34.3	39.6	356
1981	20.2	47.5	67.7	430
1982	5.4	57.5	63.1	494
1983	− 30.2	52.1	21.9	514
1984	− 48.6	57.2	8.6	534
1985	− 50.2	53.6	3.1	553
1986	− 32.7	50.2	17.5	573
1987	− 27.8	45.7	17.9	586

Source: IMF *World Economic Outlook.*

are the normal pattern for developing countries in which saving is low relative to investment. They are the channel through which resources are transferred from rich to poor countries to support capital formation and growth in the developing world. Private and public lending form the financial counterpart. Using the national accounts identities we can represent in (2) the financing of investment from the resource point of view.

(2)   Investment = Saving + Real Resource Transfer from Abroad

The abrupt reduction in financing of noninterest deficits, or the reduction in net inward real resource transfers has meant a sharp decline in investment for Latin America. Since 1982, by comparison with the period 1973–82, investment has declined by 5 percent of GDP which is exactly equal to the swing in resource transfers. Now debtors are transferring resources to creditors.

16.2.2   Debt Crises

Any debt crisis involves the inability of debtors to make timely payments of interest and principal. Five factors can be identified as leading to a gap between interest payments that are due and the noninterest current account:

1. With an unchanged willingness to roll over debt and provide a given flow of money, an increase in real interest rates raises the financing requirement. The imbalance between new money requirements and credit voluntarily supplied brings about a debt crisis.
2. A deterioration in the noninterest current account—because of domestic macroeconomics, a worsening in the terms of trade, or a fall in export demand—opens a financing gap.
3. An increase in world inflation leads to an increase in nominal interest rates and hence to an early *real* amortization of the external debt. Although real interest rates are unchanged, a cash flow problem for debtors results from increased nominal interest rates.
4. With an unchanged interest rate and noninterest current account, creditors decide that exposure is excessive and therefore limit new money commitments and require that maturing principal be paid off.
5. Industrial activity in developed countries affects the demand for exports from developing countries. A slowdown or recession reduces quantity demanded and lowers prices, thus impairing debt service ability.

I now proceed to identify the impact of world macroeconomic events on debtor countries. Specifically, in what way has the world macroeconomy been one of the factors leading to the debt crisis, how has it influenced the evolution of debt problems since 1982, and what implications can be anticipated from alternative scenarios of the world economy in the coming years? World interest rates, growth, and commodity price trends are at the center of the discussion.

16.3 The World Macroeconomy: An Overview

Figures 16.1 and 16.2 highlight two important external variables for debtor countries: the real interest rate and the real price of commodities. In figure 16.1 I show the London interbank offer rate for dollar deposits (LIBOR) adjusted by the rate of inflation in world trade.[2] The central role of interest rates in precipitating the debt crisis is shown by the peak level of an interest rate in excess of 18 percent in late 1981.

The interest rate effects appear through two separate channels. One is associated with the level of nominal rates, given the real rate of interest. When higher inflation increases the nominal interest rate, the effect on debtors is a shortening of the effective maturity of the debt. The *real* value of the debt is amortized at a faster pace. As a result, debtors may experience liquidity problems. In 1980–82 debtor countries were hurt both by increased nominal interest rates and by declining commodity prices. The combination implies that the real interest rate facing debtor countries was much higher than 20 percent per year. Of course, real interest rates had already reached high levels on previous occasions, as for example, in the period 1975–76. But at that time debt ratios were much lower and, accordingly, the vulnerability to interest rate shocks was less.

Figure 16.2 represents the real price of commodities. The series shown here is the IMF index of all (nonoil) commodities deflated by

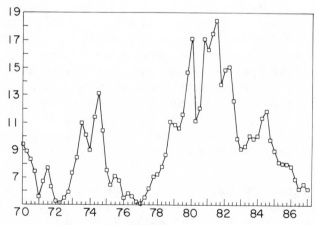

Fig. 16.1   The real interest rate

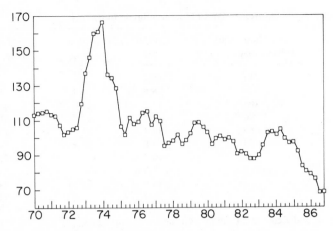

Fig. 16.2   The real price of commodities

the export unit value of industrial countries. Commodity prices have steadily declined since their peak levels in 1973–74. By late 1986 they had fallen to only 40 percent of the peak level. But in the early 1980s, when the debt crisis first broke out, the real price of commodities did not show a dramatic deterioration. Commodity prices thus were not an immediate source of the crisis, but they did become relevant later in raising the costs of adjustment for several debtor countries. In fact, to the extent that real commodity prices were high in the late 1970s, they contributed to the borrowing spree. Later, when they declined, they aggravated the debt crisis over and above what it otherwise would have been.

Table 16.2 shows data for these aggregate indices. The averages for the 1960s and 1970s are reported, as well as more detailed information on the period of the debt crisis. In addition to interest rates, real commodity prices, and economic activity in industrial countries, a further external factor influences the noninterest current account: commercial policy in developed countries and its influence on market access and hence, developing country export performance. There are no good aggregate indicators of market access or of changes in market access. But there is also no evidence that this factor was an important element in provoking the debt crisis. Of course, that does not mean that protectionism did not increase the costs and difficulties of debtor countries once the crisis had started.

16.4   The Period 1982–87

When the debt crisis emerged in 1982 there was a ready consensus that a package of adjustment and financing could see debtors and

304   Rudiger Dornbusch

Table 16.2   Aggregate World Macroeconomic Indicators

	Real Commodity Prices (1980 = 100)[a]	LIBOR (%)	Inflation[b] (%)	World Activity[c] (1980 = 100)
1960–69	115	5.2	1.0	56
1970–79	115	8.0	11.4	86
1980	100	14.4	13.0	100
1981	96	16.5	−4.1	100
1982	89	13.1	−3.5	96
1983	98	9.6	−3.3	99
1984	101	10.8	−2.5	106
1985	88	8.3	−0.4	110
1986	72	6.9	13.7	110
1987	63	6.8	12.8	112

Source: IMF and Economic Commission for Latin America.
[a]Measured in terms of manufactures export prices of industrial countries.
[b]Rate of inflation of industrial countries' unit export values.
[c]Industrial production.

creditors through the worst difficulties until the world economy turned, as was expected, in a more favorable direction. What precisely were the expectations about the external environment facing debtor countries?

16.4.1   The Beliefs of 1982

When Mexico in 1982—and shortly afterwards a host of Latin American countries—encountered acute debt service problems, the process of concerted or involuntary lending started. The prevailing philosophy of that process had three ingredients:

1. To assure an ultimate return to voluntary lending it was essential that debtor countries should service their debts, to the maximum extent possible, on commercial terms and without significant concessions other than with respect to the maturity of the debt principal.
2. Adjustments in debtor countries, specifically in the budget and exchange rates, would go far in bringing about a swing in the noninterest balance so as to service debt.
3. An improving world economy—recovery, rising real commodity prices, and declining real interest rates—would make a substantial contribution in reducing the burden of debt servicing. From the vantage point of 1982, the macroeconomy could only improve. Debtor countries could anticipate higher growth in demand for their exports, lower interest rates, and improving terms of trade.

The question of adjustment in debtor countries is beyond the scope of this chapter and has been amply dealt with elsewhere.[3] The issue of interest here is the contribution of the world macroeconomy. Certainly in 1982 the outlook must have been favorable. Specifically, the scenarios in the IMF *World Economic Outlook* of that year reflected the following views:

- The world economy was in the deepest recession since the 1930s. In the recovery period there had to be, accordingly, an expectation of growth significantly above trend. This growth would bring about two results. First, it would mean an increase in demand for manufactures exports from debtor countries. Second, it would translate into a cyclical upturn of real commodity prices. These stylized facts were quite beyond doubt, given the ample empirical evidence on the cyclical behavior of real commodity prices and export volumes.[4]
- With respect to interest rates, the outlook also had to be outright favorable. The short-term interest rate was at record high levels in American history. These high levels of interest rates were an immediate result of a deliberate attempt to use monetary policy to stop the sharply accelerating U.S. inflation of the late 1970s and early 1980s. With the success of disinflation, interest rates would decline and hence the extraordinary debt service burdens of 1982 would come down.

The expectation of declining nominal interest rates and cyclically rising nominal and real export prices for debtor countries implied an expectation of low real interest rates. Recovery and sustained growth in the industrial countries were expected to translate into significant growth in export volumes. At the time there was apparently no recognition of the real interest rate consequences of rapid disinflation and of the U.S. monetary-fiscal mix. The early scenarios are also revealing in that there was a quite explicit confidence that current account imbalances could be financed.

16.4.2 The Actual Experience Since 1982

The actual outcome differed from the IMF scenario in the following respects:

- Real interest rates continued to be far higher than expected. The U.S. monetary-fiscal mix had strong implications for the performance of countries with high debt ratios and a high ratio of floating rate debt.
- The real oil price fell dramatically and hence the relative performance of net oil exporters was due to their adjustment efforts rather than to favorable terms of trade.
- The assumption that debtor countries could afford to run significant current account deficits was overly optimistic. Financing constraints in fact limited these deficits.

Nominal interest rates did, indeed, decline significantly from their peak levels, and OECD growth was somewhat above the 3 percent threshold that had been set as a benchmark for solving debt problems. The significant difference from the 1982 outlook involved commodity prices. Rather than showing a recovery in nominal and real terms, they in fact continued to decline. The decline was so significant that in 1986 they were at a lower level than at any time in the preceding quarter of a century (see figure 16.2 above). In nominal terms they had fallen back to the level of 1977.

The belief that debt and debt service ratios would decline has not in fact been borne out. On every measure of creditworthiness debtor countries today look worse than they did in 1982, except for the debt service ratio. The reduction in interest rates since 1982 clearly helped reduce the service ratio, as did the long-term restructuring of debts. But even though there is a marginal reduction in the debt service ratio, the extent of decline falls short of the 1982 expectations.

16.5   The Outlook

In this section I ask whether important changes in the world macroeconomic outlook lie ahead that might help overcome the debt problem or whether, on the contrary, world macroeconomic developments threaten to make the solution much more difficult. On the side of macroeconomics there is certainly a possibility of two quite different scenarios, depending on the way in which the U.S. budget problem is solved and the response of interest rates and the dollar to budget cuts when they occur.

The medium-term outlook is neither outright unfavorable nor exceptionally favorable. Table 16.3 lays out the IMF's 1988 views.[5] There is an expectation of continued, moderate growth in the world economy. No major changes in relative prices are anticipated, and real interest rates are not expected to decline. This outlook represents a baseline. Sharply different scenarios are possible depending on the fiscal adjustments that lie ahead in the U.S. economy.

16.5.1   U.S. Adjustment: Implications for Debtor Countries

It is interesting to go beyond the baseline forecast and explore what consequences U.S. adjustment of the twin deficits can have for debtor countries.

Two features of U.S. adjustment can be highlighted as in table 16.4. One is whether there is a hard or soft landing. The hard landing scenario envisages a collapse of the dollar caused by a loss of confidence. This collapse in turn translates into a sharp upturn of U.S. inflation, and induces the Federal Reserve to severely tighten monetary conditions.

Table 16.3   **The IMF 1988 Outlook (percent per year)**

	1988	1989	1990–92
Industrial countries			
Growth	2.8	2.6	2.8
Inflation	4.7	4.3	3.0
Real six-month LIBOR[a]	3.0	3.1	4.3
Prices in world trade			
Manufactures	8.0	3.4	3.5
Nonoil primary commodities	9.4	1.0	3.5
Oil	−7.8	5.1	3.5

Source: IMF *World Economic Outlook* (April).
[a]Deflated by U.S. GNP deflator.

Table 16.4   **Consequences for Debtors of U.S. Adjustment Scenarios**

	Soft Landing	Hard Landing
Trade restrictions	Moderate trouble	Debt default
No trade restrictions	Major improvement	Moratoria

The result is a recession and high real interest rates. The soft landing, by contrast, assumes that fiscal policy turns increasingly restrictive, and monetary policy accomodates with a decline in interest rates. The dollar falls and thus growth of output is sustained by an improvement in net exports. Growth thus is stable and inflation rises moderately. Real interest rates clearly decline.

The second dimension concerns trade policy. Here there are two possibilities: targeted restrictions on countries with large bilateral surpluses (Japan, Korea, Brazil, Mexico) or no significant change in trade policy.

Sustained U.S. growth with low real interest rates *and* unimpaired market access means debt problems will become significantly smaller. Of course, the counterpart of U.S. external balance improvement in this case is a worsening of the net exports of Europe and Japan. But lower real interest rates have a self-correcting property in that debtor countries can reduce their noninterest surplus and still improve their creditworthiness. This feature means that there is not necessarily a conflict between U.S. and debtor country objectives. When debtor countries argue for the need to reduce U.S. deficits, they presumably have this scenario in mind.

The other extreme scenario is a hard landing with trade restrictions. The consequences are obvious: Recession and high real interest rates move debt service problems far beyond what debtor countries can make up for by domestic adjustments. Trade restrictions further worsen their ability to service debts. The almost certain consequence would be runover 1930-style debt defaults or indefinite suspension of debt service.

World growth and real interest rates are central in judging the impact of alternative scenarios for debtor countries. On the side of growth, U.S. fiscal adjustment will tend to reduce growth in the world economy. If U.S. output growth is sustained, even as the growth of domestic spending is reduced as a result of fiscal correction, this will mean that real depreciation is necessary to raise net exports and that, accordingly, foreign growth will tend to be less. It is very unlikely that Europe and Japan will provide an expansion in demand sufficient to keep world output growth constant. Thus, on the growth side, the performance of the past few years is not likely to be sustained. But on the interest rate side, there may be a favorable development. If the U.S. reduces the budget deficit and keeps growth up through lower interest rates, the dollar will depreciate. This is likely to force Europe and Japan into interest rate reductions even if that would threaten monetary discipline.

The impact of interest rates on debtors' current account balances is, of course, very significant. For Latin America a 2.5 percentage point reduction in interest rates would amount to a foreign exchange saving of nearly 8 percent of total imports. Hence the importance to debtors of the easier monetary conditions that would accompany a reduction of the U.S. budget deficit.

Trade barriers might not be applied uniformly across U.S. trading partners. They might instead be applied only to industrial countries, specifically Japan, or only to *current account* surplus countries, rather than to countries with bilateral surpluses. For debtors the implication here is that an improvement in debt service ability of countries like Mexico or Brazil might be paid for by extra restrictions on Korea or Taiwan. Thus developing countries as a group might experience an improvement, while specific countries like Korea bear the burden.

There is another way of looking at U.S. adjustment and the implications for debtor countries. Suppose that the U.S. in fact achieved a $100 billion reduction in the external deficit. Assume also that this had as a counterpart a $20 billion improvement in the U.S. bilateral trade balance with Latin America. How can Latin America experience a $20 billion reduction in the resource transfers to developed countries? There are only two ways: through much lower interest rates or significant extra financing. Thus any hard landing scenario without default necessarily involves a dramatic change in financing availability which is not apparent today.

Is there a chance that debt problems will be solved in some other fashion by the world macroeconomy? Here one would look to a pattern of terms of trade, interest rates, and inflation of the 1970–73 variety. Since the U.S. is already at full employment, continuing depreciation and monetary accommodation, without fiscal contraction, would inevitably raise inflation while sustaining growth. This policy would ease debt problems significantly. The only question is whether the process of sliding gently into the soft landing option, with a few years delay, can in fact be achieved. The monetary authorities would have to be sufficiently accommodating and impervious to inflation, and asset holders would have to be patient, sitting out dollar depreciation without a stampede. This does not seem to be a high-probability scenario.

16.5.2 The Commodity Price Problem

The final point to raise concerns the long-term behavior of commodity prices. Table 16.5 shows a long-term time series for the real price of commodities. Although exact comparisons across periods are impaired by the fact that these data are spliced from different series, the basic point is very striking.[6] Commodity prices in the mid-1980s have reached the lowest level in real terms since the Great Depression.

Several factors explain this low level of commodity prices. One is the high level of real interest rates and, until 1985–86, the other was the high level of the dollar. But these factors are not sufficient to explain the large decline as discussed in Dornbusch (1985). Others to be considered are substitution toward resource-saving technologies on the demand side, real depreciation, and hence increased levels of output at given *world* real prices. Capacity expansions in many producing countries are further factors that reduce real prices. Finally, for agricultural commodities, government support policies in industrial countries have played an important role.

But this large decline in real commodity prices that has been a decisive factor in the debt performance of several countries—as, for example, Argentina, Bolivia or Peru—has bottomed out. Indeed, over the twelve months through May 1988, commodity prices in dollars increased by nearly 40 percent! And, just as in 1973–74 or in several

Table 16.5   **The Real Price of Commodities: 1950–87 (Index 1980 = 100, period averages)**

1950–54	124	1970–74	115	1985	85
1955–59	113	1975–79	104	1986	69
1960–64	106	1980–84	94	1987	64
1965–69	108				

Source: IMF (1987).

later episodes apparent in figure 16.2, further recovery of real commodity prices may turn out to be surprisingly large and rapid. The various structural factors at work suggest that the level of real commodity prices is unlikely to return to the high of the early 1970s. But a resumption of inflation and much lower real interest rates will drive up inventory demand and thus bring about a significant rise.

16.6 Conclusion

World macroeconomic policies and commodity shocks and variables were not, until 1981–82, the major reason for the present debt crisis. Only in 1981–82 did the sharp increase in interest rates and the decline in growth help to create a crisis in the aftermath of very poor policy performance in debtor countries.

Since 1982 the world macroeconomic environment has shown an improvement. Interest rates declined in nominal and real terms and growth has been sustained, as was expected in 1982. The only surprises have been that the dollar overvaluation lasted as long as it did, that there was a smaller than expected decline in real interest rates, and that a massive decline in the real prices of commodities occurred. The world macroeconomic environment certainly did not provide a setting in which debtor countries could grow out of their debts by export booms and improving terms of trade.

In 1987, five years into the adjustment process, indicators of creditworthiness show a deterioration except for the ratio of debt service to exports. And even that indicator is barely below the 1982 level. Can we expect that the world economy in the years ahead will provide a distinctly more favorable setting? The IMF outlook for the period 1988–91 shows a no-news setting: steady, moderate growth, no changes in the terms of trade, and an increase in real interest rates. In such an environment debtor countries would have to continue making massive real resource transfers to the creditors. Any improvement in their creditworthiness would have to come primarily from further domestic adjustments.

The no-news scenario conceals the wide variation of outcomes that lie ahead which depend on the nature of U.S. fiscal and external balance adjustment. Two extreme possibilities are a soft landing with significant real interest rate reductions, improving terms of trade, and sustained growth, on the one hand, and a hard landing on the other. The soft landing would ease debt service problems in the same way as happened in 1970–73. But the hard landing, with high real interest rates and recession, possibly reinforced by protection, would certainly preclude debt service on the scale that has taken place so far. U.S. external adjustment forces the question of how a reduction in debtor countries' noninterest balances is consistent with the lack of financing of debtors' interest payments. Without the financing there cannot be any reduction in surpluses except by moratoria or default. Thus U.S. trade adjustment poses a major unresolved issue for the international debt problem.

Notes

1. Problem debtors are defined as those that have arrears in 1983–84 or have rescheduled their debts since 1985.
2. There is some question as to which deflator to use in calculating *real* interest rates for debtors. In figure 6.1 I use export prices of developing countries that represent a broad index of prices in world trade.
3. See Dornbusch (1985).
4. See IMF, *World Economic Outlook*, 1982, and Dornbusch (1985).
5. See IMF *World Economic Outlook*, April 1988, table 53.
6. See IMF (1987, 90–91) for a discussion of the data.

References

Dornbusch, R. 1985. Policy and performance links between LDC debtors and industrial countries. *Brookings Papers on Economic Activity* 2: 303–56.
———.1986. International debt and economic instability. In Federal Reserve Bank of Kansas, *Debt, financial stability and public policy*.
Feldstein, M. 1986. International debt service and economic growth: Some simple analytics. NBER Working Paper no. 2076. Cambridge, Mass.: National Bureau of Economic Research.
Goldbrough, D., and I. Zaidi. 1986. Transmission of economic influences from industrial to developing countries. In International Monetary Fund, *Staff Studies for the World Economic Outlook* (July). Washington, D.C.: IMF.
International Monetary Fund. *World Economic Outlook*, various issues.
———.1987. *Primary commodities: Market developments and outlook* (May). Washington D.C.: IMF.
Sachs, J. 1987. International policy coordination: The case of the developing country debt crisis. NBER Working Paper no. 2287. Cambridge, Mass.: National Bureau of Economic Research.
Sachs, J., and W. McKibbin. 1985. Macroeconomic policies in the OECD and LDC economic adjustment. Brookings Discussion Paper in International Economics (February). Washington, D.C.: The Brookings Institution.
Saunders, P. and A. Dean. 1986. The international debt situation and linkages between developing countries and the OECD. *OECD Economic Studies* (Autumn). Paris.

17 Resolving the International Debt Crisis

Stanley Fischer

17.1 Introduction

Since it was first recognized in August 1982, the international debt crisis has dominated economic policymaking in the developing countries, economic relations between the debtor and creditor countries, the attention of the multilateral institutions in their dealings with the debtor nations, and private-sector decisions on lending to the developing countries.

The economic difficulties of the debtors since 1982 are summarized by two facts: Per capita incomes in the Baker fifteen of heavily indebted countries fell on average 10 percent over the period 1981 to 1984 and have risen very little since; and domestic investment has fallen by an extraordinary 5 percent of GNP, significantly impairing growth prospects.

The most remarkable feature of the debt strategy followed since 1982 is that the heavily indebted developing countries have been transferring real resources of close to 5 percent of their income to the developed creditor countries. A solution of the debt crisis will either reverse the direction of this resource flow or at least significantly reduce it. Despite the virtual cessation of capital inflows, debt burden indicators, such as the debt-to-export ratio, have not improved. The picture for the debtors is not entirely bleak. Real interest rates fell between 1982 and 1987, though they appear late in 1987 to be rising again. Net exports showed extraordinary growth. Budget deficits have been reduced despite falling incomes. In 1987 commodity prices have begun to recover. The period has seen a shift toward rather than away from democracy.

Stanley Fischer is Chief Economist at the World Bank, a professor of economics at the Massachusetts Institute of Technology and a research associate of the NBER.

I am indebted to Geoffrey Carliner, Rudiger Dornbusch, and Allan Meltzer for helpful comments and discussions. This paper was completed before I joined the Bank; it is current to the end of 1987.

There has also been very real progress for the creditor banks and for the international financial system. Most important, neither the commercial nor central banks have had to deal with large-scale debt defaults. Balance sheets of creditor banks have been strengthened. There is an active secondary market in developing country debt, and debt-to-equity swaps are a reality.

But the fact remains that five years after it began, the debt crisis is very much alive. None of the major Latin American countries has restored normal access to the international capital markets. Even a country like Colombia, which has rigorously met its payments, finds it difficult to roll over its debts. At least one major debtor has been in trouble each year. In 1987 it is Brazil, whose moratorium could mark the beginning of a new phase of the crisis.

In its brief life the international debt crisis has generated an impressive variety of proposed initiatives and solutions.[1] Least radical are proposals for procedural reform and changes in the nature of the claims on the existing debt. There have been several suggestions for the creation of a facility, or new institution that would in specified ways deal with the overhang of existing debt. And finally, there are proposals for debt relief. I take up these possibilities in turn in sections 17.3 through 17.5.

17.2 Preliminaries

The debt crisis involves at least three parties: the debtor countries, the creditor countries, and the private banks and their stockholders. A more sophisticated view further distinguishes between the governments of debtor and creditor countries and their citizens, between workers in the debtor countries and portfolio holders who succeeded in moving their capital abroad, and between financial and manufacturing interests in the developed countries.

Although the point is rarely explicitly recognized, alternative solutions to the debt crisis imply different burdens for different groups involved in the crisis. Up to 1987, most of the burden has been borne by wage earners in the debtor countries. Part has been borne by bank stockholders, who have seen the value of their shares rise less rapidly than the stock market as a whole. Some will be borne by the taxpayers of the creditor countries, as the banks record portfolio losses, lower profits, and lower taxes.

Before describing and evaluating plans to solve the debt problem, I make several stipulations about the nature of the problem and its solution.

1. The debt crisis will have to be resolved in a way that differentiates among countries. Bolivia's problem is different from Brazil's, and both are different from Tanzania's.

2. From the viewpoint of the stability of the U.S. banking system, the debt problem is dominated by just a few countries. The concentration on the Baker fifteen with its heavily Latin American flavor is a result of those countries' debts being predominantly to the private sector.
3. Concentration on the Baker fifteen overlooks the debt and growth problems of sub-Saharan Africa, which will have to be taken into account in any discussion of aid.
4. Just as the debt problem arrived unexpectedly as a result of changes in the international economy, it could quietly go away. Higher prices for commodity exports, and further reductions in real interest rates, would make the entire problem look manageable. It could also intensify quickly if the international trading system seizes up as a result of growing protectionism or a worldwide recession.
5. The interested parties, the banks and the debtors, each have little interest in revealing the dimensions of whatever compromises they might ultimately be willing to make.
6. Finally, there are important political constraints on solutions to the debt problem. There is no well-defined economic sense in which a Brazil, Mexico, or Argentina is incapable of servicing and ultimately paying off its debt.[2] However the new democratic governments in several of the heavily indebted countries are certainly too weak to achieve massive reductions in consumption. The question for both their own governments and the creditor governments is how far it is possible and politically wise to push their citizens to meet debt payments.

17.3 Procedural Reform and New Debt Instruments

Some debt plans would leave the present value of claims on the debtors unchanged while changing their form. Others would reduce the present value of claims on the debtors. In this section I take up both procedural and regulatory reforms, and suggestions for new debt instruments. In neither case are the changes designed to reduce the value of claims on the debtors.

17.3.1 Procedural Reform

Several procedural reforms are listed in table 17.1. There has already been progress in the implementation of a number of these reforms, including the first, for instance in multiyear reschedulings for Argentina, Mexico, and the Philippines. Because macroeconomic management skills are in short supply, reduction of the frequency of negotiations would help improve the overall quality of macroeconomic management in the debtor countries. The creditor banks can retain some of the

Table 17.1   Procedural Reforms

Change	Initiating Agency
1. Multiyear rescheduling	Banks and debtors
2. Reduced size of banking syndicates and exit option for small banks	Banks and debtors
3. Change accounting rules to allow partial writedowns and their gradual amortization	Bank examiners and accounting standards
4. U.S. information provision on foreign accounts	Bank regulators and IRS
5. U.S. taxation of foreign accounts	Congress

control afforded by frequent renegotiation by using IMF Article IV consultations as a framework for monitoring and conditionality.

The size of the banking syndicates involved in the debt negotiations are obstacles both to efficient negotiation and to the rapid mobilization of capital after an agreement has been reached. The desire of many of the small banks to leave the international debt business is well known. The exit vehicle may be either the interbank secondary markets or, as intended in the 1987 Argentine restructuring, exit bond issues.

Two aspects of the accounting and tax treatment of sales of debt at less than face value have to be distinguished. First, it is sometimes stated that a bank selling part of its claims on a given country for less than book value has to write down its remaining claims. However, some bankers believe that is not necessary, provided a good case can be made that the bank is likely to collect on the remaining debt.[3] Certainly the creation of loss reserves against developing country debt has *not* forced the banks to carry the corresponding debt on their balance sheets at its market value.

Second, any bank taking a loss in a given period has to record that as a loss in current revenue and cannot amortize it over time. If banks are convinced that amortization is preferable to a larger one-time loss, even though there is no good economic reason they should be, they could be allowed to write off the losses over a period of several years rather than immediately.

Although some capital flight can be regarded as a natural attempt by portfolio-holders in developing countries to diversify internationally, much of it is a form of tax evasion. Procedural reforms 4 and 5 would help the debtors deal with the tax-evasion aspects of capital flight. U.S. and foreign developed country banks that hold the accounts of citizens of other countries could be required to inform the tax authorities of those countries of the existence of the accounts.

Developed countries could instead impose a uniform tax on all interest on bank accounts, and indeed on other income generated from securities holdings, that are not those of their own taxpayers. This would reduce the attraction of capital flight. An alternative would be for the taxes to be imposed by the country from which the capital fled, for which purpose the provision of better information about foreign-held bank accounts would assist the tax authorities in the debtor countries. To be effective, all these changes would require international agreement.

17.3.2   Changing the Nature of Claims

A driving force behind proposals to change the nature of claims on the debtors is the conclusion that the structure of the debt in 1982 was partly responsible for the debt crisis. With a high proportion of all payment flows linked to short-term interest rates abroad, the debtors were vulnerable to a rise in real interest rates in the developed countries, and had no protection against changes in the terms of trade. The suggestions are probably motivated also by the view that eventually the structure of debtor country liabilities should correspond more closely to the structure of underlying assets, with more long-term fixed interest debt, more equity, more direct investment, and less floating rate debt.[4]

Table 17.2 describes the proposals for changes in the form of claims on the debtors. In this summary, I focus on the more important proposals listed in the table.

Secondary and Insurance Markets

Secondary markets have already developed to some extent. They do little to solve the debt crisis other than to enable the banks—if they were to sell their claims—to reduce their vulnerability to default in particular countries. The secondary markets could eventually become the locus in which an international facility deals with the debt. And, if the market became deeper, prices in them could serve as the basis for debt renegotiation.

Private insurance of the debt is not in principle different from the provision of a secondary market, except that it would enable banks tied into the debt to reduce their vulnerability to default. Insurance rates could be deduced from the discounts on debt in the secondary market, and would be extremely high for many countries. It is therefore difficult to see private insurance markets becoming large or significant.

There have also been proposals for public sector provision of insurance or guarantees, perhaps through an agency associated with the World Bank.[5] Such an agency could help mobilize new private capital, perhaps at lower cost than through private insurance because the World Bank and other multilateral agencies have developed expertise

Table 17.2   Changing the Nature of Claims

Change	Initiating Agency
1. Development of secondary and insurance markets	Creditor financial institutions and official institutions
2. Indexed loans	Debtors and banks
3. Contingent lending obligations	Debtors, banks, and offical lenders
4. Longer debt maturities	Debtors and banks
5. Debt-equity swaps	Debtors and banks
6. Servicing of debt in local currency	Debtors and banks
7. Return of flight capital	Creditor and debtor governments, and banks
8. Country funds	Debtors and creditor financial intermediaries
9. Debt subordination	Debtors, existing and new lenders
10. Interest capitalization	Debtors and banks, plus creditor governments

in evaluating loans to developing countries. The agency need not necessarily subsidize insurance rates. To prevent the moral hazard problem of inadequate monitoring of loans by lenders that contributed to the creation of the current debt crisis, the agency would probably insist on significant co-insurance by the lenders.

Indexed Loans

Any loan that ties payments from debtors to creditors to some objective criterion is an indexed loan. Payments may be fixed in real rather than nominal terms, or may be specified as some percentage of GNP. Exchange participation notes suggested by Bailey (1983) tie payments to export earnings.[6] In well-operating markets such claims could be priced and traded, and there is no difficulty in principle in envisaging their introduction.

Direct swaps of debt for claims on commodities which the recipient exports are another form of indexed instrument. By tying the payoff of loans to a specific amount of the country's production, such agreements reduce the transfer problem.

Debt-Equity Swaps

Debt-equity swaps are the central element of most market-oriented debt restructurings, and they have also been implemented, for example in Mexico, Chile, and Argentina. The essential transaction is simply that a debt claim on a country is swapped by that country's central bank for local currency claims that should be invested in local firms.

The greatest attraction for the creditors is that debt-equity swaps often carry an implicit subsidy of the equity investment. Swaps may involve the purchase of debt in the secondary market at a discount, and redemption at face value. However there is no reason, if the debtors decide to subsidize, that they need to do so on the basis of the New York price. Another approach has been used by Chile, which auctions off the right to exchange dollar debt for peso assets.

Obviously, debt-equity swaps replace interest payments by dividend payments, and are not a source of new money for the debtor country. In addition, they may merely be subsidies for investment flows that would have taken place anyway, and they may lead to round-tripping.

None of these problems rules out debt-equity swaps as a useful supplement to handling the debt crisis. The present value of the dividend outflow is probably similar to the expected present value of interest outflows on the debt, but it does reduce the probability of debt default and does provide a payment stream that better matches the country's economic performance.

Local Currency Servicing

Closely related to the notion of debt-equity swaps is the proposal from debtors that they be permitted to service their debt in local currency, with automatic reinvestment of the proceeds in the domestic economy. Part of the servicing might be made available to the government; the remainder would be relent to the private sector, in forms chosen by the creditors.

This proposal has the benefit for the debtors of reducing the need to generate foreign currency to service the debt, though it does not reduce the need to mobilize resources to service the debt. It has the advantage for creditors that their debt is serviced in full, but the disadvantage that they would be constrained from reducing their total exposure in any given country. In addition, it establishes a simple formula by which all existing creditors provide continuing finance for a country.

Flight Capital

It would be difficult to place flight capital as the centerpiece of any debt strategy. If it would come back for reasonable interest rates and small subsidization of debt-equity deals, it would not need any special attention. It is quite likely though that especially high rates of return would be needed, because the owners of flight capital would fear the imposition of ex post sanctions of some type.

Interest Capitalization

The last item in table 17.2, interest capitalization, could change resource transfers to the debtors quite radically and rapidly. Capitalization simply limits the amount of interest that has to be paid in any one year, perhaps to a given nominal interest rate on the debt, or to a given percentage of GNP, a given percentage of export earnings, or by some formula related to commodity prices. The remainder is capitalized and automatically added to the debt, to be paid off over a specified horizon.

The obvious fear from the viewpoint of the creditors is that the amounts capitalized will grow too fast for the country ever to be able to pay all the interest without further capitalization. Whether that is a realistic fear depends entirely on the prospects of the country and the exact formula used for capitalization. But if every reasonable capitalization formula results in debt instability, then there is no chance that current claims on the country can be collected in full.

Interest capitalization has received more support in Europe than in the United States. U.S. regulators would have to change rules if capitalization were to become a practical option.

Most of the proposals discussed in this section are for changes in the form of the debt that—except to some extent in the discussion of debt-equity swaps—do not reduce the present value of debtor country obligations. Alternative proposals typically include elements of debt relief.

17.4   New Institutions

The overhang of the existing debt is the main obstacle to a renewal of resource inflows to the heavily indebted developing countries. Very early in the debt crisis both Kenen (1983) and Rohatyn (1983) proposed the formation of an international institution to buy debt at a price below the face value and provide relief to the debtor countries. The proposal has been developed by Weinert (1986–87) among others.

Kenen's 1983 proposal was for the governments of the creditor nations to set up an International Debt Discount Corporation (IDDC) to which they would contribute capital. The IDDC would issue long-term bonds to the banks in exchange for their developing country debts, at a discount on face value. If the IDDC misjudged and was unable to collect, the creditor governments would bear the losses.

The plan is elegantly simple in replacing developing country debt in banks' balance sheets with the liabilities of the IDDC, in effect requiring the banks to lend to the IDDC. The key questions about each such plan are how large a write-down the banks take, whether they would be willing, or could be made willing, to do so, and how much relief is provided to the debtors.

Any IDDC-type scheme creates a free-rider problem. If the IDDC buys up much of the developing country debt and makes some form of debt relief possible, then the credit standing of the debtors improves. Those creditors who stayed out of the IDDC agreement have a capital gain. For that reason an IDDC would have to find some means of ensuring almost complete participation by the creditors.

The IDDC notion is at the least interesting; if it could be carried off with relatively small injections of public money it would also be important. If there is to be an overall solution to the debt problem it will almost certainly involve an IDDC-type institution. But since the procedures it set up for pricing debt will determine the burdens borne by both banks and debtors, and the possible extent of creditor nation government support, its operating rules and management are bound to be the subject of protracted negotiations. It might be possible in such a negotiation to separate technical discussions on the terms and methods of buying debt from aid discussions that determine the concessions that are given to each country.

17.5   Debt Relief

The case for debt relief is that debtor countries will be unable to grow unless they can increase imports, that no solution currently in sight permits them to do that without reducing income levels to politically unacceptable levels, and that ultimately they will in any case not pay most of their debts.

The case against debt relief is that of precedent, and the view that contracts that were voluntarily entered into should not be abrogated. The question of the precedent that would be set by giving debt relief is not simple: Debt contracts involve both creditors and debtors, and the use of political authority to enforce the debts sets a precedent for creditors, whose incentives to exercise appropriate caution in lending are reduced.

Relief can come through direct negotiations between the creditor banks and each debtor country, or with the intervention of the international institutions and/or creditor governments. Or it may be imposed unilaterally by some of the debtor governments, either in the form of a moratorium which does not repudiate the debt, or in the form of unilateral action that leaves them to deal with the legal consequences of their actions. Or it could come in some combination of the above.

It might be possible for the major debtors to settle their own debt problems in direct negotiations. So long as the creditor countries permitted these negotiations to proceed without interference, and at critical stages were willing to help—for instance by changing banking regulations—agreement is quite possible. The agreement would likely be conditional on the country's economic policies, and could involve the international institutions in monitoring roles.

17.6 Scenarios

Three basic scenarios present themselves. The first is an evolution of the muddling through strategy that has been followed to date. Its benefits and costs were described in the introduction.

The second scenario would see a series of direct agreements between each debtor and its creditors, involving relief and substantial lengthening of the debt. The negotiations for such agreements would be protracted and possibly crisis-laden, and would likely involve the international institutions in monitoring roles.

The third possibility is the setting up of a large international organization, the IDDC, to attempt to dispose of the debt problem. This too has the benefits of settling the crisis and enabling economic management teams to concentrate on policies for growth. It would also provide a longer-term solution for the banks.

Of course, the scenarios are not mutually exclusive. The second and third possibilities could be combined, with the debt crisis eventually being resolved through a mixture of direct agreements between creditors and debtors with extra relief being provided for the most impoverished countries though an IDDC or the existing international institutions. Elements of the first scenario would be seen in the evolution of international lending in the direction of more equity-like claims.

In all cases the solutions would involve agreed-upon policy reforms in the debtor countries to attempt to ensure that the debt problem does not soon recur.

Notes

1. Dornbusch (1987), Feldstein et al. (1987), and Krugman (1986) present useful surveys of alternative solutions; the classification of debt initiatives used here is taken from Krugman.
2. See Feldstein (1986) for a detailed scenario.
3. This was the position taken by a panel of the American Institute of CPA's in 1985 (see "The Outlook" column, *Wall Street Journal*, 26 October 1986).
4. Lessard and Williamson (1985) provide a very useful review of alternative proposals for changing the form of finance of the debtor countries. See also World Bank (1985) and IMF (1986).
5. National export credit agencies perform some of the same functions. The World Bank has provided some investment guarantees in the co-financing of projects with commercial lenders.
6. Lessard and Williamson (1985) analyze this and related proposals which they call "quasi-equity" investments.

References

Bailey, Norman. 1983. A safety net for foreign lending. *Business Week*, 10 January.

Dornbusch, Rudiger. 1987. The world debt problem: Anatomy and solutions. Report prepared for the Twentieth Century Fund, New York.

Feldstein, Martin. 1986. International debt service and economic growth: Some simple analytics. NBER Working Paper no. 2076. Cambridge, Mass.: National Bureau of Economic Research.

———. 1987. Latin America's debt: Muddling through can be just fine. *The Economist*, 27 June.

Feldstein, Martin, Herve de Carmoy, Koei Narusawa, and Paul Krugman. 1987. Restoring growth in the debt-laden Third World. New York: Tri-Lateral Commission, mimeo.

International Monetary Fund. 1986 and 1987. *World Economic Outlook* (April).

Kenen, Peter. 1983. A bailout for the banks. *New York Times*, 6 March.

Krugman, Paul R. 1986. Prospects for international debt reform. Report to the Group of Twenty-Four, prepared for United Nations Conference on Trade and Development.

Lessard, Don, and John Williamson. 1985. *Financial intermediation beyond the debt crisis*. Washington, D.C.: Institute for International Economics.

Meltzer, Allan H. 1983. *International lending in the IMF*. Washington, D.C.: Heritage Foundation.

Rohatyn, Felix. 1983. A plan for stretching out global debt. *Business Week*, 28 February.

Weinert, Richard S. 1986–87. Swapping Third World debt. *Foreign Policy* (Winter): 85–97.

World Bank. 1985. *World Development Report*.

Contributors

Edward F. Buffie
Department of Economics
Vanderbilt University
Nashville, TN 37235

Eliana A. Cardoso
Fletcher School of Law and
  Diplomacy
Tufts University
Medford, MA 02155

Merih Celâsun
Department of Economics
Middle East Technical University
Ankara, Turkey

Susan M. Collins
Department of Economics
Harvard University
Littauer Center M-7
Cambridge, MA 02138

Juan Carlos de Pablo
Paez 2608
1406 Buenos Aires
Argentina

Robert S. Dohner
Fletcher School of Law and
  Diplomacy
Tufts University
Medford, MA 02155

Rudiger Dornbusch
Department of Economics
Massachusetts Institute of
  Technology
E52-357
Cambridge, MA 02139

Sebastian Edwards
Department of Economics
University of California
Bunch Hall, Room 8283
405 Hilgard Avenue
Los Angeles, CA 90024

Barry Eichengreen
Department of Economics
University of California
250 Barrows Hall
Berkeley, CA 94720

Stanley Fischer
S-9035
The World Bank
1818 H Street NW
Washington, D.C. 20433

Albert Fishlow
Department of Economics
University of California
Berkeley, CA 94720

Stephen Haggard
Center for International Affairs
Harvard University
1737 Cambridge Street
Cambridge, MA 02138

Ponciano Intal, Jr.
Department of Economics
University of the Philippines at Los
    Banos
College, Laguna
The Philippines

Robert Kaufman
Department of Political Science
Rutgers University
Hickman Hall, Douglass Campus
New Brunswick, NJ 08903

Allen Sangines Krause
Instituto Technologico Autonomo de
    Mexico
Rio Hondo No. 1
Tiazapan, San Angel
Mexico 20, D.F.
Mexico

Anne O. Krueger
Department of Economics
Duke University
Durham, NC 27706

Paul Krugman
Department of Economics
Massachusetts Institute of
    Technology
E52-383A
Cambridge, MA 02139

Peter H. Lindert
Director
Agricultural History Center
University of California
Davis, CA 95615

Juan Antonio Morales
Universidad Católica Boliviana
Av. 14 de Septiembra 4807
Cajon Postal No. 4805
La Paz, Bolivia

Peter J. Morton
Department of Economics
Hofstra University
Hempstead, NY 11550

Anwar Nasution
Institute for Social and Economic
    Studies
Faculty of Economics
University of Indonesia
Jalan Ray Salemba 4
Jakarta 10430
Indonesia

Won-Am Park
Korea Development Institute
P.O. Box 113, Chungryang
Seoul, Korea

Dani Rodrik
John F. Kennedy School of
    Government
Harvard University
79 Kennedy Street
Cambridge, MA 02138

Jeffrey D. Sachs
Department of Economics
Harvard University
Littauer M-14
Cambridge, MA 02138

Miguel Urrutia
Manager, Economic and Social
    Development Department
Inter-American Development Bank
1300 New York Avenue, NW
Washington, D.C. 20577

Wing Thye Woo
Department of Economics
University of California
Davis, CA 95616

Name Index

Subject Index

Adjustment programs. *See* Structural
  adjustment programs; Stabilization
  programs
African nations, 1, 266, 277, 315
Agricultural sector, 15, 269–70, 309
Arab nations, loans to, 227. *See also*
  specific country
Argentina: Austral plan, 38, 46, 47t, 264,
  273; bank exposure to, 11; capital
  flight from, 41, 43; central bank
  borrowing, 43–44; corruption in, 68;
  creditworthiness of, 50; debt and, 3,
  37–47, 233; deficits in, 37–38, 46;
  devaluations and, 44–45; economic
  performance in, 4t; economic policies
  of, 37, 41; exchange rates and, 39–45;
  fiscal policies of, 46–47, 50; IMF and,
  49; income per capita, 38, 39t; inflation
  and, 37–43; 46–47, 283; interest rates
  and, 46; investment rates in, 49;
  middle-class and, 215; politics in, 37,
  50, 273; price levels and, 46–47;
  private sector confidence in, 268;
  resource transfers of, 18; stabilization
  plans in, 38, 42; standard of living in,
  49; taxes in, 37
Australia, standard of living in, 38
Authoritarian governments, 270, 273

Baker Plan, 93, 193, 253
Banks. *See* Central banks; Commercial
  banks
Baring panic (1890), 38

Bolivia: capital flight from, 67–68; class
  conflicts in, 58, 62–63; cocaine
  industry in, 68; commodities and, 19,
  68; cotton boom in, 68; debt and, 3,
  57–79; deficits and, 73; devaluations
  and, 67, 258; economic development
  in, 60–65, 78–79; economic
  performance, 4t; employment, 78;
  exchange rate and, 67, 72–73; exports
  of, 60–62, 67–68; fiscal policies of,
  213–14; GDP growth, 67; government
  revenues, 69–73, 76–77; income
  distribution, 58–59, 63, 65, 79;
  inflation and, 27, 57, 64–65, 69, 71–76;
  interest rates and, 69; labor and, 69;
  mining sector, 58, 60–62; money
  printing, 69, 71–72; politics in, 12, 57–
  58, 60–65, 68; price levels and, 69;
  resource transfers of, 18; stabilization
  process and, 74–78
Bolivian Revolution, 62
Bonds: bank loans vs., 247; exit, 316;
  global returns on, 229–30; 1920s
  yields, 240; nominal returns on, 228;
  pricing of, 240–42
Brazil: bank exposure to, 11; Citicorp
  and, 8; creditworthiness, 50, 84;
  Cruzado plan, 85–87, 91, 213, 273;
  debt and, 3, 81–98; default of, 265,
  267, 314; deficits of, 22, 83, 87, 88–90,
  112–13; devaluations and, 83–84;
  economic development in, 81, 92–93;
  economic performance in, 4t; exchange

For dozens of developing countries, the financial upheavals of the 1980s have set back economic development by a decade or more. Poverty in those countries has intensified as they struggle under the burden of an enormous external debt. In 1988, more than six years after the onset of the crisis, almost all the debtor countries were still unable to borrow in the international capital markets on normal terms. Moreover, the world financial system has been disrupted by the prospect of widespread defaults on those debts. Because of the urgency of the present crisis, and because similar crises have recurred intermittently for at least 175 years, it is important to understand the fundamental features of the international macroeconomy and global financial markets that have contributed to this repeated instability.

Developing Country Debt and the World Economy contains nontechnical versions of papers prepared under the auspices of the project on developing country debt, sponsored by the National Bureau of Economic Research. The project focuses on the middle-income developing countries, particularly those in Latin America and East Asia, although many lessons of the study should apply as well to other, poorer debtor countries. The contributors analyze the crisis from two perspectives, that of the international financial system as a whole and that of individual debtor countries.

Studies of eight countries—Argentina, Bolivia, Brazil, Indonesia, Mexico, the Philippines, South Korea, and Turkey—explore the question of why some countries succumbed to serious financial crises while others did not. Each study was prepared by a team of two authors—a U.S.-based researcher and an economist from the country under study. An additional eight papers approach the problem of developing country debt from a global or "systemic" perspective. The topics they cover include the history of international sovereign lending and previous debt crises, the political factors that contribute to poor economic policies in many debtor nations, the role of commercial banks and the International Monetary Fund during the current crisis, the links between debt in developing countries and economic policies in the industrialized nations, and possible new approaches to the global management of the crisis.

JEFFREY D. SACHS is the Galen L. Stone Professor of International Trade at Harvard University and a research associate of the National Bureau of Economic Research. He is the coauthor, with Michael Bruno, of *Economics of Worldwide Stagflation*.

An NBER Project Report

The University of Chicago Press

Cover illustration: © Daniel Abraham 1988   ISBN 0-226-73339-4